T0331470

Fashion Business and Digital Transformation

Fashion Business and Digital Transformation provides a practical and holistic overview of the fashion industry and the key technologies impacting the fashion supply chain. It covers product design and development, production, sales and customer experiences in physical, online and virtual environments. The key technologies impacting the ecosystem are explored, including artificial intelligence, virtual reality, augmented reality, digital fashion design, NFTs, 3D textiles, and blockchain. Strategic concepts such as 'retail-tainment', 'phygital', gamification and e-commerce, are analysed, alongside the effect of these key strategies for both the retailer and the customer.

Theoretical foundations are supported by extensive use of examples, interviews and case studies drawn from a wide range of global fashion disrupters and cutting-edge brands. Engaging activities, exercises and technical step-by-step guides are incorporated throughout, which will both consolidate how technology is driving change in the industry and also equip the reader with the key skills and digital literacy capabilities required by future practitioners. Online resources include chapter-by-chapter PowerPoint slides, a test bank and links to further resources.

This examination of the digital transformation of the fashion industry will be essential reading for advanced undergraduate and postgraduate students of Fashion Management, Fashion Business and Fashion Technology.

Charlene Gallery is a Reader at the University of Manchester, UK.

Jo Conlon is a Senior Lecturer at the University of Manchester, UK.

Mastering Fashion Management

The fashion industry is dynamic, constantly evolving and worth billions worldwide: it's no wonder that Fashion Business Management has come to occupy a central position within the Business School globally. This series meets the need for rigorous yet practical and accessible textbooks that cover the full spectrum of the fashion industry and its management.

Collectively, *Mastering Fashion Management* is a valuable resource for advanced undergraduate and postgraduate students of Fashion Management, helping them gain an in-depth understanding of contemporary concepts and the realities of practice across the entire fashion chain - from design development and product sourcing, to buying and merchandising, sustainability, and sales and marketing. Individually, each text provides essential reading for a core topic. A range of consistent pedagogical features are used throughout the texts, including international case studies, highlighting the practical importance of theoretical concepts.

Postgraduate students studying for a Masters in Fashion Management in particular will find each text invaluable reading, providing the knowledge and tools to approach a future career in fashion with confidence.

Fashion Marketing and Communication
Theory and Practice Across the Fashion Industry
Olga Mitterfellner

Fashion Buying and Merchandising
The Fashion Buyer in a Digital Society
Rosy Boardman, Rachel Parker-Strak and Claudia E. Henninger

Sustainable Fashion Management
Claudia E. Henninger, Kirsi Niinimäki, Marta Blazquez Cano and Celina Jones

Fashion Supply Chain Management
Virginia Grose and Nicola Mansfield

Celebrity Fashion Marketing
Developing a Human Fashion Brand
Fykaa Caan and Angela Lee

Luxury Fashion Brand Management
Unifying Fashion With Sustainability
Olga Mitterfellner

Fashion Business and Digital Transformation
Technology and Innovation across the Fashion Industry
Charlene Gallery and Jo Conlon

For more information about the series, please visit https://www.routledge.com/Mastering-Fashion-Management/book-series/FM

Fashion Business and Digital Transformation

Technology and Innovation across the Fashion Industry

Charlene Gallery and Jo Conlon

Routledge
Taylor & Francis Group
LONDON AND NEW YORK

Designed cover image: © kirstypargeter

First published 2024
by Routledge
4 Park Square, Milton Park, Abingdon, Oxon OX14 4RN

and by Routledge
605 Third Avenue, New York, NY 10158

Routledge is an imprint of the Taylor & Francis Group, an informa business

British Library Cataloguing-in-Publication Data
A catalogue record for this book is available from the British Library

Library of Congress Cataloging-in-Publication Data
Names: Gallery, Charlene, author. | Conlon, Jo, author.
Title: Fashion business and digital transformation : technology and
innovation across the fashion industry / Charlene Gallery and Jo Conlon.
Description: Abingdon, Oxon ; New York, NY : Routledge, 2024. |
Series: Mastering fashion management |
Includes bibliographical references and index.
Identifiers: LCCN 2023056942 | ISBN 9781032428505 (hbk) |
ISBN 9781032428475 (pbk) | ISBN 9781003364559 (ebk)
Subjects: LCSH: Clothing trade. | Clothing trade–Technological innovations.
Classification: LCC HD9940.A2 G354 2024 | DDC 687.068/8–dc23/eng/20240417
LC record available at https://lccn.loc.gov/2023056942

ISBN: 9781032428505 (hbk)
ISBN: 9781032428475 (pbk)
ISBN: 9781003364559 (ebk)

DOI: 10.4324/9781003364559

Typeset in Palatino
by Newgen Publishing UK

Access the Support Material: www.routledge.com/9781032428475

CONTENTS

FIGURES

TABLES

PART I

Strategic digital transformation in the fashion industry

Part I is dedicated to the description, analysis and discussion of how new technologies are changing fashion business practice. It demonstrates how data provides a digital thread connecting the value chain. It starts by introducing the evolution of digital technologies, data sources and their associated data management in the fashion system to support the shift to data-driven decision-making. It describes the journey towards Industry 4.0 and outlines the associated technologies that are set to evolve the industry. Key terms associated with digital transformation, Industry 4.0 components and principles are outlined. The significance of data integration and connectivity across the information systems of the extended enterprise and throughout the product life cycle is detailed. The complexities of strategic change are explored and the process of integrating digital technologies into businesses to achieve business ambitions. The need for a strategic approach to digital transformation that invites all stakeholders to contribute to the digital transformation journey is explained. Theories of change management are outlined and adapted to support digital transformation. The role of enterprise solutions such as retail apparel product lifecycle management (PLM) is explored to illustrate the opportunities for change through a fully connected fashion value chain.

DOI: 10.4324/9781003364559-1

CHAPTER 1.1

Introduction to digital transformation in the fashion industry

Jo Conlon

This chapter aims to equip future fashion professionals with a foundational understanding of the key technologies of the digitally connected fashion system and an enthusiasm for the potential of the technologies of Industry 4.0 to evolve the industry further. Dramatic changes in the fashion industry have occurred in the last generation. This chapter reviews the evolution of digital technologies in fashion provide a broad perspective on the fundamental and ongoing changes impacting fashion organisations. Hence this chapter provides insight into the apparent paradox that while technology adoption by fashion consumers has been rapid, technology adoption throughout the fashion system has been cautious to date. Accordingly, there remains a need to transform traditional analogue supply chains to digital value chains to realise the full potential of digital transformation. Hence, there are many opportunities for new approaches and innovative thinking from people starting in the industry.

LEARNING OUTCOMES

After reading this chapter you should be able to:

- Explain the significance of consumer behaviour in driving change in the fashion system.
- Identify the key technologies in the evolution of the digitally connected fashion system: CAD/CAM, PDM, ERP, CRM, PLM.
- Determine the inter-relationships between infrastructure, processes and people in the process of change.
- Distinguish the difference between the terms digitise, digitalise and digital transformation within the context of the fashion system.
- Identify the enabling technologies and applications of fashion Industry 4.0 components (smart products, smart factories, smart networks) and principles (interoperability, real time capabilities, virtualisation, service orientation, modularity and decentralisation).

DOI: 10.4324/9781003364559-2

- Explain the terms data, data management and data governance in relation to supporting data-driven decision-making.

1.1.1 INTRODUCTION TO THE EVOLUTION OF TECHNOLOGY IN FASHION

The timeline (Figure 1.1.1) illustrates some of the key dates in the evolution of technology in fashion. As fashion consumers we have witnessed both the change in operating formats of fashion retailers and the increase in our own expectations as a fashion consumer. As an illustrative example, when the UK online retailer ASOS began as a start-up in 2000, it was met with scepticism of the potential of online fashion business. The prevailing thinking was that as shopping was a social activity and a tactile experience it would not be replaced. In fashion retail there was much cynicism about whether this would prove to be no more than an experiment and this reticence meant that e-commerce teams were set up separate to the core business.

The shift to online retail began in earnest from 2012 (Deloitte, 2018) as the additional sales potential through the new internet channel became visible. The shift to online retailing has provided a lucrative and additional sales channel with the online clothing and apparel industry expected to reach a value of 1.2 trillion U.S. dollars by 2027 (Statista, 2023a). Post-2010, the supply chain was still operating on a product-centric push model, and this initial phase of e-commerce became known as multichannel retailing. In fashion retail there was much scepticism about whether this would prove to be no more than an experiment and this reticence meant that e-commerce teams were set up separate to the core business. The legacy of physical and online channels operating as separate entities remains an issue for many retailers. However, time-pressed consumers embraced online retail's 'always on and always changing' aspect, along with the expanded choice of retailers, and leveraged their consumer power to demand the best price. This provoked a shift to a consumer-centric pull model of supply and the need to integrate the consumer experience seamlessly across different channels and social media.

FIGURE 1.1.1 Timeline of the emergence of the key technologies in fashion retail.

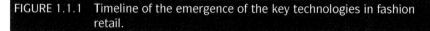

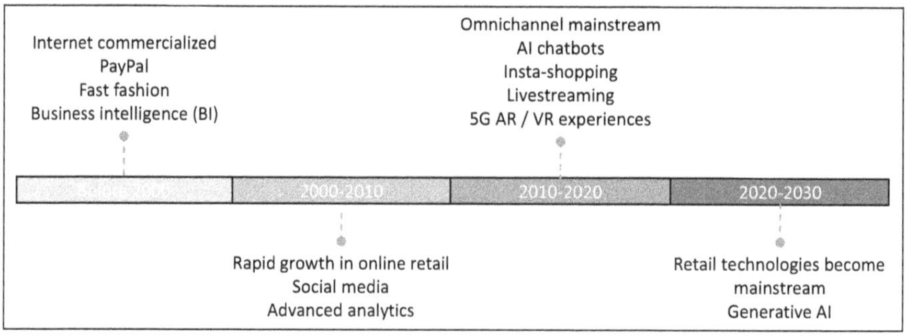

This is known as omnichannel retailing. The shift from push to pull production represents a seismic shift in retail management (OC&C Insight, 2016) prompting a fundamental rethink of processes and practices that has been described as changing retailing from 'transmit to receive' mode (Jong, 2017, p.1). Today's success is determined by the ability to be flexible and responsive to consumer demand through product and process innovation based on a deep understanding of customers, coupled with open and robust supply chain relationships throughout the extended enterprise.

However, digital transformation means much more than establishing an online sales channel. The significant success of increased sales and expanded consumer reach that resulted from this first digital initiative encouraged more long-term strategic investments. From online (PC-based e-commerce), the next stage was the introduction of mobile apps (m-commerce) benefitting from the advances in mobile infrastructure (Figure 1.1.2). Additional features such as profile creation, additional content, push messaging, loyalty schemes, etc. enhanced customer engagement and provided access to rich customer data, yielding insight into customer demographics, expectations, purchase history and buying behaviour. This illustration of the continued development of mobile software applications demonstrates that there is no end to a digital transformation journey and that each advance leads to another opportunity. Further development added further advanced features like social media login and interaction, smart search, multi-lingual support, virtual try-on, which are covered in more detail in Part III of this book. Retailers and brands can use the data to improve their products, services and operations. Access to data along the customer journey has provided new levels of customer insight resulting in data-driven responsiveness replacing efforts to forecast demand. This need for responsiveness cascades into associated supply chains. Overproduction was a consequence of the inaccuracy of demand forecasting and the associated push supply chain management approach. In pull supply chains, goods are produced to demand from consumers. With advances in technological capabilities, the fashion industry is increasingly able to apply data analytics to provide insight to support the shift away from product-centric to consumer-centric perspective of fashion businesses.

1.1.2 THE EVOLUTION OF THE DIGITALLY CONNECTED FASHION SYSTEM

Computer aided design (CAD) tools emerged in manufacturing industries in the 1980s. As global sourcing of production became established, the predecessor to product lifecycle management (PLM), product data management (PDM) emerged from the need to share product data (via electronic versions of design concepts) through globally distributed teams, including supply chain partners. PDM allowed for the establishment of procedures to manage product development processes and associated collaborative workflows which could then be automated. Simultaneously, other new technological tools to streamline and support operations were being introduced alongside the computer-aided design and manufacturing systems of CAD/

FIGURE 1.1.2 E-commerce in fashion in billions of USD (from 2010 to 2027) and associated mobile infrastructure (adapted from Statista 2020, 2022, 2023a and 2023b).

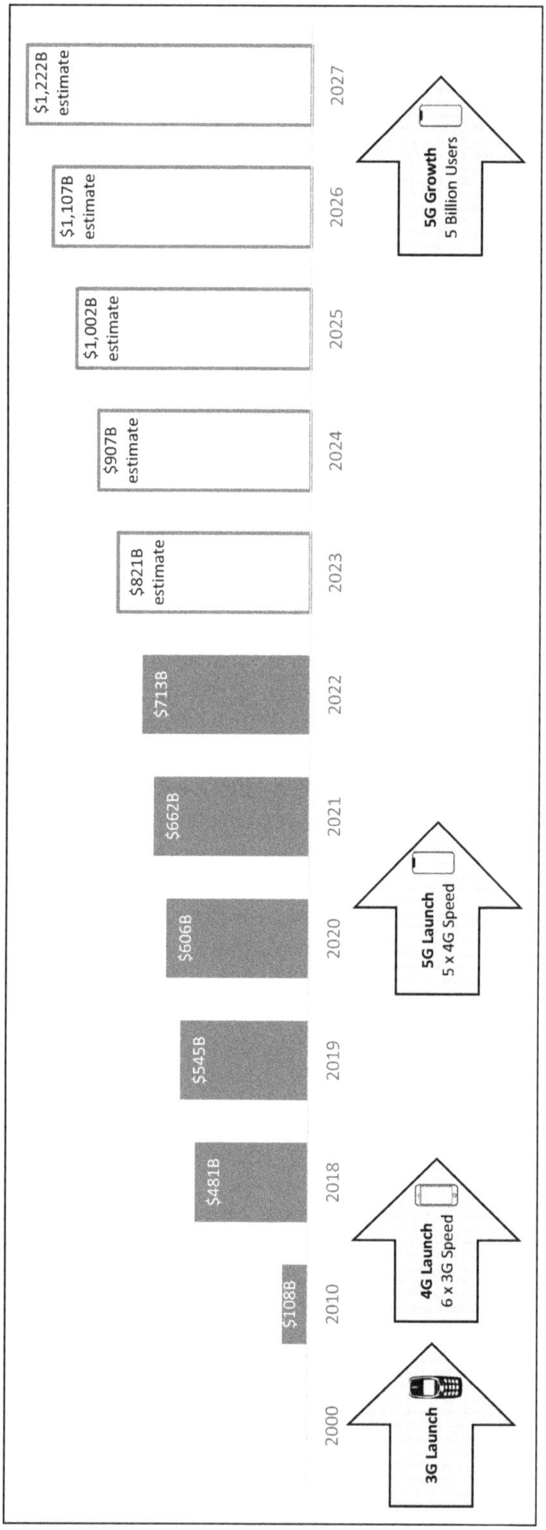

TABLE 1.1.1 Key terms in the digital transformation of fashion retail.

Term	Description
E-commerce (electronic commerce)	The buying and selling of goods and services using the internet.
M-commerce (mobile commerce)	The buying and selling of goods and services through wireless handheld devices.
Multi-channel	Retailing and marketing activities that use different channels/platforms
Product-centric merchandising	Indicating that the process starts with the product and efforts to forecast demand. Product is manufactured and stocked through a push demand and push supply chain model.
Supply chain	The activities related to the production and distribution of a product. Traditionally activities are separate or siloed.
End-to-end supply chain	Deliberate integration of functions into one continuous workflow providing visibility across the entire supply chain.
Value chain	The full range of required activities from design though production and sale, to end of use / recycling with a focus on delivering value to the customer.
Omnichannel	A retail strategy to engage customers consistently through multiple digital and physical touchpoints creating frictionless and personalised customer experiences.
Consumer-centric merchandising	Indicates a fundamental shift that puts the customer at the centre of decision-making, leading to adaptations in processes. Product is produced to pull demand through responsive or pull supply chains.

CAM and PDM systems such as Enterprise Resource Planning (ERP) and Customer Relationship Management (Conlon, 2020). ERP was first to become established within the industry for planning and transactions. PLM emerged in the 1990s as a strategic business model representing an enterprise-wide solution. ERP systems have remained dominant due the significance of on-time delivery within the fashion industry. However, as PLM supports product design, digital asset management (DAM) and innovation in products and services, it is now used in conjunction with ERP systems. Both systems share the bill-of-materials (BOM) and product data held within a PLM system can be transferred into an ERP system for financial transactions such as raining purchase orders. There is now a growing recognition of the need to integrate and consolidate enterprise systems such as PLM and ERP systems to provide accurate data to support transparency and responsiveness. This evolution is depicted in Figure 1.1.3. The capabilities of PLM solutions continue to advance; applications are discussed in Chapter 1.2.

The pandemic catalysed the adoption of many tech tools across the fashion and luxury value chain. The digitalisation of key processes meant that more data was generated providing the opportunity for additional customer insight. However, beyond pilot schemes, there are only a few fashion industry organisations that have fully implemented digitalised systems into their operations. Digital hesitancy persists due to the scale of the investment in training, operational upheaval, plus a lack of 'digital mindset' is seen as a barrier to change (Heim et al., 2022) despite the reported benefits. Mobile broadband infrastructure is one of the fundamental technologies required to leverage the capabilities of digital technologies. 5G (the most advanced mobile broadband standard) offers lower latency (reduced lag), faster data transfers and the potential to connect a huge number of devices within an area (Statista, 2022). The number of countries in which 5G is available has increased rapidly since its launch in 2020 and an estimated 4.4 billion subscribers by 2027 is predicted (Statista, 2022). The evolution of enterprise-wide technologies across all industries to meet emerging business challenges is depicted in Figure 1.1.3. However, adoption in the fashion industry lags behind other industries such as automotive. Stage 5, 'thing-centric', most closely represents the current investments of the fashion industry where a range of different sensors, connected systems and the use of cloud computing across textile and apparel manufacturing and retail environments is being established. In stage 6 'everything-centric', a data-centric, networked architecture approach to data management is realised through an interplay of networks of people, data, things and services (Panetto et al., 2016). It is in stages 5 and 6 that digital devices increasingly support organisations to identify new opportunities, make better decisions and improve operational efficiency by providing the required data to meet the requirements of a particular project or user.

TOWARDS DIGITAL TRANSFORMATION IN FASHION

> Digital fashion involves all those process that include (i)marketing and communicating tangible and intangible products; (ii) the development and implementation of processes that support the advancement of the industry; (iii) the effects of digital advances on society.
>
> Nobile et al. (2021).

Digital transformation is a strategic approach to integrate digital technology and cultural change into all business areas, with the aim of increasing profit, productivity and the agility of the company by reviewing and redesigning business processes to take advantage of these emerging technologies. The four core technologies abbreviated to SMAC (social, mobile, analytics and cloud) are driving innovation in business processes. Digital transformation has been defined as 'the use of new digital technologies . . . to enable major

FIGURE 1.1.3 The evolution of enterprise-wide technology systems to meet business challenges (adapted from Panetto et al. (2016) and Udroiu and Bere (2018)).

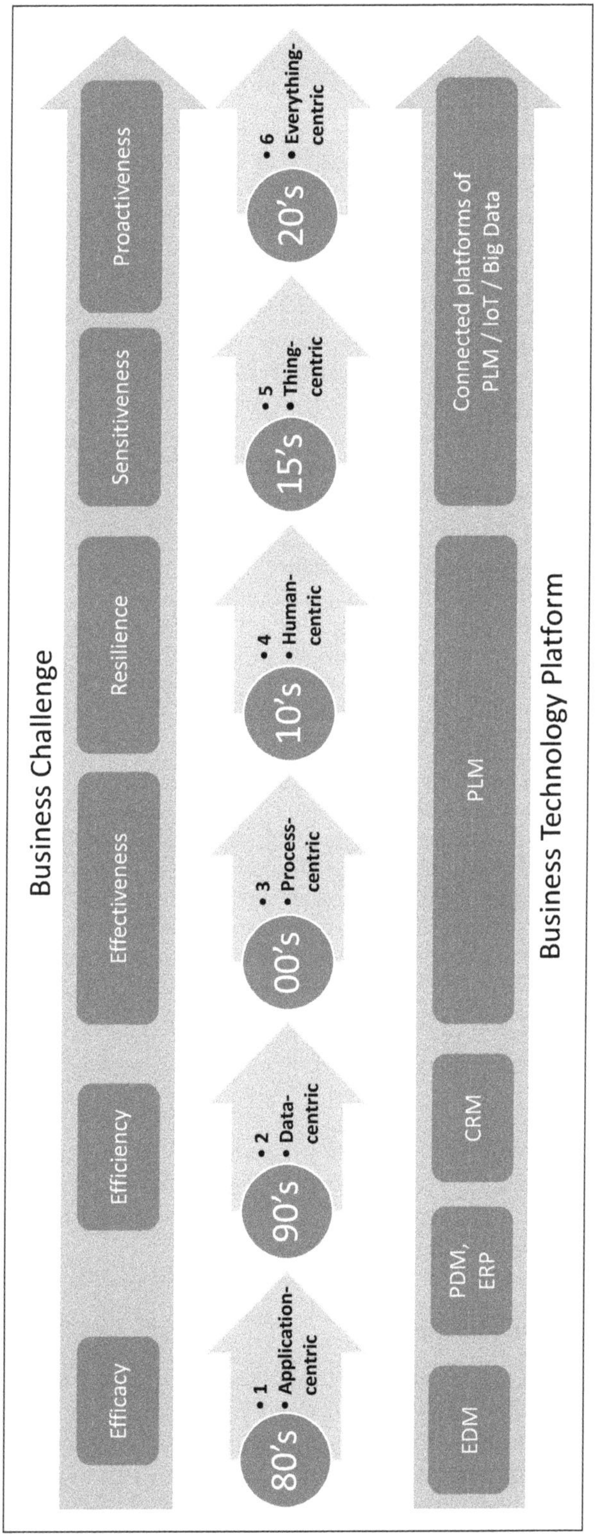

TABLE 1.1.2 Key terms associated with digital transformation, Industry 4.0 components and principles.

Digitise: the process of converting analogue to digital, i.e., the existing process remains unchanged. An example would be typing on a keyboard rather than a typewriter – the output is a digital asset rather than a physical one, but the process of typing remains the same. A **digital asset** therefore represents any content that is stored in digital form and includes files such as images, photos, videos, and text files and databases. Data from connected operations and production systems provides information to learn and to adapt.
Digitalisation: adoption or increase in the use of digital technologies such that business operating processes change to become digital and therefore people's jobs change and, in some cases, become obsolete through automation.
Digital transformation: recognises that there has been a shift in customer needs and behaviours that needs an organisational strategy in response. This means reimagining fashion retail in a digital world, rather than merely digitising the process of shopping for a physical world.
Smart: a suffix added to a variety of terms associated with Industry 4.0. **Smart products**: a collective term used to describe the evolving capabilities digital products (connected, responsive and intelligent) achieved through upgrades to hardware and software (Raff et al., 2020); **smart factories**: a vision for future developments in manufacturing facilities providing flexible and adaptive production processes (Radziwon et al.,2014) and **smart networks** 5G communication networks supporting the digitalisation of society and economy.
Principles of Industry 4.0: interoperability: the ability of devices to accept data from another system preserving the precise meaning of exchanged information; **real time capabilities**: the ability to collect and analyse data in real time; **virtualisation**: the creation of a virtual copy of the physical world so that the system can monitor physical processes; **service orientation**: using technology advancements to stay competitive and customer-focused; **modularity**: systems made of parts (modules) so they can be flexibly and easily adapted or adjusted; and **decentralisation**: physical systems can make automated decisions when equipped with sensors leading to a shift away from centralised factory control systems.

business improvements (such as enhancing customer experience, streamlining operations, or creating new business models)' (Fitzgerald et al., 2013). The key terms of change to digital transformation in the era of Industry 4.0 are summarised in Table 1.1.2.

Disruptive innovation

There is a tendency for market leaders to have their organisational focus elsewhere (maintaining margins, finding new markets/segments etc.) and to consequently underestimate the impact of new entrants. An unprecedented rate of new competitors has entered the fashion market using digital technologies. Online fashion businesses such as ASOS, Net-a-Porter and Farfetch have pioneered a new model of digital-first, sharing the common feature of fast access to reliable data that they use to drive innovation, efficiency and growth (McKinsey, 2014). This level of change in markets is termed 'disruptive innovation'. In his seminal text, Christensen (1997) defines disruptive innovation as 'a process by which a product or service takes root initially in simple applications at the bottom of a market' — that is, with customers who are not currently being served — 'and then relentlessly moves up market, eventually displacing established competitors'. Christensen himself has clarified that few technologies are intrinsically 'disruptive technologies'. Christensen's framework also describes the resistive force of 'sustaining innovations', that is, products and services that strengthen the position of the current market leader (incumbent), but it is the phrase 'disruptive innovation' that has been widely popularised. Disruption has occurred at the point at which mainstream customers are adopting the new entrants' offering in volume.

1.1.3 CASE STUDY: THE ROLE THAT ONLINE MARKETPLACES PLAY IN PROMOTING CIRCULARITY: THE CASE OF VINTED

The 'sharing economy' has disrupted established organisations and business models in many sectors by offering an alternative to ownership. The sharing economy has three core features: the business model is hosted on a digital platform; sharing, swapping or re-selling offer new ways to access goods and services; and communities develop with deeper interactions than traditional models can develop (PwC, 2014). Consumption by sharing keeps products in circulation and is part of the circular economy. Employing digital technologies to support the sharing economy can therefore accelerate the fashion industry towards greater adoption of circular business models. The overproduction, underutilisation and low recycling quality of clothing continues to have a severe environmental impact (Huynh, 2021). The Vinted case study demonstrates new thinking to address unnecessary new demand, that leads to new production and recycling, by keeping products in circulation longer through resale or exchange in communities of likeminded people. The following case uses the 5WH framework (What?, Where?, Why?, Who?, When? and How?) that is used in project and change management.

> We are contributing to a seismic shift in the second-hand fashion market, enabling more sustainable, socially responsible shopping habits. Our platform offers a great, easy-to-use product and helps people experience the benefits of second-hand trade...
>
> Thomas Plantenga, CEO of Vinted, EQT Group (2021).

The Vinted marketplace contributes to UN Sustainable Development Goal 9, 'industry, innovation and infrastructure', as it represents an innovative infrastructure and a positive force in promoting and implementing circular principles. Its success has led to the increasing relevance of circular fashion contributing to UN Sustainable Development Goal 12, 'Ensure sustainable consumption and production patterns'. The global second-hand fashion business model has grown rapidly from $14 billion dollars in 2014 and is now forecast to reach a value of $351 billion dollars by 2027 (Statista, 2023).

What?

Vinted is the largest online customer to customer (C2C) marketplace in Europe dedicated to second-hand fashion. The Vinted platform facilitates the transaction. C2C platforms are more complex than other e-commerce methods due to the greater product variation and non-standard listing. Service fees apply to buyers and cover purchase and fraud protection and customer support services to settle disputes. The buyer also pays for shipping. Additional features can be purchased by sellers to increase the likelihood of sales. Additional revenue comes from third-party advertising.

Where?

The free-to-download mobile app connects users to the online marketplace and this route drives most of the website traffic, although the proportion varies by country. The entry point is typically as a seller. Vinted has a strong social media presence, supporting its community-led brand marketing.

Why?

Users can generate value from the clothes they no longer want, rather than throwing them away. There is also a strong appeal to swapping items in the community. Vinted has offered an alternative means of enjoying the 'newness factor' of fashion at affordable prices for consumers eager to make more responsible and less wasteful fashion choices. Buying second-hand is part of the solution to addressing the environmental impact of clothes production. The marketplace is an example of circular fashion that promotes access to clothes without new production by facilitating the buying and selling of pre-owned items that extends the lifecycle of products.

Who?

In 2008 Milda Mitkute was moving house and had too many clothes and wanted a way to give them away to friends. Working to solve this common problem led to the development of a forum-style website by Vinted co-founders Milda Mitkute and Justas Janauskas. This was a joint hobby project that grew organically. The first angel investor, Mantas Mikuckas, also became chief operating officer (COO). When there was a period of financial trouble related to rapid expansion, Thomas Plantenga joined Vinted first as a strategy consultant and has since become CEO of the company. Vinted is a privately held company, with its co-founders, executives and investors as stakeholders. Vinted is now backed by six leading investment firms: EQT

Growth, Lightspeed Venture Partners, Accel, Insight Venture Partners, Burda Principal Investments and Sprints Capital. The company has over 1000 employees, of which 350+ are engineers working to develop and support continuous improvements of the platform. Vinted has more than 75 million registered users in 18 countries, most of them female and aged between 18 and 39.

When?

2008: Founded in Lithuania
2009: Launched in Germany
2011: First Angel Investor, Mantas Mikuckas became COO
2012: Partnered with Lemon labs to build a mobile app to transition from being desktop-centric to mobile-first. Following its unprecedented success, the app was then redeveloped to be more stable.
2013: Investment from Accel Partners supported expansion to new markets with a launch in the US and further development of the product.
2016: Rapid expansion led to significant financial trouble. Thomas Plantenga joined Vinted first as a strategy consultant and since became CEO of the company.
2016: The mandatory sales fee was replaced with buyer fees and optional paid services for sellers.
2019: The company reached a market valuation of $1 billion, realising unicorn status.
2021: Investment from firm EQT Growth led to expansion into new markets, and supported development of improved payment, shipping and infrastructure.
2021: Vinted partnered with Vaayu, the retail carbon-tracking platform, for an independent analysis of the carbon emissions avoided through the digital marketplace.
2022: Vinted expanded its platform to include non-clothing categories.
2022: Vinted acquired competitor Rebelle.
2022: Vinted launched new shipping platform Vinted Go focusing on PUDO (pick-up, drop-off) as a delivery option intended to reduce their operational carbon footprint.

How?

Vinted offers a mobile and social shopping experience that supports members selling and buying second-hand clothes and accessories from each other. The support team is divided into domains to focus attention into the different parts of the user journey: marketing to attract and retain consumers, onboarding, communication between buyers and sellers, payment, shipping and feedback. These specialised teams drive platform innovation and improvement across iOS, Web and Backend, Site Reliability, Data, Security and Quality Assurance. Vinted uses numerous technologies including Ruby on Rails, CentOS 7, Chef, MySQL, Vitess, ElasticSearch HTML5, jQuery and Google Analytics.

Task

1. Examine the key findings in the Vaayu x Vinted Climate Impact Report (available at: https://www.vaayu.tech/vinted-climate-change-impact-report-2021). What is consequential LCA and how is it estimated? What percentage of users were doing so out of social or environmental concerns?
2. Vinted added 'material search' to the features list. What features do you love, or would you like to see added? Send them feedback: https://www.vinted.co.uk/help/356-send-us-your-feedback

1.1.4 THE JOURNEY TO INDUSTRY 4.0 AND BEYOND

This section moves from our shared fashion experiences of online shopping to provide an overview of the fashion industries journey to today. The intention is to provide a historical perspective of the major changes that resulted in the current state of the industry to demonstrate that change has been a constant in our industry, and that the changes around us are not unique. Historically, fashion and textiles were at the heart of the first industrial revolution, when products that had previously been made by craftsmen and artisans at home began to be manufactured by machines in factories. The sector was among the first industries to use steam power and now the industry is on the brink of another industrial revolution, although this time, it is one powered by digital technologies. In the 'fourth industrial revolution' new digital technologies and internet connectivity are driving the latest wave of industrial progress.

Improving efficiency and reducing waste helps to preserve profit margins and keep prices competitive. Business performance relies on organisational efficiency. Technologies are adopted to help produce things faster and with less effort and is measured by workplace productivity. Productivity is a measure of performance that reflects output compared to inputs. Productivity increases when resources are used efficiently. Today more goods and services are produced than 50 years ago, with the same size (or reduced) workforce leading to growth and increased profitability. Productivity advances with adoption of technology, but the impact is not immediate, as processes and practices need to evolve and build through to full adoption. Additionally, the workforce also needs training, upskilling and time to learn how to maximise the effectiveness of new technologies. The advances in response to key technologies, termed 'industrial revolutions', are depicted in Figure 1.1.4. In the first, second and third industrial revolutions, a major advance in technology powered a leap in productivity when steam power (1.0) electricity (2.0) and computers (3.0) became mainstream. Note that although Industry 3.0 revolution in information and communications technology started in the 1960s, productivity lagged until the growth seen in the 1990s. Equally, today, the right skills and training to realise the benefits of digitalisation and connectivity are required.

This new digital era has become known as Industry 4.0. Industry 4.0 is a term that relates specifically to the new technologies to connect people, things, machines and systems in manufacturing. The term Industry 4.0 is

FIGURE 1.1.4 Industrial Revolutions: Industry 1.0 (mechanisation), Industry 2.0 (mass production), Industry 3.0 (automation), Industry 4.0 (connectivity) 5.0 (human-centricity).

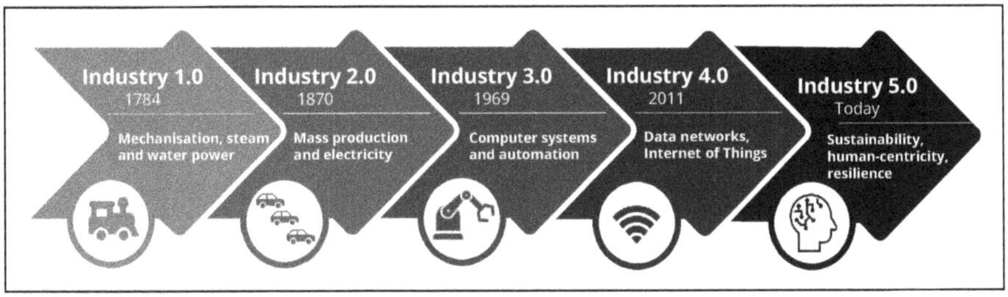

used to describe the growing trend towards automation and data exchange in processes within manufacturing. The basic premise of Industry 4.0 is that new technologies are enabling businesses to connect people, things, machines and systems to create intelligent networks along the entire value chain. The significant driver to initiate the new era technology-driven Industry 4.0 was connectivity between digital technologies, enabling data exchange. Factories are transforming, through the adoption of sensors and readers, into a fully interconnected environment tracking progress, defects, waste and downtime to support decision- makers with reliable, accurate, precise and real-time data. Activities in the retailing and consumer space are also increasingly producing data from multiple sources, including the 'voice of the consumer', and are influencing product design and the rate of manufacture. This data can be analysed for insight and improvement. The challenge for companies is how to connect and share these insights throughout the extended enterprise. This requires that all business decisions, processes and initiatives are routinely reviewed to realise the opportunities offered in the digital age. This in turn will increase manufacturing productivity, fostering industrial growth, modify the required skillset of the workforce and change the economic competitiveness of companies and regions (BCG, 2015). Industry 4.0 presents tremendous opportunities for innovative producers, system suppliers and entire regions. However, as with previous transformational developments, Industry 4.0 also poses a severe risk for individuals, organisations and regions, given the pace of change. Retailers and brands are finding that previous processes and practices are proving inadequate or obsolete in the digital age of fashion retail, where the physical and virtual worlds collide (Crewe, 2013), and many have been unable to adapt to increasingly competitive and challenging markets. Today's fashion system is increasingly digital-first, connected, in the cloud and powered by data. The adoption of new technologies and business models means new skills are required and many companies are experiencing difficulties finding qualified people who possess the required and appropriate data and analytics skills (Gartner, 2019; WEF, 2023). These changes and challenges are conceptualised as Industry 5.0, co-existing with Industry 4.0, and focus on three interconnected core values: sustainability, human-centricity and resilience (Xu et al., 2021). The aim is to ensure that industry refocuses on social fairness and sustainability to achieve social goals as the depth of cooperation between human and machine increases.

ESG – Environmental, Social and Governance – a collective term to show the impact of a business on the environment and society in general and how robust and transparent its governance practices are. It measures how a business integrates environmental, social and governance practices into its operations, as well as its business model and its sustainability.

The advances in technology that form the foundation for Industry 4.0

This section outlines the nine new technologies associated with Industry 4.0 that are enabling businesses to connect people, things, machines and systems to create intelligent networks along the entire value chain (Figure 1.1.3). Digital Transformation is the mechanism that allows the incorporation of new emerging technologies to complete the digitalisation of a business, and this is not restricted to manufacturing industries. Many of these advances in technology already used in manufacturing will not only transform production but change traditional production relationships among suppliers, producers and customers with further connectivity and real-time data exchange.

1.1.5 DATA AND DATA MANAGEMENT

> The world's most valuable resource is no longer oil, but data.
>
> *The Economist*, 6th May 2017

Data can come from sources such as enterprise resource planning (ERP) systems, customer relationship management (CRM) systems, sensors, social media and website data. PLM provides a single organised foundational data set to be shared across the end-to-end value chain.

Data – types and sources

TRADITIONAL, STRUCTURED DATA There are well-established procedures for collecting and monitoring business data for invoicing systems, product databases and contact lists. This type of data is known as structured data as it is organised in a predictable and consistent way. For example, transactional data would be stored in a relational database in structured fields like date, name, age, quantity, price and total that is easily searchable. These relational databases are well established in all types and sizes of organisations with structured query language (SQL) as the language for database queries being widely used.

NEW FORMS OF DATA, UNSTRUCTURED DATA Digital images, videos, audio files, text documents, emails, social media posts (i.e., data from humans) and sensor data (i.e., data from machines) are being created all the time and are

TABLE 1.1.3 The nine foundational technologies of Industry 4.0.

	Technologies in the foundation of Industry 4.0	Description	Current fashion state	Future applications in the fashion system
1	Big data analytics 	Big data analytics is the use of advanced analytic techniques against very large, diverse data sets. Big data analytics pulls from existing information to look for emerging patterns that can help shape our decision-making processes.	Use of data analytics is a rapid growth area (see Chapter 2.4)	Smart workflows will rapidly become standard practice for all employees. (McKinsey, 2022a).
2	Autonomous robots 	Machines that can perform tasks and operate in an environment independently.	Production of high-volume technical textiles, long seams in bedding products and packaging	Reshoring efforts supported with robots to tackle skill shortages e.g., SoftWear Automation's Sewbots (Just Style, 2023).
3	Simulation – virtual reality (VR) 	3-D simulations of products, materials and production processes.	Digital product creation reducing need for physical prototypes to an absolute minimum.	Applications in the Metaverse enhance design without constraints
4	Horizontal and vertical system integration 	Universal data-integration networks enable truly connected value chains.	Companies, suppliers and customers tend to operate with legacy systems resulting in silos of untapped potential benefits.	Data-ecosystem membership connects the extended enterprise to facilitate collaboration on data-driven projects (McKinsey, 2022).

(*Continued*)

TABLE 1.1.3 (Continued)

	Technologies in the foundation of Industry 4.0	Description	Current fashion state	Future applications in the fashion system
5	The Industrial Internet of Things 	The Internet of Things (IoT) describes the network of physical objects i.e., things, that are embedded with sensors, software and other technologies for the purpose of connecting and exchanging data with other devices and systems over the internet.	IoT traceability technologies that typically include RFID, NFC and Bluetooth low energy (BLE), are now widely available (see Chapter 2.4)	Smart manufacturing, example Alibaba's Xunxi Digital Factory
6	Cybersecurity 	Cyber security is the application of technologies, processes and controls to protect systems, networks, programs, devices and data from cyber-attacks, e.g., multifactor authentication, encryption and network segmentation.	Online retail is a target for cyberattacks often target (BoF & McKinsey & Company, 2022) Business risk for failure to protect customer data.	With the rise of valuable digital assets, the need to protect digital assets will intensify.
7	Cloud computing 	Organisations previously hosted their servers on their premises (private). Cloud services are hosted by third-party providers and users access data and run applications over the Internet. Servers on the cloud function just like traditional servers but can be located anywhere.	Companies exploring the benefits: increased flexibility, affordability, scalability and processing power. Some resistance regarding security.	Advanced practices of the cloud continuum create a seamless technology and capability foundation to support the changing needs of the business (Accenture, 2023)

8	Additive manufacturing (AM) 	Additive manufacturing is the industrial production name for 3D printing.	Printing of components and accessories e.g., sunglasses, buttons, footwear.	Further scaling of applications to produce novel and customisable products.
9	Augmented reality (AR) 	AR is an interactive experience that combines the real world and computer-generated content.	Virtual try-on	Advances to include fabric quality and texture and improve appearance of close-fitting garments.

Note: Artificial intelligence is the combination of several technologies, which allow software and machines to sense, understand, act and learn on their own or enhance human activities and this is covered in the next section.

FIGURE 1.1.5 The four V dimensions of big data: Volume (scale of data), velocity (rate of receiving data), variety (different forms of data) and veracity (uncertainty of data).

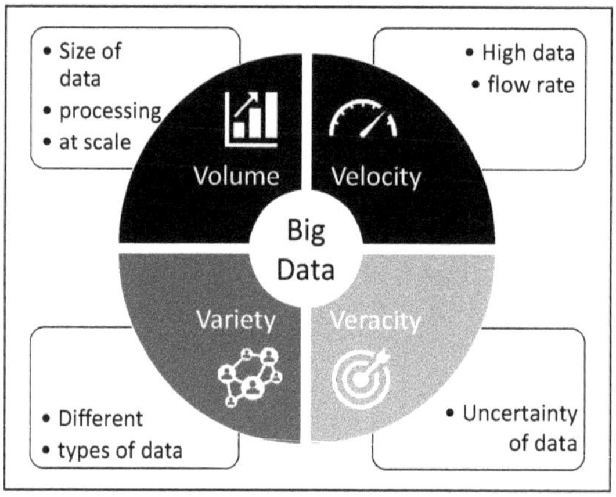

examples of unstructured data. These unstructured data sets are not organised in a consistent way but advances in data analytics are now making it possible to access these untapped data sources. Unstructured data are often richer and more detailed than structured data but may also be subjective and inaccurate.

BIG DATA The term big data refers to a dataset that is too large (given these new data sources) or too complex for ordinary computing processing devices. Big data brings together data from many disparate sources. The cost of data storage has been radically reduced with recent advances in cloud computing making it easier and less expensive to store more data. Big data is often characterised with an emphasis on quantity, but this is just one of its characteristics. IBM devised the system of the four V dimensions of big data: volume (scale of data), velocity (rate of receiving data), variety (different forms of data) and veracity (uncertainty of data) as illustrated in Figure 1.1.5. It is big data that is playing an increasingly important role in digital transformation initiatives.

Introducing artificial intelligence (AI): Its applications in fashion

Artificial intelligence is the combination of several technologies, which allow software and machines to sense, understand, act and learn on their own or augment human activities. AI applications perform specific tasks based on predefined rules and patterns. Examples of traditional AI applications are transactional and conversational chatbots. Generative AI is the field of artificial intelligence that focuses on creating new content based on existing data through cycles of making, testing and elimination to generate a useful deliverable - hence the label 'generative'. The potential positive and negative consequences and how to manage these is in much debate but AI tools are already widely deployed (Table 1.1.5). The amount of time and effort to get an acceptable outcome through extensive prompting and reworking is

TABLE 1.1.4 Example sources of data in the fashion system (adapted from The Interline, 2023).

Scanning data of bodies (to generate avatars), footwear & materials	PLM (product lifecycle management)
CAM (pattern & marker making)	ERP (enterprise resource planning)
2D & 3D CAD solutions	CRM (customer relationship management)
VR/AR/MR (virtual reality/augmented reality/mixed reality)	E-commerce
Material platforms	POS (point of sale)
Colour solutions	AI (artificial intelligence)
Digital printing & dyeing	ML (machine learning)
Inspection & sewing machines	IoT (Internet of Things)

often downplayed (The Interline, 2022b). Whilst human guidance in design and content creation is still required, currently, the degree of human authorship is not adequately regulated raising proof of copyright concerns, anti-counterfeiting and brand protections issues (The Interline, 2022b). People define the problem, identify an appropriate AI technology to solve it, train the tool with the correct data and then verify that the results are valid which means that human bias is also built into AI tools. Much discussion has focused on AI´s potential for propagating bias (Kordzadeh and Ghasemaghaei, 2021) requiring an acceleration in progress to address bias around equality, diversity, inclusion and accessibility (EDIA) and the consequences (Manyika et al., 2019).

Data governance

A key initial step in digital transformation is identification and digitalisation of the master data used across the end-to-end value chain. Core data sets are a mix of structured and unstructured data in unstandardised formats requiring data management to ensure employees have the right data for decision-making. Some examples of sources of data in the fashion system and their impact across the value chain are shown in Table 1.1.6.

Data management involves collecting (from diverse systems and technologies), organising, validating and providing access to data to support objectives such as higher productivity, greater efficiency and better decision-making. Data management relies on effective master data strategies within foundational platforms systems such as PLM; research suggests this continues to be neglected (Kalypso, 2023). Data integrity is an imperative for structured or unstructured data and is established by using data governance practices and using established data management techniques. Data management is a common problem in fashion companies requiring investment to improve visibility, reliability, security and scalability. Additionally,

TABLE 1.1.5 AI applications across the value chain (adapted from BoF, 2023).

Value chain area	Comment	Example
Design & product development	By using AI to create visual designs, brands reduce costs and product development lead times	Nike, H&M and Tapestry leverage AI for insights derived from vast data sets.
Buying & merchandising	Brands use AI to predict trends, plan assortments and create negotiation strategies.	Tommy Hilfiger use AI to manage inventory, improve sustainability practices and enhance the shopping experience
Operations & supply chain	ML optimises inventory by predicting demand, managing quality assurance and reducing waste.	Omnichannel order fulfilment solutions H&M adjusts its production levels and distribution networks to reduce waste and improve efficiency
Marketing	Automated content creation, SEO, sentiment analysis and copywriting using Shopify Magic and Salesforce Einstein GPT	Farfetch uses AI to provide shoppers with personalised product discovery. Maison Meta and Revolve's AI-driven advertising campaign blends human creativity with AI.
Sales & distribution	Product suggestions, AI-driven chatbots, virtual try-on experiences and smart mirrors enhance the shopping experience due to AI's capability in understanding natural language.	Zalando's AI-powered fashion assistant for virtual concierge services Stitch Fix is a personal styling service that uses AI to provide personalised customer recommendations

organisations are experiencing a rapid increase in both the amount and the types of data created that need to be collected, stored and processed from a growing number of sources. Data cleaning is the process of fixing or removing incorrect, corrupted, incorrectly formatted, duplicate, or incomplete data within a dataset produced by combining multiple data sources. Checks for validity, accuracy, completeness, consistency and uniformity are required to ensure the quality of data. Data is seen as key to unlocking the insights needed for businesses to adapt to change and to reengage customers. It is important to note that neither the technology nor the data provide the solution, it is through data analysis that trends or insights can be revealed.

TABLE 1.1.6 Sources of data in the fashion system and their impact (adapted from McKinsey, 2020 and The Interline, 2022a).

Stage in the value chain	**Design**	**Manufacture**	**Logistics**	**Retail**	**Consumer Use**
Sources of data	CAD (2D and 3D)	Digital printing	Returns data	IoT Deloitte connected store example	Size data from virtual try-on apps
	National Sizing Survey	IoT Sewing unit data – from cutting and sewing machines and inspection	Recording and monitoring stock	RFID tags	Consumer profile
	Materials platforms			Changing room conversion to sale	Sentiment analysis social media
	Colour solutions			Heat maps	
	PLM	PLM / ERP	ERP	ERP / CRM	
	Trend tools e.g., Edited / WGSN	IoT		PoS	
	Customer insight				
Data-informed decision-making	Range planning optimisation	Real-time inventory optimisation	Transport network and route optimisation	Inventory optimisation across network	Personalised customer care
	Product development	Supplier selection by performance	Inventory forecasts	Tailored assortments by store	Pricing and promotion

(Continued)

TABLE 1.1.6 (Continued)

Stage in the value chain	**Design**	**Manufacture**	**Logistics**	**Retail**	**Consumer Use**
	Material selection to sustainability criteria	Capacity planning	Capacity planning	Shelf optimisation at store level	
		sub-process traceability	Risk management	Stock visibility	
				Real-times sales	
				Pricing and promotion	
				Returns optimisation	
Impact*	Increased visibility of progress against targets	Overproduction detection	Reduced costs	Improved full-price sell-through	Returns reduced
	ESG			Sales growth	
	ERP				Enhanced personalised experience and loyalty
	Gross margin maintenance				

(* may come from a combination of data including AI, ML)

TABLE 1.1.7 Universal data governance principles (adapted from The Data Governance Institute, 2023).

1. Integrity	Truthful about drivers, constraints, options and impacts for data-related decisions.
2. Transparency	Clear how and when data-related decisions and controls were introduced into processes.
3. Auditability	Documentation supports compliance-based and operational auditing requirements.
4. Accountability	Define accountabilities for cross-functional data-related decisions, processes and controls.
5. Standardisation	Introduce and support standardisation of master data.

Effective data governance is critical to ensure responsible practices that build trust for the adoption and use of data (Table 1.1.7).

Data analysis and interpretation

Raw data is simply facts without context or significance – e.g., a demographic feature of consumers such as age range (from a consumer profile)– so before we start the analysis we need to consider whether it is up to date and is representative of the current situation, as if not its use may lead to further perpetuating the gender data gap (Criado Perez, 2019) and inherent bias (HBR, 2019).

Statistical data analysis techniques can be used to summarise and reveal patterns and trends. Data interpretation is the process of explaining the patterns and trends. The phrase data-driven decision making is therefore somewhat misleading as it implies a direct link between raw data (facts) to a recommendation for a decision and unfortunately it is not quite as simple as that. The missing steps are analysis and interpretation. Let's look at an example through the different levels of analysis and interpretation (adapted from Retalon, 2023).

TRADITIONAL

1. Descriptive: What happened? We can look at sales data against consumer profiles (analysis) to generate a report on best-sellers by similar characteristics e.g., age group or geographical location (interpretation).
2. Diagnostic: Why has it happened? We could then dig a little deeper to try to determine why this is the case. This common activity uses structured data like consumer reviews and CRM data to identify trends. This analysis might look for patterns in pricing, style features, colours, sizing. Our interpretation from that analysis might be that there is a price limit for certain styles or colours. This insight may prompt us to recommend action for promotional activities for these products to encourage sales.

ADVANCED TECHNIQUES

3. Predictive Analysis: What if? Fashion product assortments change rapidly and have a short-window of opportunity for full-price sale, further complicated by size and colour combinations. These models use statistics and ML algorithms for predicting future outcomes to manage risk by calculating the probability that a similar style would also sell-well or demand forecasting. Retailers have found ML and predictive analytics to be transformative. See 2.2.2. Case study M&S x First Insight
4. Prescriptive Analysis: How to make it happen? This model suggests how to optimise the desired result by using recommendations, e.g., to move stock where sales are sluggish to a different store to reduce markdowns.

Towards the data-driven enterprise

Spreadsheets such as Excel remain popular in fashion organisations as they are easy to use and have numerous functions built in for data analysis with additional features to deal with high volumes of data. However, they can be time-consuming, need updating, are open to human error and typically lack data governance. The resulting issues, the need for true collaboration and the potential value from optimisation are leading to organisations considering replacing spreadsheets with end-to-end data science platforms and built in data-supported capabilities. Smart workflows, advanced interactions and capabilities will become standard, with most employees using data to perform and optimise their work (for more, see Chapter 2.4). Table 1.1.8 details the seven characteristics of the data-driven enterprise (McKinsey, 2022a and 2022b).

TABLE 1.1.8 The seven characteristics defining the data-driven enterprise (adapted from McKinsey, 2022a and 2022b).

Characteristic	Today	From 2025
1. Data is embedded in every decision, interaction and process	Traditional ways of working are being replaced but are not yet fully connected across the end-to-end value chain. Requirement for employee upskilling.	A digital-first and data-driven culture leads to efficiencies and drives continuous improvements. Employees have more time to focus on innovation, collaboration and communication.
2. Data is processed and delivered in real time	Legacy operating systems need replacing. IT infrastructure needs modernising.	Data analytics becomes accessible and widely available through cloud-enabled data platforms. Advances in 5G enable connected infrastructures.

TABLE 1.1.8 (Continued)

Characteristic	Today	From 2025
3. Flexible data stores enable integrated, ready-to-use data	Data engineers required to refine data, explore them and establish connections using manual, bespoke, time-consuming processes.	Real-time technology and architecture advances enable data products such as 'Customer 360' and 'digital twin' by identifying critical data sets, using flexible ontologies (naming) to map relationships between different classes of data.
4. Data operating model treats data like a product	Siloed data sets make it difficult for users to access the data they need. Data ownership is challenging.	Data products ensure the data asset continues to evolve. By building data products to support a consumption archetype (models) they can be applied to multiple business applications with similar archetypes, reducing time and cost to scale.
5. The chief data officer's role is expanded to generate value	Function as a cost centre to manage data and are responsible for compliance policies and procedures.	Work in partnership with business units to find new ways to value using data and ensure revenue-generating data services are ethical and align with the business values.
6. Data-ecosystem memberships are the norm	While data is often siloed within organisations, sharing with external partners is uncommon and very limited.	Data federation allows multiple databases to function as one data-sharing platform facilitating collaboration internally and externally enabling a more holistic view of the value chain.
7. Data management is prioritised and automated for privacy, security, and resiliency	Security seen as a compliance issue. Secure access remains a largely manual process that impacts productivity.	From compliance to a core business competence. Increased automation of data-administration and AI tools improve data-quality issues.

END-OF-CHAPTER DISCUSSIONS

1. Highlight the implications for marketing and product development teams of skewed data due to sample biases. If you were a part of these teams, what could you do to ensure that these data sets were more representative?
2. Generative AI is a useful tool for business with limited resources. Evaluate the benefits of generative AI in comparison to the ethical implications of its use.
3. Data-informed decision-making is now standard practice within organisations. Statistical knowledge is necessary. How can businesses and individuals ensure that they have the essential capabilities to use digital analysis tools effectively?
4. If you are keen to explore data and AI further then learning resources and short courses are available through the Tableau Academy, available at: https://www.tableau.com/community/academic
5. Review section on 'Disruptive Innovation'. Online shopping disrupted traditional fashion retail. Do you believe that additive manufacturing (3D printing) can be identified as a 'disruptive innovation'? To what extent do you think additive manufacturing will disrupt fashion manufacturing?

Case study bibliography

Charged (2022). Vinted launches new shipping platform Vinted Go. Available at: https://www.chargedretail.co.uk/2022/07/14/vinted-launches-new-shipping-platform-vinted-go/ (accessed 8 October 2023).

Ellen MacArthur Foundation (2021). Online marketplace and community for fashion items and more: Vinted. Available at: https://www.ellenmacarthurfoundation.org/circular-examples/vinted (accessed 8 October 2023).

EQT Group (2021). EQT Growth leads investment in Vinted, Europe's largest online C2C platform dedicated to second-hand fashion, Press Release. Available at: https://eqtgroup.com/news/2021/eqt-growth-leads-investment-in-vinted-europes-largest-online-c2c-platform-dedicated-to-second-hand-fashion/ (accessed 8 October 2023).

Green Retail World (2022). Second-hand market: Vinted intends to acquire rival Rebelle for €30m. Available at: https://greenretail.world/2022/08/03/second-hand-market-vinted-intends-to-acquire-rival-rebelle-for-e30m/ (accessed 8 October 2023).

Internet Retailing (2021). Second-hand fashion boosted with €250m investment in Vinted to fuel expansion. Available at: https://internetretailing.net/second-hand-fashion-boosted-with-250m-investment-in-vinted-to-fuel-expansion-23150/ (accessed 8 October 2023).

Netguru (2023). How Vinted Has Become a Huge Disruptor in the C2C World https://www.netguru.com/blog/vinted-huge-disruptor-in-c2c (accessed 8 October 2023).

Statista (2023c). Secondhand apparel market value worldwide from 2021 to 2027. Available at: https://www.statista.com (accessed 8 October 2023).

Vaayu (2021). Vinted Climate Change Impact Report. Available at: https://www.vaayu.tech/vinted-climate-change-impact-report-2021 (accessed 8 October 2023).

Vinted (n.d.). How it works. Available at: https://www.vinted.co.uk/how_it_works (accessed 8 October 2023)

Vinted (n.d.). Vinted Engineering. Available at: https://vinted.engineering/open-source/ (accessed 8 October 2023).

Bibliography and further reading

Accenture (2023). *The cloud continuum: Be ever-ready for every opportunity.* Available at: https://www.accenture.com/gb-en/insights/cloud/cloud-continuum (accessed 27 October 2023).

BCG (2015). *Industry 4.0: The future of productivity and growth in manufacturing industries.* Available at: https://www.bcg.com/publications/2015/engineered_products_project_business_industry_4_future_productivity_growth_manufacturing_industries (accessed 27 October 2023).

BoF (2023). 'The complete playbook for generative AI in fashion', *The Business of Fashion*. Available at: https://www.businessoffashion.com/case-studies/technology/generative-ai-playbook-machine-learning-emerging-technology/ (accessed 27 October 2023).

BoF and McKinsey & Company (2022). *The state of fashion: Technology report.* Available at: https://www.businessoffashion.com/reports/news-analysis/the-state-of-fashion-technology-industry-report-bof-mckinsey/ (accessed 25 September 2023).

Christensen, C. M. (1997). *The innovator's dilemma: when new technologies cause great firms to fail.* Harvard Business Review Press.

Conlon, J. (2020). 'From PLM 1.0 to PLM 2.0: The evolving role of product lifecycle management (PLM) in the textile and apparel industries', *Journal of Fashion Marketing and Management: An International Journal*, 24(4), pp. 533–553.

Crewe, L. (2013). 'When virtual and material worlds collide: Democratic fashion in the digital age. *Environment and Planning A, 45*(4), pp. 760–780. doi:10.1068/a4546

Criado Perez, C. (2019). *Invisible women: Exposing data bias in a world designed for men.* Abrams Press.

The Data Governance Institute(2023). *Goals and principles for data governance.* Available at: https://datagovernance.com/the-data-governance-basics/goals-and-principles-for-data-governance/ (accessed 27 October 2023).

Deloitte (2018). *Connected stores: transforming store fleet through technology.* Available at https://www2.deloitte.com/az/en/pages/consumer-business/articles/connected-stores-transforming-store-fleet-through-technology.html (accessed 27 October 2023).

The Economist (2017). 'The world's most valuable resource is no longer oil, but data', 6 May. Available at: https://www.economist.com/leaders/2017/05/06/the-worlds-most-valuable-resource-is-no-longer-oil-but-data (accessed 6 February 2024).

Fitzgerald, M., Kruschwitz, N., Bonnet, D. and Welch, M. (2013). 'Embracing digital technology: A new strategic imperative', *MIT Sloan Manag. Rev*, 55(1), pp. 1–13.

Gartner (2019). *3 barriers to AI adoption.* Available at: https://www.gartner.com/smarterwithgartner/3-barriers-to-ai-adoption (accessed 27 October 2023).

HBR(2019). *What do we do about the biases in AI?* Available at: https://hbr.org/2019/10/what-do-we-do-about-the-biases-in-ai (accessed 27 October 2023).

Heim, H., Chrimes, C. and Green, C. (2022). 'Digital hesitancy: Examining the organisational mindset required for the adoption of digitalised textile supply chain transparency'. In S. S. Muthu (ed.) *Blockchain technologies in the textile and fashion industry* (pp. 47–80). Springer Nature Singapore.

Huynh, P. H. (2021). 'Enabling circular business models in the fashion industry: The role of digital innovation',

International Journal of Productivity and Performance Management, 71(3), pp. 870–895.

The Interline (2022a). *The PLM Report 2022*. Available at: https://www.theinterline.com/2022/05/27/the-plm-for-fashion-report-2022/ (accessed 27 October 2023).

The Interline (2022b). *Digital Product Creation Report 2022*. Available at: https://www.theinterline.com/2022/11/29/digital-product-creation-in-fashion-report-2022/ (accessed 27 October 2023).

The Interline (2023). *The Fashion PLM Report 2023*. Available at: https://www.theinterline.com/2023/06/15/the-fashion-plm-report-2023-available-now/ (accessed 27 October 2023).

Jong, J. Y. (2017). *The fashion switch: The new rules of the fashion business*. Rethink Press.

Just Style (2023). *Robots versus garment workers*. Available at:https://juststyle.nridigital.com/just-style_magazine_sep23/robots_versus_garment_workers (accessed 27 October 2023).

Kalypso (2023). *Digital product creation in retail research*. Available at: https://www.theinterline.com/2023/10/03/benchmarking-digital-product-creation-for-2023/ (accessed 27 October 2023).

Kordzadeh, N. and Ghasemaghaei, M. (2021). 'Algorithmic bias: review, synthesis, and future research directions', *European Journal of Information Systems*, 31(3), pp. 388–409. doi:10.1080/0960085X.2021.1927212

Manyika, J., Silberg, J. and Presten, B. (2019). 'What do we do about the biases in AI?', *Harvard Business Review*. Available at: https://hbr.org/2019/10/what-do-we-do-about-the-biases-in-ai (accessed 27 October 2023).

McKinsey (2014). *Using customer analytics to boost corporate performance: Key insights from McKinsey's DataMatics 2013 survey*. Available at: https://www.mckinsey.com/capabilities/growth-marketing-and-sales/our-insights/why-customer-analytics-matter#/ (accessed 27 October 2023).

McKinsey Global Institute (2018). *Retraining and reskilling workers in the age of automation*. Available at: https://www.mckinsey.com/featured-insights/future-of-work/retraining-and-reskilling-workers-in-the-age-of-automation (accessed 27 October 2023).

McKinsey (2020). *Fashion's digital transformation: Now or never*. Available at: https://www.mckinsey.com/industries/retail/our-insights/fashions-digital-transformation-now-or-never#/ (accessed 27 October 2023).

McKinsey (2021). *Jumpstarting value creation with data and analytics in fashion and luxury*. Available at: https://www.mckinsey.com/industries/retail/our-insights/jumpstarting-value-creation-with-data-and-analytics-in-fashion-and-luxury (accessed 27 October 2023).

McKinsey (2022a). *The data-driven enterprise of 2025*. https://www.mckinsey.com/capabilities/quantumblack/our-insights/the-data-driven-enterprise-of-2025 (accessed 27 October 2023).

McKinsey (2022b). *How to unlock the full value of data? Manage it like a product*. Available at: https://www.mckinsey.com/capabilities/quantumblack/our-insights/how-to-unlock-the-full-value-of-data-manage-it-like-a-product (accessed 27 October 2023).

Nobile, T. H., Noris, A., Kalbaska, N. and Cantoni, L. (2021). 'A review of digital fashion research: Before and beyond communication and marketing', *International Journal of Fashion Design, Technology and Education*, 14(3), pp. 293–301.

OC&C Insight (2016). *Fast forwarding fashion: Skills for the future*. Available at: https://fashionunited.uk/tags/fashion-retail-academy (accessed 4 November 2019).

Panetto, H., Zdravkovic, M., Jardim-Goncalves, R., Romero, D., Cecil, J. and Mezgár, I. (2016). 'New perspectives for the future interoperable enterprise systems', *Computers in Industry*, 79, 47–63. doi:10.1016/j.compind.2015.08.001

PwC (2014). *The sharing economy: How will it disrupt your business? Megatrends: the collisions.* Available at: https://pwc.blogs.com/files/sharing-economy-final_0814.pdf (accessed 27 October 2023).

Radziwon, A., Bilberg, A., Bogers, M. and Madsen, E. S. (2014). 'The smart factory: Exploring adaptive and flexible manufacturing solutions', *Procedia Engineering*, 69, pp. 1184–1190.

Raff, S., Wentzel, D. and Obwegeser, N. (2020). 'Smart products: conceptual review, synthesis, and research directions', *Journal of Product Innovation Management*, 37(5), pp. 379–404.

Retalon (2023). *How data analytics is saving the fashion industry*. Available at: https://retalon.com/blog/fashion-analytics (accessed 13 October 2023).

Statista (2020). *5G set to beat adoption record for new tech*. Available at: https://www-statista-com.manchester.idm.oclc.org/chart/22000/years-until-adoption-by-one-billion-users-selected-technologies/ (accessed 27 October 2023).

Statista (2022). *Moving forward with 5G.* Available at: https://www.statista.com/study/116527/moving-forward-with-5g/ (accessed 27 October 2023).

Statista (2023a). *Fashion e-commerce worldwide.* Available at: https://www.statista.com/topics/9288/fashion-e-commerce-worldwide/#topicOverview (accessed 27 October 2023).

Statista (2023b). *5G – statistics & facts.* Available at: https://www.statista.com/topics/3447/5g/#topicOverview (accessed 27 October 2023).

Udroiu, R. and Bere, P. (eds) (2018). *Product lifecycle management: Terminology and applications.* IntechOpen. doi:10.5772/intechopen.75972

WEF (2023). *Future of Jobs Report 2023: Insight report*. Available at: https://www3.weforum.org/docs/WEF_Future_of_Jobs_2023.pdf (accessed 27 October 2023).

Xu, X., Lu, Y., Vogel-Heuser, B. and Wang, L. (2021). 'Industry 4.0 and Industry 5.0: Inception, conception and perception', *Journal of Manufacturing Systems*, 61, pp. 530–535.

CHAPTER 1.2

Digital transformation strategies

Unlocking change in fashion

Jo Conlon

LEARNING OUTCOMES

After reading this chapter you should be able to:

- Justify the necessity of a strategic approach to digital transformation within the fashion industry and describe the steps involved.
- Evaluate change management models and their application within the context of digital transformation of fashion.
- Explain the concepts of digital hesitancy and digital maturity and how these apply to the digital transformation of fashion business systems.
- Identify opportunities for greater visibility and transparency in the fashion value chain enabled by digital technologies.

This chapter explores the complexities of strategic change and the process of integrating digital technologies into businesses to achieve business ambitions. Most businesses recognise that they must adopt digital technologies to remain competitive. Although companies are aware of the potential benefits of digital transformation, they face challenges reshaping their customer value proposition and reforming their processes to leverage new technologies. This chapter advocates for a strategic approach to digital transformation that invites all stakeholders to contribute to the digital transformation journey. This chapter outlines how theories of change management have been adapted to support digital transformation and how the capability maturity model (CMM) can be used to measure the maturity of a fashion organisation's processes through a digital readiness audit. Building on Chapter 1, a review of product lifecycle management (PLM) applications is employed to illustrate the potential of digital technologies to resolve industry challenges and realise new opportunities through a connected fashion value chain.

DOI: 10.4324/9781003364559-3

FIGURE 1.2.1 The connections between vision, strategy and operations.

Vision or future goal

Strategy details the long-term initiatives to be taken

Strategic objectives are high level purpose statements with measurable goals

Key performance indicator (KPI) a measurable, quantifiable and reported metric used to track progress towards a specific goal or objective (financial, customer-focused or process-focused)

KPIs are articulated for strategic and operational areas of the business with operational KPIs reported daily or monthly

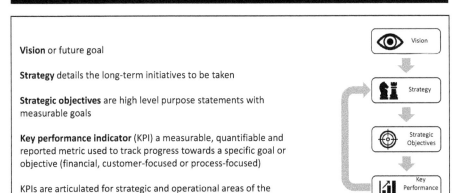

1.2.1 A STRATEGIC APPROACH TO DIGITAL TRANSFORMATION OF THE FASHION VALUE CHAIN

Digital technologies provide opportunities for doing business differently and to significantly improve the performance of a business. Strategic leadership, organisational culture and vision are described as the drivers of change and adoption of innovative new business models in conjunction with enabling technologies. Throughout the fashion value chain there are abundant opportunities for digital innovation, but organisations must maintain a holistic perspective to prevent fragmented change. Improvements to visibility throughout the value chain offers a significant advantage by joining up pockets of information for informed decision-making (McKinsey, 2020a and 2021).

A brief overview of strategic planning and operations management

Strategic planning is the process by which a company sets out its business goals and how it intends to work towards achieving them through effective use of resources (i.e., their physical, human, intellectual and financial resources) in the mid- to long-term. This period has reduced from typically 3–5 years to 1–3 years or even 12–18 months because of the high pace of change due to innovation, new market entrants and likelihood of unpredictable events. The strategy should include digital transformation as one of the approaches to achieve strategic aims given digital technologies are now deeply incorporated in achieving a unique value proposition. However, simply investing in technology does not guarantee change or success. Clearly defined business outcomes are the driver of change, and technology can be viewed as an enabler of change. The strategic plan, i.e. the holistic view of where the company is going and how it will reach its goals, is cascaded through the organisation via tactical plans and then operational plans that

FIGURE 1.2.2 How technology enables business change (adapted from Paschek et al., 2022).

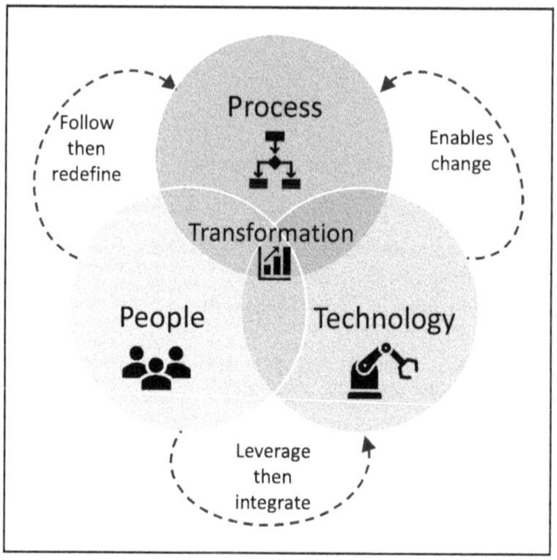

specify key performance indicators (KPIs) for the overall business operations and the functional areas. Managers then monitor actual performance against planned performance reporting if they are on track to achieve their business objectives. For some operational KPIs, especially in production processes, data needs to be captured and monitored almost in real-time, while for strategic KPIs a monthly or quarterly data gathering and monitoring frequency would be sufficient. Feedback influences ongoing decision-making and strategic planning.

Although companies are aware of the potential benefits of digital transformation, they face challenges creating a clear roadmap to reform their existing processes in line with these technologies. A digital transformation strategy is the approach to remodelling the organisation to incorporate digital technology appropriately throughout the value chain, resulting in fundamental changes to how it operates. The three factors of people, processes and technology must work in combination to achieve business success as shown in Figure 1.2.2. The purpose of this remodelling through digital transformation is to strategically position an organisation for the future. The steps required are outlined in Figure 1.2.3. The strategic plan must define how the digital transformation initiative will contribute to the key strategic goals and add value to the business. Each business will have different approaches to enhancing customer satisfaction, resulting in different strategic priorities but generally benefits include achieving greater efficiencies, improving delivery speed, reducing costs, eliminating waste, providing process transparency and enhancing collaboration between business units and business partners. New technologies require significant financial investment and therefore a compelling business case articulating the expected benefits is required. This is typically stated as return on investment (ROI). A key step involves capturing the 'AS-IS' or current position. This is typically achieved by conducting a series of

FIGURE 1.2.3 Eight steps in digital transformation (adapted from McKinsey, 2017 and PTC, 2021).

Stage 1: Define value	Stage 2: Launch and accelerate	Stage 3: Scale
• 1. Set ambitious targets that clearly define the business value and commitment from senior management • 2. Prepare for culture change with human-centric change management	• 3. Select a powerful, strategic pilot project • 4. Appoint a high-calibre and diverse change team with clear change champions and feedback and success reporting mechanisms • 5. Consider accessing external partner expertise, e.g., to perform a digital readiness audit • 6. Invest in employee upskilling and communicate successes to nurture a digital culture	• 7. Sequence new initiatives to build on momentum for further success • 8. Adopt new processes and operating models

business-wide questionnaires in a digital readiness audit, from which a baseline towards future digital maturity can be measured. An action plan of these priorities with measurable objectives 'TO-BE' over time details the roadmap to digital transformation that is then implemented by the organisation.

Change management models

Change management – systematic approach to ensure that an organisation has the skills, knowledge and confidence needed so that change and its impact on people is managed effectively, by considering, designing and applying the right processes to ensure success (Henderson, 2018, p.284).

As introduced in Chapter 1.1, new technologies and their greater connectivity have led to an explosion of possibilities for businesses to consider. Yet for many reasons, how things are done in an organisation tends to remain resistant to change (Pal and Jayrathne, 2022). An entrepreneurial mindset spots opportunities to solve problems, sees change as a positive and helps to develop resilience to thrive with constant change (for more, see Chapter 2.3). Therefore, this mindset is much needed to address business challenges as leaders and managers frequently need to take action to address underperformance (organisational or individual) or changes in the external environment (current or future). Change sounds simple but people and organisations are complex and therefore a systematic approach to understanding and implementing change is useful to avoid or limit potentially damaging effects. Organisational change now recognises the significance of employee involvement in formulating and implementing change. Adding knowledge of the principles of change management to an entrepreneurial mindset can support your personal development as an employee, manager and leader throughout your career. Change processes provide opportunities to develop skills and confidence in a diverse range of areas such as creative problem solving, flexibility, resilience, empathy, cooperation, communication, collaboration, goal setting, goal attainment, project management and leadership. Graduates should be on the lookout for the opportunity to take on additional 'stretch projects' to develop change management knowledge and skills. Organisations increasingly need experienced change leaders and often engage external change management professionals, making change management a viable career option worthy of consideration.

As digital transformation activities are typically based on change management approaches, the main models are reviewed in Table 1.2.1.

Table 1.2.2 details the change management activities that a digital transformation initiative should replicate. Organisational change management was identified as a major barrier to successfully implementing 3D digital product creation (DPC) initiatives (Kalypso, 2023). Digital transformation requires a reconsideration and definition of the organisational strategy stating

TABLE 1.2.1 Development and contribution of different change management models.

Kurt Lewin's three-stage model (unfreezing, changing and refreezing) is considered the precursor of change management models. It highlights the typical behavioural response to each step of change (threatened, resistance, confidence) so that these can be managed.
Kübler Ross' Change Curve Model depicts five stages of personal transition (denial, anger, bargaining, depression and acceptance) and remains useful to understand the emotional turmoil that some employees may face due to any change initiative in the workplace.
GE's Change Acceleration Process recognised that acceptance of the change strategy was a key part of the success of any change initiative. The Change Acceleration Process includes seven steps: 1. Lead change 2. Create a shared need 3. Shape a vision 4. Use pilots to identify success factors and barriers 5. Mobilise commitment 6. Monitor the process for progress and problems 7. Make the change permanent with new systems and structures.
The 7S framework (McKinsey) details a set of three 'hard' elements (strategy, structure and systems) and four 'soft' elements (skills, staff, style and shared values) that are interrelated and determined by shared values to help frame questions to assess an organisation's ability to change. It highlighted the difficulty in changing organisational culture.
Kotter's 8 Steps for Leading Change model is one of the most well-known and used models that details three phases: creating the climate for change (1–3), engaging and enabling the organisation (4–6) and implementing and sustaining change (7 and 8) over eight steps. 1. Create a sense of urgency and raise awareness of the need for change and establish management 'buy-in' 2. Build a change leadership team 3. Define a clear vision and strategy for change 4. Communicate the vision and strategy 5. Identify and manage barriers to change 6. Generate short-term wins 7. Build on the change through continuous improvement 8. Consolidate the change.

TABLE 1.2.2 List of digital transformation activities based on the change management approach (Bellantuono et al. 2021).

Change Management Activities	Digital Transformation Activities
Define a strong leadership	Define a strong leadership
Generate awareness on the need for change	Analyse Industry 4.0 environment to identify opportunities and threats
	Conduct a digital maturity assessment
	Generate awareness on the need for Industry 4.0 transition
Define a clear change vision and strategy	Define a clear vision, a strategy and a roadmap for the Industry 4.0 transition
Communicate change vision and strategy	Communicate the vision, strategy and roadmap for the Industry 4.0 transition
Define a change management team	Define an Industry 4.0 change management team
Identify short-term goals and pilot projects to test the change	Identify short-term goal and pilot projects of digitalisation
Identify and manage resistance to change	Identify and manage resistance to change
Train people	Define digital capabilities and skills
	Train and/or recruit people
Collect and analyse feedback and monitor change	Collect and analyse feedback and monitor the digital transformation process
Celebrate success and implement corrective actions	Celebrate success and implement corrective actions
Consolidate the change	Consolidate the change

how the organisation intends to create value in the era of Industry 4.0. Digital transformation might enable business model experimentation or reconfiguration to open new opportunities for value creation and value delivery (Lanzolla et al., 2020). This highlights that the process of digital transformation is not one of simply switching analogue systems to digital ones – a rethink is required that involves a full understanding of new possibilities and existing best practice. Accordingly, this needs an associated change management strategy to communicate and manage the proposed change in the organisation. In this stage the available technology solutions are reviewed, frequently through partnerships for specialist expertise, and mapped against the long-term strategy. An additional crucial step in digital transformation is a digital maturity assessment (section 1.2.2) to determine the current level of digitalisation of the organisation and its readiness to introduce changes. This stage considers how existing foundational technologies such as PLM will be integrated in the change initiative to fully utilise these resources and capabilities to manage DPC content effectively across the organisation. Across

TABLE 1.2.3 Effectiveness in communicating the digital vision: Percentage of leadership and employees who agree with the following statements on digital vision (adapted from Buvat, 2017).

Statement	% of leaders who agree	% of employees who agree
Our organisation's digital vision is pragmatic and can easily be translated into concrete projects and initiatives	69	36
A well-defined strategy and action plan exists for achieving our digital vision	62	37
The digital strategy and vision are well communicated to the whole organisation	61	38

any business there will be many processes all at different levels of maturity. Exactly as in change management the vision, strategy and roadmap must be effectively communicated to ensure buy-in; as seen in Table 1.2.3, communication of the digital vision frequently fails to engage leaders and employees. The appointed change team or task force project manage the change activities, starting with pilot projects to test the technology to identify quick wins and barriers to change. Change management theory posits that there will be resistance to change and that regular open communication, training and patience help. The monitoring stage assesses the performance of new processes, addresses issues and celebrates success. The new digital business model, new business processes and realigned organisational structures are documented and monitored in the consolidation stage. A culture of continuous improvement begins the next initiative. The steps in this process are summarised in Figure 1.2.3.

1.2.2 ASSESSING DIGITAL MATURITY

We covered in section 1.2.1 that a digital readiness audit or a clear assessment of the current state 'AS-IS' is an essential first step. A series of questionnaires are completed to assess the level of digital maturity across all areas and processes. Examples of questionnaires used are available through the references for Chapter 1.2, question 1. The results are typically mapped in a maturity model to identify organisational strengths and weaknesses to identify strategic priorities. The capability dimension of processes in the model comprises six levels, from level 0: incomplete, to level 5: innovating; as shown in Figure 1.2.4, 'Digital Maturity' is understood as the state of an organisation's digital transformation (Chanias and Hess, 2016). From this a roadmap is produced to detail the phases and timings for the digital transformation initiative.

FIGURE 1.2.4 Capability maturity model: Capability and process dimensions of digital transformation.

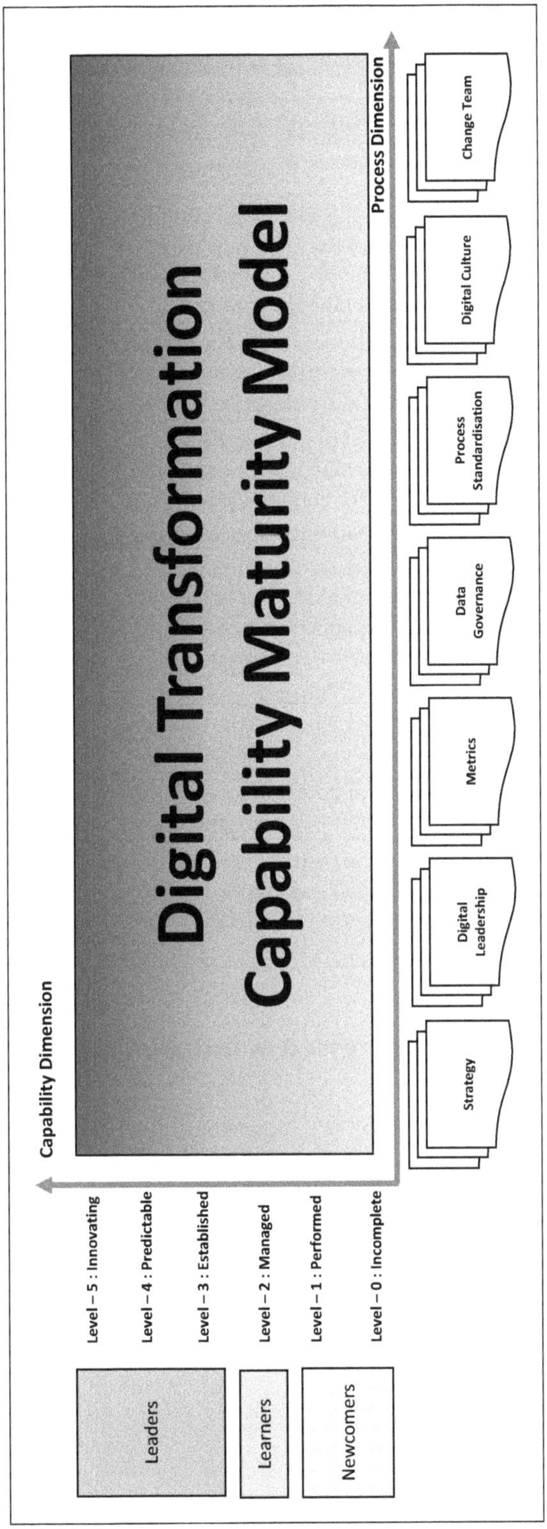

TABLE 1.2.4 Prevalence of the seven digital culture dimensions (adapted from Buvat et al., 2017).

Dimensions of a 'digital culture'	Description	Whole Organisation %	Culture Leaders %
Customer centricity	The use of digital solutions to expand the customer base, transform the customer experience and co-create new products	59	91
Collaboration	The creation of cross-functional, inter-departmental teams to optimise the enterprise's skills	51	96
Open culture	The extent of partnerships with external networks such as third-party vendors, startups or customers	35	37
Agility and flexibility	The speed and dynamism of decision-making and the ability of the organisation to adapt to changing demands and technologies	31	77
Digital-first mindset	A mindset where digital solutions are the default way forward	31	75
Data-driven decision- making	The use of data and analytics to make better business decisions	25	60
Innovation	The prevalence of behaviours that support risk-taking, disruptive thinking and the exploration of new ideas	20	53

Cultural attributes addressed in included digital maturity models

The growing importance of organisational culture as an enabler of digital transformation efforts is being recognised, with calls for it to be developed as a dedicated dimension to be integrated into digital maturity models through the addition of clearly defined attributes of a digital culture (Teichert, 2019). Digital culture has been defined as a set of seven key dimensions/attributes. As shown in Table 1.2.4, organisations are making the most progress in collaboration and adopting a customer-driven mindset, but still need to make progress to the level of the digital culture leaders.

1.2.3 HOW INTEGRATED PLM AND DIGITALISATION ENABLES A FULLY CONNECTED SUSTAINABLE FASHION VALUE CHAIN

Background to the retail apparel PLM

The fashion industry is characterised by product range complexities (size, colour and dual sourcing) and the need to respond quickly to ever-shortening time frames of interest in the era of instant gratification and a consumer demanding a streamlined personalised shopping experience. Traditional PLM has supported the standardisation of processes within the fashion system and helped to tackle the persistent challenges of cost, quality and speed, and the need to establish organisational cultures of continuous improvement. However, access to accurate product-specific supply data is difficult and time-consuming as product data are typically generated in a range of diverse, disconnected applications (The Interline, 2023a). Advances in PLM integration, coupled with improved global connectivity speeds, now offer the means to accelerate the process of digitally connecting and optimising all parts of the fashion system and the generation of actionable insights through shared reliable data. The pandemic highlighted the strategic importance of the supply chain prompting renewed efforts to connect the extended enterprise. The three cases illustrate the potential of digital value chains to have higher visibility and greater optimisation of the supply chain and how an integrated PLM approach offers a solution to the persistent issues of transparency, fairness and sustainability.

Traditional PLM initially helped to manage product design, development and sourcing by consolidating core product information and enhancing communication through supply chains. Traditional PLM offered advantages beyond Excel spreadsheets and emailed updates and signalled a shift towards greater collaboration within the extended enterprise. However, a disappointing level of collaboration and transparency still exists. Highly competitive and fragmented supply chains have fostered a lack of trust that has resisted the potential of unlocking collaborative benefits. Many partners in the extended supply chain are SMEs and communication with retail PLM has been via a portal for document upload/download rather than data exchange via secure access to an authorised level. The lack of full integration leads to issues with accuracy, delays and additional IT costs. Fashion continues to operate with very limited visibility of the extended supply chain and is therefore largely ill-equipped to monitor and manage social and environmental practices despite being held increasingly accountable for their impact (BoF & McKinsey & Company, 2022).

Around 2015 brands and retailers recognised the value of data flow and began to make investments in PLM and other solutions to support even faster, real-time responsiveness, visibility, transparency and sustainability in the supply chain (Figure 1.1.3). The pandemic highlighted the significance of transparency and robust collaborative partnerships in supply chains and accelerated several emerging consumer trends, e.g., greater engagement with online channels, the demand for more personalised experiences and the rise of conscious consumerism (Euromonitor, 2020). This period also highlighted that those organisations that had invested in digital were far more resilient during the pandemic and subsequently accelerated their digital transformation initiatives, which has prompted others to move more rapidly to digital transformation. However, the functional profile of retail apparel PLM is much broader than more mature PLM applications (aerospace, automotive, etc.) and consequently a proportionally broader number of other systems are required to send or receive data (Digital Solution Group, 2022). The expanded common set of functional product data operations supported in retail apparel PLM is presented in Table 1.2.5.

PLM facilitates access to the data from all these processes using the tools of collaboration, workflow and automation. PLM has evolved to become a tactical solution for improving processes and connecting other business systems (e.g., ERP, CRM CAD/DPC, e-commerce). Managing these integrations as they evolve over time is complex and often hampered by legacy system configuration management, meaning that there remain product data accuracy issues due to manual re-entry or operational delay due to cross system re-entry and increased IT support costs to facilitate integration of essential business systems (Digital Solution Group, 2022). Only relatively recently have PLM vendors worked with other solution vendors to create integration

TABLE 1.2.5 Typical components or modules found in retail apparel PLM solution that require integration (adapted from The Interline, 2023a and Digital Solution Group, 2022).

PLM libraries (product types, seasons, patterns and size charts, components, materials, suppliers, colours, etc.)
Industry trends presented as story and mood boards.
CAD and DAM (digital asset management)
Assortment planning (i.e., range or line planning)
BOM (bill of materials)
BOL (bill of labour)
Costing
Sourcing for products and components (supplier approval, audits and performance)
Document & file management (secure vaulting for IP, user authentication for supply chain collaboration)
Release or change management (recording modifications in design)
Access or organisation management (managing permissions for access by use role)
Product configuration & template management (reflecting bespoke or industry-standard configuration)
Critical path management of delivery logistics and lifecycle management (through IoT)

frameworks for specific applications (The Interline, 2023a). As technology ecosystems become broader and more complex, the ability to integrate best-in-class tools is becoming increasingly more important to manage multiple and sophisticated demands. The efficiencies gained through traditional PLM have reached a limit and full digitalisation of the extended enterprise to achieve a fully connected value chain is now required to bring the visibility and collaboration needed to optimise processes further. The digital applications along the fashion value chain are shown in Figure 1.2.5.

Switching from analogue supply chains to digital value chains

> It never makes sense to develop tomorrow's products with yesterday's tools.
>
> (CIMdata, 2017)

PLM has emerged as a strategic business model representing 'an integrated approach for the creation, organisation, and management of product related knowledge across an enterprise, its network of suppliers, and its partners . . .' (Cantamessa et al., 2012). The discipline of PLM can drive operational excellence and support planned future business transformation (Suleski and Toncheva, 2016) and many organisations have employed the implementation of PLM to provide a framework to support their digital transformation ambitions (Figure 1.2.6). PLM can be employed as a methodology to drive organisational excellence and to address the challenges of the industry (Suleski and Toncheva, 2016) by supporting a holistic approach to connect multiple technologies and share data across the value chain. Initially at the enablement stage, PLM acts as a hub connecting digital and physical assets across enterprise systems such as enterprise resource planning (ERP), customer relationship management (CRM) and vendor portals. PLM provides a single organised foundation across the value chain. Businesses advance to the differentiation stage by integrating best-in-class applications to achieve strategic ambitions such as faster product development by providing data feeds by role to support decision-making, and enhanced visibility to highlight problems and improve efficiencies and margin. A data-driven approach that allows all roles in the supply chain to make informed decisions is key to optimising the supply chain. The scale and pace of digital transformation taking place across fashion has underlined the importance of PLM as both a source of critical, centralised product information and as an engine for integration across everything from 3D digital product creation to supply chain transformation (The Interline, 2023a).

One of the core functionalities of PLM software is to provide the data governance framework to store, manage and share common data between each solution (Figure 1.2.7). The data from all these processes are collected within the central PLM data model and shared to roles across all processes, using the mechanisms of collaboration, workflow and automation. However, the explosion of additional data from diverse online channels, RFID and IoT devices (from both retail and manufacturing) signalled the limit of the capacity of traditional product-centric PLM and a central single version or hub

FIGURE 1.2.5 Connecting the fashion value chain with digital applications (adapted from BoF Technology).

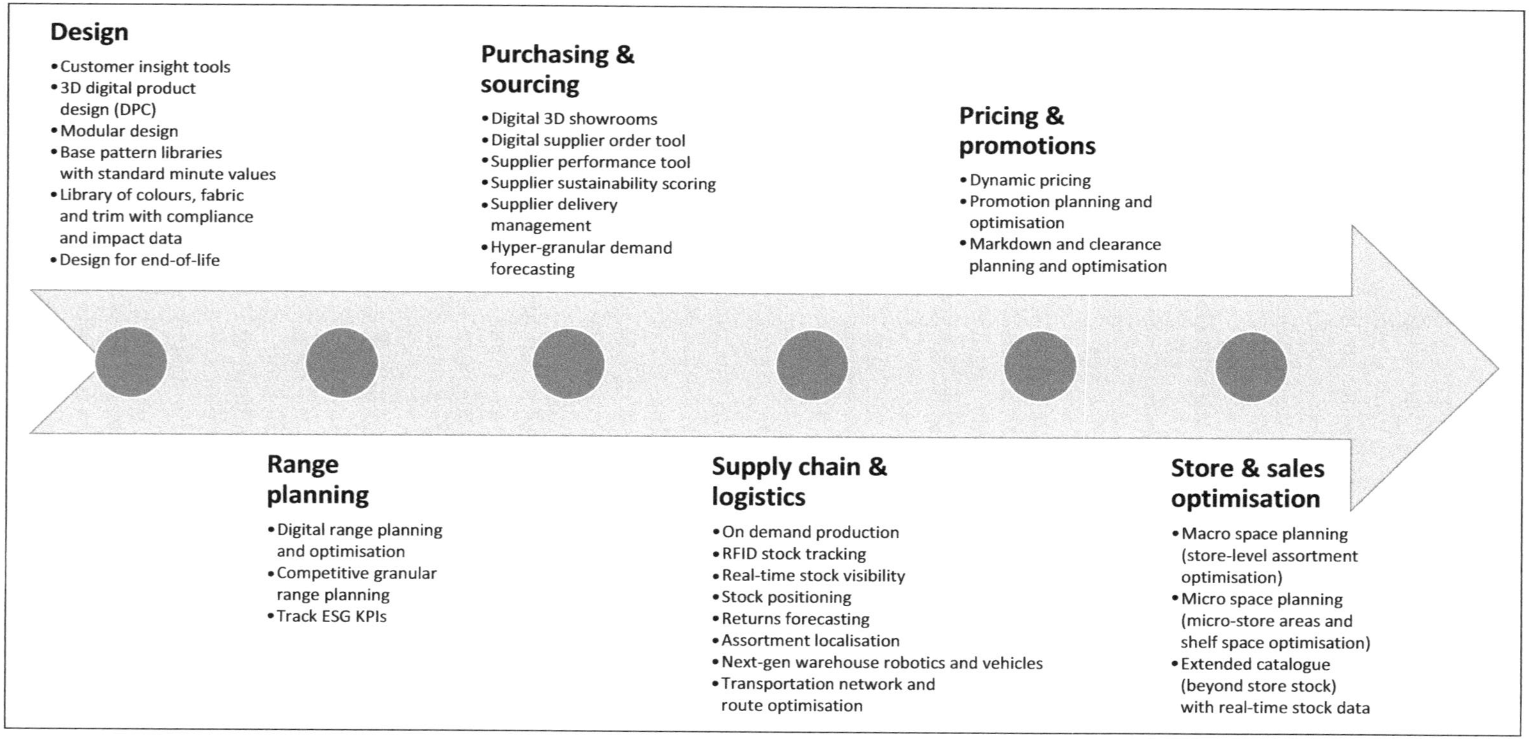

Design
• Customer insight tools
• 3D digital product design (DPC)
• Modular design
• Base pattern libraries with standard minute values
• Library of colours, fabric and trim with compliance and impact data
• Design for end-of-life
Range planning
• Digital range planning and optimisation
• Competitive granular range planning
• Track ESG KPIs
Purchasing & sourcing
• Digital 3D showrooms
• Digital supplier order tool
• Supplier performance tool
• Supplier sustainability scoring
• Supplier delivery management
• Hyper-granular demand forecasting
Supply chain & logistics
• On demand production
• RFID stock tracking
• Real-time stock visibility
• Stock positioning
• Returns forecasting
• Assortment localisation
• Next-gen warehouse robotics and vehicles
• Transportation network and route optimisation
Pricing & promotions
• Dynamic pricing
• Promotion planning and optimisation
• Markdown and clearance planning and optimisation
Store & sales optimisation
• Macro space planning (store-level assortment optimisation)
• Micro space planning (micro-store areas and shelf space optimisation)
• Extended catalogue (beyond store stock) with real-time stock data

FIGURE 1.2.6 The role of PLM in digital transformation (Conlon and Narayanaswamy, 2017).

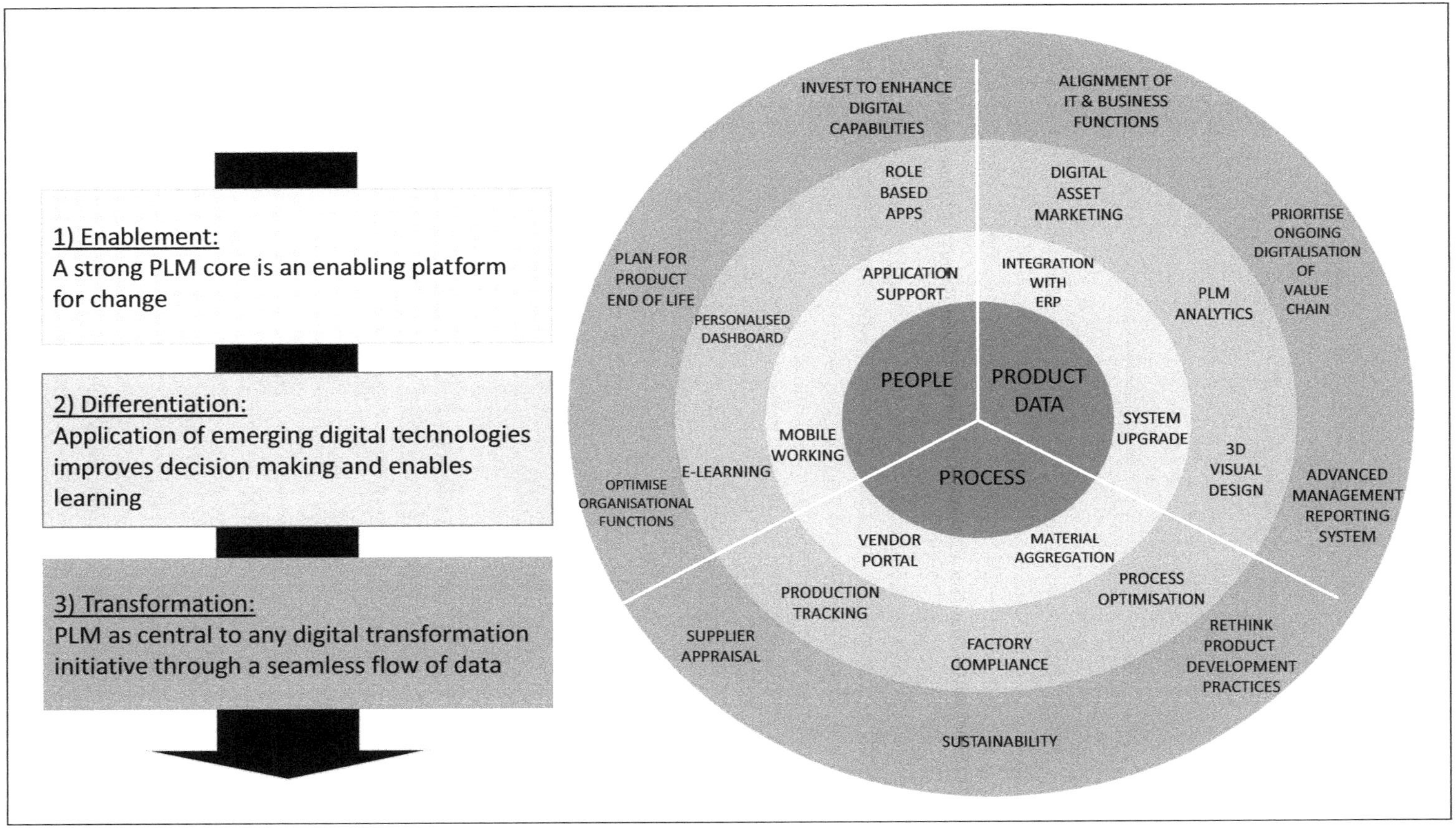

FIGURE 1.2.7 Key attributes for digital transformation supported by PLM.

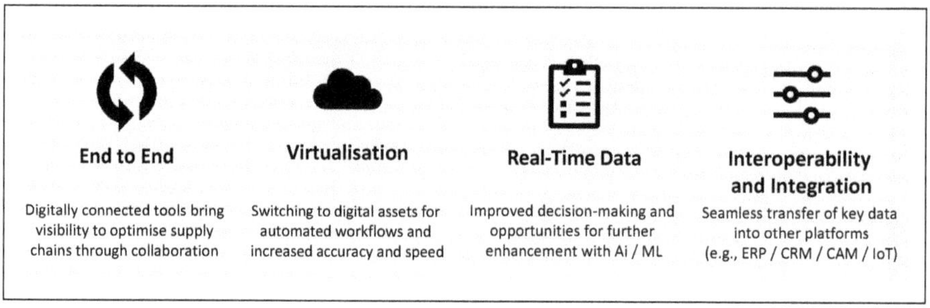

approach. This issue of storage has been resolved with a shift away from data consolidation to data federation. Traditional PLM used a data consolidation approach to bring information together into a single repository. However, cloud-based, big data analytics tools have significantly weakened the case for this approach. Data federation is an alternative approach that works to provide access to reliable data rather than bringing information together. It provides users with a means to query and analyse information from multiple systems through a unified view as if it all resides within a single, harmonised data store. A robust approach to standardisation is essential to connect multiple systems together in an ecosystem. A key advantage of the federation approach is that it allows for real-time information access although concerns about IP protection persist.

End to End
Digitally connected tools bring visibility to optimise supply chains through collaboration
Virtualisation
Switching to digital assets for automated workflows and increased accuracy and speed
Real-Time Data
Improved decision-making and opportunities for further enhancement with Ai / ML
Interoperability and Integration
Seamless transfer of key data into other platforms (e.g., ERP / CRM / CAM / IoT)

The launch of multi-tenant, software as a service (SaaS) environments and modular license options is now making it more viable for other tiers of the value chain including SMEs to realise the benefits of PLM. PLM today is typically deployed remotely with minimal implementation and services, low-code configuration, modularity and on an affordable monthly subscription basis (The Interline, 2023a).

1.2.4 CASE STUDY: THE ROLE OF PLM IN DIGITAL TRANSFORMATION: THE CASE OF BORTEX CLOTHING INDUSTRY LIMITED

Synopsis:

This case seeks to illustrate that manufacturers with retailing operations now have an opportunity to optimise their processes and practices through lower cost, modular subscriptions for PLM. This case seeks to highlight that by embarking on digital transformation with PLM, manufacturers can gain an advantage in achieving supply chain transparency. The digital readiness audit conducted during preparation for PLM investment reveals where manual processes are slowing productivity and where the areas of poor visibility hinder operations management, collaboration and communication across the full value chain. Manufacturing companies like Bortex have reported that activities to evaluate and subsequently implement PLM have not only set them on course to integrate best practice processes but also enabled digital transformation of key business processes in their product and supply chain to transform their end-to-end operations, creating efficiencies and momentum for future change.

Background to the company

Bortex Clothing Industry Limited was established in Malta in 1964 and today consists of two business units: manufacturing and retail. The company is predominantly focused on its own 'Gagliardi" menswear brand and employs over 800 staff. All knowledge-based activities, such as creative, technical design and production planning are carried out in Malta. Made to Measure tailoring is also produced in Malta whilst Bortex production units are in Morocco, Turkey and the Far East. Private label production is shipped direct to end client whereas all Gagliardi production is brought to Malta and distributed to retail and wholesale partners worldwide. Bortex Retail operates online and in ten multi-brand stores in Malta, offering a complete menswear proposition of its own label brand alongside premium brands such as Ralph Lauren, Gant, Lacoste, Hackett, Barbour, etc.

Background to the case

Bortex were clear that their digital transformation strategy was a huge undertaking but recognised that 'data is the key to success' and sought a specialised industry specific tool as a single accessible solution to give visibility to their key business processes and resolve three key business issues:

- Increasing speed to market.
- Replacing legacy systems and processes.
- Reducing internal complexity across product, sales and logistics teams.

DeSL software was selected from an initial longlist of eight providers. DeSL's core database is Microsoft SQL Server. A key factor in the selection process was the capability to offer a multi-tiered service-oriented architecture that enables users to connect to third parties, customers, suppliers, partners, and use external services. This architecture facilitated the association of three internal systems to be brought together as one and ensured access to the design tool Adobe Illustrator.

Change management was handled internally. Bortex found that having senior team buy-in and highly visible use of the new system was a powerful source of momentum. Superusers and champions promoted the milestones achieved and established a buddy system for the sharing of 'hacks'. Importantly, a safe place for all feedback was established so that concerns could be addressed patiently with support and training. The company culture now actively recognises and celebrates the positive mental attitude required to deal with constant change.

ROI outcomes

- Faster: the replacement of legacy systems has streamlined processes and enabled removal of duplication and some automation. The shared system is more viable and interactive, enabling faster decision-making, with tracked change history further reducing time to market.
- Reduced costs: increased visibility has enabled cost savings through optimisation of stock transport network and routes.
- More time for value-added activities through clear and streamlined processes, reduction in error corrections, duplication, etc. The company is on target to achieve their three-year growth plan with a reduced staff overhead.
- Increased visibility has also enabled cost savings through real-time data supported decision- making.
- Clearer communication with suppliers has reduced errors, saved time, enhanced collaboration and other mutual benefits through symbiotic ecosystems are becoming evident.
- An onward trajectory of continuous improvement is now established in the company culture.

Summary

- The replacement of analogue processes and practices with digitally connected tools has brought in advanced alternatives that offer a competitive advantage.
- The future integration of digitalised fabrics at source and digital product creation will advance design, development and retail processes still further.
- The digital transformation project aligned with business sustainability goals has prepared the company for new legislation pertaining to sustainability, traceability and reduction in carbon.

Sources: Borg (2023), Bortex Holdings (n.d) and DeSL (n.d).

HOW PLM CAN SUPPORT SUSTAINABILITY INITIATIVES

Given the urgent need to address poor labour practices and the high environmental impact of fashion and textiles (McKinsey, 2020b), the following cases illustrate how PLM-integrated software solutions are supporting brands and retailers to make their supply channels more transparent and sustainable. These cases demonstrate how supply chain transparency can be achieved through digitalisation. Combining PLM with sustainability initiatives can help businesses design and understand their social and environmental impacts. The drivers for this shift are the impending extension of due diligence obligations, additional mandatory reporting and new regulations to mitigate the risk of mis-selling and 'greenwashing' (Syrett, 2023). The triple bottom line is a well-known framework (Elkington, 1997) to broaden the measure of business success by evaluating business success across three parts: profit, people and planet and thereby commit to address social and environmental issues. However, as each part is typically reported separately, it is important for consumers to think about what is missing in progress reports. For example, does a company only report on the great work they are doing in communities towards a global living wage and neglect environmental reports, whereas another company may report on biodiversity and neglect the workers in their supply chain? Sustainability reporting can be challenging and there is an expectation that robust ESG (environmental, social and governance) frameworks and global standards for reporting will be introduced in time. Without a standardised way of mandatory reporting that ensures reports include all aspects, self-regulation and self-reporting allow greenwashing to continue, eroding consumer trust. There was an expectation that the EU would lead on mandatory reporting but there has been a regression in the regulations due for adoption in 2023. There has been a shift from 'mandatory universal disclosure' to discretionary reporting on materiality, making certain disclosures voluntary. Although this is in line with the International Sustainability Standards Board (ISSB) and thus avoids duplication of effort, many are disappointed given the urgent need for action on fashion's social and environmental impacts. More positively, this does allow businesses more time to change and improve supply chain visibility and transparency, with the expectation that reporting requirements and regulations will become stricter over time.

1.2.5 CASE STUDY: NIGMA BY NATIFIC: ACCURATE ENVIRONMENTAL REPORTING AT THE PRODUCT LEVEL

This case study discusses nIGMA, the latest advancement from the parent company natific. The privately owned company natific was founded in 2008 and has established solutions for digital colour management and compliance that can be integrated into commonly used PLM systems. Many countries and governing bodies are adopting or are in the process of adopting new domestic environmental laws and regulations. Textile companies are intensely reliant on water, chemicals and energy to treat and dye fabrics. Pressure to report on how they are managing their environmental footprint is increasing. Brands and retailers who have committed to sustainably manage their impact need a way to compare the same product when sourced through different global suppliers even before more stringent regulation. When brands and retailers are working to understand the environmental impact (water, energy and greenhouse gases) of their products, they need accurate, verifiable information based on the actual production processes of an item. The factors in the nIGMA process are shown in Figure 1.2.8. With accurate data, brands and retailers can make comparisons between suppliers to inform where they source products from and reward more energy efficient and less polluting suppliers. There is an expectation that accurate reporting will become mandatory in time rather than the current practice of using typical values for fabrics. These typical values for a process or product are likely to be inaccurate for a number of reasons – it is outdated (e.g., 10–15 years old) and generic. New

FIGURE 1.2.8 The nIGMA process (adapted from natific).

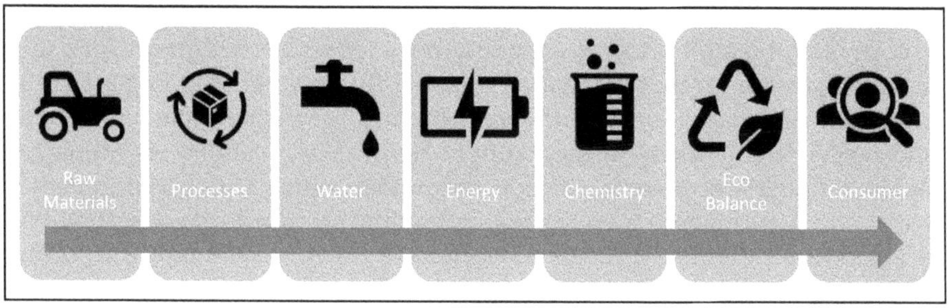

equipment and operating practices are designed to save energy and water. Typical values do not take into account these advancements or the energy type of the actual site (coal or renewables, for example) and accordingly are subject to wide variation from the actual value.

NIGMA CALCULATION TOOL – HOW IT WORKS Verified datasets for standard equipment have been built into the nIGMA module through the close cooperation with leading machine manufacturers. The supply partner then modifies the existing machine base data with local values for energy type, location, efficiency, substrates and chemicals to calculate the eco-balance summary. Each material and production process is entered into the system, where nIGMA calculates the energy, water, CO2 and waste for each process. This approach ensures that calculated data reflects real consumption values that can be approved by comparing results to known standards or by validating results with independent testing, providing brands and retailers with accurate data. Supply partners can use the nIGMA module to enter their existing production processes to determine usage data, including water and energy, and to calculate their eco-balance summary that can be used internally or shared through the Bomler supply chain transparency platform; see Figure 1.2.9. Transferring nIGMA data by product into Bomler makes transparency and consumer visibility simple by building up the eco-balance from each component supplier to the specific product at the retail level. The Bomler tool establishes a marketplace where environmentally responsible producers can promote themselves to retailers looking to source responsibly. Visibility can also be extended to consumers via QR codes that enable a view of manufacturers and the total environmental impact of each product.

1.2.6 CASE STUDY: SOCIAL COMPLIANCE WITH GSDCOST^{V5} BY COATS DIGITAL X C&A

GSDCost^{V5} by Coats Digital is a unique fair wage tool to bring transparency to global apparel sourcing through a common costing methodology based on standardised time management data of sewing operations. In terms of wider integration, GSDCostV5 is a SaaS solution, hosted in Microsoft Azure and designed to seamlessly integrate into existing digital platforms and systems

FIGURE 1.2.9 Synchronising resource data in the Bomler Eco Balance product mapping tool (adapted from natific).

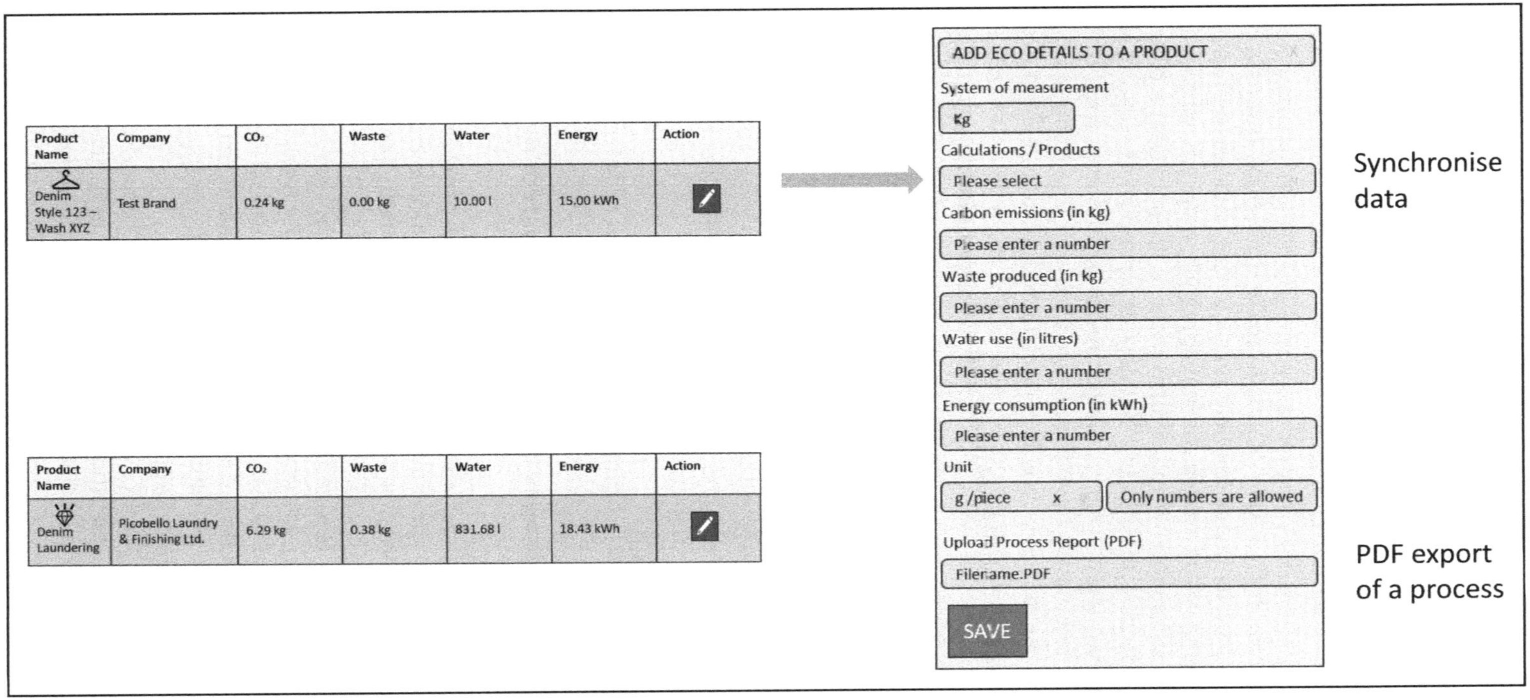

used by apparel manufacturers such as Enterprise Resource Planning (ERP) systems or a Manufacturing Execution Systems (MES). The General Sewing Data (GSD) motion codes can be used as building blocks to create thousands of sewing operations to generate the time for any sewing task, known as standard minute value (SMV), and thereby build up the total time for any style and generate the information required for product costing, pre-production planning, scheduling, delivery and profitability. This approach provides a more consistent SMV to produce any style, bringing visibility, accuracy and the potential for scrutiny of cost to make quotations from supply partners. This common language can help reveal inconsistencies in proposed methods highlighting where a more efficient approach, more advanced skills or investment in automation could reduce costs. With knowledge of the SMV, factory efficiencies (recognising that new styles and short runs are less efficient), contracted hours and agreed wage rates (local minimum wage or living wage), retailers and brands have the facts available to drive operational excellence through fair negotiation with suppliers and make informed decisions, with the ability to benchmark quotes against international fair wage standards.

C&A, the 180-year-old family managed clothing retailer with stores throughout Europe, has started the phased adoption of GSDCost^{V5} by Coats Digital. C&A was challenged by the lack of common costing and sourcing methodology amongst its suppliers, which resulted in inconsistent and disparate Cost to Make quotations. Through the optimisation of method and discussion on achieving efficiencies, both C&A and their supply chain partners can benefit from a more transparent, connected and profitable way of working and provide evidence of fair working practices. This ensures high standards of corporate and social responsibility (CSR) and ethical compliance for brand and manufacturer.

Sources: Coats (2020), Coats Digital (2022) and The Interline (2023b).

Remaining challenges for the fashion system in the era of integrated PLM

As shown through the case studies, PLM can provide fashion and textile organisations with the ability to achieve operational excellence through the creation of new work practices and business processes and provide a strategic platform for future change towards a more sustainable and consumer centric offer. The weak understanding of human and managerial dimensions of PLM systems is a barrier to companies leveraging the transformational potential of PLM (David and Rowe, 2015). PLM frequently struggles to shake off the legacy of having emerged from product data management (PDM), meaning the huge advances in features and connectivity are frequently downplayed. PLM also has an image problem when compared to more obvious and accessible solutions such as DPC and e-commerce. Accordingly, there is an increased urgency to expand the understanding of PLM as a strategic concept, rather than a system, with a pivotal role in the digital transformation of the industry. There is much potential for organisations of all sizes to consider PLM firstly as methodology to prepare processes and employees for digital transformation.

This step of establishing a clear picture of current business processes and capabilities (AS-IS) and future strategic ambitions (TO-BE) is fundamental to the success of digital transformation initiatives. A business-wide digital readiness audit with maturity assessment can then help to establish the priorities, metrics and timeline for the change initiative. The development of a highly qualified workforce acquainted with new technologies and business models is a key success factor in improving competitiveness and innovation performance of the textile and clothing sector (European Textile Technology Platform, 2016). Many organisations do not know where to start, resulting in a state of inaction known as digital hesitancy (Heim et al., 2022). Therefore, a more collaborative and open interface between higher education, industry and industry bodies is needed to meet the demands of the future industry. The perspective of the next generation has much to contribute to the development of an industry in transition. Higher education institutes could help to foster a transformative mind-set, harnessing the energy of the younger generation, who have a 'digital first' attitude, to design for the consumer more holistically and develop new practices accordingly that address end-to-end lifecycle sustainability issues.

The rise of e-commerce and the omnichannel retail model has ushered in a seismic change in fashion retail management. This shift requires a fundamental rethink of how businesses will create value in the future and of the digital technologies that can be integrated to advance processes and practices to support those ambitions. Whilst traditional PLM has supported retailers and brands with new product creation, there has remained a limited integration of supply chains. The pandemic highlighted the strategic role of the supply chain. Recent advances in the openness of PLM solutions means that best-in-class tools can be integrated to open a new frontier for innovation based on greater collaboration and democratic access to robust data for decision-making. Openness is achieved by emphasising accessibility over ownership of data through a data federation approach. Three cases were included in the chapter to illustrate how integrated PLM facilitates digital transformation, brings visibility to optimise operations, enhances collaboration through the extended enterprise and supports strategic sustainability management commitments. PLM has the potential to bring visibility to achieve optimisation of operations and transparency to realise social and environmental commitments. Finally, an aim of this chapter was to make the significance and potential of PLM more visible and accessible to fashion and textiles professionals so that it can be employed as a methodology to address digital hesitancy in businesses.

END-OF-CHAPTER DISCUSSIONS

1. Watch the YouTube clip of PwC's Digital Operations Maturity Assessment available at: https://www.youtube.com/watch?v=RIGCJkQGQR0 This clip outlines PwC's diagnostic tool for assessing digital maturity. It walks you through their proprietary online evaluation. This service helps businesses evaluate their end-to end operations to better

understand risk, priorities and return on investment. Compare with online self-check tools, e.g. The Readiness Model, available at: https://www.industrie40-readiness.de/?lang=en that was developed to give businesses the ability to check their own Industry 4.0 readiness. What are the advantages and disadvantages of proceeding wither either an internal or external audit?

2. The pandemic accelerated digital transformational initiatives. Identify a brand that utilised the circumstances of the pandemic positively, implemented this and consequently, became more successful. Contrast this with an example of a company which declined financially due to the pandemic. Evaluate what can be learned from both companies.
3. Access The Sustainability Report 2023 by The Interline, available at: https://www.theinterline.com/2023/10/05/fashion-sustainability-report-2023/ Critically evaluate the barriers to adoption of these solutions. Consider how ESG reporting may accelerate adoption.
4. For an international fashion organisation of your choice, provide an overview of their digital strategy and list the digital tools they use. What new initiatives would you recommend?
5. Compare the UK retail environment (physically and digitally) to another you have personally experienced to identify significant differences and suggest improvements to each location. How would you manage a change initiative to implement these improvements?

Bibliography and further reading

Arribas, V. and Alfaro, J.A. (2018). '3D technology in fashion: From concept to consumer', *Journal of Fashion Marketing and Management: An International Journal*, 22(2), pp. 240–251.

Bellantuono, N., Nuzzi, A., Pontrandolfo, P. and Scozzi, B. (2021). 'Digital transformation models for the I4. 0 transition: Lessons from the change management literature', *Sustainability*, 13(23), pp. 1–40. doi:10.3390/su132312941.

BoF and McKinsey & Company (2022). *The state of fashion: Technology report*. Available at: https://www.businessoffashion.com/reports/news-analysis/the-state-of-fashion-technology-industry-report-bof-mckinsey/ (accessed 25 September 2023).

Borg, S. (2023, June 20th). *Digital transformation and process improvements with Bortex'* [Webinar]. ASBCI.

Bortex Group Holdings (n.d.). *Business sectors*. Available at: https://bortexgroupholdings.com/business-sectors/ (accessed 25 September 2023).

Buvat, J., Solis, B., Crummenerl, C., Aboud, C., Kar, K., El Aoufi, H. and Sengupta, A. (2017). 'The digital culture challenge: Closing the employee-leadership gap', Capgemini Digital Transformation Institute Survey. Available at: https://www.capgemini.com/wp-content/uploads/2017/12/dti_digitalculture_report.pdf. [Accessed 26 October 2023].

Cantamessa, M., Montagna, F. and Neirotti, P. (2012). 'Understanding the organizational impact of PLM systems: Evidence from an aerospace company', *International Journal of Operations & Production Management*, 32(2), pp. 191–215. doi:10.1108/01443571211208623

Catlin, T., Lorenz, J.-T., Sternfels, B. and Willmott, P. (2017). 'A roadmap for a digital transformation',. McKinsey & Company. Available at: https://www.mckinsey.com/industries/financial-services/our-insights/a-roadmap-for-a-digital-transformation (accessed 26 October 2023).

Chanias, S. and Hess, T. (2016). 'How digital are we? Maturity models for the assessment of a company's status in the digital transformation', LMU Munich Management Report, 2, pp. 1–14.

CIMdata (2017). 'Product innovation platforms: Definition, their role in the enterprise, and their long-term viability', CIMdata Position Paper, CIMdata, Inc. Available at: https://www.cimdata.com/en/resources/about-plm/a-cimdata-dossier-plm-platformization (accessed 25 September 2023).

Coats Digital (n.d.). *Calculate garment SMV through method-time-cost analysis for sustainable garment manufacturing with GSDCost*. Available at: https://www.coatsdigital.com/en/manufacturer/gsdcost/ (accessed 25 September 2023).

Coats (2020). *Coats Digital launches GSDCost[v5] with fair wage tool and digital feedback loop.* Available at: https://www.coats.com/en/news/2020/09/coats-digital-launches-gsdcostv5-with-fair-wage-tool-and-digital-feedback-loop (accessed 25 September 2023).

Coats Digital (2022). *Adopting a sustainable fashion strategy to combat labour cost inflation.* Available at: https://www.coatsdigital.com/en/blog/fashion-supply-chain-trends/ (accessed 25 September 2023).

Conlon, J. and Narayanaswamy, S. (2017). 'A vision for the future using product lifecycle management (PLM) as a platform for operational excellence and business transformation'. In: *The circular economy from a fashion and textiles perspective*, 15th June 2017, University of Huddersfield, UK (unpublished). Available at: https://eprints.hud.ac.uk/id/eprint/32272/ (accessed 25 September 2023).

Crewe, L. (2013). 'When virtual and material worlds collide democratic fashion in the digital age', *Environment and Planning A*, 45(4), pp. 760–780.

David, M. and Rowe, F. (2015), 'Le management des systèmes PLM (product lifecycle management): Un agenda de recherché', *Journal of Decision Systems*, 24(3), pp. 273–297. doi:10.1080/12460125.2015.1030352

De Carolis, A., Macchi, M., Negri, E. and Terzi, S. (2017). 'Guiding manufacturing companies towards digitalization a methodology for supporting manufacturing companies in defining their digitalization roadmap', *2017 International Conference on Engineering, Technology and Innovation (ICE/ITMC)* (pp. 487–495). IEEE.

DeSL (n.d.). *Digital transformation.* Available at: https://www.desl.net/fashion-retail-apparel-footwear-digital-transformation/ (accessed 25 September 2023).

Digital Solution Group (2022). *The need for a systems integration strategy / tactical plan.* Available at: https://www.digitalsolutiongroup.net/valueofstratacticalplan.html (accessed 25 September 2023).

Elkington, J. (1997). The triple bottom line. *Environmental management: Readings and cases*, *2*, pp. 49–66.

Euromonitor (2020). *The Coronavirus era: "Hometainment" and the new experiential consumer.* Available at: https://www.euromonitor.com/ (accessed 25 September 2023).

European Textile Technology Platform (2016). *'Towards a 4th industrial revolution of textiles and clothing: A strategic Innovation and research agenda for the European textile and clothing industry'*. Available at: http://www.textile-platform.eu/ (accessed 25 September 2023).

Gökalp, E. and Martinez, V. (2021). 'Digital transformation capability maturity model enabling the assessment of industrial manufacturers', *Computers in Industry*, 132, p. 103522.

Hammer, M. (2002). 'Process management and the future of six sigma', *MIT Sloan Management Review*, 43 (2), pp. 26–32.

Heim, H., Chrimes, C. and Green, C. (2022). 'Digital hesitancy: Examining the organisational mindset required for the adoption of digitalised textile supply chain transparency', in S. S. Muthu (ed.) *Blockchain technologies in the textile and fashion industry* (pp. 47–80). Springer Nature Singapore.

Henderson, L. (2018). 'People management in fashion'. In R. Varley, A. Roncha, N. Radclyffe-Thomas, and L. Gee (eds.) *Fashion management: A strategic approach*. Bloomsbury Publishing.

Hoong, V. and Boermann, M. (2018). 'Connected stores: Transforming store fleet through technology', *Deloitte Digital*. Available at: https://www2.deloitte.com/az/en/pages/consumer-business/articles/connected-stores-transforming-store-fleet-through-technology.html (accessed 25 September 2023).

Hussain, S.T., Lei, S., Akram, T., Haider, M.J., Hussain, S.H. and Ali, M. (2018). 'Kurt Lewin's change model: A critical review of the role of leadership and employee involvement in organizational change', *Journal of Innovation & Knowledge*, 3(3), pp. 123–127.

IBM (2023). *What is cloud computing?* Available at: https://www.ibm.com/topics/cloud-computing (accessed 26 Oct. 2023).

The Interline (2023a). *The Fashion PLM Report 2023*. Available at: https://www.theinterline.com/2023/06/15/the-fashion-plm-report-2023-available-now/ (accessed 25 September 2023).

The Interline (2023b). *European fashion retailer C&A adopts Coats Digital's GSDCost to create a more transparent, responsible & sustainable supply chain*. Available at: https://www.theinterline.com/2023/06/07/european-fashion-retailer-ca-adopts-coats-digitals-gsdcost-to-create-a-more-transparent-responsible-sustainable-supply-chain/ (accessed 25 September 2023).

Jong, J. Y. (2017). *The fashion switch: The new rules of the fashion business*. Rethink Press.

Kalypso (2023). *Benchmarking digital product creation for 2023*. [online] The Interline. Available at: https://www.theinterline.com/2023/10/03/benchmarking-digital-product-creation-for-2023/ (Accessed 26 October 2023).

Lanzolla, G., Lorenz, A., Miron-Spektor, E., Schilling, M., Solinas, G. and Tucci, C.L. (2020). 'Digital transformation: What is new if anything? Emerging patterns and management research', *Academy of Management Discoveries*, 6(3), pp. 341–350.

McKinsey (2017). *A roadmap for a digital transformation*. Available at: https://www.mckinsey.com/industries/financial-services/our-insights/a-roadmap-for-a-digital-transformation#/ (accessed 27 October 2023).

McKinsey (2020a). 'Fashion's digital transformation: Now or never'. [Online]. Available at: https://www.mckinsey.com/industries/retail/our-insights/fashions-digital-transformation-now-or-never#/ (accessed 27 October 2023).

McKinsey (2020b). *Fashion on Climate Report*. Available at: https://www.mckinsey.com/industries/retail/our-insights/fashion-on-climate (accessed 25 September 2023).

McKinsey (2021). *Jumpstarting value creation with data and analytics in fashion and luxury.*. Available at: https://www.mckinsey.com/industries/retail/our-insights/jumpstarting-value-creation-with-data-and-analytics-in-fashion-and-luxury (accessed 27 October 2023).

natific (n.d.). *Bomler by natific*. Available at: https://natific.com/bomlerbynatific/ (accessed 25 September 2023).

OC&C Insight (2016). *Fast forwarding fashion*. Available at: https://www.fashionretailacademy.ac.uk/media/320353/26994_fast-forwarding-fashion_fra.pdf

Pal, R. and Jayarathne, A. (2022). 'Digitalization in the textiles and clothing sector'. In B. L. MacCarthy and D. Ivanov (eds) *The digital supply chain* (pp. 255–271). Elsevier.

Paschek, D., Luminosu, C.T. and Ocakci, E. (2022). 'Industry 5.0 challenges and perspectives for manufacturing Systems in the Society 5.0.'. In A. Draghici and L. Ivascu (eds) *Sustainability and innovation in manufacturing enterprises: Indicators, models and assessment for Industry*. 5.0 (pp. 17–63). Springer Singapore.

PTC (2021). *7 tenets of an effective digital transformation strategy.* Available at: https://www.ptc.com/en/blogs/corporate/digital-transformation-strategy (accessed: 27 October 2023).

PTC (2023). *Digital transformation solutions to unlock the value of IIoT.* PTC. Available at: https://www.ptc.com/en (accessed 26 October 2023).

Suleski, J. and Toncheva, A. (2016). 'A fresh look at PLM technology: Role and realism is under way', *PLM for Apparel, 2016* .Available at: https://risnews.com/secure-file/25885 (accessed 25 September 2023).

Syrett, L. (2023). *Around the world in fashion due diligence legislation.* Available at: https://juststyle.nridigital.com/juststyle_magazine_sep23/around_the_world_in_fashion_due_diligence_legislation (accessed 25 September 2023).

Uriarte, F. A. (2008). *Introduction to knowledge management: A brief introduction to the basic elements of knowledge management for non-practitioners interested in understanding the subject.* Asean Foundation.

PART II

Digital product development, manufacturing and innovation in the fashion industry

Part II consists of four chapters relating to the 'digital for physical' product development processes. Collectively, these chapters outline the argument for a digital asset-first approach to replace traditional approaches to production within fashion supply chains. The generation of a digital prototype that builds through material digitalisation, pattern construction and evaluation as a source of collaborative decision-making is described together with the associated processes of digital production creation (DPC) in production and merchandising which are innovating to advance the industry. These chapters aim to illustrate the benefits of working virtually in fashion product development to simultaneously build digital assets in collaboration with merchandising, marketing and manufacturing to reimagine traditional fashion systems in a connected way. The first chapter in this part introduces raw materials and emphasises the importance of an accurate digital representation of the 'digital twin' as input for DPC and collaborative discussions with supply chain partners. The precision in simulating the mechanical and physical behaviour of fashion textiles is crucial for enabling accurate virtual fitting, a significant topic in the forthcoming section on digital fashion product creation. The chapter starts with an overview of traditional new product creation (NPD) processes to provide the background to the current context of a rapid shift to digital product creation (DPC). Pattern construction techniques are illustrated to demonstrate the advantages of the parametric approach to improve garment fit and support the creation of customisable garments at scale. The process of digital fit evaluation and digital workflows are described. Opportunities to produce customised and made-to-measure fashion products are explored. The third chapter focuses on the impact of digital technologies in manufacturing, and the resulting business process optimisation, automation and new manufacturing approaches. One of the

DOI: 10.4324/9781003364559-4

key improvements that data from digital technologies enables is visibility, thereby providing accuracy and insight for decision-making. The third chapter seeks to demonstrate how better visibility facilitates the optimisation of processes and workflows and allows sustainability objectives to be met. It emphasises that it is workforce capabilities that leverage digital technologies by applying an entrepreneurial mindset of opportunity spotting and problem solving to generate new processes that contribute to competitive advantage and advance the industry. These topics continue into the final chapter of this part, about fashion merchandising detailing the production, promotion, and distribution of final products to the end consumer. This chapter further explores how fashion companies are redesigning supply chains using innovative technologies such as blockchain, artificial intelligence (AI) and predictive planning tools, which support on-demand production, with an emphasis on how these approaches are essential in future-proofing fashion business, managing demand, preventing waste and boosting a brand's sustainability, agility and transparency.

CHAPTER 2.1

Material digitalisation for digital product creation

Jo Conlon

This is the first of three chapters on digital product creation (DPC). DPC is the broad category of all the tools and processes in the construction and use of digital assets. The outputs of DPC are either 'digital for physical' or 'digital for digital'. Chapters 2.1, 2.2 and 2.3 introduce the digital tools and their use to optimise the processes of the manufacture of physical products representing 'digital for physical' processes of digitalisation. Collectively, these three chapters outline the argument for a digital asset-first approach to replace traditional approaches to production within fashion supply chains. This chapter outlines the technical aspects of fibres, fabrics and textiles processes as the critical data inputs of the digital twin. Although these chapters are sequenced one after another in alignment with the traditional processes it is important to emphasise that these processes are being re-envisioned as joined-up digital cycles. The aim is to illustrate the benefits of working virtually in fashion product development to simultaneously build digital assets in collaboration with merchandising, marketing and manufacturing to reimagine traditional fashion systems in a connected way. Collectively the chapters in Part II demonstrate that a digitally enabled shift to more connected and sustainable fashion system is underpinned with technical knowledge and precise data of the diverse inputs and complex processes. However, this is only part of the full scope of digitalised products, and Chapters 3.2 and 3.3 illustrate the processes of 'digital for digital' to demonstrate the new opportunities for digital fashion products in the metaverse, where there are no design constraints and new possibilities are imagined.

This chapter starts this digital product development journey with a focus on textiles. The virtual prototype must be a precise digital twin, i.e., a full counterpart incorporating all the technical and aesthetic characteristics of the physical product. The digital twin must be both technically accurate enough so that important decisions can be taken within the fashion product development process and represent a manufacturable garment or product as 3D solutions can produce virtual products that look real but are physically incorrect. The first asset required is the base material. Although currently

DOI: 10.4324/9781003364559-5

there is no standardisation of fabric measurements for digital materials, this chapter will describe how textiles are digitalised using fabric specification data, fabric testing and process of scanning. As both digital technologies and AI algorithms advance, they facilitate data-driven decisions, which means that the precision of inputs is important for creation of accurate digital outputs to support the decisions made from these assets. The accuracy of the digitalised mechanical and physical behaviour of fashion textiles materials is a key requirement to enable true virtual fitting (Chapter 2.2) and photo-realistic rendering effects. Equally, the accurate rendering of fabrics opens digital marketplaces for fabric sourcing where textile manufacturers can present their latest innovations, and brands looking for sustainable fabric options can search digital marketplaces to find new potential suppliers.

LEARNING OUTCOMES

After reading this chapter you should be able to:

- Understand how fibres and fabrics are classified and processed.
- Understand the significance of the main physical and mechanical properties of fashion fabrics such as weight, thickness, bend (drape) and stretch to garment aesthetics and performance.
- Explain how the physical and mechanical properties of fashion fabrics are captured as digital materials.
- Evaluate the significance of an agreed technical standard for digital materials and the interoperability of files.
- Identify future opportunities for haptic communication devices which could be used virtual fashion marketplaces.

2.1.1 INTRODUCING THE FASHION FABRICS BASICS

The accuracy of virtual garment simulations is dependent on the mechanical model of the simulation system derived from fabric physical and mechanical properties. Table 2.1.1 shows the different characteristics that need to be factored into 3D simulation for the digital product for it to accurately represent the original physical material. Therefore, this section starts with a review of each of these to provide a basic understanding of textile materials. Other quality features of textiles would be considered e.g., colour fastness and dimensional stability to washing, but these are beyond the scope of this chapter.

Fibres form the basic building blocks for the yarns and fabrics that are used in the fashion industry today. Fibres can be divided into several categories depending on their origin and type, and can also be blended with each other, depending on the product and user requirements. Understanding the properties, qualities and characteristics of fibres plays an important part in aligning fibres, yarns and fabrics for specific end-uses and users. Fabric properties such as cost, comfort, drape, durability and easy care are an inherent feature from fibre selection. Fibres are spun into yarns for fabric manufacture through weaving or knitting. The fabric then has colour or print added with

TABLE 2.1.1 The different characteristics of textiles to be factored into 3D simulation.

Data Fabric specification: fibres, construction and finish	Physics Physical properties	Scanned Images Texture maps from scanned images
• Fibre composition • Filament or spun • Yarn details • Woven or knit structure • Dye or print type • Finishing details	• Weight • Thickness • Stretch and recovery • Bending properties • Material sheerness • Tensile strength	• Colour / Base / Diffuse • Roughness / Glossiness • Opacity / Transparency • Normal • Displacement • Future advancements

FIGURE 2.1.1 Map of key processes, inputs and outputs in the textile production chain (adapted from Fletcher, 2008).

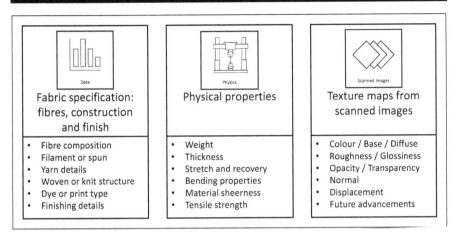

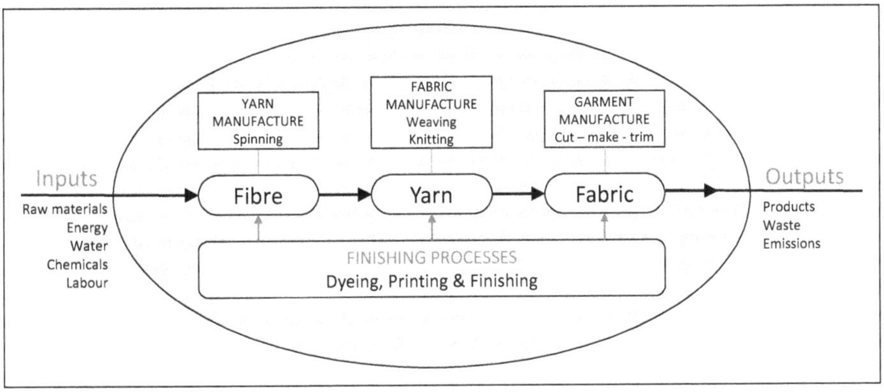

other finishes before it is despatched for cutting and sewing in apparel factories. A base knowledge of these key processes, inputs and outputs in the textile production chain (Figure 2.1.1) is needed to facilitate communication and collaboration. Increasingly this knowledge is also needed so that environmental compliance and sustainability improvements are considered and designed in at the concept stage and effectively communicated in marketing.

Fibre basics: Fibre classification

The fibre raw materials of textile fabrics for fashion are typically classified as in Figure 2.1.2. There are fibres that derive from natural plant and animal sources and those that are manufactured or synthesised from other raw

FIGURE 2.1.2 Classification of textile fibres.

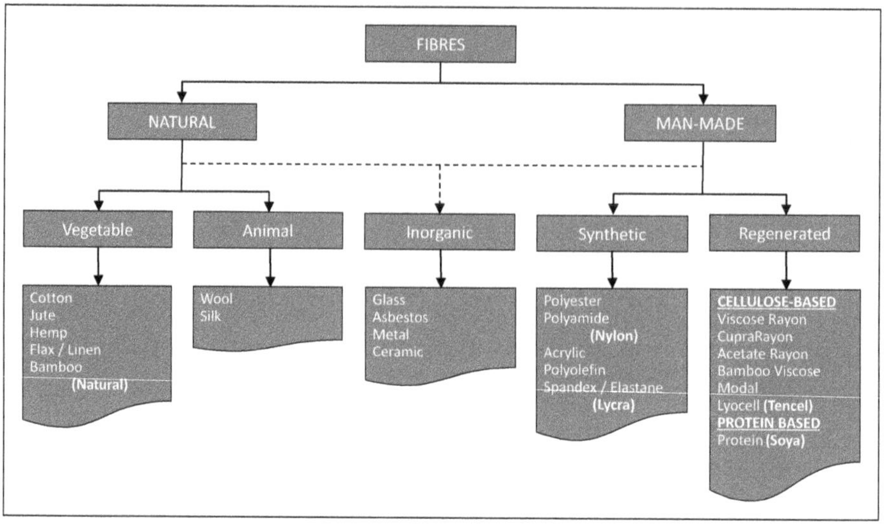

materials. Each fibre has an inherent set of physical, mechanical, chemical and environmental properties which determines how it can be used. Humankind has a long history of using diverse materials to make clothes; however, we have lost much of that diversity in our fibre consumption today, with polyester and cotton dominating world fibre. Polyester alone had a market share of around 54% of total global fibre production in 2021 with cotton as the second most important fibre in terms of volume with a market share of approximately 22% (Textile Exchange, 2022) The result of producing large volumes of limited fibres is to concentrate impacts and make the sector less resilient whereas more sustainable fashion systems promote diversity (Fletcher, 2008). Therefore, a holistic understanding of the diversity of potential raw materials is an important factor in accelerating change.

Fabric specification: Properties considered in fabric selection

Most fashion fabrics are produced through either the process of weaving, weft knitting or warp knitting. The specifics of the fabric production method also contribute to the aesthetic, physical and mechanical properties of the fabric as summarised in Table 2.1.2. Different finishes can also be applied to the fabric to enhance performance or aesthetics e.g., softeners, enzyme finishing, brushing etc. A detailed fabric specification should be included with the bill of materials (BOM) as a formal agreement between buyer and seller. This would typically detail the fibre composition (and possibly origin or brand name), the yarns used to construct the textile (fineness), fabric structure and construction details, weight (g/sq. m), width, finishes applied, as well as the agreed test methods for evaluating the specification and the agreed quality standards. Fabric hand, or how the fabric feels (also called handle or drape), is

TABLE 2.1.2 Performance and quality properties for fabric selection.

Aesthetic properties	Functional properties	Comfort properties
Handle	Strength	Absorbency
Drape	Durability	Breathability
Colour	Crease resistance	Elasticity
Appearance	Flame resistance	Softness
	Stain resistance	Stretch
	Water resistance	Warmth
	Aftercare	
	Cost	

an important characteristic to the textile industry; it is influenced by different fibre, yarn parameters and fabric structure. Evaluating fabric hand is also subjective and an agreed physical sample may be added to the fabric specification as a reference.

Fabric physics: The physical properties of textiles to be captured for accurate digital representation

The accuracy of the virtual prototype is dependent on the inputs from which it is derived, i.e., the physical (the fabric specification) and mechanical (performance when tested) fabric properties together with the algorithms within the simulation software. The extent of recent advances in the optimisation of the algorithms means that there is an imperative for accuracy in the input parameters of fabric properties. The set of measurements describing the fabric's properties, often referred to as 'physics' (Figure 2.1.3) are taken using standard or proprietary testing kits or made available as presets in 3D design software solutions. Many software applications offer a wide range of predefined material pre-sets which may suit some users. Although the presets are useful, only by testing each fabric's physical properties is the data generated to accurately reflect the fabric's movement and drape on the body. Although this makes the workflow more complex, importing the physical results for each individual fabric improves accuracy and organisations need to evolve their processes to meet their specific needs (The Interline, 2020). Currently there is no standard for digital fabric file extensions that is suitable for seamless exchanges between different software systems (Kuijpers et al., 2020). Therefore, many brands, retailers and suppliers are currently testing fabric physics multiple times for multiple 3D software solutions. Agreeing a universal set of methods would therefore be welcomed as it would lead to a reduction in time and associated costs (3D Retail Coalition, 2021). Approaches towards standardisation focus on agreeing how to test weight, bending, tensile, shear and friction properties because these are widely considered to be among the most important fabric properties determining fabric behaviour (Kuijpers et al., 2020).

FIGURE 2.1.3 The key fabric properties captured for accuracy in digital physical assets.

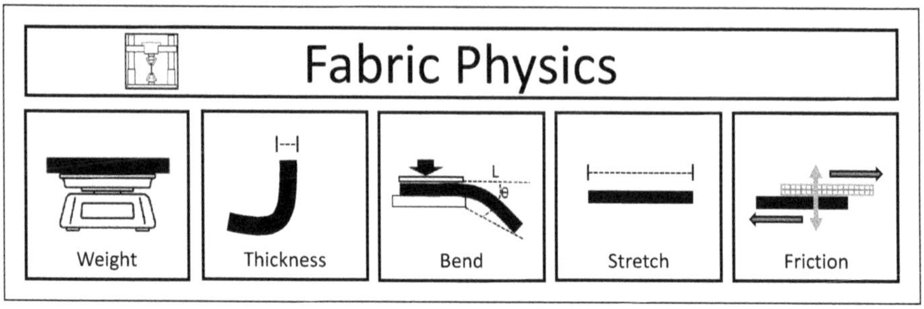

THE MEASUREMENT OF FABRIC PROPERTIES FOR VIRTUAL SIMULATION An important aspect of following a standard test method is the standardisation of the testing conditions. Following standard methods improves the accuracy, reliability and transferability of results. The standard conditions for a textile testing laboratory are 20°C and 65% relative humidity. Fabrics should be kept flat and tension-free for 24 hours before testing. Textile materials come with inherent variability, and it is strongly recommended that multiple specimens for each property are used to obtain an accurate measurement (Kuijpers et al., 2020). Taking samples from various points across and along the fabric sample increases accuracy, as an average result can be calculated.

1. WEIGHT Fabric weight affects many of the fabric properties and is expressed as the weight of the fabric in grams per m2. Fabric weight influences other fabric properties such as thickness, rigidity, drape, air permeability and thermal properties (Das, 2013). A circular sample cutter is used to cut specimens of precisely 100 cm2, which are then weighed on electronic scales. The result is multiplied by 100 to give the mass per unit area in g/m2.

2. FABRIC THICKNESS Fabric thickness is an important variable in determining fabric stiffness which in turn informs the extent to which the fabric will drape and conform (Cooke, 2011). Fabric thickness also has associated performance aspects in terms of warmth, air permeability, absorbency and abrasion resistance. Fabric thickness is normally reported in millimetres (mm). To determine the thickness of a textile fabric, the test sample is placed between two parallel plates before a known pressure between the plates is applied and maintained, allowing for the precise measurement of the distance between two plates to be measured (Das, 2013).

3. BENDING Fabric rigidity or stiffness relates to important aesthetic characteristics of handle and drape and is related to the inherent properties from the fibres, yarns and fabric structure. Bending stiffness properties are typically determined using a simple manual cantilever method where fabric specimens are pushed over the edge of the instrument and allowed to fall under their own weight until a certain angle is reached (Kuijpers et al., 2020). The length of the overhanging part is then measured and reported in centimetres with stiffer fabrics having a higher value than more flexible fabrics. Samples tested in all directions for accuracy, i.e., woven fabrics are taken in warp, weft and bias direction, and courses and wales for knitted fabrics, and should be tested face-up for consistency. Knitted single jersey fabrics tend to curl impacting the accuracy of testing.

4. TENSILE ELONGATION (STRETCH AND SHEAR) Tensile properties are important as they align with comfort and movement in the garment (Kuijpers et al., 2020). Fabric samples are prepared to a size of 5x25cm for all fabric directions (length, width and bias), with each end placed in a clamp in the tester at a set distance apart. The clamps move at a known speed to a point of maximum load. The percentage elongation is recorded. The shear is measured following the same procedure but is a recording for the bias sample.

5. FRICTION Friction is a difficult parameter to define as fabrics will have a different value on each side and in different directions (across or along the fabric). It is important, as it represents the ease with which a fabric will move over the body or against other fabrics, but this brings in another factor to consider. As there is no clear standard method or measurement unit for friction, many software providers do not state requirements for this parameter.

In summary, the data from the fabric specification and the fabric physics summarise the variety of unique physical and mechanical attributes determine the way a single fabric appears and behaves. Texture maps derived from the digital scanning of the physical fabric provide the final part to complete the data set for a 3D digitalised fabric.

2.1.2 DIGITAL SCANNING OF TEXTILES

The fabric surface is captured using high quality 3D surface scanning devices. A set of images of the fabric's surface known as texture maps are extracted from the scan data. These multiple layers of texture combine to provide a detailed editable representation of the physical fabric making a limited range of changes possible after scanning. Different software solutions have different approaches to collecting the scan data and the number and type of texture maps that are extracted. These maps are critical in achieving high-quality PBR (physically based rendering) images of virtual prototypes. A small sample of the material is simulated using these editable texture maps. This sample is then replicated and tiled to scale into a digitalised version of the physical fabric. Types of texture map layers applied to the 3D model (Figure 2.1.4) include, but are not limited to:

- Colour/base/diffuse map (colour variation)
- Roughness/glossiness map (how light scatters on the surface)
- Opacity/transparency map, also known as alpha (where parts the image need to be transparent)
- Normal map (adds depth to texture)

FIGURE 2.1.4 3D model texture map layers.

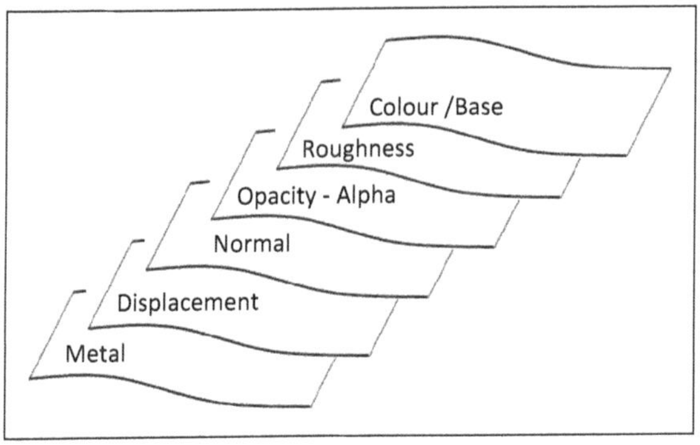

- Displacement maps (enables more detailed mapping of textured surfaces)
- Metal map (to define metallic parts)

Further advances in 3D tools and processes used in the gaming and film industries are being integrated into fashion solutions with the purpose of enabling the creation of materials and models that are almost infinitely editable in a completely digital way (The Interline, 2022). An alternative approach known as procedural generation does not use a scan-based approach to create digital materials opening more creative possibilities. There is early-stage research underway to enable manufacturing to use the data from procedural digital materials to produce a physical product. However, it is important to note that the gaming and animation industries create materials and models that will only ever be digital ('digital-for-digital'). Whilst this applies equally to fashion applications in the metaverse (for more, see Chapter 3.3) the fashion industry predominantly uses digital processes to produce products that are physical, and control is required to maintain accuracy so that the digital materials accurately reflect the physical product.

Workflow of material digitalisation

The amount of information stored within digital fabrics is growing at a rapid pace. This has created a need for fashion companies to effectively store and manage fabric libraries and other digital assets. Most organisations have already invested in DAM or PLM systems to provide an enterprise-wide data platform (for more, see Chapters 1.1 and 1.2). DAM and PLM platforms systemise data management and data flow so that fashion companies can streamline their workflows and effectively utilise the valuable information stored within their digital fabrics. The workflow for material digitalisation is shown in Figure 2.1.5. Tiling is the process of creating a seamless pattern from a smaller element without visible seams. The output is typically a U3MA (Unified 3D Material Archive) file; while not universal, they are the current standard for 3D texture mapping in fashion. The open-source nature of U3M

FIGURE 2.1.5 Workflow of material digitalisation.

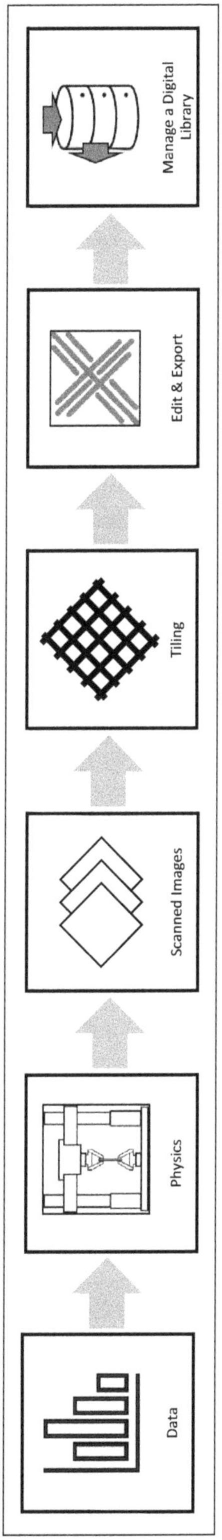

and its ability to continue to improve makes it an attractive proposition (The Interline, 2022). U3MA files supported across a range of applications through applications from 3D design tools to popular CAD (computer aided design) and PLM (product lifecycle management) software allowing for sharing of data internally and externally.

2.1.3 CASE STUDY: HOW AI IS SUPPORTING MATERIAL DIGITALISATION

Material digitisation is a critical step in the digital product creation process. Although new tools are emerging to speed up the material digitalisation stage, significant bottlenecks still exist due to high demand, manual processes, specialised equipment and lack of collaboration. Consequently, insufficient material data is one of the biggest hurdles faced during the 3D clothing design process. Frontier launched its solution to meet the demands for digital materials in 3D design and DPC.

The Frontier 3D Fabric Creator converts 2D fabric swatch images into 3D digital material. It uses machine learning to automate and accelerate the creation of digital materials at scale. The 3D Fabric Creator makes it easy to convert 2D material files into the U3M format as shown in Figure 2.1.6. The Lasagna AI Engine Converts 2D Fabrics to 3D by analysing 2D digital fabrics layer-by-layer then generates the 3D fabric layers which are saved in U3M format (Frontier, n.d).

As the solution only requires the internet and a flatbed scanner, it makes material digitalisation more accessible. Importantly for fabric mills it provides a way to protect their intellectual property (IP) by taking back control of this step. This approach where fabric mills take responsibility for their own material digitalisation is known as a 'digitise at source' approach and creates a collaborative workflow. Fabric mills also benefit with a reduction in cost associated with producing and distributing physical samples. The digital marketplace also provides visibility of the mill's ranges to fabric sourcing teams and potentially opens new business opportunities. Accordingly, Frontier.cool provides a solution to connect brands to Tier 2 suppliers transparently for co-creation. It can also transform the traditional fabric trade show as outlined below.

FIGURE 2.1.6 The Frontier 3D Fabric Creator x Made2Flow Eco-Impactor®.

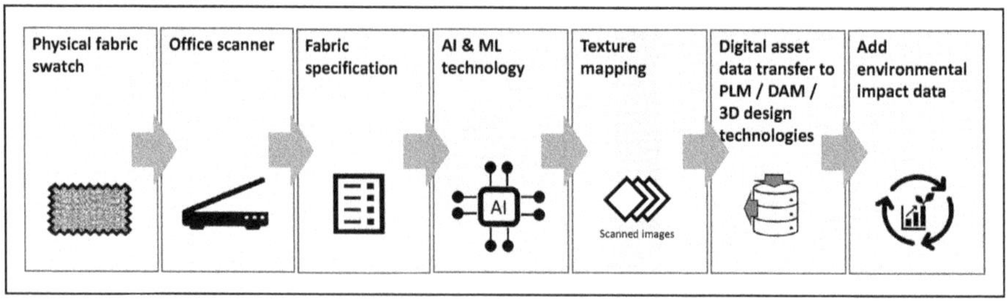

FabriSelect™ by Frontier.cool is a solution that blends the online and offline exhibition spaces to create a more immersive, interactive experience at trade shows. Each fabric has a unique QR code meaning trade show attendees can access all the digital fabric information. After the event, exhibitors can take advantage of valuable post-event data analysis to optimise their strategies for new product developments, plan future events and follow up with attendees.

Eco-Impactor® by Made2Flow x Frontier.cool is an environmental impact estimator tool that provides an accurate environmental footprint on a material / metre basis. Made2Flow is a supply chain transparency and traceability solution (for more, see chapter 2.3). The collaboration means that all fabrics on the Frontier.cool platform display their environmental impact, calculated using Made2Flow's proprietary technology, alongside the data for visual and physical properties for DPC and commercial information (lead-time and price) (The Interline, 2022). This data provides brands with key information to design new products to meet sustainability commitments. To reduce the impact of the fashion industry, validated, granular detail is required from throughout the supply chain referred to as 'Scope 3'. Again, this enhancement is a sourcing power tool, connecting producers of sustainable materials with brands.

Material digitalisation as a service

Vizoo provides an on-demand material digitalisation service through their offices in Germany and the United Sates using their xTex™ scanning system in combination with xTex™ software to automatically tile and generate high-quality PBR texture maps from a material's visual properties (Vizoo, n.d.). Their physX™ platform can generate plausible fabric properties by entering data from the fabric specification or by using a default fabric from the fabric library database (Vizoo, n.d.). The outputs can be converted to be compatible with many 3D CAD applications.

The xTex™ scanning system has been exported globally and Vizoo now offers an accreditation service for global partners to endorse standards and quality in the accuracy of the digitalisation process of providers of material digitalisation as a service. In 2023, the MAS Holdings digitisation unit in Sri Lanka became the first service partner globally to be accredited by Vizoo in addition to their existing 3D and other quality control capabilities (The Interline, 2023).

Cotton Incorporated has demonstrated how material digitalisation as a service can be used as a marketing tool. Cotton Incorporated is funded by US cotton growers and operates as a not-for-profit organisation to promote cotton products. Cotton Incorporated offers a fibre specific library of digital fabrics in the industry. New products developed by Cotton Incorporated are made available both physically and digitally in the FABRICAST™ collection and are made available for download via free registration (Cottonworks, n.d.).

In-house material digitalisation can be costly, putting it out of reach of many smaller brands, independent designers and students. Material digitalisation as a service provides accessibility for a wider range of users. Other digital materials online libraries and services include SEDDI, SwatchOn and SwatchBook.

2.1.4 THE KEY PLAYERS IN MATERIAL DIGITALISATION AND 3D SIMULATION IN FASHION

There are over 20 providers of solutions and services in the fashion DPC arena representing a range of approaches to the tasks of pattern creation, material digitalisation and 3D prototype visualisation. Equally, different areas of the value chain have different strategic aims and operational objectives leading to different requirements of the outputs from these solutions. Consequently, achieving the organisational strategy is likely to require the use of multiple solutions. This introduces the important element of enterprise architecture into the complex process of selecting solution partners. The enterprise architecture defines the components of the system and how this will develop over time (Chen et al., 2008). Within enterprise architecture there are two key terms: integration and interoperability. Two systems are considered as integrated if there is a detailed standard format to bring coordination, coherence and uniformisation. Interoperability is the ability for two systems to coexist autonomously but to understand and use functionality of one another i.e., to function jointly by giving access to their resources in a reciprocal way or 'inter-operate' (Chen et al., 2008). Although the concept of interoperability is not new, the ability to achieve it is (Accenture, 2022), with the potential to seamlessly connect technology, people and processes. A total integration between DPC solutions represents an opportunity to combat unsustainable practices, use resources more efficiently and reduce the impact of manufacturing (Papachristou and Bilalis, 2017).

The available commercial 3D fashion design software solutions are summarised alphabetically as Accumark3D (Gerber) CLO3D, Modaris 3D (Lectra), Optitex3D, Style3D, V-Stitcher (Browzwear) and Tukatech and (Papachristou and Anastassiu, 2022). These either contain libraries of digital fabric assets or can integrate with external source libraries. Although material digitalisation is time-consuming, this upfront invest pays back over the long term and through accuracy. The systems that allow users to measure and simulate new fabric assets in 3D based on its physical and visual properties are listed below and are presented in alphabetical order.

Adobe Substance

The French software developer, Allegorithmic, a leader in 3D editing and authoring for the gaming industry was acquired by Adobe in 2019, adding Allegorithmic's Substance 3D design tools to Adobe's Creative Cloud's imaging applications. Key drivers for the gaming industry are real-time performance and rapid realisation of ideas influencing and advancing fashion workflows and processes. Substance is a suite of tools that allow users to design in 3D with generative programming without the need for scan data. Developments to Substance 3D Sampler Substance add a layer of image-to-material capability by using photogrammetry techniques to capture physical materials to convert into a digital material. Substance materials can be directly integrated into several other software tools used in the apparel industry (DPC report).

Browzwear

Browzwear was founded in 1999 and is considered a pioneer of 3D digital solutions for the fashion industry and operates on an open platform approach that facilitates integration with other software solutions (DPC). As part of this ethos and commitment to the development of the industry, interested individuals wishing to explore and upskill can sign up for Browzwear's Indie Program to access on-demand learning to explore their 3D apparel design software VStitcher and showcase designs and ask questions in the learning community. In 2017 they introduced the Fabric Analyzer by Browzwear (FAB), a single instrument to measure and calculate fabric properties which although conceptually attractive has received critique about transparency, range and accuracy of method (Kuijpers, 2020)

CLO Virtual Fashion

CLO Virtual Fashion was founded in 2009 and their portfolio includes CLO (for fashion apparel), Marvelous Designer (gaming and animation) and Jinny (non-professionals) and has over 30 technology partnerships (DPC). From the beginning there was an emphasis on using digital assets as fuel for enterprise-wide change that extended the benefits of 3D tools beyond the design team to all participants in the production creation process (merchandising, marketing, manufacturing, etc.) (DPC). This approach led to the advancement CLO-SET for real-time collaboration with additional features like automated tech-packs and virtual showrooms. Integration with PLM solutions is via the plugin CLO-Vise. CLO-Vise provides access to PLM libraries of fabrics, trims and colour plans. CLO also offers its own materials measurement tool in the form of the CLO Fabric Kit 2.0, accompanied by an instruction video. Again, this proprietary system has been criticised for not using established standard methods, single sample testing (not an average) and allows scope for manual error (Kujipers, 2020). CLO argues that standardisation could potentially lead to new problems given that each 3D software algorithm is different and consequently a standardised input would not guarantee a consistently generated digital material (DPC). CLO also offers a library of preassigned fabric properties that can be edited based on the designers' needs through sliders in the software.

Optitex

Optitex was founded in 1988 and is now a global provider of software solutions that include 2D design and 3D visualisation platforms that cover the entire supply chain with an ecosystem of over 40 partners. Additional recent partnerships are with Sizer Technologies (Sizer), a global leader in contactless digital body measuring solutions and Bandicoot Imaging Services (Bandicoot), an innovative material digitisation solution provider. Optitex O/Cloud facilitates collaboration across the supply chain sharing assets with fully controlled permissions. Optitex focuses on 2D pattern accuracy, 3D simulation and collaborative tools and predicts the industry will move toward made-to-order and made-to-measure products. Optitex also has a proprietary approach to fabric testing and management that is well aligned with recommended test methods and standards (Kuijpers,2020).

Style 3D

Style3D was founded in 2015. The products within the solution are:

Style3D Studio, with embedded resource market providing fabrics, garment blocks, etc. Style 3D studio is compatible with mainstream 2D CAD software, facilitating a seamless transition from design to production. In 2023, Style3D acquired Assyst and the well-established software solutions Assyst.CAD (2D pattern, grading and fitting), Assyst.Automarker (pattern nesting and optimisation) and Assyst. Autocost (planning and cost efficiency) became part of the platform (PRNewswire, 2023).

Style3D Fabric. The company has invested heavily in researching the digitisation of fabrics with the result of a realistic representation and simulation of optics, texture and physical parameters (density, weight, stretch, elongation), not only for digital fabric swatches but also for 3D garments in motion (Assyst, n.d.).

Style3D One (previously Cloud) enables users to store, search, edit and showcase 3D assets for collaborative decision-making and asset management. The solution supports standard 3D file formats (Linctex, n.d.).

Style 3D Market provides an extensive online library of 3D assets that can be purchased to support diverse fashion applications, ranging from design, and pattern making to NFT, Metaverse or marketing content creation (The Interline, 2022).

2.1.5 CASE STUDY: DIGITISING FABRIC TOUCH AND THE FUTURE OF HAPTICS

Research to find a digital solution to represent the sense of touch in virtual experiences is being explored to make up for the loss of information and interaction that occurs when products are presented digitally (Casciani et al., 2022). This field is known as haptics (from the Greek for 'able to touch'). The gaming industry has advanced this field leading to the development of a variety of devices, namely VR headsets, vests, chairs and gloves to artificially provide users with a sensory experience of touch. There are clear opportunities for haptic devices in fashion but as the e-commerce interface (i.e., mobile or tablet) is not worn, a suitable interface would need to be developed and purchased by the end-user to adopt this technology. Haptic technology researchers and developers are actively working on understanding the role that touch plays in shaping consumer attitudes and potential fashion applications (Ornati and Kalbaska, 2022). Currently consumers use their previous experience, brand and product knowledge, and available information (i.e., videos and size charts) to inform their judgement of product texture and fit. Interestingly most sensory experiences are built from a combination of an individual's senses and an estimate of texture can be generated through audio-visual stimulation (Bruno and Pavani, 2018).

The development of textile-based haptic communication devices has several evident opportunities:

- Within DPC, textural haptic information could be added to the fabric properties to enhance the digital prototype. This additional sensory information would support designers and decision-makers in product development, but also communication throughout the value chain including through marketing to the consumer. Haptic devices (e.g., gloves) could become a standard element of 3D design investment within organisations to accelerate adoption.
- Tactile attributes could become an additional feature of online shopping to support product selection through filters and product recommendation, however a solution is required to support the adoption of devices by consumers.
- The industry has many skilled manual jobs requiring manual dexterity and discernment in touch that is learned through experience. Haptic devices provide a means to capture this tactile expertise and support a learning experience. The development of textile-based devices, systems and practices for haptic communication could easily expand to influence the end consumers' purchasing decisions as well as fashion industry professionals.

Examples of research applications in the field of haptics can be found on the MIRALab website https://www.miralab.ch/index.php/completed-projects/. These were developed from an EU-funded project coordinated by MIRALab. The HAPTEX project pioneered the development of a computer interface and a glove embedded with sensors and actuators or 'virtual fabric' with which users could manipulate and feel the physical properties of a textile (MIRALab, n.d).

END-OF-CHAPTER DISCUSSIONS

1. Conduct a wardrobe audit by either searching your own wardrobe or online for the following items and identify the fibre composition used:
   - A crisp formal shirt.

- A winter scarf.
- A luxurious blouse.
- A men's tailored suit.
- Gym wear.
- Hosiery.
- A beach towel.
- A T-Shirt.

2. Find the Textile Exchange online at https://textileexchange.org/ and review their 'responsible materials' list. Select one fibre from your wardrobe audit and review its level of sustainability. The Preferred Fiber And Materials Market Report full report is available at https://textileexchange.org/knowledge-center/reports/preferred-fiber-and-materials/
3. Explore the United Nations SDGs (https://sdgs.un.org/goals). For the textile industry, 'SDG 12: responsible consumption and production is a gateway to many other SDGs'. Discuss this in relation to a fibre of your choice.
4. Why is it important for professionals in the fashion industry to understand fibres and textiles?
5. Search online for a textile trade show. Examples are Premier Vision, Texworld, and MAGIC USA. What are the advantages in terms of cost and accessibility of making these events virtual? What are the disadvantages? How might a hybrid solution be created?
6. Finally, a book club suggestion for those of you interested in knowing more about textile history, *The Fabric of Civilisation: How Textiles Made the World* by journalist and social scientist Virginia Posterel (Basic Books, 2020).

Bibliography and further reading

3D Retail Coalition (2021). *Standard operating procedures for digital fabric physics interoperability.* Available at: http://3drc.pi.tv/2023/07/20/3drc-materials-sop/ (accessed 19 October 2023).

Accenture (2022). *Interoperability: Value untangled accelerating radical growth through interoperability.* Available at: https://www.accenture.com/gb-en/insights/technology/interoperability (accessed 27 October 2023).

Assyst (n.d). *Fabric and digital fabric.* Available at: https://www.assyst.de/en/products/style3d-fabric/index.html (accessed 27 October 2023).

Atkinson, D. (2017). 'Post-industrial fashion and the digital body'. In S. Broadhurst and S. Price (eds) *Digital bodies: Creativity and technology in the arts and humanities* (pp. 147–160). Palgrave Macmillan.

Bruno, N. and Pavani, F. (2018). *Perception: A multisensory perspective.* Oxford University Press.

Burns, L.D., Chandler, J., Brown, D. M., Cameron, B., Dallas, M. J. and Kaiser, S. B. (1995). 'Sensory interaction and descriptions of fabric hand', *Perceptual and Motor Skills*, 81(1), pp. 120–122.

Business of Fashion and McKinsey & Company (2023). *The state of fashion: Technology*. Available at: https://www.businessoffashion.com/reports/news-analysis/the-state-of-fashion-technology-industry-report-bof-mckinsey/ (accessed 27 October 2023).

Casciani, D., Chkanikova, O. and Pal, R. (2022). Exploring the nature of digital transformation in the fashion industry: opportunities for supply chains, business models, and sustainability-oriented innovations. *Sustainability: Science, Practice and Policy*, 18(1), pp. 773–795.

Chen, D., Doumeingts, G. and Vernadat, F. (2008). 'Architectures for enterprise integration and interoperability: Past, present and future', *Computers in Industry*, 59(7), pp. 647–659.

Cooke, B. (2011). 'The physical properties of weft knitted structures', in K. F. Au (ed.) *Advances in knitting technology* (pp. 37–49e). Woodhead Publishing .

Cottonworks (n.d.). *FABRICAST™*. Available at: https://cottonworks.com/en/resources/fabricast/ (accessed 27 October 2023).

Das, A. (2013). 'Testing and statistical quality control in textile manufacturing', in Majumdar, A. and Das, A. (eds.) *Process control in textile manufacturing* (pp. 41–78). Woodhead Publishing.

El Mogahzy, Y. (2008). *Engineering textiles: Integrating the design and manufacture of textile products*. Woodhead Publishing.

Fletcher, K. (2008). *Sustainable fashion and textiles: Design journeys*. Routledge.

Frontier (n.d.). *The Frontier 3D Fabric Creator – get your 3D material in just one click*. Available at: https://lasagna.frontier.cool/ (accessed 27 October 2023).

The Interline (2020). *Going 3D, part 2: Draping fabric digitally*. Available at: https://www.theinterline.com/2020/04/23/going-3d-part-2-draping-fabric-digitally/ (accessed 25 September 2023).

The Interline (2022). *Digital Product Creation Report 2022*. Available at: https://www.theinterline.com/2022/11/29/digital-product-creation-in-fashion-report-2022/ (accessed 26 October 2023).

The Interline (2023). *MAS becomes the first material digitization services partner globally to be accredited by Vizoo*. Available at: https://www.theinterline.com/2023/10/11/mas-becomes-the-first-material-digitization-services-partner-globally-to-be-accredited-by-vizoo-2/(accessed 25 October 2023).

Kuijpers, S., Luible-Bär, C. and Gong, H. (2020). 'The measurement of fabric properties for virtual simulation—a critical review', *IEEE Standards Association, Industry Connections Report*, pp. 1–43.

Linctex (n.d). *What you see is what you get*. Available at: https://www.linctex.com (accessed 27 October 2023).

MIRALab (n.d.). *HAPTEX – 'HAPptic sensing of virtual TEXtiles'*. Available at: https://www.miralab.ch/index.php/rushmore_event/haptex-haptic-sensing-of-virtual-textiles/ (accessed 27 October 2023).

Ornati, M. and Kalbaska, N. (2022). 'Looking for haptics. Touch digitalization business strategies in luxury and fashion during COVID-19 and beyond', *Digital Business*, 2(2), p. 100035.

Papachristou, E. and Anastassiu, H.T. (2022). Application of 3D Virtual Prototyping Technology to the Integration of Wearable Antennas into Fashion Garments. *Technologies*, 10(3), p. 62.

Papachristou, E. and Bilalis, N. (2017). 'Should the fashion industry confront the sustainability challenge with 3D prototyping technology?' *International Journal of Sustainable Engineering*, 10(4–5), pp. 207–214.

PRNewswire (2023). *Style3D announces acquisition of Assyst*. Available at: https://www.prnewswire.com/news-releases/style3d-announces-acquisition-of-assyst-301718576.html (accessed 27 October 2023).

Sinclair, R. (ed.) (2014). *Textiles and fashion: Materials, design and technology*. Elsevier Science & Technology.

Textile Exchange (2022). *Preferred Fiber and Materials Market Report*. Available at: https://textileexchange.org/knowledge-center/reports/preferred-fiber-and-materials/ (accessed 27 October 2023).

Vizoo (n.d.). *3D material resources.* Available at: https://www.vizoo3d.com/resources/ (accessed 27 October 2023).

VMOD (2023). *Fabric digitization service*. Available at: https://vmod.xyz/fabric-digitization (accessed 27 October 2023)

CHAPTER 2.2

The shift to digital in fashion product development[1]

Jo Conlon and Hailah Al Houf

This is the second of three chapters on digital product development and manufacture. This chapter continues the digital product development journey and focuses on digital fashion product creation using the material digital asset from Chapter 2.1. The chapter starts with an overview of traditional new product creation (NPD) processes to provide the background to the current context of a rapid shift to digital product creation (DPC). It then focuses on the generation of patterns for apparel production before discussing the opportunities within the fashion industry for body scan systems which could support virtual try-on and the production of customised and made-to-measure fashion products based on an individual's digital measurements. This chapter also highlights the significance of new skills to scale 3D capabilities, framing this as an opportunity for digitally trained fashion graduates to develop digital assets and lead on process improvement.

LEARNING OUTCOMES

After reading this chapter, you should be able to:

- Compare the two methods to make a garment pattern: the standard approach as embedded in most CAD solutions and the advanced digital approach of pattern parametrisation.
- Identify how digital product creation could help future proof fashion brands and accelerate the adoption of digital design and visualisation technologies.

1 This chapter has been developed in collaboration with Hailah Mana Al Houf, Lecturer in Clothing and Textile Education at The Faculty of Education, Najran University, Saudi Arabia, and PhD Researcher at the University of Manchester, UK.

DOI: 10.4324/9781003364559-6

- Understand the role of the digital prototype as a means of communication and shortening the product development process.
- Identify the opportunities of mass-customisation within fashion.
- Evaluate the skills needed to manage the product offering within the 3D DPC fashion eco-system.
- Examine the fit evaluation processes of 3D virtual prototypes and how this might extend into the consumer space through virtual try-on.

2.2.1 INTRODUCTION TO THE TASKS AND PROCESSES OF TRADITIONAL NEW PRODUCT DEVELOPMENT (NPD)

The buying cycle was a term used to describe the key events in the standard design and the production processes of range development within a trading period (Goworek and McGoldrick, 2015). In the depiction of the traditional industry, the process of new production creation and introduction is presented with a clear start point of initial research (market, trends, materials) from which the range is developed and confirmed before manufacture and retail, as illustrated in Figure 2.1.1. The five main tasks characterising the traditional NPD process in the apparel industry are planning, concept development, detailed design, testing and production ramp-up (d'Avolio et al., 2015). The process started with a planning stage that involved a review and analysis of consumer needs and trends, current events and previous sales. The next stage of NPD process was concept development, where materials, trims, colours and silhouettes were investigated and refined into the detailed designs of a final product range. The proposed new garments, fabrics and trims were made into physical samples for a testing phase to confirm fit, quality performance and for use in promotional activities. Although depicted as a later stage of sourcing, the planned product range was simultaneously negotiated with suppliers in terms of cost and delivery, supported by technical and global sourcing specialists. Products were sourced from less economically developed countries to benefit from cost savings. A final preproduction test lot would be produced and evaluated before going into full production. Completed orders were shipped to distribution centres and then to retail stores. Shipping from a global production unit, processing and distribution typically took six to eight weeks. Once the product was in store, sales figures were monitored closely to react to changes in demand with cancellations or repeat orders. A decline in sales against the forecast resulted in residual stocks and loss of profit margin. Any existing stock that does not sell well is marked down in price to encourage sales. The performance of each cycle was monitored and reviewed in terms of production quality and delivery accuracy, the sales against the plan, quality issues, etc. to inform the next planning stage.

Although different models exist giving a different emphasis on each function within the value chain processes, across the key areas of creative, technical, production and distribution, the overall impression is one of a straightforward process (Armstrong and Lehew, 2011, p. 38). This impression is misleading as the actual retail apparel value chain is highly complex, with

FIGURE 2.2.1 The new product development (NPD) processes within the value chain.

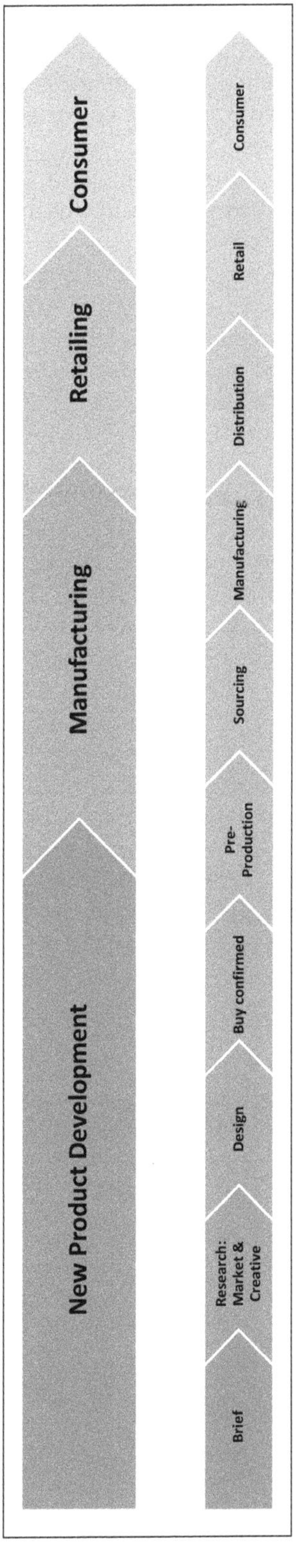

multiple critical dates, numerous points of communication and with limited process visibility. Furthermore, the sequential and functional independence of new product development from manufacturing had long been identified as a major area for improvement (Tyler et al., 2006). Consequently, the traditional processes inadequately addressed the collaborative and creative nature of the industry, leading to multiple versions of a product, needless duplication of effort and a lack of control of the process resulting in delays, excessive costs and rework.

In the past the apparel industry was categorised as predominantly operating with a push supply chain strategy (Figure 2.2.2). Push manufacturing is based on forecasted demand and is suitable for basic, high-volume, low-cost products with consistently known demand (certain core products). However, the forecasting of the demand for fashion products is notoriously inaccurate (Hines, 2013, p. 83), meaning that there is no guarantee that a fashion product would achieve the sales forecast even if delivered on time and to the right quality. The inaccuracies of forecasting demand have led to a growing issue of 'deadstock' or goods that remain unsold despite markdowns due to overproduction. The scale of the problem can be illustrated with the statistic that H&M is estimated to have $4.3 billion deadstock (Paton, 2018). Equally, cheaper global sourcing quickly became the standard, eroding the cost-competitive advantage it had achieved. A new operating model was clearly required, where success is determined by the ability to be flexible and responsive to consumer demand (Christopher et al., 2004). Such strategies in supply chain management are known as quick response (QR) or the pull-model of supply (Figure 2.2.2), which relies on all parties in the supply chain using consumer demand information. In this model the entire supply chain is flexible and responsive, i.e., able to alter production quantities, styles, sizes and colours in line with market demand (Hines, 2013). There are, of course, advantages and disadvantages to each approach. The pull system strategy has the disadvantage that it does not benefit from efficiencies achievable through economies of scale attainable with the push-system approach. However, the push-system frequently fails to deliver the cost benefits associated with economies of scale

FIGURE 2.2.2 Push vs pull supply chain strategies.

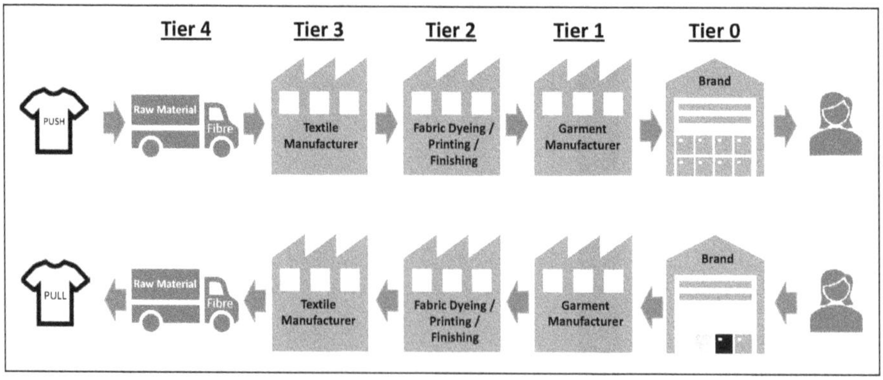

FIGURE 2.2.3 Flow diagram of the First Insight approach within their Voice of the Customer retail solution.

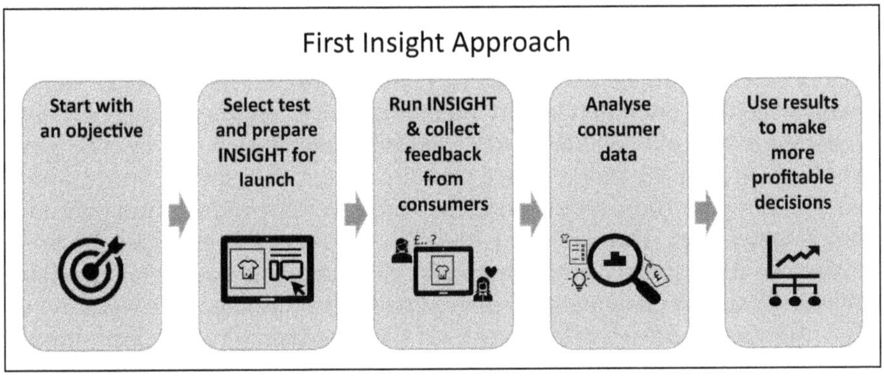

and mass-manufacturing when actual sales are less than forecasted resulting in markdowns to clear overproduction. Accordingly, the choice depends on the company's strategic approach to its market, customers and products and three kinds of supply chain management (push, pull and hybrid) co-exist in the apparel industry. However, remaining competitive increasingly relies on the ability to be responsive to consumer demand coupled with robust supply chain relationships.

New processes within connected solutions provide the ability to deliver greater design options and speed of development as garments that are digitally created and rendered, enable production approval from virtual prototypes saving time and the cost of physical samples. We saw in Chapter 1.2 how PLM solutions act as a collective hub of product data for collaboration and decision-making. Over the last 15 years, the NPD process has become increasingly digitalised; new tools and processes have reshaped new product development activities by providing new ways to collaborate and communicate to support decision-making and reduce product risk by testing ideas rapidly without the need for physical samples (Parker-Strak et al., 2020). Emerging processes promote collaborative and interdisciplinary working, leading to increases in creativity and innovation (for more, see Chapters 2.3 and 2.4).

2.2.2 CASE STUDY: M&S X FIRST INSIGHT

The case illustrates how M&S is working with First Insight for Voice of the Customer solutions to enable improved product testing and reduce product risk.

First Insight is a US technology company specialising in Voice of the Customer retail solutions that transform how retailers make product investment and pricing decisions (First Insight, n.d.). First Insight predictive analytic software offers solutions to optimise strategy, product, pricing, planning and marketing decisions. First Insight's platform enables retailers and brands to boost revenues and profitability by informing product development with consumer data, rather than relying on historical data or intuition. Traditionally retailers would have used focus groups to illicit this type of consumer sentiment. This type of solution represents an advancement of that practice that is also faster, more precise, easier to arrange and typically includes 250 consumers rather than 12. First Insight collects feedback from the retailers' consumers (often loyalty members) using gamified digital surveys. Consumers typically evaluate five to ten products in each survey. The game involves selecting the market price for a product or choosing between similar product designs. There are additional features to rate products and give additional comments. Through First Insight's online social engagement tools, preference data on new products can be gathered from consumers to shape collections so that customers are offered the best products at the right prices.

Marks and Spencer (M&S) started their partnership with First Insight in 2016 to assist in determining design, buying and pricing for lingerie products. Bringing in the voice of the consumer was seen as an essential measure to support the management of product development when operating in fast-paced, competitive markets (Staff, 2021). The UK-based retailer has subsequently expanded the consumer-driven predictive analytics software platform to more than 50 departments, testing tens of thousands of products in clothing, homeware and footwear, covering both its own private label brands and third-party brands. Through First Insight, M&S now speaks to one customer every five seconds and this direct consumer input is reflected in their buying decisions. Some of the tests are designed to understand what styles resonate with different consumer profiles. In terms of impact and return on investment (ROI), M&S, have reported that products incorporating First Insight's consumer feedback sell through at full price at a 12 percent higher rate than those that go untested.

Task

This task encourages you to think critically about using customer feedback. Consider the much-quoted statement from Henry Ford about customer input in the development of the Ford Model T: 'If I had asked people what they wanted, they would have said faster horses.' How accurate do you think the quote and sentiment are? Do you agree or think that it demonstrates the need to structure questions and interpret responses carefully? Note that the word 'faster' is clearly stated. Investigate techniques to help consumers articulate their unmet needs, e.g. 'How might we…?' questions.

2.2.3 PATTERN CONSTRUCTION

This section introduces garment measurement, garment fit and pattern construction fit to provide students and practitioners with the foundational knowledge that underpins the creation of 3D patterns that are technically accurate and manufacturable. As the fashion industry's digital transformation continues to unfold, patterns remain at the forefront of this evolution. They were the first link in the supply chain to embrace digital technology, embarking on this journey in the early 1980s (Moore, 2020). This transformation aimed to effectively overcome the limitations of traditional manual practices and bridge the gap between age-old techniques and groundbreaking innovations. This section emphasises a key point: digital pattern construction goes beyond adopting new technologies. It's the fusion of tradition and technology, rooted in applying pattern construction's foundational theories and technical principles to innovative technologies. This dynamic interaction between time-honoured craftsmanship and cutting-edge technology equips pattern makers with a digital toolkit, providing efficiency and precision.

As future professionals, it's crucial to perceive technology as an extension of tradition, not a replacement. By integrating technology into established theories and technical foundations, a harmonious synergy is achieved, where the pattern construction process is streamlined, empowering users to harness technology's capabilities to solve industry's key problems and open new opportunities. It is useful to remember that technology acts as a conduit, while the knowledge, skills and artistry of pattern construction remain the driving forces behind the industry's progress.

This section explores digital systematic methods in each phase of pattern construction, built upon traditional manual techniques. It starts with accurate body measurements and then moves to suitable measurement systems for pattern application. Next is digital pattern construction and adjustments, with insights from traditional methods that influence the digital phases. The section ends with a digital fit evaluation, a crucial step for completing the construction process. The starting point in pattern construction is precise body measurement-taking. There are several digital methods commonly employed in measurement-taking technologies. This section provides an overview of each one of them, outlining their advantages and limitations. However, before delving into the digital methods, the manual method is detailed, as it serves as the foundation for the development of digital methods and is still used as a supplementary method to acquire measurements not provided by the technology.

Manual measurement method

The manual method uses a sewing plastic tape measure (Rumbo-Rodríguez et al., 2021). Figure 2.2.4 illustrates the positioning of the measuring tape for measurements taken manually for a variety of garment patterns including skirts, dresses, foundation shell, trousers and sleeves.

While this manual method is known for its simplicity and cost-effectiveness (Rumbo-Rodríguez et al., 2021), it is important to also acknowledge the limitations which led to a significant shift towards alternative digital methods to address them and bring a new level of precision and standardisation to the field. The limitations are inconsistent data collection even by the same measurer, subjectivity in interpretation measurement and the inherently time-consuming and labour-intensive nature of the process, particularly challenging when dealing with mass production, where all measurements shown in Figure 2.2.4 are manually collected from thousands of individuals.

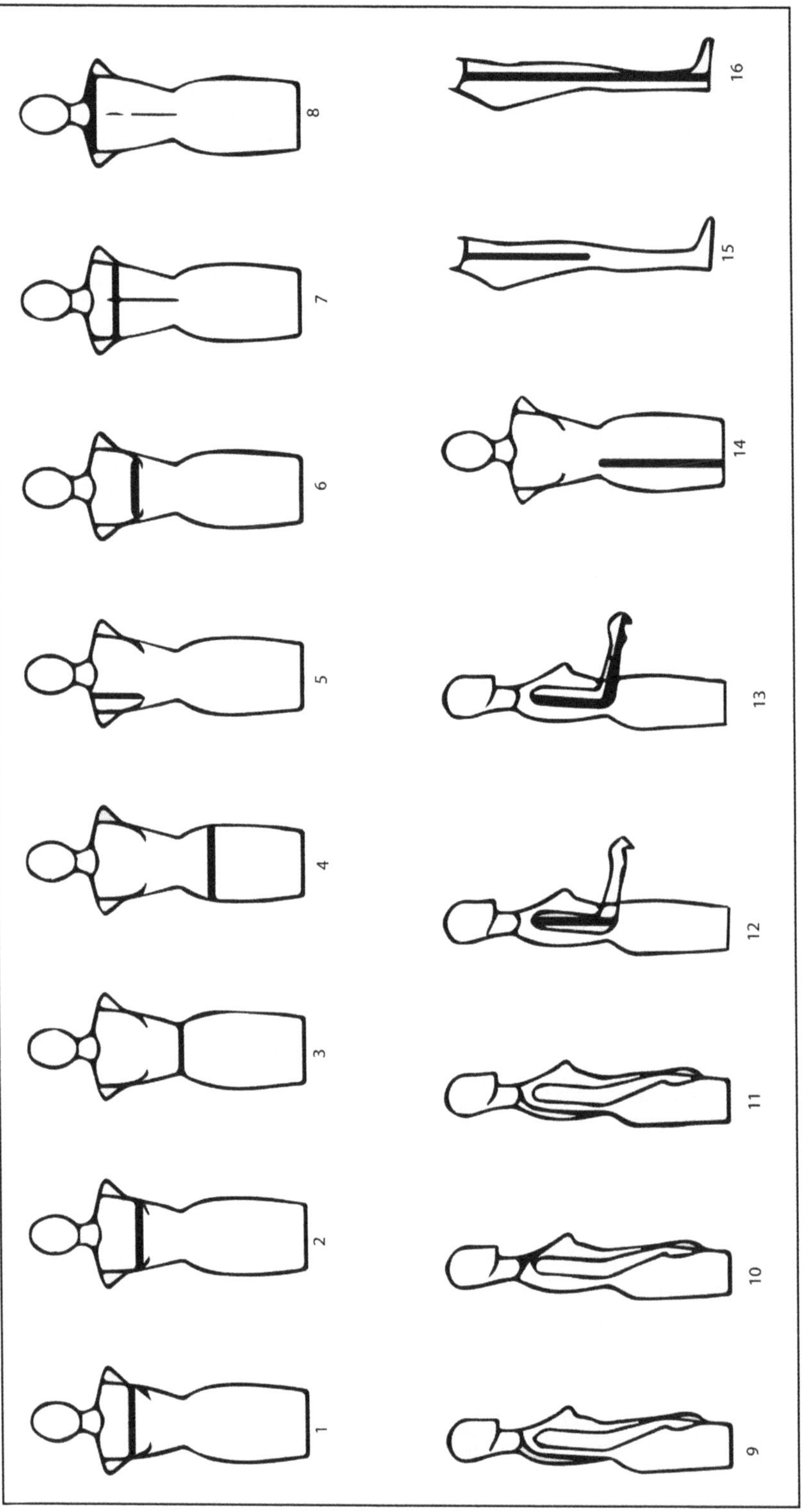

FIGURE 2.2.4 Positioning the manual tape measure.

FIGURE 2.2.5 An example of a digital tape.

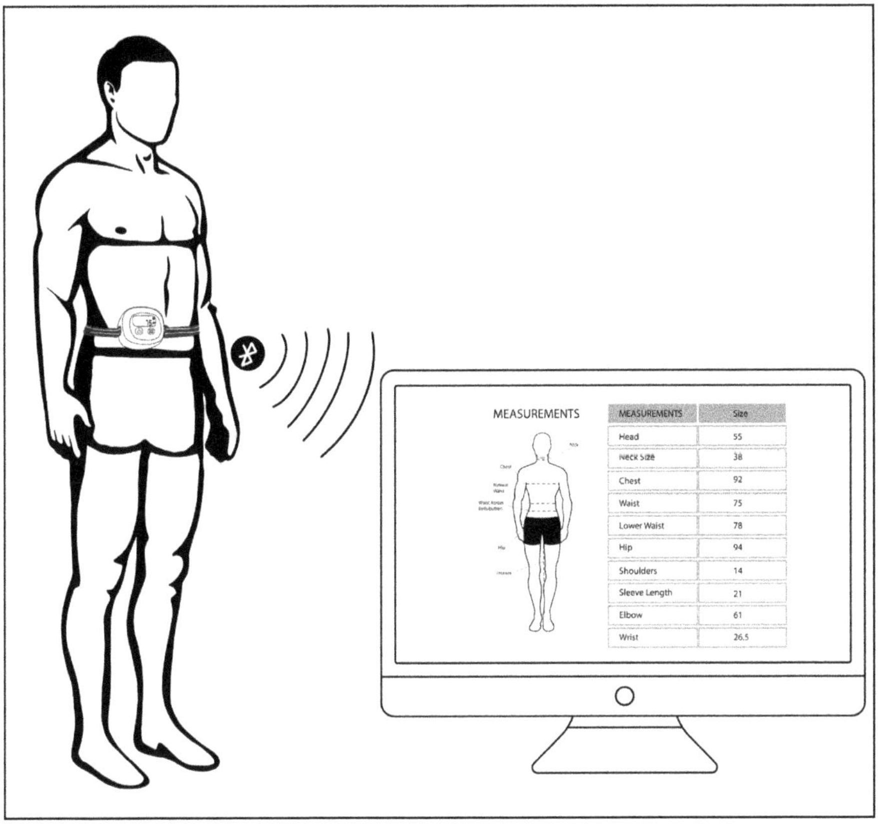

MEASUREMENTS
Chest
Hip
MEASUREMENTS
Size
Head
55
Neck Size
38
Chest
92
Waist
75
Lower Waist
78
Hip
94
Shoulders
14
Sleeve Length
21
Elbow
61
Wrist
26.5

Digital measurement methods

In addition to the convenience over the manual method, digital methods also provide the advantage of automatic data generation, which enhances the efficiency of creating standardised size charts for mass production (Bartol et al., 2021). This section outlines five distinct digital measurement methods using illustrative examples to showcase their respective advantages and the limitations often associated with the technologies employing them.

DIGITAL TAPES Digital tapes are simple and cost-effective electronic devices equipped with wireless data transmission capabilities to communicate with computers (D'Apuzzo et al., 2007). The following figure (Figure 2.2.5) depicts an example of a digital tape commonly used in the fashion industry. While digital tapes are more efficient than their manual counterparts, they can still be time-consuming in the context of mass production.

IMAGE PROCESSING AND MODELLING SYSTEM This method involves capturing two 2D images from different angles and converting them into a 3D computer model utilising user-friendly software that enables measurement analysis and storage (Zeraatkar and Khalili, 2020). The visual representation of this method is in the following figure (Figure 2.2.6).

This method offers several advantages and has some disadvantages as follows:

ADVANTAGES

1. Efficiency in collecting and processing measurements (Nariño, Becerra and Hernández González, 2016).
2. Generating 3D measurements, providing depth information.

DISADVANTAGES

1. The high cost of technology adopting this method (D'Apuzzo et al., 2007).
2. Measurement precision can be influenced by the facial and bodily characteristics of the person being photographed (Guerlain and Durand, 2006).
3. Some landmarks may be displaced due to the combination of 3D and 2D methods (Guerlain and Durand, 2006).
4. Potential errors can arise from factors like breathing and muscle contractions during the scanning process (D'Apuzzo et al., 2007).

LASER-SCANNING METHOD In this method, eye-safe laser stripes, generated from a single laser beam and multiplied through mirrors and optical systems, illuminate the body's surface while light sensors capture the scene to determine the body dimensions through basic geometric rules (D'Apuzzo et al., 2007). This method, shown in Figure 2.2.7, shares similar advantages and drawbacks with image processing and modelling systems.

WHITE LIGHT PROJECTION METHOD White light metrology is a noncontact method that uses a familiar, safe light source –simple white light. Simplicity and accuracy may make white light the system of choice in many applications. Structured white-light systems project shadows of lines onto the body and acquires the surface's shape by measuring the light stripes deformation (Figure 2.2.8) to calculate the structure of the subject through triangulation. This method is also known as the structured light method. This method is incredibly fast, taking measurements within less than a second, minimising the risk of data errors due to uncontrolled movements (D'Apuzzo et al., 2007). However, it's limited to measuring specific body parts, like the upper torso. Multiple scanning devices are necessary to measure the entire body, but they cannot be used simultaneously due to interference from their lights, which extends measurement time when used sequentially (D'Apuzzo et al., 2007).

PHOTOGRAMMETRY Photogrammetry is another method used to create 3D models but uses photographs taken from a range of angles to replace the light

FIGURE 2.2.6 Image processing and modelling system.

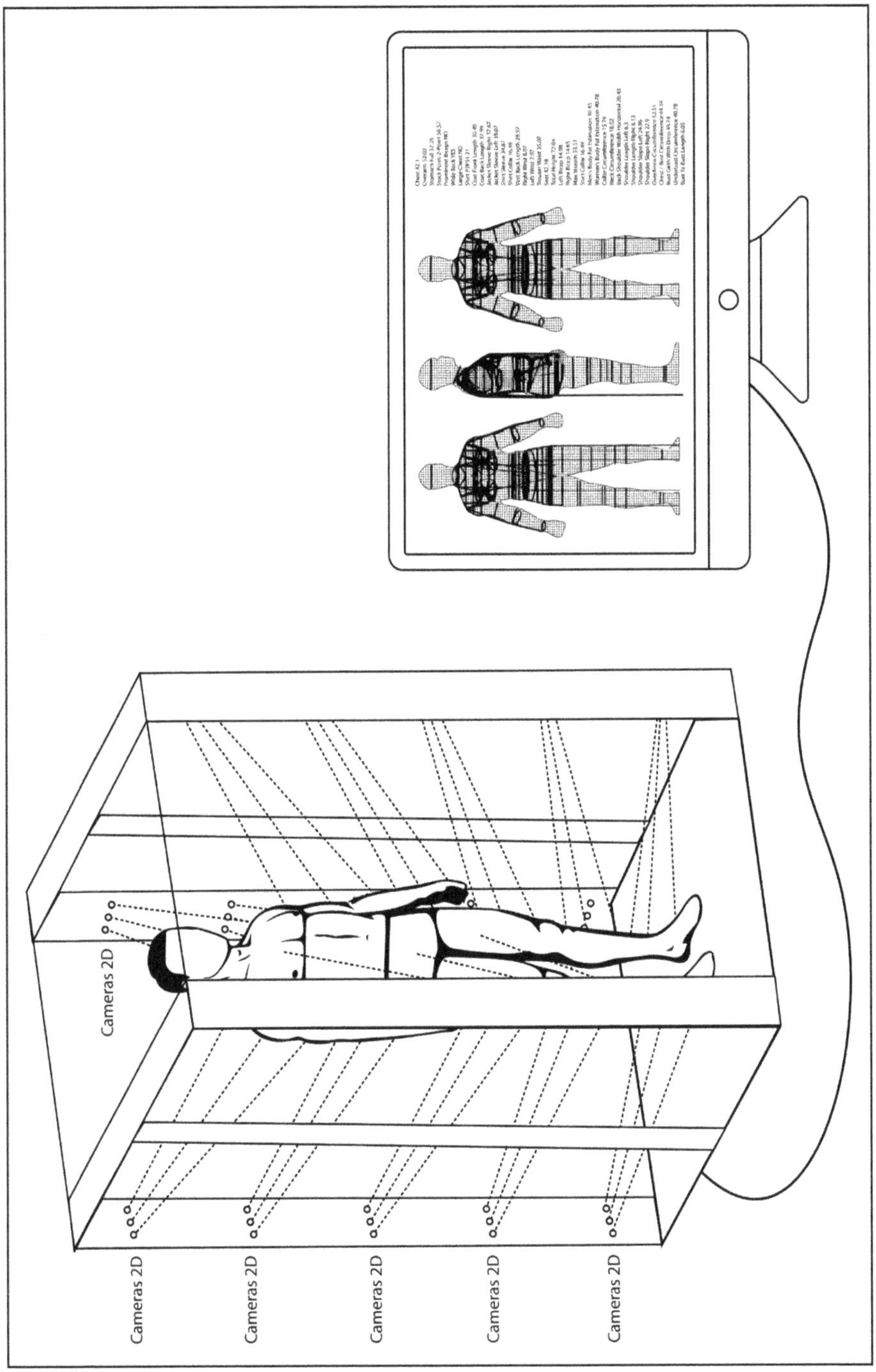

FIGURE 2.2.7 Laser-scanning method.

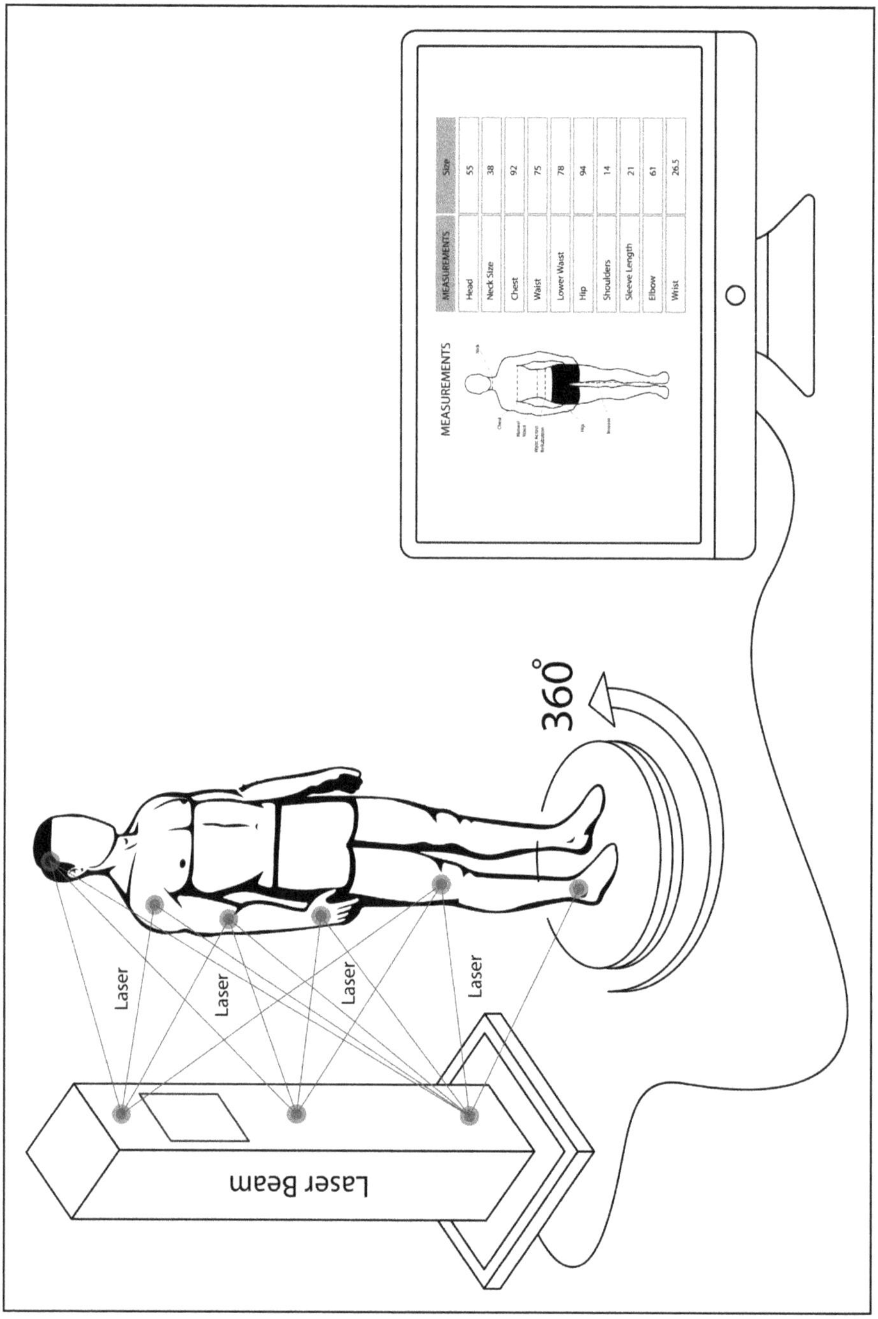

FIGURE 2.2.8 White light projection method.

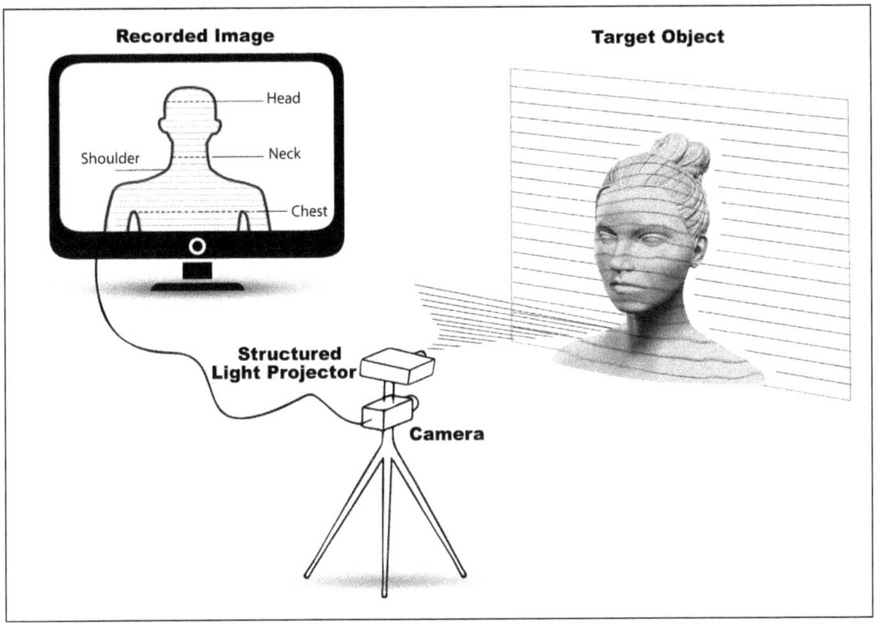

source used in scanning. The aligned photographs and an algorithm build a 3D point cloud just like 3D scanning. This method is quick but lacks detail and is therefore used in conjunction with the structured light method.

These digital methods allow the acquisition of two types of measurements: individual and average. Individual measurements are precise measurements taken for a single individual (Kim et al., 2019). These are used for the bespoke production model, in which patterns are uniquely created and cut for each wearer (Anderson, 2009), whereas average measurements involve measuring various body dimensions of thousands of individuals, summing them and then dividing them by the total number to calculate an average (Aldrich, 2015). Large-scale sizing surveys (for example SizeUK and SizeUSA) took advantage of 3D body scanning advances to generate the size data set from thousands of participants of both sexes and across different ages. The process of average measurements results in grouping of individuals with similar body dimensions into clusters termed standard size charts (Balmer and Keat, 2009; Aldrich, 2015). The use of standard size charts poses a significant challenge in the fashion industry because they are based on the measurements of a portion of the population and fail to account for the diverse body shapes and proportions found within the broader populace. Consequently, this practice has given rise to a growing issue of ill-fitting garments, significantly increasing the rate of returns and customer dissatisfaction. The type of measurement used indicates the production model and dictates the measurement systems used to apply these measurements to the pattern (Moore, 2020), as elaborated upon in the following section.

TABLE 2.2.1 The dominant measurement systems.

System	Definition	Advantages	Disadvantages	Production Model
Direct systems	Direct application of individual body measurements to the pattern, along with precise allowances to insure comfort and a custom fit (Hulme, 1946).	Offering high accuracy and precision, making them ideal for custom tailoring	Accuracy hinges on the skills of the measurers (Bray,1985)	Bespoke model (Campbell,2010)
Hybrid systems	A combination of direct system and proportional system that scales body dimensions proportionally from key measurement such as bust (Kidwell, 1979; Geršak, 2022)	Balances accuracy and efficiency and is suitable for various production scales.	Requires expertise in both direct and proportional methods.	Mass production and mass customisation models (Kidwell, 1979)

Applying measurements to the pattern using a suitable measurement system

Measurements are converted to patterns following rules and calculations termed measurements systems (Hulme, 1946). There are three main systems: direct measurement, proportional and hybrid systems, from which over 40 drafting methods are driven (Campbell, 2010). However, two systems dominate in different market sectors: direct and hybrid, as outlined in the following table (Table 2.2.1).

Selecting the correct system is crucial, as it forms the foundation for evaluating fit and addressing its issues. A common mistake involves the improper selection of drafting methods, including hybrid techniques developed by Beazley(1997), Armstrong (2014) and Aldrich (2015), originally intended for mass production. Employing these methods in bespoke tailoring leads to patterns still influenced by average measurements, which can compromise the intended custom fit.

Pattern construction and adjustment

There are choices of pattern construction approaches: manual, traditional digital and advanced digital approaches, each with associated adjustment techniques as follows.

FIGURE 2.2.9 The Aldrich foundation shell manual pattern.

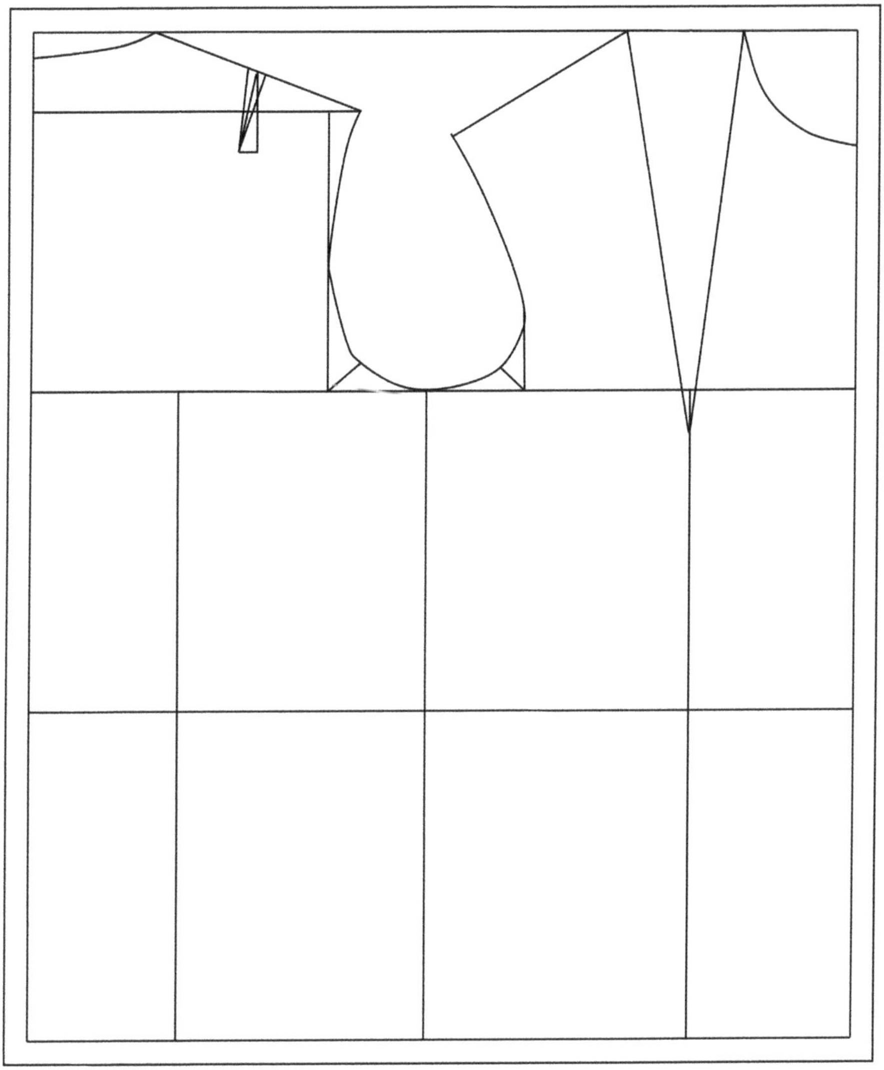

TRADITIONAL MANUAL APPROACH This approach refers to the construction of a 2-D pattern on a paper sheet by hand. The following figures (Figure 2.2.9 and Figure 2.2.10) show the Aldrich foundation shell pattern constructed manually.

This paper pattern can be manually adjusted to the desired size and shape using manual techniques such as slashing-and-spreading and the pivot (Datta and Seal, 2018; Almond and Power, 2018). In the slashing-and-spreading technique, the paper pattern is strategically cut and spread apart or overlapped to accommodate different measurements (Moniruzzaman and Rita, 2022). In the pivot technique, however, the paper pattern is anchored,

FIGURE 2.2.10 Techniques to adjust the Aldrich foundation shell manual pattern.

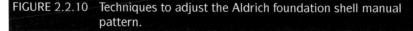

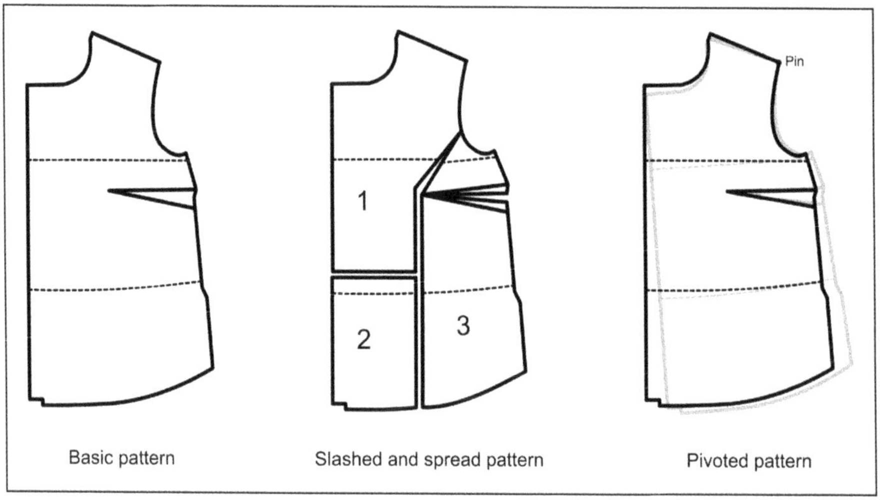

and its width is adjusted by moving it in various directions (Zieman, 2008). The following figure (Figure 2.2.10) shows how a pattern can be slashed and spread or pivoted.

These manual adjustment techniques necessitate skill, precision and a comprehension of pattern construction principles to ensure proportionality with the original pattern.

Traditional digital approach

This approach represents a transformation from the manual method to digital methods. This method is deeply rooted in the foundational concepts and technical principles of traditional manual construction. With exemplary precision, it replicates the manual approach in a digital environment, seamlessly replacing physical tools with digital alternatives. When adjusting an element within a traditional digital pattern, all associated elements must be manually adjusted. This process demands both expertise in pattern construction and CAD skills. For those who developed the skills, pattern recreation is easier, but the method is inefficient. While it has successfully bridged the gap between the past time-honoured practices and the use of patternmaking technology, its adherence to traditional manual fundamentals has posed challenges in fully exploiting the advanced capabilities of patternmaking technology, holding the potential to promote greater efficiency and sustainability within the fashion industry.

Advanced digital approach (parameterisation)

Pattern parametrisation is an advanced digital approach allowing the construction of dynamic, geometrically associative patterns that are responsive

FIGURE 2.2.11 Aldrich parametric foundation shell pattern.

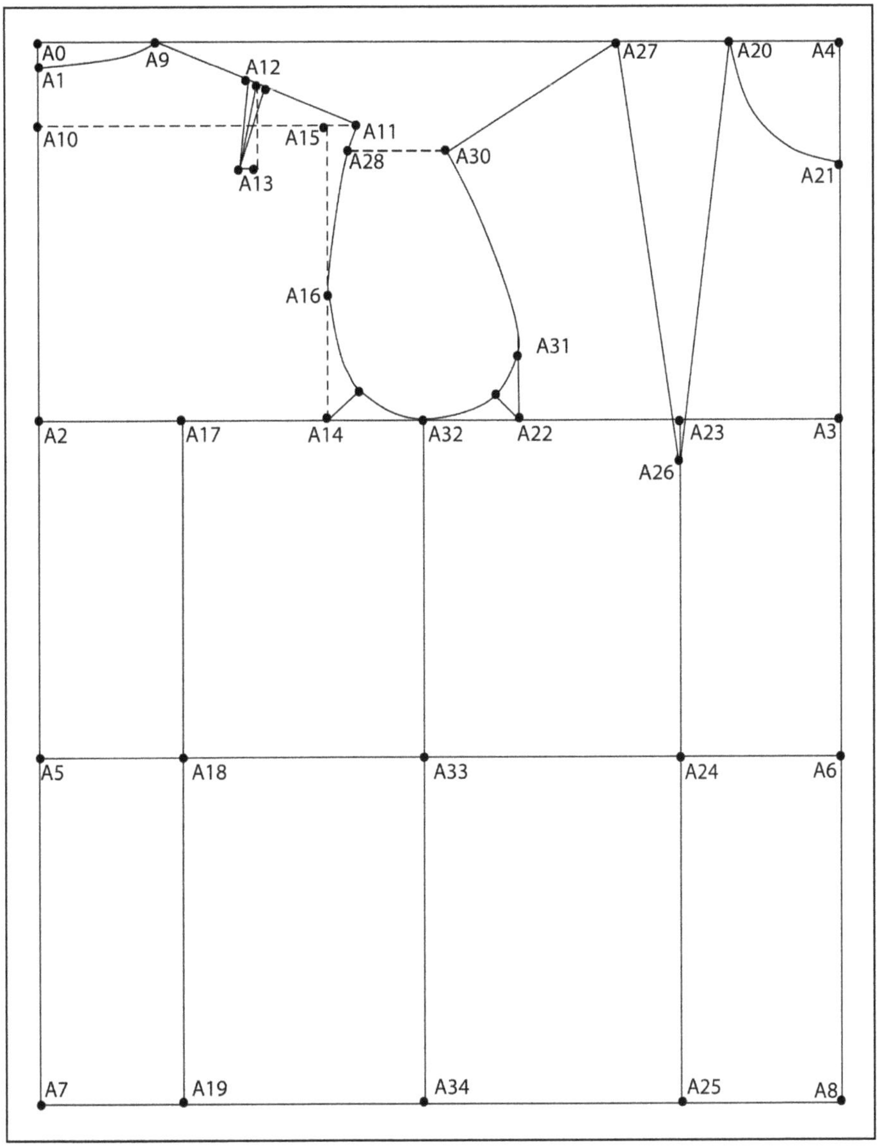

to input-properties. Parametrisation is the key approach in advanced digital construction. This approach's concepts and technical fundamentals are different to the traditional approach. Figure 2.2.11 shows the Aldrich parametric foundation shell pattern, illustrating the difference between it and the traditional digital pattern in Figure 2.2.9.

The numbers on the pattern represent the key parameters, which are the pattern's fundamental points developed where the body-to-pattern relationship exists. Clicking on any parameter opens a window displaying all the geometric rules used to create it. These parameters serve as the crucial link between input (body measurements) and output (the pattern). The significant advantage of this connection is that any alterations in the measurements lead to an automatic adjustment in the associated pattern. Consequently, this system allows for the rapid generation of new and highly customisable patterns. Parameterisation, in conjunction with AI systems, facilitates the automatic generation of resizable parametric patterns.

The traditional digital and parametric approaches reviewed in this section form the foundation for other pattern-generation and customising techniques. The table below (Table 2.2.2) outlines the key differences between the traditional and parametric approaches, explaining the superiority of the parametric approach over the traditional one.

TABLE 2.2.2 Significant differences between the traditional and parametric approaches.

Criteria	**Traditional approach**	**Parametric approach**
Editability	Not editable	Editable
Reusability	Not reusable	Reusable
Construction calculations	Manually	Automatically
Alteration for an entity	Manually	Automatically
Time/effort consuming	Less but the pattern is recreated for each new purpose.	Initially time consuming but forms an adaptable basis
Reusability of blocks geometry	Not reusable	Reusable
Resizing	Only grading at fixed points	Entirely resized based on individual measurements and modifiable variables
Creativity opportunities	Limited due to repetitive pattern recreation	Unlimited due to the pattern editability and reusability
Ease of adjustment	Requires significant effort to adjust individual elements	Allows for easier and more efficient adjustments
Versatility	Limited in versatility for different styles and sizes	Highly versatile, accommodating various styles and sizes
Sustainability	Less sustainable due to repeated pattern creation consuming energy.	More sustainable, reducing energy consumption due to pattern reusability

2.2.4 PATTERN FIT EVALUATION

Fit evaluation is a critical approval stage before a garment proceeds to production. Its significance lies in its potential to substantially diminish return rates and consumer dissatisfaction, thereby also contributing to the elimination of waste within the fashion industry. Therefore, the pattern construction process remains incomplete until the fit has undergone thorough scrutiny and has been confirmed by the decision-makers as satisfactory, aligning precisely with the final product's design and fit specifications.

Traditionally, fit evaluation involves a manual process that requires physically cutting patterns and fabric, followed by the labour-intensive assembly of fabric pieces through stitching, often resulting in the production and fitting of numerous garment prototypes. This approach was not only time-consuming but also wasteful and therefore unsustainable. However, cutting-edge patternmaking technologies, particularly those providing 2D-to-3D methods, have revolutionised this paradigm by allowing photorealistic prototype production simulations (Figure 2.2.12). This virtual simulation includes the capacity to virtually stitch 2D digital patterns on 3D parametric models, that can be resized to the exact measurements used in pattern construction. Furthermore, it enables the application of fabric properties to the pattern and a comprehensive assessment of the garment's drape, movement and overall aesthetics in a digital environment. This feature is known as a garment fit map or heat map.

Garment fit maps are visual representations of data overlaid on a 3D model or scene. They use colour gradients to indicate the values of data at different points on the model, providing a visualisation of complex datasets on top of 3D geometry. These may be colour-coded from red to blue, i.e., as a heat map display, to draw attention to hot spots and variations that may not be obvious from looking at the raw data. Heat maps are useful for identifying patterns, trends and areas of interest in large datasets for review and modification. Four layers: stress, strain, fit and pressure points make up the complete map. The stress map shows the external stress causing garment distortion by area of the fabric where the red colour indicates the highest stress while the blue colour indicates zero distortion (Teyeme et al., 2023). The strain map is also represented as a heat map to indicate the rate of clothing distortion due to external stress and is quantified as a percentage. The fit map shows how tight clothes are on the user's body and the pressure point map shows the exact point of contact, i.e., from next to the skin or flowing. It becomes evident that accuracy in the physical parameters of the fabric input is fundamental to achieving an accurate fit evaluation. With an accurate set of data for the fabric or a true digital twin, the scale parameters of the maps can be adjusted for different levels of stretch from the default setting. For performance products, e.g., sportswear, where compression and support are essential to the performance of the product, knowledge of both fabrics and fit is required to achieve a good fit. Equally, this type of garment needs to be checked in a variety of dynamic poses to check for fit comfort during use.

The digital fit evaluation method empowers designers to thoroughly assess their pattern's fit across the size range, make necessary adjustments

FIGURE 2.2.12 Digital fit evaluation.

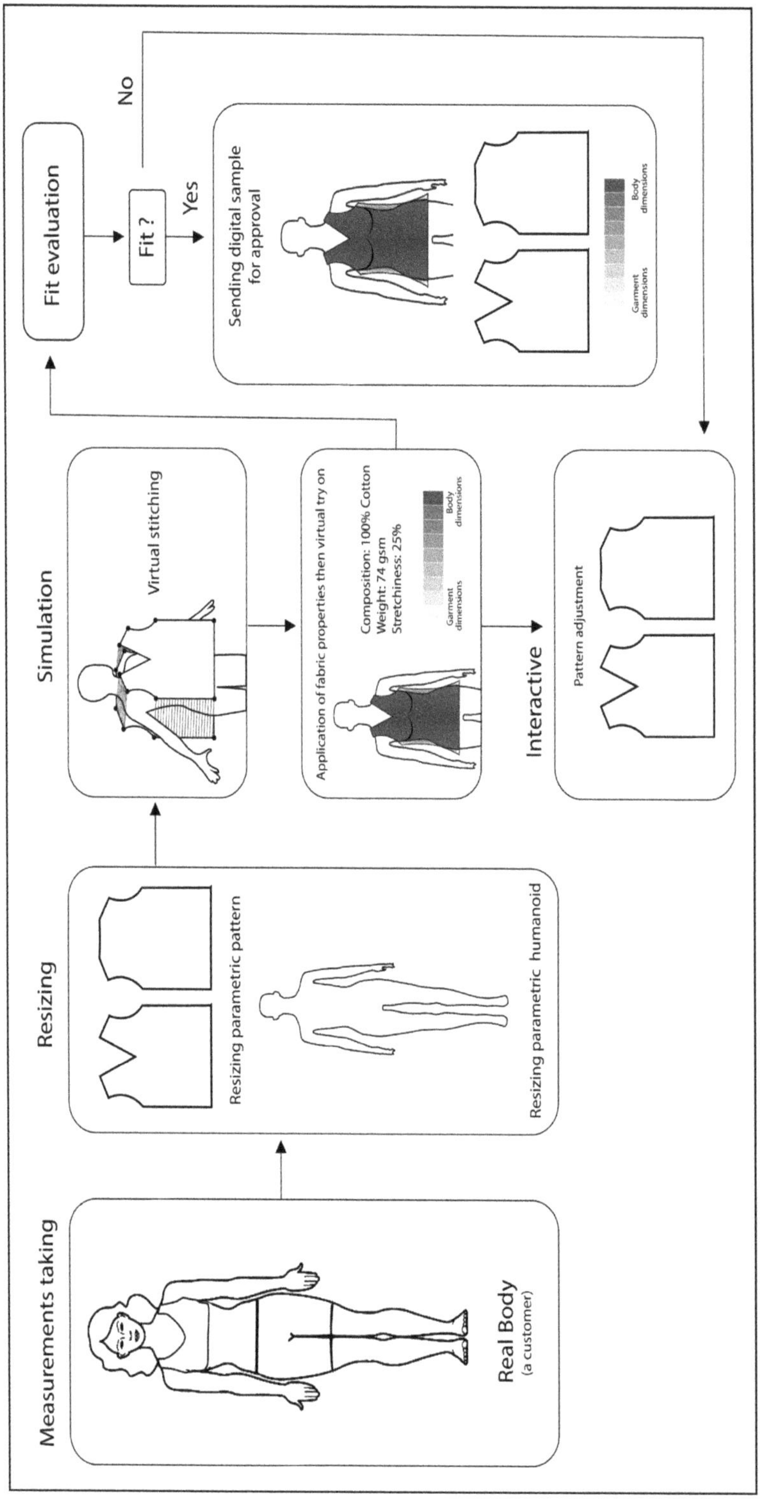

FIGURE 2.2.13 Digital fit evaluation workflow (adapted from Teyeme, 2023).

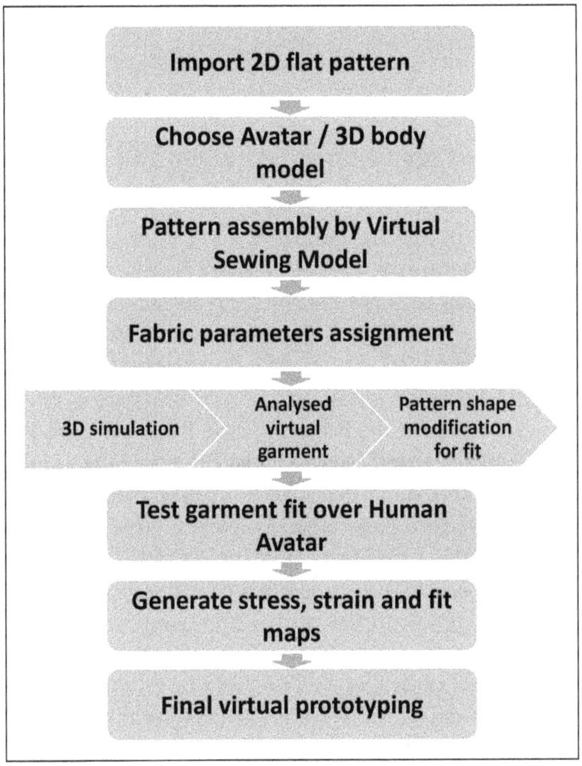

to pattern pieces or to add ease of wear at specific points to accommodate different body shapes and realise fashion products that are truly size inclusive. Speed to market is achieved through swiftly obtaining approval from decision-makers using 3D virtual samples. This not only reduces the time and material required for physical prototype development but also enhances the efficiency and sustainability of the fashion product development process. The figure below (Figure 2.2.13) illustrates the workflow of this digital method, depicting how it streamlines the pattern fitting process, saving time and resources while promoting sustainability.

The industry is currently in a state of transition where DPC is facilitating a reduction in physical protypes and a more optimised workflow. However, most brands continue to operate using a relatively small range of sizes based on averages to optimise efficiencies. This approach has led to inaccurate pattern shapes that are not truly representative of target consumers, producing garments that simply do not fit, contributing to high rates of return and unsold goods (The Interline, 2023a). Advancing DPC working practices could resolve these issues. DPC can use body scanned data as the basis for creating digital twins that better represents the target consumer and supports consistency across global manufacturing. Digital assets that are based on the brands' technical specifications for size and fit, accommodating known differences in body shape due to ethnicity or age of consumers has far-reaching potential beyond merchandising and marketing activities (The Interline, 2020) (for more, see chapter question 1).

Mini case study

Made to measure – Crea Solution IRIS vision and cutting system

Digital measurements or body scan data could give rise to new business models including 'made to measure' (MTM) and 'made to order' (MTO), informed by those individualised scans reducing inventory and waste. They open up new routes for personalisation in fit through use of these precise customer's measurements (Casciani et al., 2022). As outlined in Chapter 2.3, when this approach is coupled with near shoring through an agile small batch manufacturing model, brands can advance customisation and personalisation initiatives. The Crea Solution case example involves men's MTM and MTO suiting but this must not be confused with bespoke tailoring (see Table 2.2.1). Crea Solution has its headquarters and innovation hub in Bologna, Italy and partners with the industry's leading brands, providing a knowledge exchange for innovative solutions that meet the specific needs of the luxury sector (Crea Solution, n.d.). The Crea Solution combines AI MTM pattern generation with automatic cutting with artificial vision. An artificial vision system consists of sensors, high-definition cameras and advanced algorithms that interpret images making it possible to automatically recognise fabric details such as texture, patterns, repeated motifs, checks, stripes or fabric defects. Most men's tailored suits are made from checked or striped fabrics which requires pattern matching and precise pattern matching is a feature of luxury products. This technology can then signal to the cutting machine where the fabric needs to be cut. Applications include any MTM garment that requires pattern matching of fabrics with printed motifs, stripes, or checks. The process starts with the customer's measurements and order placement. Artificial intelligence algorithms for MTM within the Crea Solution systems then modify the models automatically to these. The system has an automatic panel placement feature that automatically accommodates checks and stripe matching in cutting, using cameras and adjustments during the cutting process. The cut panels are then sewn together by machinists completing the MTM/MTO garment production.

END-OF-CHAPTER DISCUSSIONS

1. This question explores the barriers to adoption of virtual fitting and styling apps. Research a virtual try-on application, for example StyleMe, Zyler, 3DLook and Size Stream, then answer the following questions:

a) How can virtual fitting and styling apps make shopping more accessible, and for whom?
b) How have they standardised sizing, and is this representative?
c) How could this affect the consumer's shopping experience and the likelihood to purchase, in comparison to physically trying clothes on?
d) What improvements would you make to the app?
e) Are there shared features between these apps?
f) How might businesses utilise the input of data, ethically, to improve sizing and fitting?
g) How might consumers be incentivised to participate to build scan data for instant fit recommendations?

2. Investigate the i-mannequin research project for 2D pattern parametrisation and 3D simulation, available at https://i-mannequin.iti.gr/en/home-en/ How does the proposal of fast pattern modelling and semi-automatic digitisation of existing garments advance the product development workflow?
3. As 3D design tools become more accessible, consumers can design their own personalised products; how might a start-up business explore this opportunity?

Bibliography and further reading

Aldrich, W. (2015). *Metric pattern cutting for women's wear*. John Wiley & Sons.

Almond, K. and Power, J. (2018). 'Breaking the rules in pattern cutting: An interdisciplinary approach to promote creativity in pedagogy', *Art, Design & Communication in Higher Education*, 17(1), pp. 33–50. doi:10.1386/adch.17.1.33_1.

Anderson, R. (2009). *Bespoke: Savile Row Ripped and Smoothed*. Simon & Schuster.

Armstrong, C. M. and LeHew, M .L., 2011. Sustainable apparel product development: In search of a new dominant social paradigm for the field using sustainable approaches. *Fashion Practice*, 3(1), pp.29–62.

Armstrong, H. J. (2014). *Patternmaking for fashion design*. Pearson Education/Prentice Hall.

Arribas, V. and Alfaro, J. A. (2018). '3D technology in fashion: From concept to consumer', *Journal of Fashion Marketing and Management: An International Journal*, 22(2), pp. 240–251.

Balmer, R. and Keat, W. (2009). *Exploring engineering: An introduction to engineering and design*. Elsevier Science.

Bartol, K., Petkovic, T., Bojanic, D. and Pribanic, T. (2021). 'A review of body measurement using 3D scanning', *IEEE Access*, 9, pp. 67281–67301. doi:10.1109/ACCESS.2021.3076595.

Beazley, A. (1997). 'Size and fit: Procedures in undertaking a survey of body measurements', *Journal of Fashion Marketing and Management: An International Journal*, 2(1), pp. 55–85.

Bray, N. (1985). *Dress pattern designing (4th Edition metric)*. Oxford. B.S.P. Professional Books.

Campbell, M. (2010). 'The development of a hybrid system for designing and pattern making in-set sleeves', PhD thesis, RMIT University.

Casciani, D., Chkanikova, O. and Pal, R. (2022). 'Exploring the nature of digital transformation in the fashion industry: opportunities for supply chains, business models, and sustainability-oriented innovations',

Sustainability: Science, Practice and Policy, 18(1), pp. 773–795.

Christopher, M., Lowson, R. and Peck, H. (2004). 'Creating agile supply chains in the fashion industry'. *International Journal of Retail & Distribution Management*, 32(8), pp. 367–376. doi: 10.1108/09590550410546188

Court, F. (2015). 'Embracing digital is a matter of survival', *The Business of Fashion*, 9 April. Available at: www.businessoffashion.com/community/voices/discussions/is-fashion-missing-the-technology-revolution/op-ed-embracing-digital-is-a-matter-of-survival (accessed 21 June 2017).

Crea Solution (n.d.). *Technologies for the fashion industry*. Available at: https://www.creasolution.it/en/industries/fashion/ (accessed 28 October 2023)

D'Apuzzo, N. et al. (2007). '3D body scanning technology for fashion and apparel industry', *Videometrics IX*, 64910O(6491). doi:10.1117/12.703785.

d'Avolio, E., Bandinelli, R. and Rinaldi, R. (2015). 'Improving new product development in the fashion industry through product lifecycle management: A descriptive analysis', *International Journal of Fashion Design, Technology and Education*, 8(2), pp.108–121.

Datta, D. and Seal, P. (2018). 'Various approaches in pattern making for garment sector', *Journal of Textile Engineering & Fashion Technology*, 4. doi:10.15406/jteft.2018.04.00118.

De Silva, R. K. J., Rupasinghe, T. D., and Apeagyei, P. (2019). 'A collaborative apparel new product development process model using virtual reality and augmented reality technologies as enablers', *International Journal of Fashion Design, Technology and Education*, 12(1), 1–11.

First Insight (n.d.). *Unlock the power of your customer: Next-gen retail decision platform*. Available at: https://www.firstinsight.com/ (accessed 28 October 2023)

Geršak, J. (2022). *Design of clothing manufacturing processes: A systematic approach to developing, planning, and control*. The Textile Institute Book Series. Elsevier Science (Woodhead Publishing).

Gill, S., Januszkiewicz, M. and Ahmed, M. (2022). 'Digital fashion technology: A review of online fit and sizing'. In Norsaadah Zakaria (ed.) *Digital manufacturing technology for sustainable anthropometric apparel*, Woodhead Publishing, pp. 135–163.

Gill, S., Al Houf, H., Hayes, S. and Conlon, J. (2023). 'Evolving pattern practice, from traditional patterns to bespoke parametric blocks', *International Journal of Fashion Design, Technology and Education*, pp. 1–18. doi:10.1080/17543266.2023.2260829

Goworek, H., and McGoldrick, P. (2015). *Retail marketing management*. Harlow: Pearson Education.

Guerlain, P. and Durand, B. (2006). 'Digitizing and measuring of the human body for the clothing industry', *International Journal of Clothing Science and Technology*, 18(3), pp. 151–165. doi: 10.1108/09556220610657925.

Hines, T. (2014). *Supply chain strategies: Demand driven and customer focused*. Routledge.

Hulme, W. (1946). *The theory of garment-pattern Making*. 2nd edn. National Trade Press.

The Interline (2020). *Going 3D, part 3: How fashion fits*. [online] The Interline. Available at: https://www.theinterline.com/2020/05/12/going-3d-part-3-how-fashion-fits/ [accessed 26 October 2023].

The Interline (2022). *Digital Product Creation Report 2022*. Available at: https://www.theinterline.com/2022/11/29/digital-product-creation-in-fashion-report-2022/ (accessed 28 October 2023)

The Interline (2023a). *The billion dollar return dilemma: Does body data hold the answer?* Available at: https://www.theinterline.com/2023/02/09/the-billion-dollar-return-dilemma-does-body-data-hold-the-answer/ (accessed 28 October 2023)

The Interline (2023b). *The environmental case for digital fashion.* Available at: https://www.theinterline.com/2023/02/01/the-environmental-and-sustainability-case-for-digital-fashion/ (accessed 26 October 2023).

Kalbaska, N. and Cantoni, L. (2019). 'Digital fashion competences: Market practices and needs'. In R. Rinaldi and R. Bandinelli (eds) *Business Models and ICT Technologies for the Fashion Supply Chain: Proceedings of IT4Fashion 2017 and IT4Fashion 2018* (pp. 125–135). Springer International Publishing.

Keiser, S., and Garner, M. (2012). *Beyond design: The synergy of apparel product development*. 3rd ed. Fairchild Publications.

Kidwell, C. B. (1979). 'Cutting a fashionable fit: Dressmakers' drafting systems in the United States', *Smithsonian Studies in History and Technology*, 4(42), pp. 1–163.

Kim, H. S. et al. (2019). 'Standardization of the size and shape of virtual human body for apparel products', *Fashion and Textiles*, 6(1), p. 33. doi:10.1186/s40691-019-0187-z.

Marion, T. J. and Fixson, S. K. (2021). The transformation of the innovation process: How digital tools are changing work, collaboration, and organizations in new product development, *Journal of Product Innovation Management*, 38(1), 192–215.

Moniruzzaman, M. and Rita, A. (2022). 'An approach to design solutions for garments using a CAD system', *Journal of Textile Engineering & Fashion Technology*, 8, pp. 145–148. doi:10.15406/jteft.2022.08.00313.

Moore, J. (ed.) (2020). *Patternmaking history and theory*. Bloomsbury Visual Arts.

Nariño, R., Becerra, A. and Hernández González, A. (2016). 'Anthropometry. Comparative analysis of technologies for the capture of anthropometric dimensions', *Revista EIA*, pp. 47–59.

Papachristou, E. and Bilalis, N. (2017). Should the fashion industry confront the sustainability challenge with 3D prototyping technology. *International Journal of Sustainable Engineering*, 10(4–5), 207–214.

Parker-Strak, R., Barnes, L. Studd, R. and Doyle, S. (2020). Disruptive Product Development for Online Fast Fashion Retailers Fashion. *Journal of Fashion Marketing and Management: An International Journal 124* (3): 517–532. doi:10.1108/JFMM-08-2019-0170

Paton, E. (2018). 'H&M, a fashion giant, has a problem: $4.3 billion in unsold clothes', *New York Times*, 27 March. Available at: https://www.nytimes.com/2018/03/27/business/hm-clothes-stock-sales.html (accessed 26 October 2023).

Rumbo-Rodríguez, L. et al. (2021). 'Comparison of body scanner and manual anthropometric measurements of body shape: A systematic review', *International Journal of Environmental Research and Public Health*. doi:10.3390/ijerph18126213.

Staff, S. J. (2021). 'Product testing lifts full-price sales at Marks & Spencer', *Sourcing Journal*. Available at: https://sourcingjournal.com/topics/retail/first-insight-marks-spencer-video-elaine-wheeler-next-gen-xm-285123/ (accessed 26 October 2023).

Sun, L. and Zhao, L. (2018). 'Technology disruptions: Exploring the changing roles of designers, makers, and users in the fashion industry', *International Journal of Fashion Design, Technology and Education*, 11(3), 362–374.

Teyeme, Y., Malengier, B., Tesfaye, T., Vasile, S. and Van Langenhove, L. (2023). 'Fit and pressure comfort evaluation on a virtual prototype of a tight-fit cycling shirt', *Autex Research Journal*, 23(2), pp.153–163.

Tyler, D., Heeley, J. and Bhamra, T. (2006). 'Supply chain influences on new product development in fashion clothing', *Journal of Fashion Marketing and Management*, 10(3), 316–328.

Van Laar, E., Van Deursen, A. J., Van Dijk, J. A. and De Haan, J. (2017). 'The relation between 21st-century skills and digital skills: A systematic literature review', *Computers in Human Behavior*, 72, pp. 577–588.

Wang, B. and Ha-Brookshire, J. E. (2018). 'Exploration of digital competency requirements within the fashion supply chain with an anticipation of Industry 4.0', *International Journal of Fashion Design, Technology and Education*, 11(3), 333–342.

Zeraatkar, M. and Khalili, K. (2020). 'A fast and low-cost human body 3D scanner Using 100 cameras', *Journal of Imaging*. doi:10.3390/jimaging6040021.

Zieman, N.L. (2008). *Pattern fitting with confidence*. Krause Craft.

CHAPTER 2.3

Process innovation in fashion manufacturing

Jo Conlon

New digital technologies serve as an important means to develop process innovations in the fashion industry (Jin et al., 2019). Process innovation can be found at different levels and stages in the value chain as illustrated with Figure 1.2.5, 'Connecting the Fashion Value Chain with Digital Applications'. Chapter 1.2 discussed the need for end-to-end connectivity and how greater collaboration and improved communication could be facilitated through digital asset management (DAM) and product lifecycle management (PLM). Chapters 2.1 and 2.2 demonstrate the impact of 3D design tools on the processes of new product development. Process innovation builds new ways of working across the whole value chain with digital assets, where each stage of the value chain provides interoperable digital assets as inputs for the next stage. This chapter emphasises that it is workforce capabilities that leverage digital technologies by applying an entrepreneurial mindset of opportunity spotting and problem solving to generate new processes that contribute to competitive advantage and advance the industry. One of the key improvements that digital technologies deliver is data to enable visibility, as decisions and improvements need to be based on accurate information. This chapter seeks to demonstrate how better visibility facilitates the optimisation of processes and workflows and allows sustainability objectives to be met. Data can bring greater transparency to the supply chain to support the shift to a more sustainable fashion system and enable circular economy business models. This topic continues in Chapter 2.4.

LEARNING OUTCOMES

After reading this chapter, you should be able to:

- Identify how innovation is vital for the future development of the fashion industry.
- Describe how process innovation contributes to competitive advantage within the context of the fashion industry.
- Examine the need for businesses to foster organisational entrepreneurship and how these capabilities can be supported in the workforce.

DOI: 10.4324/9781003364559-7

- Evaluate how digital tools, techniques and solutions are used to optimise and advance manufacturing within the context of fashion.
- Explain how digital tools enable process innovations to achieve business sustainability objectives.

2.3.1 UNDERSTANDING THE ROLE OF PROCESS INNOVATION FOR COMPETITIVE ADVANTAGE AND CHANGE

Process innovation is an improved way of performing tasks across the entire value chain including how operations are managed (Jin et al., 2019). Upgrading through investment in digital technologies has led to developments in process innovation. Six Industry 4.0 design principles (Table 2.3.1) provide a framework for businesses to pilot change initiatives whilst building a digital ecosystem: Interoperability, Virtualisation, Decentralisation, Modularity, Service Orientation, Real Time Capability (Hermann et al., 2016). Process innovation is increasingly seen as an important source of competitiveness and organisational renewal. The driver for investment is to yield benefits from associated process innovation, this ROI (return on investment) may be in terms of enhanced efficiency and productivity, reduced costs, improved quality, greater value and improved service. Improvements can be incremental or radical and will require change management as discussed in Chapter 1.2.

As process improvements are internally developed and become part of the business capabilities, these internal 'how things are done' techniques are not visible to competitors and are less easy to emulate rapidly and are therefore a source of competitive advantage. Therefore, businesses need to invest to foster digital capabilities to fully explore what is possible and how the business could adapt to make the most of emerging possibilities

TABLE 2.3.1 Six Industry 4.0 design principles to build a digital ecosystem (adapted from Hermann et al., 2016).

Design Principle	Comment
Interoperability	Standards are a key success factor for open communication.
Virtualisation	Sensors monitor operations and are linked to virtual models to manage rising complexity.
Decentralisation (of control)	RFID tags support greater automation and provide data to track progress and quality.
Real-time capability	Data is collected and analysed in real time.
Service orientation	Service advanced both internally and externally. Customer requirements can be fulfilled by requirements provided on the RFID tag.
Modularity	Systems are made of flexible and adaptable modules that can be added to or replaced when based on standardised interfaces.

TABLE 2.3.2 Key terms related to supply chain processes.

Term	Description
Business model	How the business creates and generates value.
Business process	How the operational aspects of the business work (typically by function).
Operational capabilities	Unique internal skills that develop and maintain competitive advantage.
Agile supply chain	Characterised by flexibility and resilience; meets known demand through an emphasis on efficient processes and collaborative partnerships.
Responsiveness	The ability to respond to demand as it happens.
Transparency	Disclosure of validated information about supply chains regarding areas of concern such as product, raw materials, sourcing, labour practices, environmental impacts etc.
Visibility	Ability to track products and reduce risks.
Traceability	The ability to map the entire product journey.
Seamless	Where the end-to-end supply chain functions as if it were a single business.
Mass customisation	A technique to produce personalised products at costs equivalent to mass-production flexibility.

and opportunities. Table 2.3.2 details the key terms related to supply chain processes. These strategic organisational abilities and needs drive process innovation within a business.

As discussed in section 1.2.1 and illustrated in Figure 1.2.2, process innovation comes from the interaction of people, processes and digital technologies. The sources of innovation are presented in Figure 2.3.1. It is interesting to note that creative inspiration is only one of ten sources of innovation, demonstrating there are many ways to bring forward innovative ideas. The skills associated with entrepreneurship can be developed through practice (for more, see question 2 at the end of this chapter).

Another one of the sources of innovation in Figure 2.3.1 is regulation. All businesses are increasingly aware of the likelihood of new legislation in response to climate change. Familiarity with the UN Sustainable Development Goals (SDGs) is now an imperative for all business professionals and these can be accessed online: https://sdgs.un.org/goals. More information on how the Sustainable Development Goals are coordinated into action in the fashion sector can be accessed online: https://unfashionalliance.org/. For fashion and textiles companies, legislation like the 'Fashion Act' and the 'EU Green Deal' represent a call for action and change to current business models. For example, the EU's Waste Framework Directive mandates that EU member states must set up separate collections for used textiles and garments by January 1st, 2025, and that this waste can no longer be sent to landfill or be incinerated. There are many industry-specific reports generated to help

FIGURE 2.3.1 Sources of innovation (adapted from Tidd and Bessant, 2020).

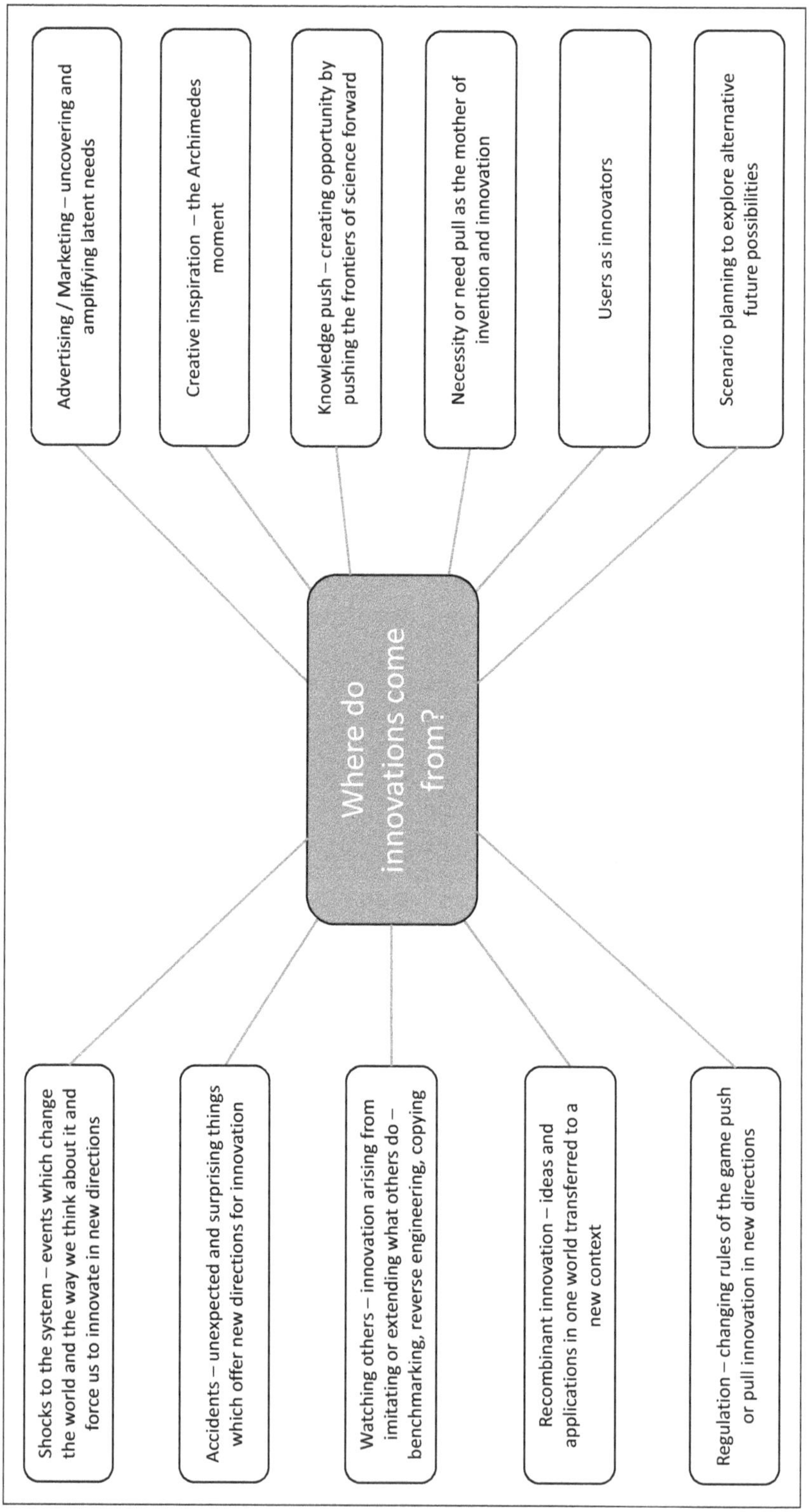
Where do innovations come from?
Advertising / Marketing – uncovering and amplifying latent needs
Creative inspiration – the Archimedes moment
Knowledge push – creating opportunity by pushing the frontiers of science forward
Necessity or need pull as the mother of invention and innovation
Users as innovators
Scenario planning to explore alternative future possibilities
Shocks to the system – events which change the world and the way we think about it and force us to innovate in new directions
Accidents – unexpected and surprising things which offer new directions for innovation
Watching others – innovation arising from imitating or extending what others do – benchmarking, reverse engineering, copying
Recombinant innovation – ideas and applications in one world transferred to a new context
Regulation – changing rules of the game push or pull innovation in new directions

fashion businesses develop strategic initiatives to navigate these changes, for example McKinsey (2020) and The Interline (2023a). This will open new career opportunities for those with a solid foundation in sustainability, product and process knowledge and passion to see the fashion industry change. The essential components of this skill set include comprehensive knowledge of materials and manufacturing processes (Chapters 2.1 and 2.2), good communication skills and proficiency in circular economy principles and waste reduction strategies. These jobs are interdisciplinary and collaborative and a good way to find out more is through networking events and by staying up to date through industry associations and organisations. One online community that is free to join is the Common Objective (https://www.commonobjective.co/), although there are many more. These platforms provide valuable opportunities to stay informed (Econyl, n.d.).

Fostering organisational entrepreneurship

Entrepreneurial activity might be evidenced by innovations in product, processes and marketing (Burns, 2022). The levels of entrepreneurial activity can be described in two dimensions: level and frequency. The level of change within businesses can be low and incremental or high and radical and it can happen frequently or infrequently within the business. Entrepreneurial intensity is high within organisations where there are radical changes happening frequently. Businesses try to foster organisational entrepreneurship to enable the business to transform for the future and to be more resistant to threat and risk. However, as discussed in Chapter 1.2, constant change initiatives can be difficult to work under if pursued relentlessly and periods of (relative) stability are needed during large and ongoing change management projects.

Large organisations have tended to struggle to be responsive and innovative, despite the greater access to resources they have compared to small and medium size enterprises (SMEs). All businesses make choices about what is important to them. There is a tendency for more focus on control using measures of efficiency and effectiveness to manage resources as organisations grow. However, in rapidly changing markets, the ability to innovate and manage change is now seen as vital to help rejuvenate large corporations (Burns, 2022).

For fashion organisations, this is evident in the shift to more customer-focused approaches to business. 'Entrepreneurial architecture' is a term used to show how the organisational architecture might be structured to encourage entrepreneurship and innovation on a sustainable basis (Burns, 2022). It is typically built upon four pillars: leaderships and management, culture, structure and systems and strategy.

The characteristics of an entrepreneurial mindset are shown in Table 2.3.3. The challenge for larger organisations is how to replicate the characteristics of an entrepreneur at scale. Certainly, there must be mechanisms for open communication to encourage challenge to the 'dominant logic', i.e., to be able to question the status quo or accepted way of doing things. One approach is through the constant learning and willingness

TABLE 2.3.3 The key traits of an entrepreneur (adapted from Burns, 2022).

Key traits	Comment
Character traits	Need for autonomy and achievement, highly determined, willingness to take measured risks and willing to take advantage of opportunities.
Relationships	Informal approach to management, uses network to support decision- making and minimise risk.
Decision-making	Appears intuitive, but information is collected constantly; willing to act with incomplete information; sets challenging but achievable goals.

for unlearning of practices that are no longer viable to the business. The techniques of design thinking and reflection are useful to reframe thinking. This type of organisational learning takes time to build; however it is a valuable source of competitive advantage. Organisational ambidexterity is an alternative approach to meet the challenge of maintaining an entrepreneurial spirit within a business. This is where departments are deliberately segregated to work in parallel to the core business (O'Reilly and Tushman, 2004). The sub-unit explores adaptations while the core continues without distraction; senior management support and coordinate activities at both sub-units.

How process innovation can support businesses to achieve their sustainability objectives

Fashion apparel value chains do not have a codified set of best practices that are standard in other manufacturing and this lack of process maturity is a barrier to getting full value across the digital value chain (The Interline, 2022). Establishing industry standard forms of measuring within clear processes would help bring transparency to de-risk supply chains, streamline costs and deliver on sustainability commitments. Additionally, most of the activity of digital technologies has been directed to the consumer-facing space, with limited applications in supply chains making this a source of untapped potential to improve resilience and sustainability and stimulate new sustainable business models (Casciani et al., 2022).

Sustainability is a wide concept that is subject to change over time and has proven difficult to operationalise. However, in applied terms, **sustainable development** is most frequently described with reference to the Brundtland Report definition of 'meeting the needs of the current generation without compromising the needs of future ones' (WCED, 1987).

TABLE 2.3.4 How process innovation supports sustainability objectives (adapted from (Stulga et al., 2022).

Mechanism	Comment
Manufacturing process optimisation	Modernising equipment and collecting and analysing data are under-utilised techniques to fully optimised manufacturing. Water and energy resources used in textile manufacture have a significant impact that requires more focused effort.
Value chain transparency	Transparent disclosure of labour, raw materials, energy source and waste management at the product level.
Circular economy model	The circular economy concept has great potential in fashion and textiles, through efforts to extend the life of products. It is estimated that only 1% of textiles are recycled.

Process innovation can support businesses to achieve their sustainability objectives in three ways (Table 2.3.4): process optimisation, increasing value chain transparency and supporting circular business (Stulga et al., 2022). The case studies of this chapter seek to illustrate three aspects. The next section presents the direction of travel for manufacturing through five commentaries. The sections start with a depiction of the concept of 'smart factory' and detail two examples of conceptual pilot schemes. The return of manufacturing to developed economy countries is known as reshoring or onshoring. The Alliance Project Report (2015): 'Repatriation of UK Textiles Manufacture' highlighted the viability of growth in the UK textiles industry, along with ways of supporting it through investment in manufacturing technology and automation to bring cost benefits and reduce response times, to make UK manufacturing more viable. To illustrate the opportunities of reshoring, the launch of the partnership of Fashion Enter with Style3D is presented to detail how manufacturing is enhanced through 3D design and digital workflows to support reshoring initiatives. The potential use of robots and IoT devices is then outlined. The chapter ends with a review of pioneering supply chain transparency and traceability tools.

2.3.2 CASE STUDY: SMART FACTORIES

The smart factory is the result of the successful implementation of Industry 4.0 technologies to automate production and logistics systems with minimal human intervention (Deloitte, 2017) as shown in Figure 2.3.2. Smart manufacturing is the process that employs computer controls, modelling, big data and other automation methods to improve manufacturing efficiencies. The physical factory is linked to its digital model through transmitters and sensors. This integrated system gathers and analyses data to connect people

FIGURE 2.3.2 Smart factory (adapted from IMPULS Foundation (n.d.)).

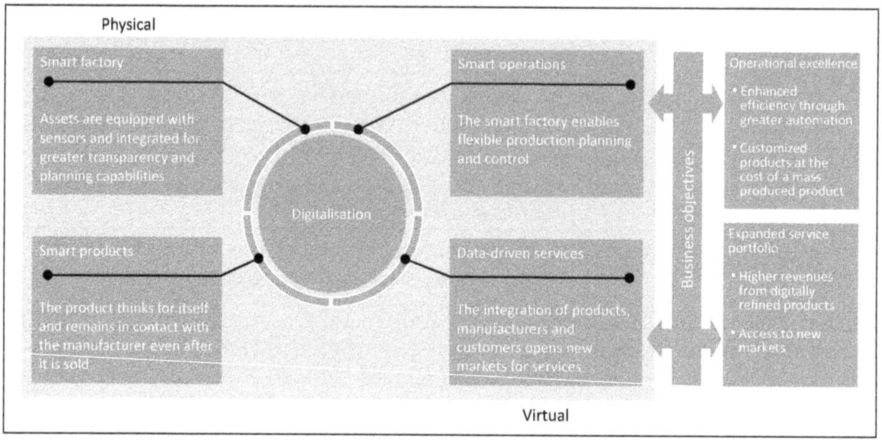

and production information through IT and is fed into decision-making models. Production can be tracked through use of barcodes or QR codes, but RFID tags are easier and quicker to read. RFID tags can store and transmit a small amount of data. The fashion industry has yet to make the shift to the smart factory beyond pilots due to a lack of understanding and progress on the principles of interoperability and virtualisation (Table 2.3.1) (Bertola and Teunissen, 2018). The creation of an integrated digital infrastructure would generate a totally transparent replication of all production processes and provide real time control. In this scenario, this real-time capability means design and production processes can be informed by data from internal functions (sales and marketing), supply partner networks and consumers. The smart factory therefore enables mass customisation but needs all processes to be streamlined and integrated to receive the input of the customer and to arrange timely delivery through logistics (Jin et al., 2019).

Factory of the future example 1: Xunxi digital factory pilot by Alibaba (source: Just Style, 2020)

The factory unit of this pilot is equipped with cutting and sewing machines, and conveyor belts that can be tracked remotely. The facility offers small and medium size manufacturers access to Alibaba's customer insights data from their retail marketplaces so that production can be responsive to consumer demand.

> Data is the core of New Manufacturing and harnessing data insights is key to capturing new opportunities in the shift in consumer preference for personalized rather than mass-produced goods.
>
> Alain Wu, CEO of Xunxi Digital Technology Company, Alibaba Group

Factory of the future example 2: Amazon's patent for on-demand apparel manufacturing (source: WWD, 2017)

Amazon hold a manufacturing patent to create on-demand clothing through a smart factory that will print and cut patterns, then assemble the garments without need of human assistance. The system is also designed to aggregate product orders to maximise productivity and limit waste of personalised orders and would involve technologies such as digital printing, 3D printing of trims and accessories, and robotics for packaging and distribution. However, the sewing of complex fashion products has not yet been automated, although advances are being actively researched as in Case 2.3.4.

2.3.3 CASE STUDY: RESHORING WITH A STRATEGIC PARTNERSHIP: FASHION ENTER X STYLE3D

Fashion Enter Ltd (FEL) is an award-winning social enterprise and a centre of ethical garment manufacturing in the UK and Style3D is a global provider of digital fashion solutions (see section 2.1.4). This collaboration was officially launched in 2023 with the opening of a Styleverse Innovation Centre within Fashion Enter's Haringey factory (Figure 2.3.3). The Styleverse Innovation Centre provides an immersive experience of 3D DPC from fabric sourcing, 3D designs, collection review and virtual store experiences demonstrating how digital assets can be managed to streamline workflows, increase productivity and reduce costs. By seamlessly connecting with Fashion Enter Ltd's current manufacturing centre of excellence, the digital garment journey progresses to the production of a physical garment. This yields a complete physical product pathway that can readily adapt to consumers' requests;

FIGURE 2.3.3 Eric Liu, CEO Style 3D presenting the Styleverse concept at Fashion Enter.

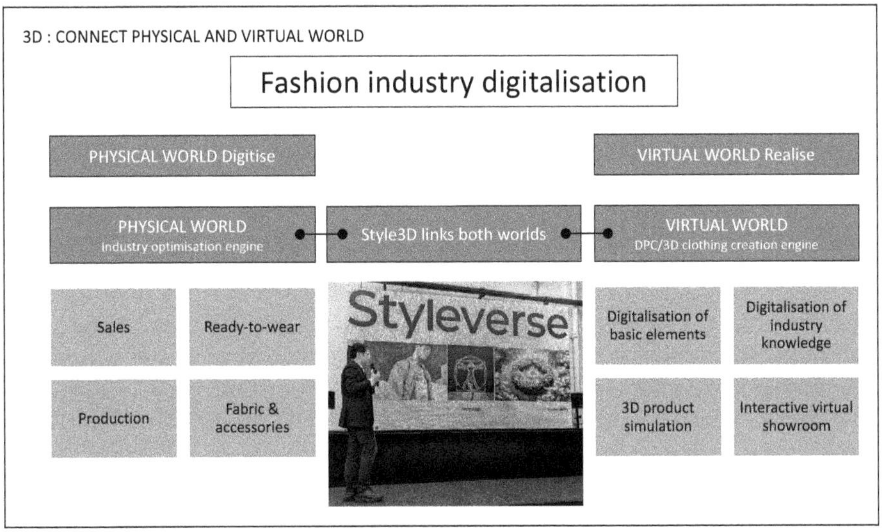

permitting on-demand production, which represents a sustainable model for the future (for more, see Part III).

> Our collaboration with Fashion Enter Ltd brings together unparalleled technical expertise and a shared vision for a digitally empowered future in fashion.
>
> Eric Liu, CEO of Style3D

Further example: Innovation centres and micro factories

In the operation of a micro factory, products are not made until they are ordered, i.e., they are entirely demand-driven. The benefits of on-demand production include increased speed to market increased personalisation, improved fit, guaranteed transparency, full target-price sell through and no requirement to hold inventory. Both Nike and Adidas have used the concept to enable mass-customisation. Another example is US company Ministry of Supply, who use thermal imaging, 3D printing and 3D knitting technologies (zero waste) to create personalised, custom-fit knitted products. Although micro factories have yet to become mainstream, they generate much interest and highlight the interest in personalised products (for more, see Chapter 3.1).

2.3.4 CASE STUDY: USE OF ROBOTS AND IOT FOR AUTOMATION OF MANUFACTURING

Automation is now standard in distribution centres with autonomous mobile robots (AMRs) that can process orders accurately and efficiently. The main barrier to automation adoption in the textile & apparel industry is a lack of proficient automated fabric gripping technology for the handling of fabric after cutting, as further automation has proven difficult due to textile materials being dimensionally unstable, limp and permeable (WTiN, 2022). The high skill and dexterity of sewing operators is currently unmatched by robotic fabric handling devices. In highly economically developed countries, sewing skills are in limited supply and are a barrier in efforts to scale the reshoring of apparel manufacturing; with rising global labour costs and high demand for skilled workers, there is renewed interest in textile grippers.

Example 1: Sewbots (source: BoF, 2017 and WTiN, 2022)

Softwear Automation are based in Atlanta USA. Their system of automated 'Sewbots' are a proprietary combination of advanced robotics, AI and IoT technologies that has enabled on-demand manufacturing where cut panels are transported and manipulated by a system of controlled rollers. The research was initially prompted by a 2002 legal requirement for US military clothing to be made in the USA despite insufficient skilled workers and high costs. Although complicated products are still not possible, relatively simple t-shirt type products are now manufactured. With the costs and impacts of unsold products or deadstock becoming more visible, the potential for this type of fast-response and customisable product is an attractive solution.

Example 2: Sewbo

Sewbo is another solution developed to meet the demand of US produced military clothing. In this process the fabric is first temporarily stiffened and transported, held, and sewn by robots. The stiffening agent is water soluble and is later removed by washing and can be recovered for reuse.

Task

Consider the challenge of balancing reshoring efforts, reducing transportation impacts with the high-risk of job losses in developing-economy countries due to automation. Try to consider both positive aspects and risks of disruptive technologies (for more, see Chapter 1.1)

Example 3: Flexciton: How factory IoT sensors and machine learning optimise scheduling

IoT devices are embedded with internet connectivity, software, sensors and other hardware that enable them to connect and exchange data with other systems and devices over the web, providing analytical capabilities. IoT devices are replacing existing technologies such as barcodes and QR codes with radio frequency identification (RFID) tags and global positioning systems (GPS) for equipment management. Sensors collect the data from the manufacturing environment for processing in the IoT system and make it available to users. Faults in machinery can be quickly identified to engineers for action. Automation means some repetitive, manual tasks are actioned without operator involvement, which reduces costs.

The Flexciton platform analyses factory data for improved scheduling and predictive maintenance. Although factories have worked to optimise their production, as complexity increases and orders are under more time pressure, the permutations are beyond the scope of traditional scheduling processes. Flexciton has clients across the food, textiles and automotive industries but now focuses on the semiconductor industry (Techcrunch, 2019). One example given by the company is of a UK textile company who manufacture over 2000 products but can only make 100 in a week. Data from operations is collected and processed with AI to come up with an optimised plan that significantly increases the efficiency of the factory.

The next section presents how digital technologies could be employed to support sustainability objectives. The section starts with a depiction of the concepts of digital ledgers and digital product passports and then reviews examples of pioneering supply chain transparency and traceability tools.

2.3.5 CASE STUDY: DIGITAL LEDGERS, DIGITAL PRODUCT PASSPORTS AND DIGITAL CATALOGUES

The supply chain is typically described through labelling of each tier – starting with tier zero or the brand HQ, working back through the supply chain to clothing manufacture (tier 1), fabric manufacture (tier 2), yarn manufacture (tier 3) and raw materials / fibres (tier 4). There is currently limited visibility beyond tier one (Fashion Revolution, 2023). This lack of reliable data is a serious barrier to producing accurate lifecycle assessments (LCA), which limits the identification of priority areas and the scaling of efforts to reduce impacts. Digital ledgers like blockchain may make the origins of products more transparent and enable better traceability. As shown in Figure 2.3.4, data from the physical supply chain is collected through various digital tools and transferred into a series of ledgers. The blockchain is a digital record of transaction and was originally developed to record cryptocurrency transactions but is now being used to track products including textiles. Through a blockchain or other records, a product can have its own digital passport where all information is stored. The advantage of blockchain technologies is that the ledger is immutable (cannot be modified after it is created) but still requires verification of the initial input. A combination of factors are challenging brands to take action to gain full visibility of how their products are manufactured and how their supply chains are managed. ESG financial reporting on investments includes non-financial factors relating to sustainability which prompted the need for standard reporting and the establishment of ESG standards and the expectation of new regulations. The disruptions during the pandemic demonstrated the strategic importance of supply chains, highlighting their significance, but pressure from investors, consumers and the likelihood of new regulations mean that solutions for supply chain transparency are being actively sought. An overview of Textile Genesis™ is presented below. Other companies targeting the fashion industry with digital solutions are Arianee, Provence, Trust Trace and Aura (for more, see Chapter 3.4).

Example 1: Textile Genesis (source: Textile Genesis, n.d.)

Textile Genesis™ is a blockchain platform that was set up to ensure the traceability of textiles from fibre into textile production, garment manufacture and into retail distribution. The Textile Genesis™ platform allows digital tokens (block chain assets) to be issued in direct proportion at the physical fibre shipment. The blockchain authentication mechanism provides a secure traceability of fibres across the supply chain.

The Textile Genesis™ platform captures shipments through the supply chain but importantly starts at the fibre source working forwards and not the traditional backward, garment route. In this way, product level traceability is captured in real time with each transaction monitored in blockchain. The platform continues to develop in line with emerging ESG standards. It has added partners such as the Textile Exchange to its collaborative ecosystem. The Textile Exchange is a global non-profit committed to driving responsible sourcing of raw materials (tier 4) and the reduction of GHG emissions in

FIGURE 2.3.4 An illustrative example of a digital value chain showing information and physical flows and how digital ledgers could provide traceability (adapted from BoF, 2022).

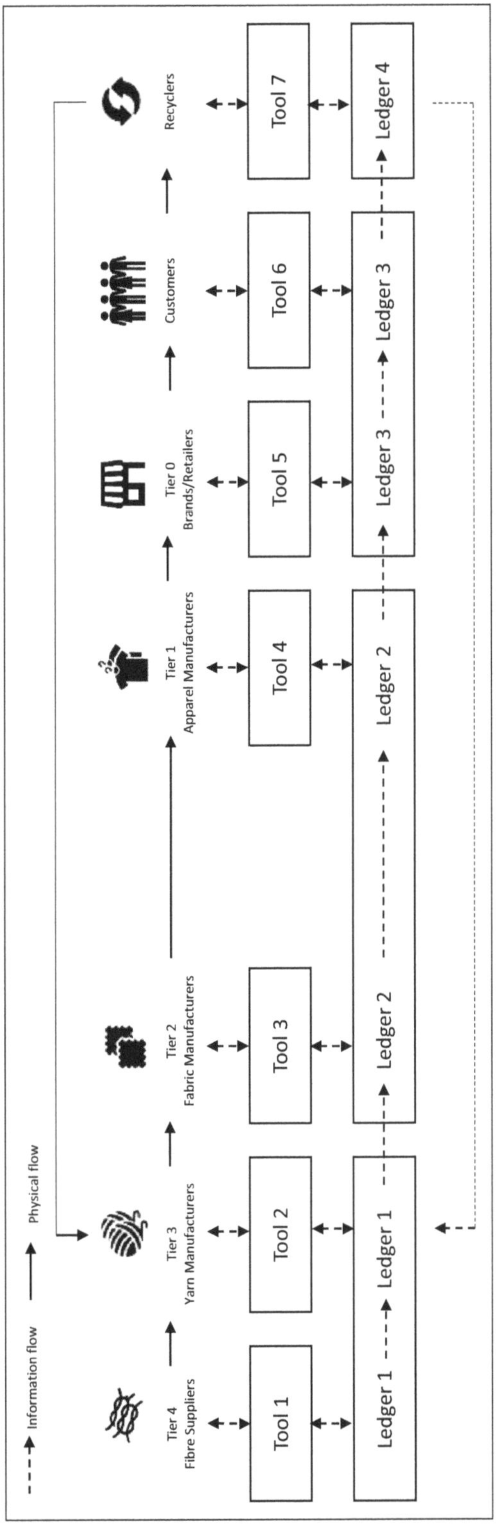

fibre and raw material production (Textile Exchange, n.d.). Another strategic partnership is with fibre producer Lenzing for their fibres TENCEL™ and ECOVERO™ (Lenzing, 2020). This involved an initial pilot, subsequently followed by phased roll-out with key brands and then a global roll-out of on-boarding most of Lenzing supply chain partners.

Example 2: Made2Flow

Made2Flow is another supply chain transparency and traceability solution that specialises in the collection and validation of environmental data. Their main applications are data collection and validation, Scope 3 reporting (activities the brand is indirectly responsible for in its value chain) and a design decision-making application to evaluate different design and sourcing scenarios. Validated data and decision tools at the granular level support brands to reduce their impacts. A new tool in the Made2Flow application facilitates insetting (investment in carbon reduction projects within their supply chains) and the identification of priorities.

Example 3: Digital product passports

Digital product passports (DPP) cover the entire product lifecycle, i.e., extending into post-purchase use stage and end-of-life disposal. To create effective DPP data, the following information is required: material, production process, transport, product care, end-of-life options, environmental data and compliance to regulation. Digital care labels with QR codes and RFID tags are already part of the retail landscape and offer a route to digitally connect products through their retail, use, resale or buy-back and disposal stages. The care label provider Avery Dennison offers an accessible route to prepare for DPP by populating their atma.io platform with data from supply chains. A benefit of this type of solution is that it follows interoperability standards for the exchange of data, including with Partnership for Carbon Transparency (PACT) for product-level emission accounting and exchange, to create transparency on emissions across their value chains (Scope 3). Another solution is ettos, a SaaS (Software as a service) platform developed from the founders of the app Lyfcycle, that facilitates the tracking of entire garment manufacturing process with real-time data, evidence for environmental and ethical claims and the creation of digital product passports (for more, see Chapter 3.4).

Example 4: Grid by Suuchi

Improvement initiatives involving technology have previously tended to streamline and optimise within rigid functional boundaries which had led to siloed information, limited automation and workflow optimisation between solutions (The Interline, 2023b). The industry has repeatedly sought ways to increase visibility in supply chains, including investments in technology-enabled platforms like enterprise resource planning (ERP) and PLM. However, such systems were often over-customised and without industry protocols for interoperability, and gaps in data either remained or were filled manually. The Suuchi: GRID platform intends to address this problem with a universal connected workflow, meeting the demand for dataflow, and it builds on the origins of the company as a sourcing platform. The GRID platform can be employed to work with established PLM systems or as a PLM system and extends existing capabilities and functions through the entire supply chain. The addition of supply chain partners to the ecosystem brings a unique perspective and insight from tiers 4, 3 and 2. It aims to support traceability goals through real-time tracking of raw materials, products and information.

Example 5: PlatformE 'RealTime'

Real-time capabilities provide the opportunity to intervene in the system of supply. This solution leverages the capability to use sales information to intervene to prevent overproduction. Online shopping has made impulse buying and returning items easier and much of the clothing produced is never worn. This solution operates in two ways to reduce impacts from overproduction. Firstly, it tackles waste by accurately listing all the products (materials, accessories and trims) already produced in a searchable digital catalogue. This encourages and facilitates the collaborative design use of current hidden waste, rather than ordering more, which also saves time and reduces costs. The virtual prototype developed can then be shared with targeted clients. The second part involves providing real-time information during product development by connecting stakeholders in active production systems to share information about cost and delivery.

END-OF-CHAPTER DISCUSSIONS

1. Select a case study from Chapter 2.3 to investigate. What criteria would you use to evaluate available solutions before recommending one for investment? Imagine you are at work and you would like to pitch the case study solution to your boss. What are the benefits, barriers and risks to this solution you have chosen?
2. Draw a mind map or spider diagram to evaluate your entrepreneurial skills, reflecting on how you can practise and implement the following:
   - Practise projecting positivity.
   - Build connections, e.g., through societies, sports, part-time work, internships and volunteering.
   - Join a professional body or community relevant to the industry.
   - Schedule time for reading industry news and reports.
   - Acceptance and re-framing of perceived failures into experimentation and opportunities for learning.
   - Build resilience.
   - Prioritise down-time and understanding burn-out.
   - Keep learning active by attending events and networking opportunities.

3. Social entrepreneurs create innovative solutions that focus on solving community-based problems, rather than generating a profit. Review the links below:
   - https://consciousfashion.co/guides/fashion-social-enterprises
   - https://ethicalfashioninitiative.org/business-development/social-enterprises

   What type of products and collaborations are there? Imagine you are setting up a social enterprise; outline the products you would produce and which charitable cause you would support if you had the opportunity.

4. Cancelled orders leads to deadstock fabrics and products. Propose a start-up business concept to generate profit from industry waste.

Bibliography and further reading

The Alliance Project Report (2015). *Repatriation of UK textiles manufacture.* Available at: https://www.ukft.org/business-advice/industry-reports-and-stats/ (accessed 25 October 2023).

Bertola, P. and Teunissen, J. (2018). 'Fashion 4.0. Innovating fashion industry through digital transformation', *Research Journal of Textile and Apparel*, 22(4), pp. 352–369.

BoF (2017). *The Sewbots are coming!* Available at: https://www.businessoffashion.com/articles/technology/the-sewbots-are-coming/ (accessed 26 October 2023).

BoF (2022). *The State of Fashion: Technology Report*. Available at: https://www.businessoffashion.com/reports/news-analysis/the-state-of-fashion-technology-industry-report-bof-mckinsey/ (accessed 26 October 2023).

Burns, P. (2022). *Entrepreneurship and small business: Start-up, growth, and maturity*. Bloomsbury Publishing.

Casciani, D., Chkanikova, O. and Pal, R. (2022). 'Exploring the nature of digital transformation in the fashion industry: Opportunities for supply chains, business models, and sustainability-oriented innovations', *Sustainability: Science, Practice and Policy*, 18(1), pp. 773–795.

Deloitte (2017). *The smart factory: Responsive, adaptive, connected manufacturing*. Available at: https://www.deloitte.com/global/en/our-thinking/insights/topics/digital-transformation/industry-4-0/smart-factory-connected-manufacturing.html (accessed 25 October 2023).

Econyl (n.d.). 3 *Must-have dkills for the booming green jobs market in fashion & design*. Available at: https://www.econyl.com/magazine/3-must-have-skills-for-the-booming-green-jobs-market-in-fashion-design/ (accessed 26 October 2023).

Fashion Revolution (2023). *Fashion Transparency Index 2023: Fashion Revolution*. [online] Available at: http://www.fashionrevolution.org/about/transparency. (accessed 26 October 2023].

Hays, K. (2017). 'Amazon prepares for on-demand fashion production with patent. *WWD*. Available at: https://wwd.com/business-news/technology/amazon-going-deeper-into-fashion-with-new-on-demand-manufacturing-patent-10869520/ (accessed 26 October 2023).

Hermann, M., Pentek, T. and Otto, B. (2016). 'Design principles for Industrie 4.0 scenarios.' *2016 49th Hawaii*

International Conference on System Sciences. HICSS. IEEE. pp. 3928–3937. doi:10.1109/HICSS.2016.488

IMPULS (n.d.). *Industry 4.0 readiness online self-check for businesses*. Available at: https://www.industrie40-readiness.de/?lang=en (accessed 25 October 2023).

IMPULS (2019). *Industry 4.0 readiness check*. IMPULS. Available at: https://www.industrie40-readiness.de/?lang=en (accessed 26 October 2023).

The Interline (2022). *Digital Product Creation Report 2022*. Available at: https://www.theinterline.com/2022/11/29/digital-product-creation-in-fashion-report-2022/ (accessed 26 October 2023).

The Interline (2023a). *The Sustainability Report 2023*. Available at: https://www.theinterline.com/2023/10/05/fashion-sustainability-report-2023/ (accessed 26 October 2023).

The Interline (2023b). *Efficiency, optimisation, and order: The strategic importance of supply chain technology*. Available at: https://www.theinterline.com/2023/09/19/efficiency-optimisation-and-order-the-strategic-importance-of-supply-chain-technology/ (accessed 26 October 2023).

Jin, B.E., Cedrola, E. and Kim, N. (2019). 'Process innovation: Hidden secret to success and efficiency'. In B. E. Jin and E. Cedrola (eds) *Process innovation in the global fashion industry* (pp. 1–23). Palgrave Studies in Practice: Global Fashion Brand Management. Palgrave Pivot.

Just Style (2020). 'Apparel centre of Alibaba's new 'smart manufacturing' drive', *Just Style*. Available at: https://www.just-style.com/news/apparel-centre-of-alibabas-new-smart-manufacturing-drive/ (accessed 26 October 2023).

Lenzing (2020). *New level of transparency in the textile industry: Lenzing introduces blockchain-enabled traceability platform*. Available at: https://www.lenzing.com/newsroom/press-releases/press-release/new-level-of-transparency-in-the-textile-industry-lenzing-introduces-blockchain-enabled-traceability-platform (accessed 25 October 2023).

LinkedIn (2023). *Style3D on LinkedIn: Style3D x Fashion Enter Ltd*, Press Release. Available at: https://www.linkedin.com/posts/style3d_style3d-x-fashion-enter-ltd-press-release-activity-707798058602 7462656-lcKW/ (accessed 26 October 2023).

McKinsey (2020). *Fashion on climate. How the fashion industry can urgently act to reduce its greenhouse gas emissions*. Available at: https://www.mckinsey.com/industries/retail/our-insights/fashion-on-climate (accessed 26 October 2023).

O'Reilly, C.A. and Tushman, M. L. (2004). 'The ambidextrous organization', *Harvard Business Review*, 82(4), pp. 74–83.

Pereira, M., Pina, L., Reis, B., Miguel, R., Silva, M. and Rafael, P. (2020). 'Digital technology for global supply chain in fashion: A contribution for sustainability development'. In G. Vignali, L. F. Reid, D. Ryding, C. E. Henninger (eds) *Technology-driven sustainability: Innovation in the fashion supply chain* (pp. 117–136). Palgrave Macmillan.

Stulga, P., Whitfield, R. I., Love, J. and Evans, D. (2022). 'Towards sustainable manufacturing with Industry 4.0: A framework for the textile industry'. *Proceedings of the Design Society* (2), pp. 283–292.

Style3D (2023). *Style3D and Fashion-Enter Ltd Announce Strategic Partnership to Open Innovation and Training Center*, Press Release. Available at: https://www.linkedin.com/posts/style3d_style3d-x-fashion-enter-ltd-press-release-activity-707798058602 7462656-lcKW/

TechCrunch (2019). *Flexciton is using AI to help factories optimise production lines*. Available at: https://techcrunch.com/2019/01/21/flexciton/ (accessed 26 October 2023).

Textile Exchange (n.d.). Available at: https://textileexchange.org/ (accessed 26 October 2023).

Tidd, J. and Bessant, J. R. (2020). *Managing innovation: integrating technological, market and organizational change*. John Wiley & Sons.

WCED (1987). *Our Common Future (The Brundtland Report)*, World Commission on Environment and Development. Oxford University Press.

WTiN (2022). *New, effective textile gripping systems.* Available at: https://www.wtin.com/article/2022/november/21-11-22/new-effective-textile-gripping-systems/. (accessed 26 October 2023).

WWD (2017). *Amazon prepares for on-demand fashion production with patent.* Available at: https://wwd.com/business-news/technology/amazon-going-deeper-into-fashion-with-new-on-demand-manufacturing-patent-10869520/

CHAPTER 2.4

Merchandising innovation[1]

Digitalising the supply chain and ethical sourcing

Charlene Gallery and Fiona Velez-Colby

Fashion merchandising is the strategic coordination of product design, promotion and distribution to the consumer, acting as the crucial conduit between product creation and consumption in the fashion industry. At its core, successful merchandising hinges on a deceptively simple equation – delivering the right product, at the right price, at the right time, to the right place. Traditional merchandising has been underpinned by intuitive decision-making, but the rise of digital technologies is streamlining these processes significantly. As the digital age accelerates consumer trend turnover, leveraging technology in merchandising strategies is no longer optional but essential. By integrating data analytics and artificial intelligence (AI), merchandisers can more accurately predict product demand and optimise inventory. Furthermore, there is an increasing imperative to adopt sustainable and ethical practices within the industry, driven by technology's ability to track and manage supply chains more responsibly.

This chapter examines how emerging technologies such as blockchain, radio frequency identification (RFID) tags, AI and predictive analytics are being employed in fashion merchandising. It will evaluate these technologies' effectiveness in streamlining the merchandising processes. The chapter will also address how these advancements support sustainable practices, increase operational transparency and contribute to the sector's resilience and long-term viability.

LEARNING OUTCOMES

After reading this chapter, you should be able to:

- Identify and discuss driving factors impacting the role of a fashion merchandiser.

1 This chapter has been developed in collaboration with Fiona Velez-Colby, Lecturer at the University of Manchester, UK.

DOI: 10.4324/9781003364559-8

- Understand existing and emerging technologies in fashion merchandising and how they function in the creation, promotion and distribution of fashion ranges.
- Understand how superior data management tools can drive business growth for fashion brands.
- Understand the potential and implications of on-demand production in the fashion industry.
- Appreciate the role of technology and sustainability in the evolution of fashion merchandising.

2.4.1 DRIVING FACTORS IMPACTING THE ROLE OF FASHION MERCHANDISERS

Within the fashion industry, the roles of buying and merchandising are inextricably linked, where one informs and impacts the other and vice versa, and often buying teams and merchandising teams will operate as a multidisciplinary team facilitating fast and accurate communication of vital information across these two key operational areas. To understand the role of buying and merchandising we can return to the well-known phrase of delivering the right product, at the right price, at the right time, to the right place (Morgan, 2011). Additionally, from the buying and merchandising perspective, we must also consider the need to ensure products are delivered in the 'right quantity' and to the 'right customer', and with the widely accepted need for dynamic change in the way the fashion industry operates towards a sustainable future, we can also add 'in the right way' (Boardman et al., 2020).

The buying and merchandising function within the fashion organisation is responsible for delivering balanced commercial and financially viable fashion product ranges. In the past these functions could be divided whereby the function of the buying department was to develop product ranges and the function of the merchandising department was to realise product ranges to ensure they achieved sales and profits for the business (Boardman et al., 2020). However, these distinctions no longer hold true and in many of today's fashion businesses there is no separate department, job role or function within the business for buying or merchandising as distinct activities. This chapter will not examine the ways in which the buying and merchandising function has evolved, although this evolution is in the main due to technological advancements, but rather identifies the merchandising activity itself and will discuss how this function alone has changed and developed into the one found in many fashion businesses today.

There are many external pressures exerted on the contemporary fashion business, for example, national and international policy, innovations in textiles, production and manufacturing, consumer trends and political instability affecting supply chains, all of which affect the merchandising function in some way. This section will focus on four direct drivers and consider the impact of the purchasing power of the technology-enabled consumer, social connectivity and the role of social media, technology-enabled merchandising decision-making, and the impact of sustainability, so we can understand some of the challenges facing the merchandising function in the fashion industry.

The customer journey is no longer easy to track and predict; it flows through touchpoints facilitated by the omnichannel environment and has now become extremely complex, as touchpoints multiply and duplicate as customers interact across an ever-growing range of data points. Chapter 3.1 explores how today's fashion industry is experiencing a shift in consumer behaviour and how contemporary consumers are displaying a higher level of discernment compared to previous generations. We know that the supply chain of fashion brands must be able to react to the considerable speed of customer demand for products and services 24 hours a day and with a full range of products to meet customer expectations. Where consumer expectations are not met, their ability to go elsewhere has never been stronger. Empirical evidence from the clothing sector demonstrates a noticeable increase in spending on clothing and footwear over the last 15 years. This rise can primarily be attributed to the global adoption of fast fashion production and manufacturing, which enables fashion brands to gain the advantages of huge levels of production.

In this production model, the cost per single item significantly decreases as more items are produced, thereby enabling brands to meet the ever-growing demand from consumers for cheap and readily available products. In 2005, the expenditure of UK households on clothing was approximately £30 billion, which doubled to reach £68 billion in 2022 (Office for National Statistics, 2023; Statista, 2023). Currently, in the UK, we purchase more clothes per person than in any other European country, with the average UK resident purchasing around 70 garments per year (Wiseman, 2023). Interestingly, this only accounts for a modest 3.5% of their annual expenses, due in large part to the abundance of mass-produced, affordable products available in the market. Predicting and managing the production of fashion product ranges with these dynamic and challenging market conditions places considerable stress on merchandising decision-making, making what was already a difficult job much harder. However, there has been a significant rise in revenue from prominent fast-fashion companies such as Boohoo plc (UK £1.7Bn in 2022), Shein (China$30Bn in 2022) and Fashion Nova (USA). Notably, these retailers have generated billions in annual revenues primarily by targeting women under the age of 35 (Ndure, 2023).

Within contemporary culture, adapting to the constantly changing trends that permeate society has become of utmost importance to many consumers. There is a noticeable increase in the emergence of fashion trends, which has fundamentally shifted how the fashion industry approaches marketing and the development of fashion product ranges. The rise of social media and influencer-driven marketing has been particularly transformative for the fashion industry. As of 2023, there are an astounding 4.9 billion global users on social media platforms (Statista, 2023), which represents almost half of the world's population. In contrast, back in 2010, there were only around 970 million users, highlighting the rapid growth of these platforms. In fact, fashion remains one of the key industries in which influencer marketing has played a significant part in the growth and spread of trends. Therefore, the ability to identify new trends and react quickly in the development of new product ranges that meet the demand of these fashion-sensitive consumers has led to the development of technologies to support the merchandising activity within the ever-quickening, ever-shortening fashion supply chain.

The integration of technology in the field of fashion merchandising, particularly AI, the Internet of Things (IoT) and advanced analytics, has significantly revolutionised the merchandising operation. AI-powered merchandising software offers predictive insights into market trends and consumer behaviour, empowering merchandisers to make informed decisions based on data. This aids in optimising inventory management strategies along with enhancing online product placement techniques. Additionally, IoT-enabled devices enable real-time tracking of inventory while improving supply chain efficiency and promoting a more personalised shopping experience for consumers. Furthermore, advanced analytics plays a vital role in understanding and predicting intricate consumer preferences and monitoring sales performance. Consequently, brands can tailor their product offerings according to market demands, demands which are becoming more discerning. Technology has not only altered the way fashion merchandisers operate but has also played a crucial role in addressing and meeting the growing demand for ethical sourcing and sustainable fashion.

In conjunction with the advancement of technology, there has been an evident shift towards ethical sourcing and sustainability in the fashion industry. This transformation is fuelled by a growing awareness among consumers regarding the environmental impact of fashion manufacturing, growing industry recognition of the need for more responsible production practices, and an overwhelming global demand for more sustainable practices to ensure the viability and longevity of the fashion industry. It is important to consider what factors will shape consumers' behaviours and preferences going forward. Today's consumers are increasingly informed and discerning, prioritising brands that exhibit transparency, ethical sourcing and environmentally conscious business models. (Henninger et al., 2016). This societal shift is placing increasing pressure on merchandisers to ensure the brands they represent align their sourcing and production processes with these consumer values.

Despite this societal shift in consumer behaviour, the current situation remains dire. According to a 2021 study commissioned by the European Parliament, the apparel and footwear industry contributes significantly to global carbon emissions by approximately 10%, superseding emissions from the shipping and aviation industries combined (Filho et al., 2022). This issue is further compounded by patterns of excessive production and consumption. The fashion industry production model is one that has traditionally predicted consumer demand based on past sales patterns, market research and macro factors such as economic, social and cultural influences, and trends. Overproduction is common practice as high levels of competition, the guesswork of prediction, long lead times, rapidly changing trends and economies of scale inherent to the production model, encourage overproduction on a massive scale, representing a monumental flaw in the merchandising model. Then, in response to the buying and merchandising requirements of brands, throughout the production cycle, apparel and their component parts travel around the world racking up CO2 emissions, water consumption, chemical byproducts and energy use, until they are brought together and the final products are assembled, and then distribution further adds to the environmental weight of the item.

Overproduction provides a buffer for brands, waste is built into merchandising strategies and, while overproduction carries its own costs, these are weighed against possible reputational risk and the financial impact of items being unavailable, so it is clear to see which is considered the greater risk. The true scale of overproduction in the industry remains extremely difficult to measure, with 88% of major fashion brands failing to publish their annual production volumes (Fashion Revolution, 2023). With a mountain of clothing, mainly manufactured in China and Bangladesh, that failed to sell in US, European and Asian markets, being discarded in the Atacama Desert, Chile, a mountain so large that it is visible from space, it is clear the system is very broken indeed.

In order to address these concerns effectively it is crucial that companies adhere to Environmental Social and Corporate Governance (ESG) standards and metrics and substantially invest in sustainable transformation across all areas of their business and operations. ESG concepts were explored in Chapter 1.1, providing a definition of the term and case studies to highlight, ESG adoption within environmental reporting in product development and social compliance within sustainable manufacturing processes. These measures should drive improvements not only in efficiency and accuracy in merchandising strategies, but in working conditions, sustainable sourcing of materials and changes to manufacturing processes, all working towards significantly shortening the geographic journey of apparel, efficiency of distribution and movement towards circular models of disposal and reuse. The dual dynamic of technology integration and sustainability presents both a challenge and an opportunity for fashion merchandisers. Embracing these developments will enable merchandisers to improve their strategies, manage consumer demands and contribute to a more sustainable future in the fashion industry.

2.4.2 EXISTING AND EMERGING TECHNOLOGIES IN FASHION MERCHANDISING

In the current era of the fashion industry, marked by digital transformation and the need for sustainable practices, the role of a fashion merchandiser is evolving, from reactive predictions based on past performance and attempts to make sense of multiple data, to predictive strategic planning backed by AI-enabled data-centric decision-making. As technology continues to advance, the fashion merchandising function expands in scope, improves in accuracy, and further integrates into all areas of the supply chain. By embracing technological advancements, fashion brands and suppliers can enhance operational efficiency, support business growth and navigate the dynamic fashion industry with agility. Understanding how technology is being utilised throughout the supply chain becomes essential for anticipating future technological advancements within the fashion industry (Casciani et al., 2022).

In the fashion and retail-tech sectors, financial investments have shown an optimistic trajectory towards improving supply chain processes, however, a joint report by Fashion for Good and the Boston Consulting Group (2020) estimates that at least $20 billion USD needs to be invested each year until 2030 in order to meet the ECG targets. Technological advancements are already evident in the industry and developments such as predictive demand forecasting, efficient production planning and innovative design operations offer the potential to reduce waste, streamline production workflows and minimise the time-consuming process of creating physical samples. The convergence of emerging technologies and data-driven analysis creates new opportunities for advancement in fashion merchandising, and systems such as integrated product lifecycle management (PLM) (Chapter 1.1), product visualisation software, eye-tracking applications and Web3D (Chapter 3.3) all provide unprecedented resources for innovation, process optimisation and enhanced customer experiences. This section will explore remarkable technologies and applications such as blockchain, radio frequency identification tags and product passports, and their revolutionary effects on both merchandising and the fashion industry more broadly.

Blockchain technology

Blockchain technology is an emerging innovation that is increasingly being utilised in the field of fashion merchandising. A blockchain is a type of database or ledger that is decentralised, distributed and public, storing transactions, or blocks, across a peer-to-peer network. The decentralised nature of blockchain provides a high level of transparency and traceability, which plays a crucial role in verifying product authenticity and ensuring ethical sourcing practices. From a merchandising standpoint, it can be employed to establish a secure and unalterable record, documenting the entire journey of products from their origin to the end consumer. This fosters trust among consumers while enhancing accountability within the supply chain. By offering an immutable and transparent account of a product's lifecycle, blockchain technology holds great potential for validating authenticity and promoting ethical sourcing practices, ultimately benefiting brands, consumers and the environment alike. Blockchain technology is discussed in greater depth within the 'product passport' section below.

Radio frequency identification (RFID)

The use of RFID tags presents a technological solution that fashion merchandisers can utilise to enhance their operations through better inventory management and logistics, and enhanced customer engagement. RFID tags enable real-time tracking and monitoring of inventory and supply chain movements. This real-time information can be used to optimise the production and distribution processes, reducing overstocking and understocking of items. Therefore, implementing RFID tracking not only facilitates more efficient management of inventory but also contributes to reducing waste and improving overall supply chain efficiencies. Beyond offering benefits related to inventory management, utilising RFID tags empowers merchandisers with valuable insights into consumer shopping behaviours. The incorporation of RFID tags in retail stores allows for enhanced consumer engagement by providing product details, availability information and even personalised recommendations upon scanning.

Product passports

There has been a growing focus in academic and industry discourse on the benefits of incorporating serialised data into company operations. From a technical perspective, serialised data refers to the process of assigning or generating unique identifiers to individual product units. This strategic shift is driven by the potential of this data to provide more detailed and specific insights into the entire product lifecycle, and an examination of key players in the apparel industry reveals they are increasingly implementing infrastructure that enables comprehensive data collection as products move through different stages of the supply network.

A digital product passport (DPP) is an advanced tool driven by blockchain technology. Its purpose is to enable thorough traceability, allowing businesses to record and share information about a product's origin and its environmental sustainability credentials. The concept of a digital product passport helps to illuminate the unique worth that a product brings to the market, particularly within the luxury sector.

A digital product passport serves as a comprehensive repository of information concerning a product's entire lifecycle, starting from inception, throughout the manufacturing process, to its eventual disposal. This collected data is extensive and covers various aspects including the origin of materials (such as specific cotton farms or countries), details regarding manufacturing processes for both raw materials and final products, logistics involved in transportation, distribution channels in markets and additional procedures like product returns, repairs and resale activity. To handle and organise this large volume of data efficiently utilising unique identifiers such as RFID or QR codes throughout the product lifecycle is crucially important.

Product passports serve multiple purposes, including enhancing product authentication measures to prevent counterfeiting that can lead to brand dilution, as well as facilitating efficient inventory management practices. As a result, consumer trust is strengthened, and supply chain operations are better understood. The incorporation of serialised data serves as a pivotal step towards enhancing transparency within the fashion industry.

This shift is characterised by two key components: traceability and authenticity.

In addition to promoting transparency and ensuring authenticity, the utilisation of serialised data plays a critical role in optimising operations. It enables real-time tracking of inventory, reducing redundancies and

TABLE 2.4.1 Components of product passports.

Traceability	Authenticity
Serialised data provides an extensive view of the entire life cycle of a product, starting from its initial stages of raw material sourcing to its final disposal after consumption. This heightened level of transparency has significant implications for sustainability efforts and ethical sourcing practices, allowing stakeholders to ascertain the origin and journey of each individual product.	The issue of counterfeit products presents a significant challenge to brand reputation and consumer confidence. By incorporating distinct markers into their merchandise, brands can provide assurance to consumers regarding the authenticity of their purchase, thus strengthening brand credibility and fostering customer loyalty.

inefficiencies which ultimately leads to significant cost savings. This is especially relevant within the fashion industry where product lifecycles are short-lived and demand accurate inventory management.

The rising utilisation of serialised data in the fashion industry is a purposeful and strategic shift towards enhanced openness, responsibility and operational efficiency. All stakeholders involved in the supply chain must acknowledge and incorporate this new approach as an essential foundation for their operations and ethical standards. Failing to embrace this technological advancement would mean missing out on numerous opportunities to transform transparency and cost dynamics within the modern fashion industry.

This section has looked at some of the ways in which the fashion retail industry is undergoing significant transformation through the adoption of technological advancements such as blockchain technology, RFID tags and product passports. These innovations are reshaping the role of merchandisers in the field. By leveraging these technologies, fashion merchandisers can effectively meet consumer demands, streamline inventory management processes and contribute to sustainability efforts. Fashion brands can harness the potential of emerging technologies to drive innovation in merchandising. These advancements offer opportunities for improved efficiency, enhanced customer experiences and the establishment of higher standards for sustainability and ethical practices in the industry. In an era where sustainability and ethical practices are increasingly important to consumers, fashion merchandisers must embrace innovation in order to remain competitive.

2.4.3 CASE STUDY: ADVANCEMENTS IN LUXURY MERCHANDISING – AURA BLOCKCHAIN CONSORTIUM

The luxury goods market has long been targeted by counterfeiters, causing immense loss of revenue and dilution of brand value. The problem has been particularly acute for leading European luxury groups like LVMH

(Louis Vuitton Moët Hennessy), Prada Group and Compagnie Financière Richemont. In 2017, the loss from the sales of counterfeit goods was estimated to be $323 billion USD (Fontana, 2019). To combat this issue, these erstwhile competitors have embarked on an unprecedented collaboration: the Aura Blockchain Consortium. This initiative exemplifies innovation in the merchandising arena, particularly in leveraging technology to secure the authenticity and provenance of products.

The Aura Blockchain Consortium has developed a single, universal blockchain solution that all luxury brands worldwide can utilise. This secure, flexible and adaptive 'multinodal private blockchain' offers direct consumer access to a product's historical data, proof of ownership, warranty and maintenance service record. The technology is open to all luxury brands, regardless of their size or geographical location.

The Aura Blockchain Consortium is a significant step in dismantling the 'counterfeit goods' industry. The technology offers a secure method to trace and verify the identity of luxury goods, thus protecting consumers and brands from counterfeits and illegal counterfeit operations. A critical side effect of the Consortium is the potential disruption of the counterfeit goods supply chain, helping obstruct the trafficking of counterfeits and blocking fake goods from reaching consumers.

One of the brands adopting this technology is the Italian luxury label Loro Piana. Famed for its quality luxury materials like cashmere and ethically sourced vicuña, Loro Piana is embracing blockchain technology to digitally certify the authenticity and traceability of its products. Customers can scan a QR code to learn more about the product's journey, from the farms in Australia and New Zealand to the storefront. This showcases the practical application of the Aura Blockchain Consortium and exemplifies the type of transparency and traceability that can be achieved through this technology.

Beyond authenticity – sustainability and circularity

Aura Blockchain Consortium is not only a tool for authentication. Brands are also utilising it to enhance transparency and trust. For instance, the De Beers Group uses blockchain technology to track the journey of each diamond throughout its value chain, demonstrating ethical sourcing (De Beers Group, 2023). Additionally, the Sustainable Markets Initiative Fashion Task Force (FTF), launched by Prince Charles in 2020, is building a digital ID system to inform consumers about the sustainability credentials of their garments. The Aura Blockchain Consortium is a partner in this endeavour, using its technology to help FTF members achieve their sustainability goals.

Blockchain technology aids the circular economy by facilitating ethical resale of luxury products. High-end watch brand Vacheron Constantin uses Arianee, a blockchain solution, to register its watches and provide buyers with a digital passport which can be transferred between owners.

The Aura Blockchain Consortium has the potential to revolutionise the luxury goods industry by enhancing the security, transparency and ethical standards of the market. By forming an alliance to combat the counterfeit goods market, major luxury brands have demonstrated that through technological innovation, traditional competition can be put aside for the greater good of the industry.

Discussion questions

1. How does the Aura Blockchain Consortium aid in battling counterfeit luxury goods? How might this approach impact the industry at large?
2. How is the Aura Blockchain Consortium beneficial for smaller luxury brands struggling to combat counterfeiting?
3. Explore Loro Piana's implementation of Aura's technology. How does this case highlight the potential benefits for other brands?
4. Discuss how the Aura Blockchain Consortium's technology contributes to transparency and sustainability in the luxury goods market.
5. How can blockchain technology facilitate the circular economy in the luxury goods sector? Consider the example of Vacheron Constantin.
6. Given the potential benefits, what challenges might brands face in adopting this technology? Discuss any potential solutions to these challenges. (Source: Aura Luxury Blockchain, 2023)

2.4.4 DATA ANALYTICS AND AI

What is big data?

Big data is playing a more important role than ever in fine-tuning the customer relationship as masses of data-rich information is produced by every interaction customers have with brands and retailers. Big data can be defined as heterogeneous data (meaning diverse and varied), time-series data that is regularly generated by virtually all IT systems and regularly stored, and real-time data. The term 'big' is used to describe the available quantity of the data. Volumes of big data available to retailers daily is in the hundreds of terabytes of diverse, varied, time-series and real-time data, gathered across multiple platforms, and by many different IT systems. Time-series data is a sequence of data points collected over time intervals, giving the ability to track changes over time, and time-series data can track changes over milliseconds, days or even years. Real-time data is fast-moving data that's often messy or unstructured and is available as soon as it's created; it is seen as very valuable, especially to the fast-paced fashion industry.

The management of all this big data is being generated, stored, collected and analysed by AI. Big data is stored in a data lake (rather than in databases), which is a centralised repository that allows for the storage of raw (unstructured) data at any scale. This is important as it means retailers and brands can store all the data they can access without having to structure it, then run analytics as and when needed. However, without meaningful analysis to transform it into usable information and insights, big data has no value. Data mining is the analysis of big data to uncover patterns and other valuable information from very large data sets. Data mining techniques accelerated very rapidly over the past few years but, with the recent explosion in AI capabilities and application, that acceleration has seen unprecedented growth. Structured and raw data are being very effectively and efficiently processed by AI and transformed into extremely useful information that can be leveraged for competitive advantage, informing strategic and operational decisions throughout organisations, enabling the development of strategies for improvements and to manage operations including finance, human resources, security, and sales and marketing.

With meaningful and targeted analysis big data gives brands better insights into their customer behaviour, which in turn helps them to meet the needs and wants of their customers more effectively. In merchandising and marketing, data is information about consumer behaviour across multiple platforms. This information becomes useful information strategically applied to improve merchandising decision-making and customer experience.

2.4.5 PREDICTIVE ANALYTICS, MACHINE LEARNING AND AI IN FASHION MERCHANDISING

Predictive analytics and machine learning (ML) triggered a revolution in the fashion merchandising sector, with merchandising functions integrated into a wide range of integrated PLM platforms. Recent and very rapid advancements in AI capabilities and further implementation into existing platforms throughout the fashion industry have seen these advanced algorithms enabling even more precise prediction of fashion trends, sales forecasts and inventory management.

By using AI to analyse large volumes of consumer behaviour data, such as shopping movements across multiple platforms, including abandoned baskets and products not purchased, purchasing habits across the globe and within countries, and location-based instore sales through point of sale transactions, for example, fashion merchandisers can anticipate consumer purchase decision behaviour, predict trends and tailor their product offerings accordingly. This enables them to manage inventory and order processes with increased precision, resulting in improved full-price sales and higher-value item transactions. However, and most importantly, it also facilitates the integration of highly personalised customer relationship management processes (CRM) with the merchandising function. This level of accuracy enables fashion merchandisers to effectively implement the 'right product, right place, right time, right price' strategy.

Mini case study

Stitch Fix

One excellent example of the strategic use of big data and AI in fashion retail is Stitch Fix, a pioneering technology-driven fashion brand. Stitch Fix harnesses the power of advanced algorithms, combined with AI-driven insights, which considers the customer's distinct fashion style inclinations, their fit specifications and their financial constraints to tailor a bespoke collection of five garments, or 'Fixes' for each customer through an on-demand or subscription-based retail model. As customers engage more with the platform, ML improves the accuracy of its recommendations. This AI-supported approach effectively emulates the personalised service of a fashion style consultant, enhancing the brand's unique selling proposition. To achieve this, Stitch Fix conducts thorough data collection, capturing specifics about users' fashion tastes, body measurements and feedback on prior purchases. The amassed data informs their ML systems which, when coupled with the expertise of human fashion stylists in place at the final curation stage, deliver the tailored 'Fixes', resulting in collections of clothing tailored to resonate with the consumer's distinct style and needs. This harmonisation of tech innovation with a human touch has cemented robust customer affinity towards Stitch Fix. A testament to their success is their revenue for 2022 tallying up to $2.1 billion USD, marking a commendable surge of 22.8% since 2020.

In addition to data-driven personalisation, AI-powered solutions such as visual search and recommendation systems also significantly enhance the customer shopping experience. By identifying individual tastes and preferences, these tools analyse individual preferences and deliver a more personalised shopping journey, resulting in higher levels of customer satisfaction and loyalty. Modern technological advancements such as these continue to redefine the way we perceive and experience fashion merchandising and are discussed in greater detail in Chapter 3.3.

2.4.6 ON-DEMAND PRODUCTION

As discussed in Chapter 2.3: 'Process innovation in fashion manufacturing', the fashion industry is increasingly adopting a demand-centric approach which responds to real-time sales, underlined by the need for efficient inventory handling, a sharper focus on flagship brands or products and a decisive move towards minimising, if not wholly eliminating, waste (Verhoef et al., 2017). In the smart factory concept (Chapter 2.3), manufacturing is managed by a fully automated production model, informed and managed by data from internal business functions and supplier networks. The advantages of this model, compared to the demand-centric approach, are evident.

As previously discussed, a pertinent issue plaguing the sector is overproduction, resulting in a staggering 40% of the apparel produced being sold at discounted rates, eroding profit margins, not to mention the high levels of waste textiles and disposal of unsold goods causing further criticism of the unsustainable nature of the fashion industry. Nevertheless, there is hope that innovations in demand forecasting, AI-enhanced inventory control and astute pricing and promotional strategies could potentially offset these challenges. The concept of on-demand production has the potential to revolutionise the fashion landscape, enabling manufacturing to be triggered by genuine customer demand, thereby eliminating excessive inventory expenses and minimising overproduction.

On-demand manufacturing can be summarised simply as a system which allows manufacturers to produce products based on customer demands, not on predictions, but in response to orders. While on-demand manufacturing systems are technically possible for certain products, there are strong opposing factors inhibiting the successful widespread and scaled adoption of on-demand manufacturing. Challenges such as consumers' demand for immediate availability and delivery of products they have ordered, combined with the complexities of sewing fashion products with a variety of fabrics and trims within fully automated systems, mean true on-demand manufacturing in the fashion industry is still some way off. However, breakthroughs in technologies like digital apparel printing, 3D printing and automated production systems (smart factories) present opportunities for greater adaptability and responsiveness to evolving market trends, whilst simultaneously shrinking the design-to-delivery window.

An area of the industry that has proved very successful in the adoption of on-demand production principles (although it does not achieve on-demand production) is direct-to-garment (DTG) printing, where clothing items remain as blanks until a customer order prompts a design to be printed and then shipped direct to the consumer. An industry sector in which this has proved extremely successful is sports merchandise.

Mini case study

Agile fashion merchandising utilising on-demand direct-to-garment (DTG) print technology

Within the fast-moving, ever-changing world of sports, and fanatic sports fans wanting to display both their commitment to their team and the team's latest sporting achievements, the world of sports merchandise is an ideal market for on-demand production. Product ranges for sports merchandise are fairly static and apart from specific sports team branded items like football, basketball, rugby, baseball strips and kits, etc., entire product ranges based on core items like T-shirts, sweatshirts, hoodies, shorts, joggers, jackets, hats and caps, can be delivered to customers and to stores, through on-demand, direct to garment (DTG) printing facilitated by online inventory management systems, and all in a matter of hours leading up to or following an important sporting event. And since DTG digital apparel printing has long matched the quality, durability and brand standards of major apparel retailers and sports teams (Whaley, 2023), smaller retailers are able to efficiently fulfil demand for localised sports merchandise. Setup costs are extremely low and margins profitable regardless of the number of items being printed. Benefits of this model are that customers' needs can be fulfilled locally and extremely quickly and overproduction of unwanted merchandise can be almost eliminated.

Successful examples of fully on-demand production within the fashion industry remain scarce and are often short-term, very small-scale, research-type projects conducted by brands to test the viability of new manufacturing and production systems.

Mini case study

Adidas Knit for You

In 2017 Adidas was investigating a range of strategies to decentralise its manufacturing and distribution operations in the wake of supply chain challenges. Alongside the launch of its Speedfactory concept (a recently terminated project of introducing onshore robotic manufacturing to shorten production cycles and introduce environmentally friendly manufacturing and distribution to Western consumers), a small 3-month long, truly on-demand, initiative was launched. 'Knit for You' was a flexible and automated in-store production concept for knitted customised merino wool sweaters (Buecher et al. 2018). First the customer was invited into a dark room filled with sensors to detect hand gestures, enabling the customer to generate patterns and, guided by the design software, to co-create a final design for their sweater. Body scanning ensured exact measurements and customers could specify the style and fit of their sweaters. Once satisfied with the final product, the customer sent the final design to 'print'. Using industry-standard industrial knitting machines, a high-quality bespoke merino wool sweater was produced within two hours. Whilst short-lived, this innovative on-demand project, which was partly funded by a consortium of private and public entities and supported by the German government (Knitting Industry, 2017), enabled the brand and its partners to investigate and test localised on-demand manufacturing and reduce time to market, which is one of the factors leading to overproduction and loss of profits in the industry.

A shift towards on-demand production resonates with the growing demand for a fashion industry that prioritises environmental responsibility alongside customer desires. More wide-scale adoption of on-demand manufacturing will form a key strategy for the future and will amplify the industry's commitment to sustainability by drastically reducing waste within the supply chain and levels of unsold stock. By harnessing the power of digital production and manufacturing technologies through on-demand manufacturing fashion, brands could produce just what is needed to fulfil genuine customer demand, leading to a transformative move towards a sustainable fashion industry.

2.4.7 MERCHANDISING INNOVATION IN PRODUCT DEVELOPMENT: SUSTAINABILITY AND ETHICAL SOURCING

In light of increasing consumer awareness regarding the environmental and social consequences of their purchases, there has been a surge in demand for sustainable and ethically sourced fashion. Technology plays a crucial role in enabling transparency throughout the supply chain, ensuring responsible sourcing practices and promoting circular economy initiatives like reselling or recycling. Consequently, modern fashion merchandisers must leverage technology not only to cater to consumer preferences but also to foster a more environmentally conscious and socially responsible industry.

Everlane, a US-based contemporary fashion brand, highlights how the incorporation of an eco-friendly and ethical sourcing model can be effectively leveraged within the realm of fashion retail. Founded in 2010 as a direct to consumer (D2C) brand on a strong online platform, Everlane's commitment to 'radical transparency' was evident from its foundation. It has always advocated a transparent approach through its disclosure of cost breakdowns and supply chain information, including factory details for each product. This level of openness enables customers to gain insight into the production process behind their clothes, building trust and nurturing an environment rooted in honesty. By leveraging technology to track and trace its manufacturing processes and to deliver product cost information, Everlane effectively communicates its vision and principles to its customer base, ultimately encouraging more conscientious consumption habits.

Another disruptor in the sustainable fashion landscape is Patagonia. This outdoor clothing brand has been at the forefront of environmentally responsible business practices for years. They use the latest technologies to trace the sourcing of their materials, track chain-of-custody of sustainable materials and to ensure fair trade practices, which is shared on their website and product tags. Patagonia also actively encourages consumers to repair, reuse and recycle their products. Their Worn Wear initiative, an online platform for buying and selling used Patagonia gear, utilises e-commerce to promote a circular economy within the fashion industry.

A problem at the other end of the supply chain is the industry's upstream carbon emissions, which account for more than 70% of the greenhouse gases attributed to the fashion industry (Granskog, 2020). One contributing factor is the huge amount of deadstock fabrics unused by brands when buying and merchandising plans change course, which, given the quantities of these fabrics, happens relatively often. Sourcing these fabrics has traditionally been an extremely labour-intensive and slow process only accessed by the most dedicated brands, a challenge exacerbated by the fact they often need direct relationships with other designers or mills to get information about their overstock (Bain, 2023). Queen of Raw has developed a digital platform that converses directly with a brand's inventory management systems, enabling them to share their deadstock inventory directly through the Queen of Raw's platform, providing an e-commerce marketplace for deadstock fabrics. In its

2023 sustainability report, Ralph Lauren reported it had diverted 11.8 metric tons of unused materials from landfill using Queen of Raw's global network of recyclers (Bain, 2023).

These examples serve as a testament to how technology is transforming fashion merchandising to meet consumer demand for sustainability and ethical sourcing. By leveraging technology to promote transparency, fairness and circularity, fashion merchandisers can contribute to a more sustainable and socially responsible fashion industry.

As consumer awareness of the environmental and social consequences of their purchases grows, there is a rising demand for fashion that is both sustainable and ethically sourced. Technology plays a crucial role in this shift by facilitating transparency in the supply chain, promoting ethical material sourcing and encouraging circular economy practices such as reselling or recycling. As a result, contemporary fashion merchandisers must harness technology, not only to meet consumer expectations, but also to contribute to the development of a more sustainable fashion industry.

Through the development and implementation of product ranges that respond to the needs of the market fashion, merchandisers can enhance retail experiences, meet the growing expectations of consumers and adjust to the dynamic fashion industry. These practices have been significantly improved and streamlined by adopting technological advancements across merchandising activities. This flexibility in the role necessitates a combination of creative, analytical and technical abilities that will be further examined in upcoming sections.

END-OF-CHAPTER DISCUSSIONS

1. Reflect on the current relationship between buying and merchandising functions in the fashion industry. How do you think technological advancements and the increasing importance of sustainability are influencing these roles?
2. In what ways do you believe social media and the 'technology-enabled consumer' have redefined the landscape for fashion merchandising?
3. Considering the significant rise in expenditure on clothing and the growth of fast fashion, what strategies should merchandisers adopt to balance the increasing consumer demand with the need for sustainable practices?
4. How does the role of a fashion merchandiser change when dealing with an omnichannel environment where consumer journeys are complex and unpredictable?
5. How do you think innovations such as blockchain, RFID tags and digital product passports could transform traditional fashion merchandising practices to promote environmental responsibility and ethical consumerism? Consider potential challenges that fashion merchandisers might face when integrating these technologies and suggest strategies for overcoming these hurdles.

6. Discuss how AI and big data are transforming the fashion industry in terms of customer relationship management, inventory control and production processes.

Bibliography and further reading

Aura Blockchain Consortium CEO announcement (2023). *AURA*. Available at: https://auraluxuryblockchain.com/news/aura-blockchain-consortium-ceo-announcement (accessed 4 August 2023).

Bain, M. (2023). 'Can technology build a better market for fashion's unused fabrics?', *Business of Fashion*. Available at: https://www.businessoffashion.com/articles/technology/can-technology-build-a-better-market-for-unused-fabrics/

Boardman, R., Parker-Strak, R. and Henninger, C. E. (2020). *Fashion buying and merchandising: The fashion buyer in a digital society*. Routledge.

Buecher, D., Gloy, Y. S., Schmenk, B. and Gries, T. (2018). 'Individual on-demand produced clothing: Ultrafast fashion production system'. In S. Hankammer, K. Nielsen, F. Piller, G. Schuh and N. Wang (eds) *Customization 4.0: Proceedings of the 9th World Mass Customization & Personalization Conference (MCPC 2017), Aachen, Germany, November 20th–21st, 2017* (pp. 635–644). Springer International Publishing.

Casciani, D., Chkanikova, O. and Pal, R. (2022). 'Exploring the nature of digital transformation in the fashion industry: Opportunities for supply chains, business models, and sustainability-oriented innovations', *Sustainability: Science, Practice and Policy*, 18(1), pp. 773–795, doi:10.1080/15487733.2022.2125640

De Beers Group (2020). *The Diamond Insight Report 2023 – De Beers Group*. Available at: https://www.debeersgroup.com/reports/insights/the-diamond-insight-report-2023 (accessed 4 August 2023).

Fashion for Good (2020). *Financing the transformation in the fashion industry: Unlocking investment to scale innovation*. Available at: https://fashionforgood.com/wp-content/uploads/2020/01/FinancingTheTransformation_Report_FINAL_Digital-1.pdf (accessed: 16 February 2024).

Fashion Transparency Index (2023). *Fashion Transparency Index 2023: Fashion Revolution*. Available at: https://www.fashionrevolution.org/about/transparency/#:~:text=88%25%20of%20major%20fashion%20brands,of%20new%20items%20they%20produce (accessed 13 February 2023).

Filho, W. L., Perry, P., Heim, H., Dinis, M. A. P., Moda, H., Ebhuoma, E. and Paço, A. (2022). 'An overview of the contribution of the textiles sector to climate change', *Frontiers in Environmental Science*, 10. doi:10.3389/fenvs.2022.973102

Fontana, R. (2019). 'How luxury brands can beat counterfeiters', *Harvard Business Review*. Available at: https://hbr.org/2019/05/how-luxury-brands-can-beat-counterfeiters?utm_medium=social&utm_campaign=hbr&utm_source=twitter (accessed: 4 July 2023).

Granskog, A. (2020). 'The fashion industry can reduce emissions across the entire value chain', *McKinsey Sustainability*. Available at: https://www.mckinsey.com/capabilities/sustainability/our-insights/sustainability-blog/the-fashion-industry-can-reduce-emissions-across-the-entire-value-chain

Henninger, C. E., Alevizou, P.J. and Oates, C. J. (2016). 'What is sustainable fashion?', *Journal of Fashion Marketing and Management*, 20(4), pp. 400–416. doi:10.1108/JFMM-07-2015-0052

Knitting Industry (2017). *Flat Knitting: Adidas explores localised production with 'Knit for You' pop-up store*. Available: https://www.knittingindustry.com/adidas-explores-localised-production-with-knit-for-you-popup-store/

Lea, R. (2022). 'High fashion! Mountain of discarded clothes in Chilean desert is visible from space', Space.com. Available at: https://www.space.com/mountain-discarded-clothes-chile-satellite-photo

Morgan, T. (2011). *Visual Merchandising* (2nd Edition). Laurence King Publishing.

Ndure, I. (2023). 'Boohoo swings to FY loss but boss assures 'clear path' to margin recovery', *Just Style*. Available at: https://www.just-style.com/news/boohoo-swings-to-fy-loss-but-boss-assures-clear-path-to-margin-recovery/?cf-view (accessed 4 August 2023).

Office for National Statistics (UK) (2023). 'Annual expenditure on clothing and footwear in the United Kingdom (UK) from 2005 to 2022, based on volume (in million GBP)', Statista. Available at: https://www.statista.com/statistics/300845/annual-expenditure-on-footwear-in-the-united-kingdom-uk/ (accessed 19 February 2024).

Verhoef, P. C. et al. (2017). 'Consumer connectivity in a complex, technology-enabled, and mobile-oriented world with Smart Products', *SSRN Electronic Journal* [Preprint]. doi:10.2139/ssrn.2912321.

Whaley, D. (2023). 'For sports fans and athletes, on-demand apparel production captures that winning feeling: Agile digital fashion and merch print means scoring on wins in the World Cup, Super Bowl, March Madness – and community', *Ink World Magazine*. Available at: https://www.inkworldmagazine.com/issues/2023-04-01/view_online-exclusives/for-sports-fans-and-athletes-on-demand-apparel-production-captures-that-winning-feeling/ (accessed 19 February 2024).

Wiseman, D. (2023). 'Fast fashion environmental impact facts 2023', Green Heart Collective. Available at: https://www.greenheartcollective.uk/blogs/news/fast-fashion-facts-environment (accessed 3 July 2023).

PART III

Fashion retail and the digital customer experience

Part III presents a detailed examination of the interplay between digital innovation and the fashion value chain, specifically focusing on marketing and retail operations. It consists of three structured chapters, each contributing to a comprehensive understanding of the evolving landscape in fashion due to technological advancements.

Chapter 3.1 commences with a detailed analysis of how digital innovation influences consumer behaviour within the fashion industry. This chapter offers an in-depth exploration of the factors influencing consumer behaviour, including the significant role of social media and the acceptance of emerging technologies. A comparative analysis of digital adoption, influenced by regional infrastructure and cultural attitudes, provides a foundational understanding of contemporary consumer dynamics. The chapter progresses to examine the evolution of marketing strategies, transitioning from traditional product-centric approaches to a more technology-integrated customer experience. This segment of the chapter underscores the importance of hyper-personalisation and immediate gratification in the current economy, emphasising the need for brands to adopt data-driven, consumer-centric marketing strategies. The effectiveness of various engagement strategies, such as social listening and digital clienteling, is evaluated. Additionally, the chapter explores the increasing interest in immersive experiences, assessing the long-term commercial potential of platforms like the metaverse. It concludes with a focused case study on the application of photorealistic avatars in virtual identity creation, featuring insights from the experts at I AM HUMAN.

In Chapter 3.2, the focus shifts to the transformation of in-store environments within the retail sector. This chapter introduces the concept of 'phygital' retail, a synthesis of physical and digital experiences, and its application in enhancing customer service. The discussion elaborates on how technologies like augmented reality (AR), smart technologies, AI and radio-frequency identification (RFID) are being integrated into retail operations. This analysis is crucial in understanding the transformation of consumer experiences and the

DOI: 10.4324/9781003364559-9

modernisation of traditional retail functions. The final chapter, 3.3, addresses the progression of online retail, highlighting the growth facilitated by technological innovations such as AI, machine learning (ML), and extended reality (XR). This chapter provides a thorough assessment of the influence of technologies like 3D product visualisation and augmented reality on online retail strategies. It offers a detailed examination of how these technologies are reshaping consumer interactions and advancing virtual fashion. The chapter also includes an illustrative case study on Brandlab-360, offering insights into the future trajectory of online fashion retail.

Throughout these chapters, the work consistently integrates themes such as the digital transformation in marketing and retail, the shift towards consumer-centric approaches and the incorporation of technology in retail environments. This analysis delves into the transformative impact of digital technologies on the fashion industry. It emphasises the notable shifts in market engagement, consumer interaction and the evolution of retail environments due to technological advancements. This comprehensive exploration in Part III offers valuable insights into the current and future dynamics of the fashion industry in the digital era.

CHAPTER 3.1

Marketing to the hyper-connected consumer

Charlene Gallery

This book underscores the transformative impact of digital technology on the fashion industry, with earlier discussions focusing on sustainable innovation in product development and manufacturing. It is essential, however, to recognise that consumers are the driving force propelling these technological advancements. With the advent of the digital era, consumers have gained unparalleled access to global brands and are actively reshaping market dynamics. Empowered by technology, their revolutionary interactions with brands catalyse a new wave of connectivity, necessitating that brands adopt agile, data-driven and consumer-centric marketing strategies.

This chapter investigates the evolution of consumer behaviour within the digital marketing landscape and the emergence of the 'right now' economy. It examines the critical role of hyper-personalisation in marketing, evaluates the integration of data-driven approaches such as digital clienteling and considers how brands can utilise social listening and data analytics to bring them closer to the hyper-connected consumer. As consumers pursue extraordinary and immersive brand experiences, there is a growing desire for enhanced digital interactions and social connectivity; therefore, the chapter will conclude with an exploration of the metaverse and the proliferation of virtual self-identities. In a marketplace where customer expectations are escalating and evolution is constant, a profound understanding of these shifts is essential for brands to navigate the challenges ahead, forge significant connections and maintain prominence in a tech-centric fashion world.

LEARNING OUTCOMES

After reading this chapter, you should be able to:

- Demonstrate an understanding of the impact of the technology on consumer behaviour.
- Understand how marketing has evolved in response to technological advancements.

DOI: 10.4324/9781003364559-10

- Understand the necessity for brands to exhibit data-driven agility and the importance of adopting consumer-centric marketing strategies in the digital age.
- Understand how brands use data intelligence and analytics to deliver personalised services and strengthen connections with fashion customers.
- Examine the consumer shift towards immersive experiences and the rise of virtual self-identities in marketing.

3.1.1 THE DIGITAL CONSUMER: BEHAVIOURAL INSIGHTS AND STRATEGIC IMPLICATIONS

The fashion sector, traditionally viewed as a reflection of social progress and innovation, has consistently demonstrated adaptability and responsiveness to evolving consumer tastes and market shifts. Chapter 1.1 highlights how digital technologies are fundamentally changing the way fashion companies operate. Instead of just adding new tools, the industry is rethinking its entire approach to business, affecting everything from product creation to how items are marketed and sold (Alexander & Kent, 2022).

In the past, value chains in fashion were relatively straightforward, with companies controlling the process from raw materials to the final consumer. Now, the rise of digital technology has complicated these chains. Data analytics, online platforms and consumer-centric technologies have allowed different stakeholders, including customers, suppliers and competitors, to contribute in significant ways, leading to a collaborative, more democratic approach to creating value. This change means that companies need to adapt to a more interconnected system that can respond quickly to consumer feedback and market changes.

Digital tools have shifted the role of consumers from end-users to active contributors in their relationships with brands. Through their interactions on various platforms, consumers are not just buying products; they are also influencing how those products are developed and how they are perceived by others, effectively blurring the boundaries between creation and consumption (Alexander & Cano, 2020). This level of involvement means that understanding consumer needs and responses is more important than ever for businesses wanting to succeed in this new digital fashion environment (Park & Lim, 2023). The modern fashion industry must view consumers as partners, engaging with them to influence the range of products and services offered. This approach extends beyond simple sales; it's about fostering relationships, providing interactive experiences and aligning the brand's messaging with consumer values (Peña-García et al., 2021).

Recent technology advancements such as artificial intelligence (AI), machine learning (ML), natural language processing (NLP), the Internet of Things (IoT), blockchain, sensor technologies, extended reality (XR) and mixed reality (MR) are significantly influencing consumer interactions and operational strategies within the fashion industry. These technologies, often seen as extensions of human capability, are central to enhancing the consumer experience, offering a blend of personalisation and efficiency (Grewal et al., 2020; Venkatachalam et al., 2022). Technologies designed to replicate human-like interactions, for example, AI-based recommendation engines, deliver tailored suggestions aligning with individual preferences, streamlining the shopping process. Interfaces employing voice and gesture recognition enable more engaging product interactions, and augmented reality (AR) or virtual reality (VR) platforms simulate in-store experiences remotely, allowing for virtual fittings.

This technological integration is not just about consumer engagement but also aligns with operational adaptability in response to economic and trend shifts within the sector. Brands are, therefore, required to not only adopt these technologies but to do so in a manner that remains consistent with their brand identity and values, ensuring consumer engagement remains authentic and aligned with the brand's DNA. The importance of a coherent digital presence that matches a brand's core values cannot be understated, especially when digital channels are becoming primary consumer touchpoints (Kaczorowska-Spychalska, 2018).

The following are four central determinants shaping today's fashion consumer choices:

The digital native vs. the digital architect consumers – As already highlighted, digital innovations have equipped brands with new tools to refine customer interactions that align with evolving consumer behaviour. Extended Reality (XR) technologies, including AR and VR, are significant in this regard. Brands must grasp the shifting consumer mindsets to remain relevant, particularly among two key groups as identified by LSN Global: Digital Natives and Digital Architects. Although these are two broad consumer categories, there are, of course, nuances in each segment's behaviour. For instance, Digital Natives expect immersive engagement across social media and mobile platforms, highlighting the need for mobile-optimised interfaces and AR/VR integration. Digital Architects are characterised by their capacity to shape the digital landscape to their preferences. With a deep understanding of technology, they tailor their digital interactions by fine-tuning algorithms to filter information that meets their unique requirements and selectively sourcing data that aligns with their specific inquiries. This level of digital proficiency enables them to navigate and manipulate their online ecosystem efficiently, ensuring that their shopping engagements are both purposeful and personal. However, they are cautious about brands that might infringe upon their digital privacy.

Consumer investment is increasingly directed to where they spend their time: online spaces. However, capturing the wallet share of consumers online is becoming complex. Payment methods, while already optimised for frictionless transactions, must also consider the emotional aspects of spending in the digital age. Prelec and Loewenstein's 1998 'Pain of Paying' theory highlights consumers often experience emotional discomfort when parting with their money. Brands, keeping both the native and architect consumer types in focus, should ensure their payment systems balance efficiency with this emotional aspect. Innovations like Curve's AR payments and cryptocurrencies represent a merger of convenience with emotional consideration.

The socially empowered consumer – social media has created an interconnected consumer network, which has become a fundamental part of daily life, affecting consumer behaviour and influencing purchasing decisions (Kotler, 2021). Global social media usage varies by region and demographic, with platforms like Facebook, YouTube and Instagram dominating the market, with over 6 billion daily users combined. Data from Dixon (2023) also indicates a global average of 151 minutes spent on social media per day, with the Philippines at nearly four hours and the US at over two hours. Notably, over 90% of Gen Z and Millennials are daily users, while Baby Boomer engagement sits at 74% (Statista, 2023). Given these statistics, the strategic move of fashion brands to integrate social media for consumer outreach and marketing is logical.

The transformation from a one-to-many to a many-to-many communication model signifies the democratisation of the digital space, where power dynamics now favour consumers (Kaczorowska-Spychalska, 2018). The expectations for brands to engage in wider societal conversations have grown, particularly with the politically active younger generations of recent years. This trend underscores the shifting dynamics in the brand–consumer relationship, where brands are watched closely and their actions are measured against the evolving sentiments of consumers. Social media provides significant opportunities for brand exposure and engagement, but it also presents challenges in anticipating consumer behaviour. Today's consumers, equipped with digital tools, exhibit a mix of empowerment and unpredictability, making it crucial for brands to navigate these waters with care and attention.

The role of social listening has become crucial for fashion brands to navigate the complex consumer behaviour landscape. Brands monitor online discussions to detect trends, shifts in consumer preferences and cultural nuances. This information is critical for refining products and tailoring marketing campaigns to address consumer sentiment effectively (Iannilli & Spagnoli, 2021).

Social listening involves tracking discussions on social media to identify trends and sentiments using tools like Hootsuite Insights or Brandwatch. This process helps businesses monitor brand mentions, assess positive or negative sentiments, spot trending topics and identify influential voices in their industry.

Sustainability through tech – The intersection of sustainability and technology is becoming increasingly critical in the fashion industry. With a focus on ethical practices, brands like Stella McCartney are utilising blockchain technology to enhance transparency in material sourcing, catering to the escalating demands for sustainability among global consumers. This approach is particularly effective in regions with a profound respect for nature, such as Africa, where the consumer willingness to invest in sustainable products is more pronounced. Local African brands are tapping into this sentiment by marrying sustainability with indigenous values, which resonates with the consumer base. McKinsey's 2022 report indicates that a significant 70% of African consumers are prepared to pay a premium for sustainable offerings (Hattingh & Ramlakan, 2022). This shift can be linked to a multitude of factors:

- Social media and activist platforms are bringing the negative impacts of the fashion industry, including pollution and labour exploitation, to the forefront, driving consumer awareness and demand for change.
- Economic growth on the continent has led to increased disposable incomes, empowering consumers to make more conscientious purchasing decisions.
- The intrinsic cultural principles of community and responsibility in Africa are further fuelling the call for sustainable practices.

Companies like Afrikea Rising from Kenya, Orange Culture in Nigeria and KikoRomeo in Ghana are epitomising this movement by integrating sustainability into their brand ethos (Ayesu et al., 2023). This synergy of sustainability, technological advancements and cultural heritage is redefining the African fashion industry, positioning ethical practices as a foundational element and enabling local entrepreneurs to lead the way in sustainable innovation.

Consumer acceptance of technologies – Technology's impact on consumer shopping behaviours is evident, with a significant rise in online shopping activity globally. Retailers, facing these changing trends, are increasingly turning to technology to improve, not only the in-store experience but to augment the entire customer journey. AR and VR are gaining popularity, recognised for providing unique shopping experiences and it is likely that the next decade will see these technologies become more deeply integrated into fashion retailing.

Yet, a crucial aspect for brands to assess is the consumer's interest in and willingness to use these new technologies. As the pace of technological development accelerates, today's novel concept can quickly turn into tomorrow's expectation (Iannilli & Spagnoli, 2021). Consumers, now regularly encountering new technologies, create a demand pressure that brands must meet. This suggests that a successful future retail strategy will include significant technological investment, with a focus on AR and VR. At the same time, fluctuating consumer loyalty suggests that brands need flexible strategies. While incorporating immersive technologies could be key in maintaining and enhancing consumer-brand relationships, it is critical that retailers do not simply approach digital integration as a one-size-fits-all approach, but rather implement them in ways that add real value for the consumer, ensuring that the investment translates into a tangible improvement in the shopping experience.

3.1.2 UNDERSTANDING TECHNOLOGY ADOPTION

The **technology acceptance model (TAM),** a conceptual framework adapted from the **theory of reasoned action (TRA)**, serves as a vital tool in understanding the adoption of technology. This model is particularly relevant in interpreting how users come to accept and utilise new technologies within the context of Marketing 4.0, which integrates technological innovation with consumer-centric marketing approaches. TAM is centred around two core perceptions that influence technology acceptance: perceived usefulness and ease of use. For instance, in the fashion industry, the acceptance of AR fitting room apps hinges on these elements – if users recognise the app's benefit in simulating the fit of clothes (perceived usefulness) and find it easy to navigate (perceived ease of use), they are more likely to embrace the technology.

However, it is crucial to consider that cultural differences can significantly impact technology acceptance. Research, such as the studies by Jan et al. (2022) and Srite (2006), has demonstrated that the determinants of technology acceptance, as outlined by TAM, can vary between regions like Saudi Arabia, China and the United States, with factors such as perceived usefulness, ease of use and subjective norms carrying different weights depending on cultural contexts. This suggests that in innovation-friendly regions, i.e., the US, the functional benefits of an application may be emphasised, whereas, in technologically mature markets, such as China, ease of use often emerges as a critical factor influencing adoption.

These regional and cultural preferences play a critical role in the adoption of digital tools in fashion. For instance, in a fast-moving market like South Korea, the usefulness of a digital trend-tracking tool may be particularly valued due to the rapid evolution of fashion trends. On the contrary, in markets less familiar with such technology, its ease of use may be highlighted. Acknowledging these variances is essential for brands aiming to optimise technology adoption across the global fashion industry, highlighting the importance of a tailored approach. By customising technology offerings and marketing strategies to align with the specific values and preferences of diverse consumer bases, brands can more effectively resonate with their target audiences.

Technology acceptance model (TAM): Introduced in the 1980s by Fred Davis, TAM is a reliable measure for understanding the user adoption of technology, focusing on perceived usefulness and ease of use as primary factors for adoption.

Theory of reasoned action (TRA): developed by Martin Fishbein and Icek Ajzen in the 1970s, TRA suggests that an individual's behaviour is informed by their intention, which is influenced by their attitudes toward the behaviour and the subjective norms surrounding it. If one believes a behaviour is positive (attitude) and perceives that others want them to perform it (subjective norm), they are more likely to engage in that behaviour. It's been widely applied in understanding and predicting behaviours across various sectors.

While these models highlight general tendencies in consumer behaviour, the actual landscape of digital adoption is also shaped by a multitude of factors, including technological infrastructure, economic policies and educational backgrounds. Regions like Europe, with its stringent GDPR guidelines, prioritise digital privacy, advocating for sustainable and ethical digital solutions. The Middle East is seeing a surge in e-commerce driven by the younger population, with consumption patterns changing during events like Ramadan. Innovations like Kenya's M-Pesa showcase the innovative approach of mobile money solutions in Africa, aimed to address barriers in traditional banking structures (Mpofu, 2022). Conversely, there is a growing movement towards digital minimalism in the US owing to well-being concerns, while fintech advancements in Latin America, particularly in Brazil and Mexico, reflect a regional shift toward digital wallets (Ozili, 2022).

Understanding these diverse digital adoption patterns enables businesses to develop strategies that are not only inclusive but also respectful of regional preferences, thereby fostering a more globally connected and responsive digital ecosystem.

3.1.3 COMPARATIVE ANALYSIS: DETERMINANTS OF DIGITAL ADOPTION ACROSS REGIONS

Digital adoption varies significantly worldwide, influenced by a range of factors from infrastructure to cultural attitudes. Provided is a breakdown of these influences:

Technological infrastructure

Developed vs. developing countries – In developed regions, advanced infrastructures, exemplified by Scandinavia's robust internet and 5G networks, pave the way for seamless integration of sophisticated digital applications which require high-bandwidths such as AR and VR. This contrasts with some developing nations where infrastructure may still be evolving.

Urban vs. rural – A digital divide is often observable within countries. India, for instance, demonstrates a stark contrast between the urban proliferation of digital commerce and the internet access challenges in rural areas.

Cultural acceptance

Asia (China vs Japan) – China's digital ecosystem is robust, marked by platforms like WeChat and Taobao, and with technologies like AR/VR becoming mainstream. This contrasts with Japan's more reserved uptake, where tradition often influences technological engagement.

Middle East – With regions like the UAE exhibiting high mobile usage rates, there is a marked difference in the technological landscape across the Middle East, where cultural and religious values can significantly shape digital adoption patterns.

Africa – Despite the widespread use of social media platforms, the continent's diverse cultural and linguistic distinctions necessitate tailored approaches for digital outreach. Localisation, in this regard, becomes key.

Economic factors

Disposable income – Wealth discrepancies affect technology access; while affluent societies may take smartphone ubiquity for granted, some regions of Africa or India show a preference for basic mobile phones and related innovations such as mobile money.

Economic policies – In places with protectionist policies, local digital ecosystems might thrive. China's tech giants Alibaba and Taobao, for instance, thrived partly because of limited competition from Western companies.

Education and awareness

Higher educational levels correlate with faster adoption and more discerning usage of technology. Europe's comprehensive educational infrastructure has facilitated the widespread adoption of e-learning technologies.

Age demographics

Young populations – Countries with a younger demographic profile, such as India and some African nations, are more likely to quickly embrace new digital platforms and immersive technologies.

Aging populations – Contrastingly, nations with a higher proportion of older adults, like Japan, have a demand for digital innovations tailored to the needs of the elderly.

Understanding the diverse determinants of digital adoption is crucial for businesses aiming to navigate the complex global landscape. While some factors such as technological infrastructure present clear benchmarks for digital strategy, others like cultural attitudes and economic policies require a more nuanced approach to effectively engage with various consumer segments. Adapting digital strategies to cater to these variances is not only strategic but necessary for global market resonance.

3.1.4 MARKETING INNOVATION: MOVING BEYOND THE ORDINARY

Marketing in the fashion industry has long been recognised for its vital role in enhancing customer experiences (CX). According to Kotler's Marketing 3.0 paradigm, the strategic development of CX is central to fostering brand loyalty and, ultimately, contributing to a firm's profitability. Defined comprehensively, CX encompasses all interactions between a consumer and a brand, starting from initial brand awareness to post-purchase engagement.

TABLE 3.1.1 Marketing 1.0 to 5.0.

Marketing 1.0 (Product-Centric)	Marketing 2.0 (Consumer-Centric)	Marketing 3.0 (Human-Centric)	Marketing 4.0 (Digital-Centric)	Marketing 5.0 (Human-Tech Symbiosis)
Anchored in the age of industrialisation, this phase was marked by a focus on product attributes. Fashion houses prioritised production efficiency, with minimal attention to individual consumer preferences	The 1980s and 1990s heralded a renaissance. Recognising the discerning consumer, brands began tailoring their campaigns to specific demographics, forging deeper emotional connections	The turn of the millennium observed a global awakening towards sustainability and ethical consumption. Brands underscored their ethical values, resonating with the conscious consumer	The advent of digital platforms revolutionised consumer-brand interactions. AR-based shopping experiences epitomised the blend of digital and offline touchpoints	A nascent era, it envisages a seamless integration of AI and emotional intelligence. Brands now harness technology to amplify the human element, ensuring personalisation at an unprecedented scale

The effectiveness of customer experiences (CX) is a critical determinant in maintaining customer retention and, subsequently, impacts a company's financial performance (Hoffman et al., 2022). Therefore, CX is an essential aspect of an effective business strategy, designed to strengthen customer engagement, guide purchasing choices and establish lasting brand loyalty.

While foundational marketing concepts are familiar to many, the imperative now is to contextualise these within the evolving digital fashion landscape. Fashion marketing, intrinsic to business strategy, has transformed in response to major societal shifts. It has transcended product-centric approaches, embracing a synergy of human touch and technological innovation. For a clearer understanding, consider the following chronological framework:

Marketing 1.0 was characterised by a concentration on the product.
Marketing 2.0 transitioned the focus toward the consumer.
Marketing 3.0 highlighted the human dimension, beyond mere transactions.
Marketing 4.0 witnessed the incorporation of digital elements into marketing strategies.

Moving beyond these earlier stages, we now explore Marketing 5.0, as formulated by Kotler et al. (2021), which synergises established principles of fashion marketing with cutting-edge technologies such as AI, ML, AR, VR, and other applicable technologies. This integration embodies a fundamental aspect of both current and future marketing paradigms. Consequently, the discourse on Marketing 5.0 is not only timely, but an essential component of the ongoing dialogue regarding the future of marketing within the fashion industry.

Marketing 1.0–5.0 traces a fascinating evolution of the marketing discipline, each phase marking a significant shift in strategy and focus.

Marketing 1.0: The product-centric genesis

Marketing 1.0 focuses on the product itself. The belief here was that a superior product would naturally lead to sales success (Fuciu & Dumitrescu, 2018). This product-centric approach, as exemplified by brands like Chanel, emphasises product quality and innovation over customer experience. However, the critique of this model pointed to its limitations. It lacked a customer-centric perspective; no matter how technologically advanced or qualitatively superior a product might be, if it did not resonate with consumer needs and desires, it would not achieve its potential in the market. This critique signalled the beginning of a shift towards a more consumer-oriented approach in marketing.

Marketing 2.0: Embracing the customer

Marketing 2.0 represented a shift to a consumer-focused approach, taking advantage of technology advancements to understand and meet customer needs better. It was a response to a more empowered consumer, thanks to the rise of the internet and social media platforms, which facilitated two-way communication and provided companies with valuable consumer feedback. Detailed market research and data-driven strategies became central to crafting marketing campaigns that delivered personalised experiences to different customer segments. This era positioned the consumer at the centre of the marketing universe, advocating that understanding and satisfying customer needs was the cornerstone of success.

Marketing 3.0: Prioritising the human element

Marketing 3.0 further evolved the concept by viewing consumers not just as buyers of products or services, but as whole human beings with complex layers of emotions, values and aspirations. This phase recognised the importance of emotional connection, authenticity and brand ethos. The trend of **servitisation** transformed the fashion industry, where the focus shifted from just selling clothes to offering a comprehensive brand experience that aligned with the consumers' values, such as sustainability and ethical production, e.g., Patagonia, Stella McCartney (Ke Zhang et al., 2023). This strategy leveraged the emotional dimension of marketing, as social platforms opened novel pathways for engaging with consumers more intimately. The objective was to align a brand's core identity with its public perception, meeting consumers' elevated expectations for brands to represent values beyond their products.

Servitisation is the shift from selling products to providing holistic services. This change is driven by evolving customer demands, technological advancements like IoT and AI and intense market competition. Benefits of servitisation include new revenue avenues, enhanced customer loyalty and a unique market position.

Marketing 4.0: The technological renaissance

In Marketing 4.0, the use of technology bridges the gap between the physical and digital worlds. This transition to a more integrated, omnichannel approach emphasises the importance of aligning brand strategy with consumer behaviour and expectations. The shift to a more horizontal, collaborative marketing framework fosters continuous consumer interaction, across all brand or retailer touchpoints (Kotler et al., 2021). Industry leaders like Nike, Adidas and Gucci have set a standard in the fashion sector by adopting advanced digital tools to enhance consumer engagement. These tools range from perfunctory mobile applications and social media platforms to more immersive platforms such as video games and virtual worlds, forming a continuous brand presence across all customer touchpoints. This strategy, termed 'brandification', represents a brand's relentless effort to remain engaged in consumers' lives (Lucarelli & Hallin, 2014).

Yet, some brands remain tentative, often due to resource constraints or a reluctance to change; it is widely accepted across both academic and industry discourse that adapting to digital advancements is crucial for brand survival and success.

Data analytics plays a crucial role in this new marketing era, allowing for an enhanced understanding of consumer behaviour and the ability to tailor marketing strategies accordingly. The integration of big data across a brand's value chain is essential for competitiveness and relevance (Suárez et al., 2017). As outlined in Chapter 3.4, big data – specifically, the accurate and relevant kind – has become the lifeblood of business strategy. The adage 'you can't manage what you can't measure' highlights the necessity of precise data in the modern marketing landscape. Brands that neglect to utilise the appropriate data risk obsolescence, highlighting the critical role of reliable data in generating meaningful marketing metrics and ensuring brand survival in the current market landscape (Forbes, 2020).

The concept of customer experience within the framework of Marketing 4.0 inherently requires a seamless integration of physical and digital interactions. Kotler (2021), highlights the importance of combining both the tangible aspects of a product and the intangible elements that resonate emotionally with consumers. For instance, Apple does not just sell a phone; they offer an entire ecosystem. While the iPhone's design and functionality (tangible elements) appeal to users, it is the sense of community, the brand image and the memories created using their devices (intangible elements) that truly anchor customers to the brand.

In the contemporary landscape of the fashion industry, where digital and hyper-connectivity are at the forefront, brands need to move beyond simply offering retail experiences to creating distinctive, memorable customer interactions. This echoes Carù and Cova's (2003) emphasis on the significance of delivering experiences that go beyond the norm to secure customer loyalty and satisfaction. Academic literature often categorises experiences into two distinct types: ordinary and extraordinary. Extraordinary experiences, often related to hedonic consumption, are characterised by their emotional depth, uniqueness and lasting impact (Carù & Cova, 2003). For instance, consumers might seek these experiences for moments of adventure, reflecting their value in the market (Varley et al., 2018; Arnould & Price, 1993).

On the other hand, ordinary experiences represent routine aspects of daily consumption. Yet, the reality is that these experiences often exist on a spectrum, therefore, what starts as a routine engagement can transition into an extraordinary one (Skandalis et al., 2019). The in-store shopping experience serves as an illustrative example of this concept. Traditionally, a customer enters a fashion retail store, picks out clothes and heads to the fitting room. This is a routine task with a clear purpose to ensure the clothing fits and looks good on the customer. Now, envision a smart fitting room equipped with AR and AI. A customer can still pick out clothes, but instead of physically trying each piece on, they can stand in front of a smart mirror. This mirror, leveraging AR, superimposes the selected clothes onto the customer's reflection, allowing them to see how they would look in different outfits without the need to change. AI can suggest sizes, colours or similar styles based on the customer's previous selections and body type. Further enhancing this experience, the system could provide real-time feedback or style advice, show the clothing in different scenarios (such as how it looks in various lighting conditions) or even allow the customer to virtually mix and match pieces they already own (by accessing a previously uploaded digital wardrobe). Customers could share their virtual fittings with friends or social media followers directly from the smart mirror for instant feedback.

By integrating this technology, the routine process of trying on clothing becomes an interactive, social and personalised experience. It transforms a mundane task into an engaging and memorable shopping event that customers might actively seek out for both its convenience and novelty, potentially driving higher engagement and customer loyalty for the retail brand. For brands, the challenge lies in transforming even ordinary interactions into experiences that convey a sense of uniqueness and emotional engagement, thereby differentiating themselves in a competitive marketplace.

Marketing 5.0: Bridging human insight with technological progress

Marketing 5.0 marks a new era in the evolution of marketing, combining advanced technology with insights into human behaviour. Kotler et al. (2021) describe this phase as focused on co-creating value with customers, emphasising sustainability, social responsibility and personalised interactions, all enhanced by tech developments. The use of big data and AI allows marketers to customise experiences, predict strategy outcomes and blend digital and physical sales spaces with remarkable accuracy.

Again, digital tools are instrumental in the transition to Marketing 5.0. AI is enabling hyper-personalisation, and VR and AR are bringing immersive experiences into physical retail spaces. The fashion sector is at the forefront, with innovations like VR fitting rooms and AR try-ons boosting customer interaction. Successful initiatives, such as RTFKT's digital sneaker releases and DressX's AR couture app, have generated significant revenue and market interest. Despite the enthusiasm for these innovations, the transition to Marketing 5.0 remains an ongoing effort. Embracing technology while preserving a human touch is an endeavour filled with complexities. While a minority of fashion brands such as Everlane and Veja are leading the way in merging marketing with social values via their commitment to ethical fashion, sustainable practices have yet to become universally embraced. This context sets the stage for Marketing 5.0, which offers an exciting yet complex future for marketing, one that necessitates a nuanced balance between technological advancements and fundamental human values.

RACE model

Technological disruption in fashion marketing represents a shift in how brands engage consumers and respond to rapidly changing market dynamics. Although we are a long way from mainstream adoption of some more advanced digital technologies, such as generative AI, or Visual Emotional AI, we are seeing the impact of more emergent technologies.

The RACE (Reach, Act, Convert, Engage) model (Chaffey, 2010) provides a framework for businesses to apply advanced technologies throughout the customer journey, enhancing digital communications and interactions.

The outline below represents how brands can integrate modern technologies within each phase of the RACE model:

Reach: Broadening brand awareness through tech-enhanced methods

- *Programmatic advertising:* Utilise real-time bidding algorithms for ad placements, ensuring high relevance and efficiency in targeting potential customers.
- *AI-enhanced SEO and content creation*: Apply artificial intelligence to analyse search trends and user data, optimizing content for improved search rankings and visibility.
- *AR advertisements*: Craft interactive augmented reality ads that allow users to experience products within their own space, enhancing engagement and interest.
- *Social media chatbots*: Implement chatbots on social platforms to instantly address inquiries, extending reach through timely and automated customer service.

Act: Stimulating interaction and lead generation with technology

- *Personalised web experiences*: Employ AI to customise website interactions based on user behaviour and preferences, creating a more personalised visit that encourages engagement.
- *VR and AR interactivity:* Incorporate virtual and augmented reality features for product demonstrations, such as virtual try-ons, which can lead to increased interaction and longer site visits.
- *Predictive analytics*: Use predictive models to forecast user actions and present tailored content or promotions, nudging users toward conversion.

Convert: Facilitating the transition from prospect to customer via tech

- *AI-driven product recommendations:* Implement systems similar to Amazon's recommendation engine to suggest items, increasing the likelihood of additional purchases.
- *Sales-assisting chatbots*: Use chatbots to guide prospects through the buying process with real-time support, addressing questions and overcoming objections on the spot.
- *Smooth payment technologies*: Incorporate frictionless payment solutions, including one-click payments or biometric authentication, to expedite the checkout process.

Engage: Deepening customer relationships through technological engagement

- *Blockchain loyalty programs*: Create transparent and secure loyalty programs using blockchain, offering customers clear visibility into their rewards and redemption processes.
- *AI-powered email personalisation*: Leverage AI for advanced segmentation and personalisation of email campaigns, ensuring relevant content delivery that aligns with individual user profiles.
- *AR post-purchase support*: Provide augmented reality tutorials or assembly guides, enhancing the post-purchase experience and reducing potential frustration with new products.
- *Chatbots for feedback and support*: Deploy chatbots for instant customer support and feedback collection, contributing to continuous improvement and customer satisfaction.

Employing these advanced technologies across the RACE framework, brands can create a more effective and engaging journey for customers, driving both conversions and sustained loyalty.

3.1.5 THE 'RIGHT NOW' ECONOMY

The 'right now' economy represents a shift in consumer behaviour towards instant gratification, driven by advancements in technology and the strategic personalisation of services. This trend, evident in the approaches of Amazon, Spotify and Netflix, demonstrates how personalised recommendations, based on data analysis of user preferences, are reset consumer expectations. For instance, Netflix harnesses sophisticated algorithms that analyse user viewing patterns to curate personalised recommendations. This data-centric approach extends beyond media suggestions; it informs Netflix's content creation strategy, leading to the production of widely popular originals like 'Stranger Things', which align with the diverse tastes of their global audience.

The growth of e-commerce, alongside the widespread influence of social media, has also altered consumer expectations, accelerated the pace of fashion consumption and promoted impulse buying. This shift towards instantaneous content access and purchasing contributes to the environmental burden by increasing clothing production, which in turn raises greenhouse gas emissions and contributes to the rapid turnover of clothing that often ends in waste. Clothing waste commonly contributes to landfill mass, where it decomposes and emits methane, or it is incinerated, leading to the release of toxic substances. The compulsion for immediate gratification often neglects the merits of sustainable fashion considerations. The Expectancy Theory (Vroom, 1964) explains this shift as a consumer's pursuit of immediate rewards, particularly when these rewards are linked to social or personal satisfaction. For example, if a consumer perceives that purchasing a specifc product will elevate their social status or resonate with their personal values, thereby enhancing their self-esteem, they are more inclined to proceed with the purchase. Consequently, it's imperative for brands to not only meet but exceed these expectations to maintain strong customer loyalty. Zara exemplifies this approach by staying ahead of fashion trends and providing value through its regularly updated product lines, thereby keeping its customer loyalty robust. In contrast, brands that fail to align with consumer expectations face the risk of diminishing their customer loyalty.

In response to these changes, businesses are tasked with providing flexible payment options, rapid shipping options and intuitive online interfaces across the web and mobile. As highlighted earlier, in this chapter, retailers must also adeptly manage and analyse consumer data to offer a personalised shopping experience. Numerous studies have explored the implications of the 'right now' economy on businesses and consumers. A 2022 *Harvard Business Review* study reports that a majority (84%) of consumers now expect immediate customer service from brands. In parallel, Deloitte's 2022 findings reveal a willingness among 79% of consumers to spend more on personalised products and services. This growth trajectory underscores the significant economic implications of the 'right now' economy.

Countries boasting advanced digital infrastructures lead this trend, whereas emerging markets with expanding middle classes - such as India, Brazil, and Mexico - are progressively demanding comparable levels of service. This shift is illustrated by the adoption of live-streaming in fashion retail, which offers an example of real-time interaction that meets consumers' expectations for immediate purchase options. The 'right now' economy reflects the critical interplay between technological advancements, evolving consumer expectations and the imperative for businesses to rapidly adapt to remain competitive in the digital marketplace.

The 'right now' economy refers to the contemporary consumer culture driven by immediacy, convenience and instant gratification. This concept captures the changing expectations of consumers who now desire immediate access to products, services and information, largely facilitated by digital technology and the rise of the internet.

3.1.6 HYPER-PERSONALISATION: RETHINKING CONSUMER SEGMENTATION IN THE DIGITAL ERA

Market segmentation, the practice of grouping consumers based on similar characteristics, has long been a mainstay in marketing. Although these tried and tested methods have been effective, traditional segmentation, which primarily relied on largely homogeneous behavioural and demographic data, may fall short of comprehensively capturing the complete picture of today's consumer behaviour. The theme throughout this chapter is how digital innovation has reshaped the interactions between brands and consumers. With a digital-first strategy, fashion brands are moving away from broad market segmentation toward a more refined **hyper-personalised** approach using micro-segmentation strategies. This method is in line with the 'segment of one' philosophy, which employs real-time data to create individualised products and experiences (Kotler et al., 2021). For instance, Zara has developed multiple buyer personas to target their customers with greater accuracy. This level of personalisation is made possible by big data, signifying a marketing shift towards catering to individual consumer preferences. However, given the fluid nature of digital trends, these consumer profiles are subject to periodic revisions.

Micro-segmentation refines this approach by subdividing the consumer market into smaller, highly specific segments based on detailed criteria, considering lifestyle, behavioural patterns, demographics, psychographics, shopping habits and individual preferences.

The emergence of big data analytics and AI has significantly enhanced the sophistication of micro-segmentation. Companies are now able to analyse vast datasets to identify patterns and trends previously unseen. This capability enables them to customise marketing messages, product offerings, and services for highly specific and niche groups within a broader market. The process can include:

- **Collect data** – Harness intricate data from diverse sources like social media, customer surveys, transactions, online behaviours and IoT devices.

- **Analyse data** – Employ ML and data mining to detect nuanced preferences and behaviour patterns.
- **Predict and model** – Construct models to forecast consumer behaviour and preferences for future needs.
- **Customise and personalise** – Craft marketing campaigns, products or services to address the distinct needs of each microsegment.

The objective of micro-segmentation is to boost customer engagement by delivering tailored products and marketing, thereby increasing marketing efficacy and potential ROI. Digital tools have revolutionised the approach to consumer interaction, from static data collection to dynamic engagement. Advanced tracking technologies grant retailers detailed consumer insights, surpassing traditional metrics. Together with third-party data repositories, these insights form elaborate and detailed consumer profiles, granting brands a competitive advantage (Shah & Murthi, 2021). This depth of insight empowers companies to not only respond to but also anticipate consumer needs, often before they are explicitly communicated. Yet, this massive influx of data brings its own challenges in effective management, storage and utilisation. Here, AI is crucial in managing this complexity, swiftly processing data to fine-tune consumer interactions. This precision gives rise to targeted promotions, smarter chatbot interactions and improved customer service, all converging to create a deeply engaged brand–consumer relationship.

Hyper-personalisation in fashion marketing employs advanced data, analytics, AI and automation to deliver uniquely tailored customer experiences. It surpasses traditional segmentation by addressing individual customer needs, preferences and behaviours. Through hyper-personalisation, companies can send highly contextualised communications to customers at the right time and place, and through the right channel.

The push for personalisation in consumer markets is supported by both academic findings and industry analysis. Research has identified that personalisation appeals to consumers' need for control and their desire for a more streamlined decision-making process (Iannilli & Spagnoli, 2021; Pangarkar et al., 2022). Personalised services make customers feel like the centre of attention, narrowing down their options to what best suits their individual needs and simplifying their choices. This sense of being prioritised fosters an emotional connection with the brand, potentially increasing customer loyalty, spending and advocacy. A 2021 McKinsey study supports this, revealing that over 70% of customers favour personalised interactions and are more inclined to purchase from brands offering tailored experiences (Arora et al., 2021). Additionally, the study indicated that companies proficient in personalisation generate 40% more revenue from similar activities when compared to their average counterparts. However, insufficient personalisation efforts can significantly dampen customer engagement. In today's market, consumers have high expectations for the use of their data to enrich their shopping experience. When these expectations are not met, it can lead to a decline in customer interaction, diminished impact of advertisements, eroded brand loyalty, and an increase in both impulsive purchases and product returns, underscoring the critical importance of adept personalisation in maintaining consumer satisfaction and loyalty.

From a strategic perspective, the application of hyper-personalisation spans the entire spectrum of the customer journey. From adaptive web designs to dynamic pricing and post-purchase personalised communications, the potential touchpoints for enhancing customer experience are extensive. Nike's ID initiative exemplifies this approach with a campaign that harnessed social media data to create highly personalised video advertisements, yielding significant improvements in engagement and conversion metrics. E-commerce giants like Amazon also demonstrate the efficacy of personalisation in boosting sales conversions. Their algorithms subtly guide consumers towards items that resonate with their past behaviour, often without the customers' conscious recognition. This method has set a precedent that customers have come to anticipate from other retailers as well, expecting proactive and intuitive product recommendations that mimic their interaction with Amazon's sophisticated personalisation engines.

An emerging trend is the rise of 'on-demand' digital clienteling services. While clienteling has historically been a cornerstone in enhancing the customer experience in brick-and-mortar stores, the surge in online shopping has compelled retailers to rethink their approaches to delivering personalised services. For years, this approach has focused on nurturing sustained relationships with frequent, high-value customers, elevating their shopping journey to a 'white-glove' standard. The luxury sector, renowned for its in-store personal shoppers and unmatched service, epitomised this high-level engagement. Yet, the traditional model of clienteling was often labour-intensive, limited by in-store staffing constraints. As consumer behaviour increasingly shifts to the online domain, fashion retailers understand the urgency of digital adaptation, transitioning from static customer service models to versatile, data-informed strategies. Gucci's innovative 'Gucci App' exemplifies this convergence, offering a suite of digital clienteling services that maintain customer engagement across shopping platforms. We are already witnessing digital tools like AI and ML facilitate real-time interactions, extending the boundaries of online shopping and creating experiences that closely mirror those found in physical stores.

Luxury retailers are adapting to online consumer behaviours by integrating advanced technology with established clienteling principles, aiming to replicate the personalised service online, that rivals the 'white glove' attention to detail offered in stores. The use of the 'Gucci App' is a clear strategy to replicate the in-store experience digitally, offering live chats, video consultations and AR fittings to enhance online shopping. This digital shift allows for sustained customer engagement and service quality, providing a wealth of data to customise the shopping experience further. For luxury brands, the introduction of these digital tools is a significant step towards improving operational efficiency and customer satisfaction. However, the challenge lies in executing this digital transition in a way that maintains the brand's reputation and the high standards that luxury consumers expect.

In the same technological advancement wave, visual recognition software is becoming a key tool in marketing innovation, especially within the fashion industry. Brands like Bestseller are at the forefront, integrating facial recognition technology in their Jack & Jones and Vera Moda stores in China. The technology is used to match customers with their WeChat ID profiles as soon as they enter a store; data of which contains existing purchasing patterns and past product searches. While this approach offers clear advantages in personalising retail experiences, it also raises questions about privacy and ethics. Fashion retailers must balance the benefits of personalised shopping with the responsibility of managing consumer data privacy responsibly, ensuring that the technological enhancements to the shopping experience do not compromise customer trust or the integrity of the brand.

Mini case studies – digital clienteling

Snapchat and New Balance's innovative clienteling

Snapchat and New Balance launched the 'Holiday Gifting Concierge Lens', blending AR and speech recognition to provide gift suggestions across footwear, apparel and accessories. The lens operates in two modes. In selfie mode, users verbally describe their recipient, utilising Snap's VoiceML technology for gift guidance. In worldview mode, an AR unboxing experience reveals product recommendations. While the lens did not support direct links, 5.8 million users could view items on New Balance's Snapchat profile under 'Shop', leading them to the brand's website for purchases (Kenan, 2022). Snap's 2022 statement highlighted the user experience: 'Using VoiceML, Snapchatters answer questions about the person they are shopping for and get matched with the ideal gift ideas. Upon answering, they can then access product recommendations through a unique unboxing experience.' This partnership showcases the evolving landscape of digital clienteling, highlighting the blend of technology and personalised shopping.

HKIA's digital Luxury Concierge service

Hong Kong International Airport (HKIA) introduced a digital Luxury Concierge service in 2023, accessible via WhatsApp, WeChat and video calls, allowing clients to shop prior to airport arrival. The platform supports 16 high-end brands including Chanel, Louis Vuitton and Gucci, with plans to expand the brand roster. With the development, HKIA says its fashion offering is an 'unmatched shopping destination for sophisticated trendsetters'. The service ensures gate delivery within 90 minutes and free global delivery to 15 destinations for purchases over HK$1,000.

Sources: Kenan, 2022; Snapchat, 2022; Sherry, 2023

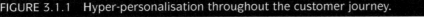

FIGURE 3.1.1 Hyper-personalisation throughout the customer journey.

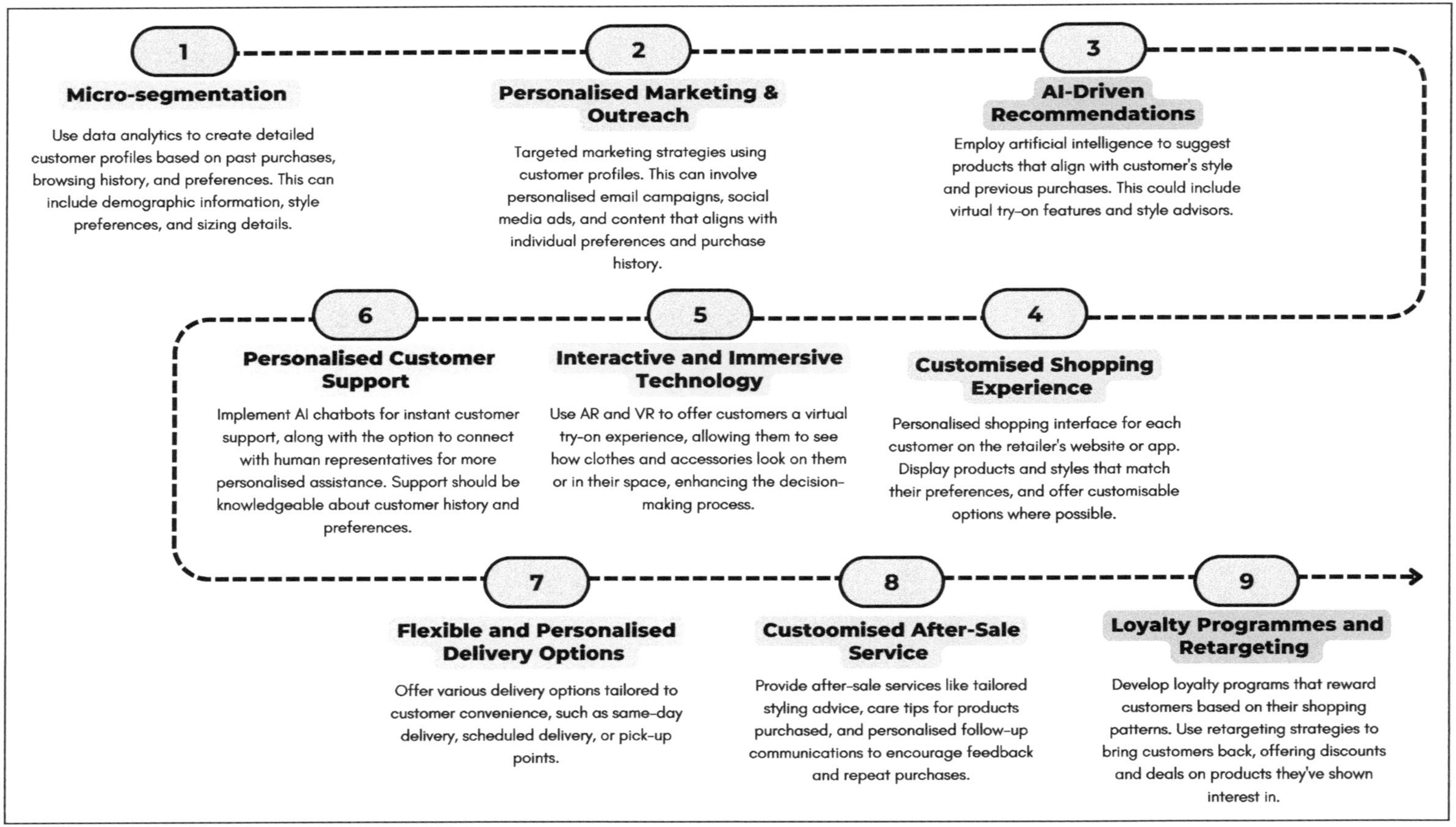

1
Micro-segmentation
Use data analytics to create detailed customer profiles based on past purchases, browsing history, and preferences. This can include demographic information, style preferences, and sizing details.
2
Personalised Marketing & Outreach
Targeted marketing strategies using customer profiles. This can involve personalised email campaigns, social media ads, and content that aligns with individual preferences and purchase history.
3
AI-Driven Recommendations
Employ artificial intelligence to suggest products that align with customer's style and previous purchases. This could include virtual try-on features and style advisors.
4
Customised Shopping Experience
Personalised shopping interface for each customer on the retailer's website or app. Display products and styles that match their preferences, and offer customisable options where possible.
5
Interactive and Immersive Technology
Use AR and VR to offer customers a virtual try-on experience, allowing them to see how clothes and accessories look on them or in their space, enhancing the decision-making process.
6
Personalised Customer Support
Implement AI chatbots for instant customer support, along with the option to connect with human representatives for more personalised assistance. Support should be knowledgeable about customer history and preferences.
7
Flexible and Personalised Delivery Options
Offer various delivery options tailored to customer convenience, such as same-day delivery, scheduled delivery, or pick-up points.
8
Custoomised After-Sale Service
Provide after-sale services like tailored styling advice, care tips for products purchased, and personalised follow-up communications to encourage feedback and repeat purchases.
9
Loyalty Programmes and Retargeting
Develop loyalty programs that reward customers based on their shopping patterns. Use retargeting strategies to bring customers back, offering discounts and deals on products they've shown interest in.

3.1.7 THE METAVERSE AND THE VIRTUAL SELF

In considering the metaverse, it is essential to understand its original core offer: a deeply immersive and interactive virtual universe (Park & Lim, 2023). Initially, this concept captivated brands and consumers alike, offering a retreat from reality into a domain of endless potential (Giang Barrera & Shah, 2023). Users imagined themselves exploring vast virtual landscapes, forging connections and revelling in a spectrum of digital activities, including shopping for virtual products. It promised a level of customisation and personalisation that had never been seen before, where one's digital persona could be as intricate or as fantastical as they wished (Yoo et al., 2023). The allure of the metaverse was its capacity to transcend the physical world's limitations, providing a platform for global interaction (Henninger et al., 2022). For users, it enabled us to meet and collaborate with a diversity of personas, cutting across geographical and societal barriers.

For some time, it seemed to deliver on its promise, facilitating the formation of digital communities, fostering shared experiences and, indeed, allowing for the creation of meaningful connections, particularly between brands and consumers (Dwivedi et al., 2022).

The fashion industry's leap into the metaverse, led by early adopters such as Nike, Tommy Hilfiger, Gucci and Balenciaga, has been both ambitious and experimental. These brands have capitalised on the metaverse as a new platform to push the boundaries of digital marketing and engagement. Nike's interactive 'Nikeland' on Roblox and Balenciaga's immersive game, *Afterworld: The Age of Tomorrow* are prime examples of this digital foray, indicating a substantial investment in virtual consumer experiences. Nike's 2021 acquisition of RTFKT, along with Balenciaga's establishment of a dedicated metaverse division, signals a strategic long-term investment in metaverse. These moves highlight a recognition of the metaverse's potential, despite the current unpredictability of returns on such ventures. It illustrates a calculated bet on the future intersection of fashion, technology and consumer engagement within virtual environments.

The inauguration of Metaverse Fashion Week (MVFW) in 2022 on Decentraland marked a significant entry of luxury brands such as Selfridges, Dolce & Gabbana and Hogan into the Web3 space. These brands set up virtual storefronts in Decentraland's Luxury Fashion District, effectively opening high fashion to a broader, global audience through digital participation in events and afterparties (Shirdan, 2022). In its inaugural four-day event, MVFW attracted 108,000 unique visitors, a number that, while modest compared to the attendance of traditional fashion weeks like New York Fashion Week, cannot be directly compared due to MVFW's emergent status and the longstanding history of its real-world counterparts. The success or lack thereof of MVFW cannot be discerned from attendance figures alone. Technical issues such as subpar graphics, slow processing speeds and browser crashes marred the experience, while catwalk shows suffered from low engagement and disarray, indicative of a platform yet to reach its peak.

Notwithstanding the hurdles, MVFW demonstrated the extensive capabilities of virtual platforms to transform consumer interaction with the fashion industry. Decentraland, in particular, has become a stage for an immersive luxury shopping experience that broadens the accessibility of high-end fashion. However, the industry must now grapple with the challenge of keeping consumer interest alive as the novelty of the metaverse begins to diminish, highlighting the need for a critical reassessment of the metaverse's long-term value and strategic importance to the fashion sector.

The initial appeal of the metaverse for fashion brands lay in its promise of an unrestricted creative world, detached from the limitations of physical retail. It offered a space where virtual showrooms, avatar skins and NFTs could be leveraged to cater to a digitally savvy consumer base eager for innovation in ownership and self-expression. The initial excitement surrounding the metaverse has been moderated by growing concerns about the sustainability of blockchain and Web3 technologies as the considerable computing power and electricity necessary for maintaining these platforms raise questions about their environmental impact (Marr, 2023). Additionally, the speculative aspect of virtual assets has sparked discussions about the long-term value and ethical considerations inherent in their trade and acquisition. These concerns underscore the importance of developing and implementing more sustainable practices within the industry to ensure that the progress in digital spaces does not come at the expense of ecological and moral responsibility.

Despite promising early engagement metrics, the long-term commercial viability of these metaverse ventures remains to be seen. The market for virtual goods and experiences, although substantial, may not align with the initially high expectations. McKinsey's (2022) report on digital assets suggests there is a market; however, the extent and persistence of consumer interest are still subject to analysis (McKinsey, 2022). Although brands like Nike and Balenciaga, however, demonstrate a more strategic approach to the metaverse, translating virtual engagement into concrete revenue remains a complex challenge amid the volatile nature of digital consumer behaviour.

Whilst interest in the metaverse has seen fluctuations, one sector within it continues to draw significant investment: virtual identities and avatars. Fashion, traditionally an avenue for self-expression, finds new opportunities in this digital landscape. The concept of a 'virtual twin', a digital replica of a physical product, is gaining traction beyond its initial industrial, automotive and gaming applications into areas such as apparel. This technology offers tangible benefits for product development and marketing by enabling the creation of customer body doubles for a variety of uses, from virtual fittings to advertising.

Companies like Epic Games are leveraging their MetaHuman technology to push the boundaries of digital identity, producing avatars that are increasingly indistinguishable from real people. The UK-based company I AM HUMAN is further disrupting the digital fashion landscape with its photo-realistic model avatars, offering a new dimension of virtual fitting and product communication (see case study 3.1.8). These capabilities are supported by significant advancements in processing power, especially in GPUs, allowing for photorealistic renderings. Similarly, improved scanning technologies such as photogrammetry, and the ability to use smartphones for both material and body scans, have democratised access to these tools, facilitating their integration into various business models.

As gaming engines evolve, they introduce sophisticated rendering techniques that benefit the entire creative spectrum, including 3D fashion systems. The expectation is that these technologies will enable more credible virtual scenes and avatars, enhancing the user experience. However, the rapid pace of these developments requires careful consideration of their impact, particularly in terms of consumer psychology and the ethics of digital representation. Fashion brands have recognised the potential of digital avatars, creating exclusive lines and using them to cultivate more intimate connections with consumers. In the virtual environment, the selection of virtual clothing and accessories is more than a personal preference; it is a statement of identity that influences how others perceive the user. This concept parallels Tajfel and Turner's (1979) social identity theory, where self-esteem is linked to the groups to which one belongs. Within the virtual environment, these groups often form around common interests in fashion, shaping an individual's self-perception and reinforcing their identity within the broader digital community. There can be a symbiosis between the identity created in the metaverse and the one lived in the physical world.

Yet, the convergence of digital and physical identities is not without its issues. The pursuit of hyper-realistic digital twins raises questions about data privacy, the potential for misrepresentation and the psychological effects on the user's sense of self. As brands navigate this space, there is a pressing need for a balanced approach that respects ethical standards and considers the long-term implications on individual identity. Companies like I AM HUMAN exemplify the delicate balance of embracing technological advancement while maintaining ethical integrity. They serve as a reminder that even in the rush to innovate, there must be a conscious effort to uphold the responsible use and regulation of these technologies to prevent potential misuse.

The path forward will require a synergy of innovation, responsibility and an unwavering commitment to authenticity, ensuring that the virtual world enhances, rather than detracts from, the human experience.

3.1.8 CASE STUDY: I AM HUMAN: BALANCING INNOVATION AND ETHICS

I AM HUMAN, the brainchild of Model Agency Founders Norv Bell and Jonny Sydes, exemplifies a revolutionary approach to fashion's digital frontier. At its core, the creation of photorealistic avatars stands as its most notable disruption, reinventing the traditional processes of product development and e-commerce presentation.

I AM HUMAN: The vision and approach

I AM HUMAN's inception is marked by its commitment to inclusivity, sustainability and technological progress. It distinguishes itself by creating digital twins that embody the physical characteristics and personalities of real humans, enabling interaction across various digital platforms. Their photo-realistic avatars, created through state-of-the-art photogrammetry and proprietary processing techniques, the company has created photo-realistic model avatars that mimic their human counterparts, not only physically, but also mirror their intricate movements and personality traits.

The vision expands to ethical considerations, ensuring remuneration for models and prioritising the security of their personal data through immutable encryption methods. These strides in protecting model identity and integrity further I AM HUMAN's goal to set a standard for ethical innovation in the industry. With digital human usage anticipated to soar within the industry, particularly within the fields of virtual fitting, entertainment and marketing, I AM HUMAN is at the forefront, leading the charge toward a digital-centric future.

The innovation: Photo-realistic avatars

I AM HUMAN's cutting-edge 'Digital Twinning Process' is its competitive edge, involving a sophisticated photogrammetric 3D scanning system that captures models in extraordinary detail. The system accurately records anthropometric data of their physical counterparts, thus rendering a unique and highly precise 3D avatar. This method seamlessly integrates avatars into existing design workflows, revolutionizing the process and enhancing efficiency. The company's avatars are meticulously optimised for immediate use, facilitating collaborative design, development and buying processes. This represents a substantial leap over traditional methods, offering cost-effective solutions and addressing challenges associated with physical modelling.

The integration of these avatars can also significantly reduce online return rates, offering personalised virtual fitting experiences. I AM HUMAN is a testament to the evolving capabilities of technology in fashion, continually pushing the boundaries and reimagining what's possible. As I AM HUMAN carves its niche, it redefines the synergy between fashion and digital environments, proving that the future of the industry is not just about adaptation but about radical transformation.

Interview: I AM HUMAN

Interviewer: What inspired you to start I AM HUMAN, and what was the vision behind it?

Norv Bell: The original idea was born over ten years ago in collaboration with my business partner, Jonny Sydes. We also run a model agency called The Bureau and wanted to find a way of accurately and consistently measuring the models that we supplied to our clients. We saw many flaws in the conventional way, as garment technicians would often vary where they took the measurements from on the body. We thought that a body scan would eradicate these inconsistencies and decided to have a few models

FIGURE 3.1.2 I AM HUMAN photo-realistic model avatar (Image credit: I AM HUMAN, 2023).

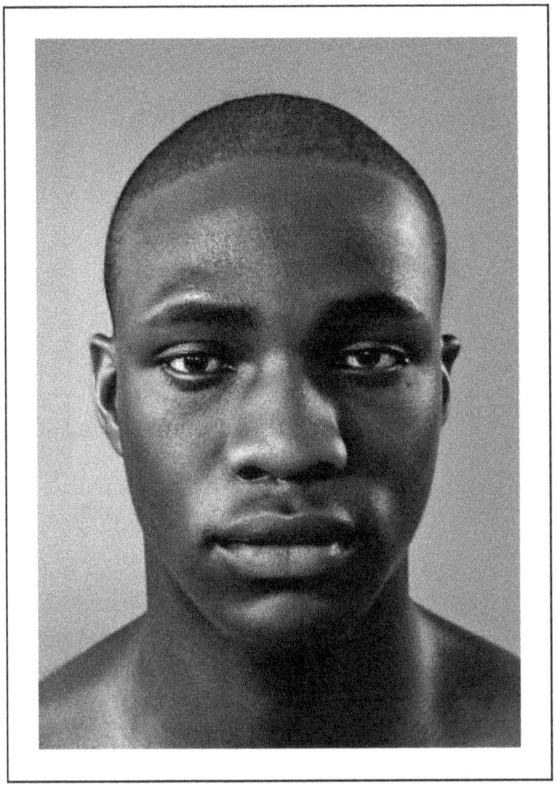

3D scanned. Unfortunately, the scans resulted in the measurements being too different when compared with measurements taken manually. We therefore decided that the timing was not right for scanning our models on mass, because it could be detrimental to our business. Garment technicians may have perceived a model as being the incorrect size, even though the scanned measurements were actually a more accurate reflection of the model's body. We found, however, that speciality foot scanners produced measurements for the feet that deviated much less from the physical measurements. These results prompted us to collaborate with Volumental, a company providing highly accurate foot scanners for retail environments. We like to say that this was us 'dipping our toes' into 3D scanning. The results and feedback from our footwear clients were extremely encouraging and gave us the confidence to further pursue the body scanning.

FIGURE 3.1.3 3D foot scan (Image credit: I AM HUMAN, 2023).

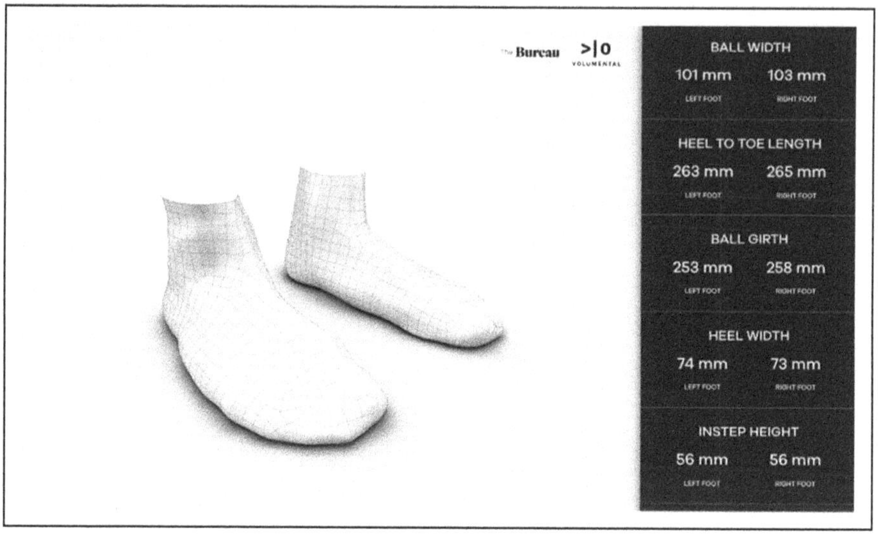

Just a few years later, advances in 3D garment design and fitting software gave us further impetus to invest heavily in this area. What started as simply being a tool that provided brands with a more accurate and consistent measurement has evolved into something much bigger. We quickly realised the impact of providing our clients with both a physical model and their 'real human' avatar counterpart within their chosen 3D platform. Not to mention the huge reduction in the financial and environmental costs associated with physical sampling. Therefore, we decided to seek out and form a new business with the best photogrammetry and character creation company in the UK and I AM HUMAN was formed.

Interviewer: How does the process of creating a virtual model work?

Norv Bell: Without getting too technical, it starts with scanning the model's body using photogrammetry. We have over 150 cameras that take the initial scan, each focussed on different parts of the body. From this data, we can ascertain both the size and shape of the subject and build their hyper-realistic digital twin for use across multiple platforms. Then, the post-processing is where the magic happens! It is a very complex sequence of processes which we are continuously working on to make more efficient. We tend to capture and process the model in multiple different poses so that the avatar can be rigged with a virtual skeleton to enable animation synonymous with real-life movement. This enables brands to get the most out of our avatar in a digital space. Once complete, the avatars are then integrated into various 3D platforms, which involves creating specific base meshes for each platform respectively for optimal compatibility. Should a brand decide they want one of our avatars for a campaign, we can dress the avatar within the 3D platform then export the data to apply more look development on to the avatar. This enhances the realism even further. These avatars can then be integrated into virtual environments, giving brands boundless creative freedom.

Interviewer: How do you see the use of virtual models revolutionising the fashion industry?

Norv Bell: We believe that virtual models will change the landscape of the fashion industry dramatically. For us, it is a question of ethics and consumer relatability. There is no doubt that using a Meta Human saves money in some areas for a brand, but are they losing value elsewhere? Can consumers truly relate to a Meta Human enough to make purchase decisions and become brand loyal? These are just a couple of the questions we ask ourselves daily when considering whether the market is ready to buy from 3D assets or AI generated content. By means of example, recently a well-known luxury fashion brand created their SS23 fashion campaign utilising AI. The brand claimed that the campaign harmonised their sense for aesthetics and point of view on design to inform digital dreamlike imagery; 'AI powered by human emotion'. The collection itself took inspiration from Mexican culture, with the campaign featuring undoubtedly 'Mexican' landscapes and fashion models generated by AI. Whilst visually impactful the campaign was fiercely divisive. It drew a significant amount of media attention due to its use of AI, but an equal amount of scrutiny on social media platforms, with many commenters identifying the lack of real Mexican talent featured or involved in the creation of the campaign. 'Imagine if you actually hired Mexicans, as opposed to profiting off our culture and humanity?', writes one follower. Most posts featuring this campaign by the brand have now had the comments switched off.

We feel that real models have intrinsic value that cannot be replaced entirely by a virtual model. This is because they are real by nature; they have personalities, emotions and characters that consumers can relate to. Whilst it is incredibly exciting to be able to utilise such advanced technology to create elaborate campaigns at the click of a button, it could be seen as deprived of human creativity, sensitivity, realism and craft. Furthermore, real models can add value to a brand after a campaign has been produced, by connecting with consumers on their own social media. Brand partnerships and influencer relations are powerful and direct secondary marketing tools.

This is why we are excited about I AM HUMAN because the avatars are human; they have personalities, and they've had highs and lows, which is all a part of life that people can relate. We think there is still a huge space between the present and the fully-fledged metaverse where people still want the human element, and not someone or something that does not exist.

Interviewer: Can you share some of the initial challenges you faced, and how you overcame them?

Norv Bell: Where do we start! Aside from creating the guidelines for a completely new part of the industry, in terms of data security, model remuneration and licensing contracts, there have been a couple of challenges that are worth mentioning in a bit more detail. Firstly, getting the models on board has been key. Educating them on where the fashion industry is heading has been a large undertaking, as well as empowering them with the knowledge that we are working to protect their data and ultimately their careers. Models are understandably concerned about Metahumans taking their place, so it has been our responsibility to explain to them how important it is for them to protect themselves from being exploited. We have heard a few horror stories, where brands have scanned the models with rudimentary data usage agreements in place, essentially having the models sign over all their rights to the data in perpetuity. Once we have advised the models, they become excited because they soon realise that once they have been scanned there is the potential of being in multiple places at once, without having to physically be there. This is delightful news to a model! Remaining on the subject of data protection, security has been another large project. It is vital that we can demonstrate to the models that their data is secure. To do this we have had to both encrypt our avatars and build our own ecosystems within the major 3D design platforms. Encrypting the avatars means the files cannot be exported and shared unlawfully, which is paramount for compliance with GDPR regulations. Lastly, creating hyper-realistic digital twins that are able to perform within multiple 3D design platforms efficiently has been a challenge. Each platform has its own technical specifications, resulting in a lot of work and dedication to ensure each avatar performs optimally. This has been no easy task. The feedback we have had from brands and the 3D platforms themselves has been extremely positive, with everyone noting that our avatars are the best quality and most life-like.

Interviewer: Which key advancements in technology have been instrumental in enabling the creation of hyper-realistic models?

Norv Bell: The technology in creating virtual humans has been available for a while if you look at the film industry. However, producing something that is both affordable and functional and provides real value for fashion brands has not always been possible. The process for a game developer or film producer to incorporate avatars into their environment typically takes months, even years. Our ready-made portfolio of human avatars is functional across multiple platforms and as such will add huge value for fashion brands, as well as across the gaming and film industry. In addition to this, the fact our models are real humans adds even more value because companies or brands don't need to worry about the moral or ethical issues of 'hiring' Meta or AI-generated humans. The featured model will be getting remunerated for the use of their image, just as they would if physically modelling. This is not to say that the process has been easy; our proprietary processing allows for faster results but there is still a lot of work involved. Although, bespoke ML helps us create more efficiencies in the pipeline.

Also, 3D garment creation software has caught up with the avatar creation more recently, and both technologies have become more aligned. This has opened more opportunities within fashion, not just with the creation of digital assets and how they interact, but also within the workplace and in education. We can see a new generation of talented workers entering the marketplace equipped with the skills to use 3D platforms.

Interviewer: How do you envision I AM HUMAN evolving alongside rapid technological advancements?

Norv Bell: It's difficult to predict what the future holds, as everything is moving so quickly. Fortunately, we feel we have a unique proposition and are focussing on delivering the best solution for our clients here and now, whilst keeping our eyes on future evolution. The technology that is likely to change the most quickly is the method of data capture. Advanced scanning capabilities are becoming available on smartphones and ML is enabling the captured data to deliver impressive results. The advancements in technology should result in greater efficiencies for IAH.

We know that the accumulation of accurate biometric data that we will be obtaining from our scans will provide immense value to brands. This can be applied for use at several stages of their production process, whether it is to inform better accuracy for their size blocks, align sizing between ranges or even from brand to brand, which ultimately helps to reduce returns due to sizing inconsistencies. The valuable biometric information and hyperrealistic visual data that we capture could eventually lead to an elevated and more accurate virtual fitting room environment for the consumer.

Interviewer: What impact do you believe virtual influencers will have on the future of the fashion industry?

Norv Bell: We're looking to provide the human element to virtual fashion, so perhaps we are a bit biased. We feel that a virtual influencer that does not exist in real life will have less influence over consumer behaviour than a digital twin of a person that does exist. In recent years, digital influencers have been popular, as they were something new and exciting. The consumer response to this has been mixed, however. In October 2022, Marks & Spencer revealed their first virtual influencer on social media –sp 'Mira', which stands for Marks & Spencer, Influencer, Reality, Augmented. Whilst a handful of comments praised the brand for embracing future technologies and appealing to a younger market, many had severely adverse reactions to Mira, openly stating their loss of brand loyalty in response to the decision not to feature real humans in this particular marketing endeavour. 'This is so wrong, we should be promoting real, imperfect people – not creating "flawless" avatars that create impossible "beauty standards". Marks & Spencer, I'm disappointed in you for investing in this marketing strategy that will exacerbate issues of poor body image. Why didn't you use this budget to invest in promoting real, honest influencers who celebrate the diversity of what human beings look like?' writes one commenter whose sentiment we share.

Brands need to be keenly aware of the potential impact this content can have on consumers. Whilst still undoubtedly imperfect, the fashion industry has made great progress in recent years when it comes to representation, diversity and inclusion. We are further away from the unrealistic and unattainable beauty standards that were glorified by fashion brands in the past. Therefore, are virtual influencers a backwards step? Do consumers now have to wrestle with the standards set by beings who don't even exist? What impact will this have on consumer wellbeing, and is it responsible for brands to be influencing consumers in this way? We believe that consumers will continue to value authenticity and maintain emotional connections to those they are influenced by and will therefore have a greater response to human avatar influencers.

Norv Bell, 2023; Josie Pearson, 2023

END-OF-CHAPTER DISCUSSIONS

1. Choose a contemporary fashion brand and analyse how it utilises technology to engage with consumers and adapt to the fast-changing fashion environment.
2. Considering the various factors that influence technology acceptance, how might a fashion company devise a market entry strategy in a country of your choice? Discuss the strategy in terms of market research, adaptation to local consumer behaviour and potential barriers to adoption.
3. With the transition to Marketing 5.0, how do you envision the balance between personalisation and privacy will be managed?
4. How do you think retailers can balance the demand for instant gratification and personalised experiences with the ethical considerations surrounding consumer data privacy and the environmental impact of increased consumption?
5. How does the integration of digital identities within the metaverse challenge our traditional understanding of self and social interaction?
6. What might be the long-term psychological and/or social impacts of engaging with digital twins and avatars?

Bibliography and further reading

Alexander, B. and Cano, B. M. (2020). *Store of the future: Towards a (re) invention and (re)imagination of physical store space in an omnichannel context*. Available at: doi:10.1016/j.jretconser.2019.101913.

Alexander, B. and Kent, A. (2022). *Change in technology-enabled omnichannel customer experiences in-store*. Available at: https://scite.ai/reports/10.1016/j.jretconser.2020.102338

Arnould, E. J. and Price, L. L. (1993). 'River magic: Extraordinary experience and the extended service encounter', *Journal of Consumer Research*, 20(1), p. 24. doi:10.1086/209331.

Ayesu, S. M., Acquaye, R., Howard, E. K. and Asinyo, B. (2023). *Promotion and preservation of indigenous textiles and culture in Ghana*. Available at: https://scite.ai/reports/10.46606/eajess2023v04i01.0252

Bain, M. (2023). 'H&M Group's new AI tool lets anyone play designer', *The Business of Fashion*. Available at: https://www.businessoffashion.com/articles/technology/hm-group-is-using-ai/

BRC (2022). *Footfall rises as consumers shop around*. (2022) Available at: https://brc.org.uk/news/corporate-affairs/footfall-rises-as-consumers-shop-around/

Bruno, P., Denecker, O. and Niederkorn, M. (2020). *Accelerating winds of change in global payments*. McKinsey & Company. Available at: https://www.mckinsey.com/industries/financial-services/our-insights/accelerating-winds-of-change-in-global-payments

Carù, A. and Cova, B. (2003). 'Revisiting consumption experience', *Marketing Theory*, 3(2), pp. 267–286. [online]. doi:10.1177/14705931030032004.

Chaffey, D. (2010). *RACE Planning Framework*, Smart Insights. Available at: https://www.smartinsights.com/tag/race-planning-system/ (accessed 16 February 2024).

Chaffey, D. and Ellis-Chadwick, F. (2019). *Digital marketing: Strategy, ImplementationandPractice*.PearsonUK.

Chrimes, C. and Boardman, R. (2023). 'The opportunities & challenges of the metaverse for fashion brands'. In M. Brandstrup, L-P. Dana, D. Ryding, G. Vignali and M. Caratù (eds) *The garment economy: Understanding history, developing business models, and leveraging digital technologies* (pp. 389–410). Springer, Cham.

Chowdhury, B.H. (2018). 'China's tech giants spending more on AI than Silicon Valley', *The Telegraph*. Available at: https://www.telegraph.co.uk/technology/2018/10/07/chinas-tech-giants-spending-ai-silicon-valley/?WT.mc_id=tmgoff_psc_ppc_generic_articles_technology&gclid=CjwKCAjw-eKpBhAbEiwAqFL0mlocG1gcDIJuM0FP0zF2RzYzeYMxMiDRxK8cTmBOJYAS4J5Nm6YmMRoCmfYQAvD_BwE

Cohen, D. (2022). 'Snap, New Balance team up on holiday gifting concierge lens', *Adweek*. Available at: https://www.adweek.com/social-marketing/snap-new-balance-team-up-on-holiday-gifting-concierge-lens/#:~:text=answer% 20questions% 20about% 20the% 20person% 20 they% 20are% 20shopping% 20for% 2C% 20and

Deterding, S., Sicart, M., Nacke, L., O'Hara, K. and Dixon, D. (2011). 'Gamification: Using game design elements in non-game contexts', *Proceedings of the 15th International Conference on the Foundations of Digital Games*, 9–15.

Dixon, S.J. (2023). 'Global daily social media usage 2023', Statista. Available at: https://www.statista.com/statistics/433871/daily-social-media-usage-worldwide/ (accessed 13 February 2024).

Dubbelink, I. S., Herrando, C. and Constantinides, E. (2021). *Social media marketing as a branding strategy in extraordinary times: Lessons from the COVID-19 pandemic*. Available at: https://scite.ai/reports/10.3390/su13181 0310

Dwivedi et al. (2022). 'Metaverse beyond the hype: Multidisciplinary perspectives on emerging challenges, opportunities, and agenda for research, practice and policy', *International Journal of Information Management*, 66, p. 102542. doi:10.1016/j.ijinfomgt.2022.102542.

Enoch, M., Monsuur, F., Palaiologou, G., Quddus, M. A., Ellis-Chadwick, F., Morton, C. and Rayner, R. (2022). 'When COVID-19 came to town: Measuring the impact of the coronavirus pandemic on footfall on six high streets in England', *Environment and Planning B: Urban Analytics and City Science*, 49(3), pp. 1091–1111. doi:10.1177/23998083211048497

Fuciu, M. and Dumitrescu, L. (2018). 'From Marketing 1.0 To Marketing 4.0 – the evolution of the marketing concept in the context of the 21st century', International conference KNOWLEDGE-BASED ORGANIZATION, 24(2). doi:10.1515/kbo-2018-0064.

Giang Barrera, K. and Shah, D. (2023). 'Marketing in the Metaverse: Conceptual understanding, framework, and research agenda', *Journal of Business Research*, 155, p. 113420. doi:10.1016/j.jbusres.2022.113420

Goasduff, L. (2020). *How gamification boosts consumer engagement*. Gartner. Available at: https://www.gartner.com/smarterwithgartner/how-gamification-boosts-consumer-engagement.

Grewal, D., Hulland, J., Kopalle, P. K. and Karahanna, E. (2019). 'The future of technology and marketing: A multidisciplinary perspective', *Journal of the Academy of Marketing Science*, 48(1), pp. 1–8. doi:10.1007/s11747-019-00711-4.

Hamari, J., Koivisto, J. and Sarsa, H. (2014). 'Does gamification work? A literature review of empirical studies on gamification'. In *Proceedings of the 49th Hawaii International Conference on System Sciences*, 3025–3034.

Hattingh, D. and Ramlakan, S. (2022). 'Stretched South African consumers put health and sustainability on the shopping list', McKinsey & Company. Available at: https://www.mckinsey.com/za/our-insights/stretched-south-african-consumers-put-health-and-sustainability-on-the-shopping-list (accessed 14 February 2023).

Henninger, C. E., Niinimäki, K., Blazquez, M. and Jones, C.(2022). *Sustainable fashion management*. Taylor & Francis.

Hoffman, D. L., Moreau, C. P., Stremersch, S. and Wedel, M. (2022). 'The rise of new technologies in marketing: A framework and outlook', *Journal of Marketing*, 86(1), 1–6. doi:10.1177/00222429211061636

Iannilli, M, V. and Spagnoli, A. (2021). *Phygital retailing in fashion. Experiences, opportunities and innovation trajectories*. Available at: https://zmj.unibo.it/article/view/13120

Jan, J., Alshare, K. A. and Lane, P. L. (2022). 'Hofstede's cultural dimensions in technology acceptance models: a meta-analysis', *Univ Access Inf Soc*. doi:10.1007/s10209-022-00930-7

Kaczorowska–Spychalska, D. (2018). 'Shaping Consumer Behavior in Fashion Industry by the Interactive Communication Forms', *Fibres and Textiles in Eastern Europe*, 26(4), pp. 13–19. doi:10.5604/01.3001.0012.1307

Kenan, J. (2022). *Metaverse examples: The brands to watch across industries, Sprout Social*. Available at: https://sproutsocial.com/insights/metaverse-examples/ (accessed 16 February 2024).

Kotler, P., Kartajaya, H. and Setiawan, I. (2021). *Marketing 5.0*. John Wiley & Sons.

Lau, O., Ki, C. W. (2021). 'Can consumers' gamified, personalized, and engaging experiences with VR fashion apps increase in-app purchase intention by fulfilling needs?', *Fash Text* 8, 36. doi:10.1186/s40691-021-00270-9

Logaugh, K., Stephens, B., Simpson, J. (2019). *The consumer is changing, but perhaps not how you think*. Deloitte Insights. Available at: https://www2.deloitte.com/us/en/insights/industry/retail-distribution/the-consumer-is-changing.html

Lucarelli, A. and Hallin, A. (2014). Brand transformation: A performative approach to brand regeneration. *Journal of Marketing Management*, 31(1–2), pp. 84–106. doi:10.1080/0267257x.2014.982688

Marr, B. (2023, January 13). 'Why blockchain, NFTs, and Web3 have a sustainability problem', *Forbes*. https://www.forbes.com/sites/bernardmarr/2023/01/13/why-blockchain-nfts-and-web3-have-a-sustainability-problem/?sh=6cd6b6735b0b

Mogaji, E., Dwivedi, Y.K. and Raman, R. (2023). 'Fashion marketing in the metaverse', *Journal of Global Fashion Marketing*, pp. 1–16.

Mpofu, Y, F. (2022). *Industry 4.0 in financial services: Mobile money taxes, revenue mobilisation, financial inclusion, and the realisation of sustainable development goals (SDGs) in Africa*. Available at: https://scite.ai/reports/10.3390/su14148667

Nikolopoulos, S. and Epifano, M. (2023). *H&M, Zara, fast fashion turn to artificial intelligence to transform the supply chain*. Available at: https://www.thomasnet.com/insights/zara-h-m-fast-fashion-ai-supply-chain/

Ozili, K. P. (2022). *CBDC, Fintech and cryptocurrency for financial inclusion and financial stability*. Available at: https://scite.ai/reports/10.1108/dprg-04-2022-0033

Pangarkar, A., Arora, V. and Shukla, Y. (2022). 'Exploring phygital omnichannel luxury retailing for immersive customer experience: The role of rapport and social engagement', *Journal of Retailing and Consumer Services*, 68, p. 103001. doi:10.1016/j.jretconser.2022.103001.

Park, H. and Lim, R. E. (2023). 'Fashion and the metaverse: Clarifying the domain and establishing a research agenda', *Journal of Retailing and Consumer Services*, 74, p. 103413. doi:10.1016/j.jretconser.2023.103413

Peña-García, N., Otàlora, M. L., Juliao-Rossi, J. and Orejuela, A. R. (2021). *Co-creation of value and customer experience: An application in online banking*. Available at: https://scite.ai/reports/10.3390/su131810486

Poenaru, A. (2015). 'Is market segmentation dead? A conceptual model of the effect of segmentation choices on marketing performance'. In L. Robinson, Jr. (ed.) *Proceedings of the 2009 Academy of Marketing Science (AMS) Annual Conference. Developments in Marketing Science: Proceedings of the Academy of Marketing Science*. Springer, Cham. doi:10.1007/978-3-319-10864-3_22

Polakoff, S. (2020). 'Why small business can no longer ignore big data', *Forbes*. [online]. Available at: https://www.forbes.com/sites/forbestechcouncil/2020/05/20/why-small-business-can-no-longer-ignore-big-data/?sh=6a1d95367639

Popowska, M. and Sinkiewicz, A. (2021). *Sustainable fashion in Poland—too early or too late?*. Available at: https://scite.ai/reports/10.3390/su13179713

Ratchford, T. B., Soysal, G., Zentner, A. and Gauri, D. K. (2022) 'Online and offline retailing: What we know and directions for future research', *Journal of Retailing*, 98(1), pp. 152–177. doi:10.1016/j.jretai.2022.02.007.

Ross, K. (2023). 'Summer holidays drive surge in high street footfall', *Drapers*. Available at: https://www.drapersonline.com/news/summer-holidays-drive-surge-in-high-street-footfall

Shah, D. and Murthi, B. P. S. (2021). 'Marketing in a data-driven digital world: Implications for the role and scope of marketing', *Journal of Business Research*, 125, pp. 772–779. doi:10.1016/j.jbusres.2020.06.062.

Sherry, K. (2023). 'HKIA launches fashion-focused Luxury Concierge Digital Service', *TRBusiness*. Available at: https://www.trbusiness.com/regional-news/asia-pacific/hkia-launches-fashion-focused-luxury-concierge-digital-service/233254 (accessed: 16 February 2024).

Shirdan, L. (2022, May 11). 'Metaverse Fashion Week was a promising prototype for the future. Here's why', *Entrepreneur*. https://www.entrepreneur.com/living/metaverse-fashion-week-was-a-promising-prototype-for-the/424308

Skandalis, A., Byrom, J. and Banister, E. (2019). 'Experiential marketing and the changing nature of extraordinary experiences in post-postmodern consumer culture', *Journal of Business Research*, 97, pp.43–50. doi:10.1016/j.jbusres.2018.12.056

Snap Inc. (2023). *Snap AR Try-On Study: Middle East*. Retrieved from https://ar.snap.com/intermediate-courses

Snapchat (2022). 'New Balance success story', Snapchat for Business, Snapchat Ads. Available at: https://forbusiness.snapchat.com/inspiration/new-balance-wins-with-ar-powered-gifting-concierge (accessed 16 February 2024).

Srite, M. (2006). 'Culture as an explanation of technology acceptance differences: An empirical investigation of Chinese and US users', *Australasian Journal of Information Systems*, 14(1). doi: 10.3127/ajis.v14i1.4

Suárez, G. M., Martínez-Ruiz, P. M. and Martínez-Caraballo, N. (2017). *Consumer-brand relationships under the Marketing 3.0 Paradigm: A literature review*. Available at: https://scite.ai/reports/10.3389/fpsyg.2017.00252

Tajfel, H. and Turner, J. C. (1979). 'An integrative theory of intergroup conflict'. In W. G. Austin and S. Worchel (eds), *The social psychology of intergroup relations* (pp. 33–48). Brooks/Cole.

Yoo, K., Welden, R., Hewett, K. and Haenlein, M. (2023). 'The merchants of meta: A research agenda to understand the future of retailing in the metaverse', *Journal of Retailing*, 99(2), pp. 173–192. doi:10.1016/j.jretai.2023.02.002

Williams, G. A. (2022). 'From 2017 to 2022: Five years of Tmall Luxury Pavilion so far', *Jing Daily*. Available at: https://jingdaily.com/tmall-luxury-pavilion-five-years/

Vargo, S. L., and Lusch, R. F. (2004). 'Evolving to a new dominant logic for marketing', *Journal of Marketing*, 68(1), 1–17.

Varley, R., Roncha, A., Radclyffe-Thomas, N. and Gee, L. (2018). *Fashion management: A strategic approach*. Bloomsbury Publishing.

Venkatachalam, K., Abouhawwash, M. and Bacanin, N. (2022). *Artificial intelligence and blockchain technology enabling sustainable and smart infrastructure*. Available at: https://scite.ai/reports/10.18267/j.aip.203

Zhang, K. et al. (2023). 'Servitization in business ecosystem: a systematic review and implications for business-to-business servitization research', *Technology Analysis & Strategic Management*, 35 (11), pp. 1480–1496. doi: 10.1080/09537325.2021.2010698

CHAPTER 3.2

Retail innovation
The future of the physical store

Charlene Gallery

Despite the significant rise of e-commerce, physical stores remain at the heart of the retail sector, accounting for approximately 85% of sales in 2023 (Deloitte, 2023). This fact counters the bleak predictions of a 'retail apocalypse' and demonstrates the enduring importance of in-person shopping. The pandemic has not only catalysed new retail trends but also solidified certain consumer behaviours and changed our very perception of what constitutes a 'personal' shopping experience. Post-pandemic, physical stores have regained prominence, yet the convenience of online shopping, which became more popular during lockdowns, persists. What has changed, however, is the function and purpose of the physical store. This chapter offers an overview of the concept of 'phygital' and its potential to enhance customer experience in physical stores. The chapter will explore the transformation of fashion retail through digital innovations, emphasising the new functions of brick-and-mortar locations. The focus will be on how retailers are combining tangible and technological aspects to create engaging, consumer-centric spaces. The chapter will examine the impact of technologies like augmented reality (AR) and operational systems such as radio frequency identification (RFID) in revolutionising the in-store environment.

LEARNING OUTCOMES

After reading this chapter, you should be able to

- Understand the changing role of the physical store within the context of fashion.
- Identify ways in which technology can deliver highly personalised, immersive and interactive customer experiences in-store.
- Identify ways big data can be captured and used within the fashion in-store environment.
- Understand the 'phygital' concept and explain how technologies have changed the fashion customers' shopping journey.

DOI: 10.4324/9781003364559-11

3.2.1 THE TRANSFORMATIVE LANDSCAPE OF FASHION RETAIL

The fashion industry stands at a transformative crossroads, as detailed in Chapter 1.1, where technological progress, environmental concerns and shifting economic tides are reshaping the market (Grewal et al., 2017). This upheaval is altering consumer behaviour and the traditional relational dynamics between shoppers and brands, compelling a re-examination of the role of the physical store in an increasingly digital world (Varley et al., 2018. However, to paint a full picture, a brief retrospection into the evolution of the physical store will be insightful for our discourse within this chapter.

Retail has deep historical roots. From the bustling bazaars of the Middle East to the lively piazzas of Europe, central assembly marketplaces have always been a cornerstone of communities. Historically, retailers vied for customers through the competitive triad of convenience, price and product variety; yet, as retail evolved, the emergence of department stores and large-scale retailers reflected a shift to a broader offering, albeit at the expense of personalised service. Now, the digital age, punctuated by the onset of e-commerce, challenges the existence of traditional retail, with the COVID-19 pandemic accelerating the transition towards online platforms (Alexander & Cano, 2020). Terms like 'retail apocalypse' gained traction, with data from 2017–2020 highlighting a spate of store closures and company bankruptcies; however, it is important to note that the pandemic simply expedited trends that were already in motion. While some businesses struggled during this crisis, digital-first players like Amazon and Zalando exemplified resilience through technology adoption, emerging stronger where others faltered (Dubey et al., 2023).

The e-commerce revolution has altered the traditional path to purchase, creating an intertwined ecosystem of digital and physical interactions (Reinartz et al., 2019). This blend demands consistency and a heightened level of service from retailers, who must now navigate the complexities of omnichannel strategies. Today, manufacturers, third parties and consumers are more involved in retail functions, providing the value once solely offered by conventional retailers. Although traditional brick-and-mortar retail will strive to maintain its role, it is gradually being undermined as manufacturers directly reach customers through dual distribution and vertical integration (Wang et al., 2009). Yet, the persistent shift towards digital mediums has not eradicated the need for physical retail spaces; on the contrary, brands like Adidas and Apple continue to invest in these spaces, reasserting the value of in-person shopping experiences. For instance, Adidas aims to double its brand's retail space globally by 2025 by expanding its Direct-to-Consumer (DTC) stores and developing flagship and experiential store-within-store concepts (Salpini, 2021).

The modern retail landscape demands agility and a nuanced understanding of consumer behaviour. The advent of BOPIS (Buy Online Pick-Up in Store) and similar models reflects a broader trend towards personalised and convenient shopping experiences. Deloitte's (2023) study points to consumer preferences for services that blend online shopping with the immediacy of physical stores. Such innovations are crucial for retailers to stay relevant and cater to the evolving expectations of their customers. Yet, despite the obvious benefits, adopting new consumer behaviours into a unified retail strategy remains a complex endeavour (Henninger et al., 2022; Varley et al., 2019). Retailers are pressured to compete with online giants while avoiding complacency in their traditional operations. The volatility of the market, influenced by private equity, leadership changes and real estate instability, adds layers of complexity for retailers. Additionally, retailers are grappling with the financial impact of product returns, the need to meet aggressive sales forecasts and the challenges posed by a shifting economy.

However, contrary to initial assumptions related to the demise of physical retail, the retail sector experienced a surge in store openings post-pandemic, driven by **digital native vertical brands (DNVBs)** and progressive retailers who recognised the enduring value of the physical store, which still accounts for a significant (86%) portion of global sales (Fromm, 2022). Physical stores offer sensory experiences and immediate satisfaction that digital platforms cannot replicate, underscoring their continued relevance in the retail ecosystem. The challenge for retailers is to innovate continually, ensuring that the integration of online and offline channels results in a cohesive and satisfying **customer journey**.

Physical stores must now serve as experiential hubs, blending tactile experiences with digital innovations. As the British Retail Consortium's report in May 2023 indicates, footfall in physical stores has decreased, reflecting a broader trend towards online shopping. However, this shift is not uniform across all sectors or geographic locations. The modern physical store is evolving, focusing more on customer engagement, sustainability and incorporating digital technologies to enhance the shopping experience (Iannilli & Spagnoli, 2021).

Digital native vertical brands are online businesses that later expand to brick-and-mortar stores. They sell products directly to consumers without intermediaries like wholesalers or traditional retailers, using a direct-to-consumer (D2C) model. This approach streamlines product distribution, creating a more efficient connection between the brand and its consumers. The D2C model is versatile, catering effectively to both online-focused and brick-and-mortar establishments, giving them greater control over branding, customer experience and profit margins.

A **customer journey** is the process through which a customer interacts with and experiences a brand, product, or service. It includes all steps from initial awareness to purchase and beyond. The journey can be broken down into stages that reflect the customer's emotions, motivations, questions and interactions with the brand.

FIGURE 3.2.1 The physical store, past, present and future (adapted from Wright et al., 2022).

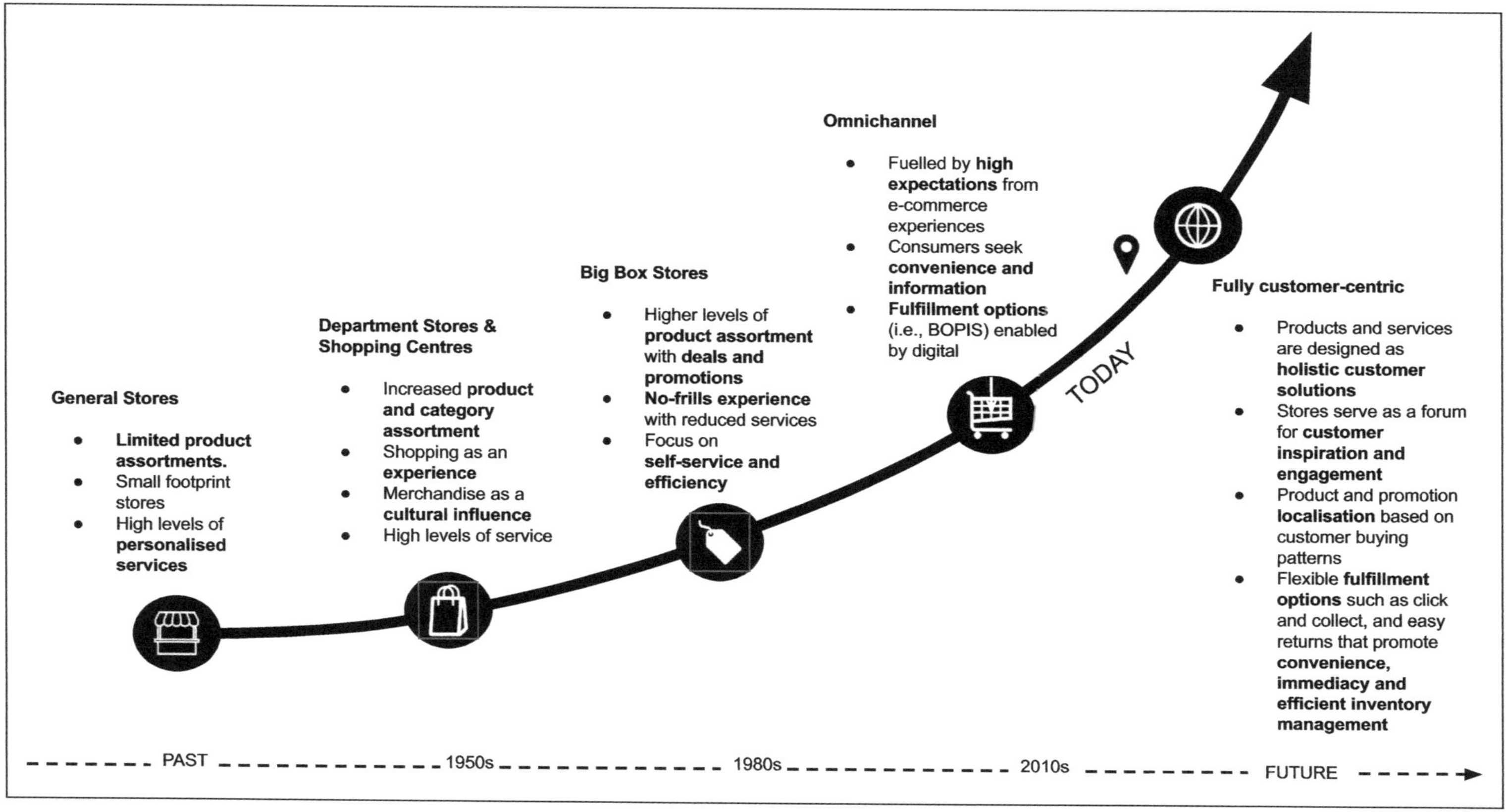

General Stores
Limited product assortments.
Small footprint stores
High levels of personalised services
Department Stores & Shopping Centres
Increased product and category assortment
Shopping as an experience
Merchandise as a cultural influence
High levels of service
Big Box Stores
Higher levels of product assortment with deals and promotions
No-frills experience with reduced services
Focus on self-service and efficiency
Omnichannel
Fuelled by high expectations from e-commerce experiences
Consumers seek convenience and information
Fulfillment options (i.e., BOPIS) enabled by digital
TODAY
Fully customer-centric
Products and services are designed as holistic customer solutions
Stores serve as a forum for customer inspiration and engagement
Product and promotion localisation based on customer buying patterns
Flexible fulfillment options such as click and collect, and easy returns that promote convenience, immediacy and efficient inventory management
PAST
1950s
1980s
2010s
FUTURE

3.2.2 DIGITAL INTEGRATION

The following segment of the chapter will explore the varied ways technology has redefined retail, particularly the implications for physical stores within the rapidly expanding digital ecosystem.

The influence of digital technology on retail has been substantial and definitive. It has catalysed an amalgamation of industries like gaming, fashion and hospitality, crafting an integrated commerce landscape ripe with opportunities for retailers that adapt and innovate. Fashion retail in particular requires a strategic embrace of digital advancements to stay competitive. Harnessing data analytics has become essential for retailers aiming to navigate the complex territory of consumer preferences, a theme thoroughly examined in Chapter 3.1. The strategic implementation of AI and cognitive technologies in retail settings is becoming increasingly prominent, acting as a force multiplier in enhancing customer experience and optimising retail operations. The fashion industry, ever so sensitive to consumer preferences, is a fertile ground for such innovations. Zara's London flagship store is a leading illustration of this trend. Here, the adoption of interactive dressing rooms, powered by RFID technology, reflects a significant leap toward a tech-enhanced retail environment.

Customers in this setting experience a unique layer of personalisation; RFID scanners read the items they intend to try on and propose additional, complementary pieces through an interactive mirror. This recommendation is not random but is smartly generated based on the analysis of vast troves of historical purchase data and feedback. The result is a highly individualised shopping experience that aligns with customer preferences and past behaviours. Beyond recommendations, AI's role in Zara's operation is manifold. The technology interprets customer interactions and purchase data to inform real-time inventory adjustments. This data can also be used to optimise store layouts and change visual displays. Such a dynamic and responsive system not only caters to individual shopping experiences but also reflects a broader shift in inventory and store management, making them more efficient and responsive to the ebb and flow of fashion trends and consumer demand.

Sustainability in product development, discussed in Chapter 1.1, has prompted retailers to adopt technologies, resulting in a ripple effect throughout the entire fashion value chain, subsequently prompting a re-evaluation of traditional retail models. For fashion retailers, this could manifest as on-site micro-factories, in-store product customisation and the introduction of recycling and take-back programs (Wu, 2022). Adidas's 'Knit for You' initiative is a practical example, merging on-demand customisation with sustainable practices. Customers had the option to design their sweaters, watch them be machine-knitted in the store within hours and subsequently take the finished product home. While this concept served to satisfy the dual demands of modern consumers for personalisation and immediacy, it simultaneously presented a sustainable approach to product development.

As highlighted early in this chapter, historically, retailers sought differentiation through service, operations or value propositions. Now, innovative technology has become the linchpin of competitive advantage, transforming mundane store visits into compelling, immersive experiences. AR-enhanced window displays are a case in point, creating an interactive engagement by bringing the visual merchandise to life and drawing customers into the store. As retailers seek to drive traffic back into the physical store, Beacon technology has become an essential tool within the retailer's arsenal, providing unidirectional communication from the brand to the customer and bridging the gap between digital convenience and in-store experience. By emitting Bluetooth signals, beacons interact with smartphone apps to deliver personalised promotions, real-time product information and tailored recommendations as customers browse within a store. This not only enhances the shopping experience but also aids retailers in gathering valuable data on consumer behaviour and preferences. In the fast-paced fashion industry, where trends and customer tastes evolve rapidly, beacons provide the agility for stores to adjust their marketing and inventory strategies promptly. They also streamline in-store navigation and enable seamless contactless payments, further elevating the customer experience to meet the expectations of the modern, tech-savvy shopper.

Technologies such as QR codes and IoT systems further extend brand content beyond the confines of the physical stores, facilitating interactive customer engagement. IoT technologies like RFID and NFC track products throughout the value chain, providing valuable data to both brands and consumers (Bertola & Teunissen, 2018). Brands like Burberry and Adidas have integrated these technologies into their products and stores to enhance storytelling, customer experience and the fusion of digital and physical retail: Adidas's flagship store on London's Oxford Street, for example, leverages RFID-equipped fitting rooms and digital displays to connect customers with a broader product range and exclusive content.

The emergence of the 'connected store' concept signifies the synergy between digital and physical retail spaces, an approach adopted with varying intensity across the industry. While some retailers incrementally integrate digital tools to augment customer service and operational efficiency, others employ them as central to a transformative business strategy. Companies like Nike and Gucci represent the latter, using digitalisation to forge new paths and redefine traditional retail frameworks.

Retailers, in response to the ongoing digital revolution, generally adopt one of two approaches:

- **Conservative integration** – Firms like JD Sports and Chanel perceive digital tools as enhancers of customer service and operational efficiency, embracing them in a measured, incremental fashion to avoid unsettling their established business models.
- **Progressive transformation** – A select few, such as Nike and Gucci, see digitalisation as an opportunity to revolutionise their business models, adopting a more disruptive and holistic approach.

The ecosystem perspective sees retail as a networked system where the retailer's role is to foster a collaborative, sustainable business model that values customer lifetime over single transactions. This calls for an agile, responsive network, adept in utilising digital tools to cater to nuanced consumer needs. Retailers are leveraging digital tools for product variety, purchasing ease, cost optimisation and customer loyalty; however, the caveat is that technology is a means, not an end. A purely technological viewpoint can be short-sighted, potentially transforming technology from a facilitator to an impediment, especially if it delivers a fragmented customer journey and a diluted brand experience (Reinartz et al., 2019).

At this point, it is worth reiterating that technology integration should not be a 'one-size-fits-all' approach and, as highlighted in Chapter 1.1, the readiness of retailers to adopt technology will be varied. However, adopting technology comes with its set of hurdles. Navigating a fragmented tech and software market, contending with significant financial investments, and addressing the distinct challenges faced by small and medium enterprises (SMEs) – who, despite their agility, may find full-scale digital integration daunting – all pose substantial obstacles.

As automation and AI become more prevalent in stores, the fashion retail sector is incorporating high-tech features like intelligent recommendation systems and robotic aides. Despite this tech-centric evolution, the intrinsic value of human interaction in retail persists. The true essence of customer brand engagement lies in the behavioural, emotional and cognitive interactions with brands, as highlighted by Hollebeek (2011) and Kaczorowska-Spychalska (2018). DNVB brands such as Matches Fashion demonstrate how to interlace technology with the physical retail experience, ensuring that digital enhancements serve to support, not supplant, the human element. Their London flagship merges immersive technologies seamlessly within a luxury ambiance. Instead of overpowering, technology complements the brand's narrative, underlining their commitment to an impeccable blend of atmosphere, digital clienteling and merchandise.

The ultimate challenge for retailers is to integrate technology in a way that amplifies the retail experience without eclipsing the personal touch that is fundamental to customer satisfaction. Technology's role should be that of an amplifier, enriching the retail experience with efficiency and insight while preserving the essential human connection that resonates with customers at a deeper level.

This metamorphosis is steering the industry towards *reimagining the store of the future.*

3.2.3 THE IMPACT OF DIGITAL DISRUPTIONS ON RETAIL STRATEGY

The disruption of digital technology in the physical store environment is reshaping retail across several operational pillars:

To holistically embrace this digital transformation, retailers must thread these components together, acknowledging the equilibrium between front and back-end mechanics while steering their strategies to align with contemporary digital retail frameworks.

FIGURE 3.2.2 The three digital pillars of in-store retail.

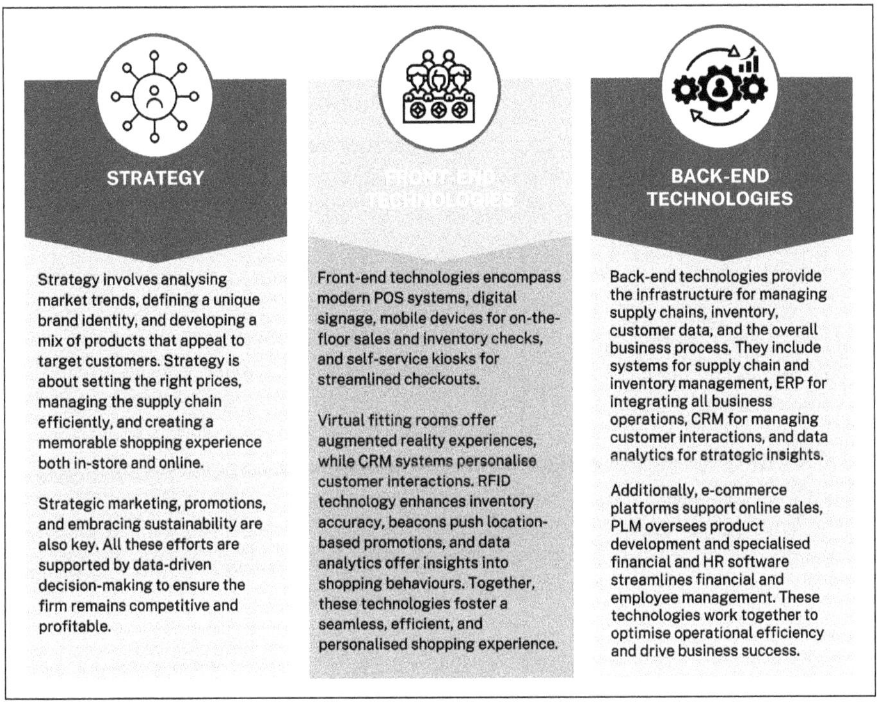

STRATEGY
Strategy involves analysing market trends, defining a unique brand identity, and developing a mix of products that appeal to target customers. Strategy is about setting the right prices, managing the supply chain efficiently, and creating a memorable shopping experience both in-store and online.
Strategic marketing, promotions, and embracing sustainability are also key. All these efforts are supported by data-driven decision-making to ensure the firm remains competitive and profitable.
FRONT-END TECHNOLOGIES
Front-end technologies encompass modern POS systems, digital signage, mobile devices for on-the-floor sales and inventory checks, and self-service kiosks for streamlined checkouts.
Virtual fitting rooms offer augmented reality experiences, while CRM systems personalise customer interactions. RFID technology enhances inventory accuracy, beacons push location-based promotions, and data analytics offer insights into shopping behaviours. Together, these technologies foster a seamless, efficient, and personalised shopping experience.
BACK-END TECHNOLOGIES
Back-end technologies provide the infrastructure for managing supply chains, inventory, customer data, and the overall business process. They include systems for supply chain and inventory management, ERP for integrating all business operations, CRM for managing customer interactions, and data analytics for strategic insights.
Additionally, e-commerce platforms support online sales, PLM oversees product development and specialised financial and HR software streamlines financial and employee management. These technologies work together to optimise operational efficiency and drive business success.

Strategy

Segmentation – The role of segmentation in the retail landscape has indeed been revolutionised by digital technology. The traditional broad-brush approach to marketing has been rendered obsolete by the capabilities that advanced analytics and AI have brought to the table. Retailers can now dissect their market into incredibly nuanced segments, thanks to the wealth of data available. (See Chapter 3.1.) With every transaction, click and social interaction, retailers gather data that, when processed through sophisticated algorithms, can identify patterns and preferences specific to individual consumers or groups of consumers. This granular segmentation allows for the curation of personalised experiences and targeted marketing initiatives. For instance, rather than viewing new customers as a monolithic group, advanced data analytics enables retailers to place them into dynamic, evolving clusters based on real-time data.

As these new customers engage with the retailer across various channels, their behaviours, preferences and even the times they are most likely to make a purchase are captured. These data points are then fed back into the analytics system, which continuously refines its segmentation models. Over time, these customer 'lakes' become increasingly accurate, allowing retailers to predict and respond to consumer needs with greater precision.

Positioning - Retail positioning has undergone significant change with the rise of online shopping. Today, physical stores must go beyond offering competitive pricing and quality merchandise. They are charged with crafting an atmosphere that draws consumers from the ease of digital purchases. This involves upgrading in-store services, offering effective conveniences and captivating customers with enjoyable activities within a cohesive shopping environment. The emergence of **destination retail** is now critical; these specialised stores provide distinctive experiences that transcend conventional shopping, cultivating more profound engagement and brand loyalty (Iannilli & Spagnoli, 2021).

A **destination store** is a specialised retail space that goes beyond the conventional shopping experience, often transcending geographical convenience. It merges attributes of department stores and recreational centres, offering innovative displays and interactive features. These stores aim to draw consumers through unique experiences aligned with a powerful brand identity or local resonance, effectively blurring the lines between retail and entertainment. This fusion not only attracts consumers but also promotes prolonged engagement.

Destination stores elevate shopping to an experiential level by merging the variety of department stores with the appeal of recreational venues. These spaces attract customers not just with their products but with the lure of a compelling brand narrative and interactive features that both entertain and educate. This model resonates with Generation Z who, despite being highly digital natives, have a pronounced affinity for tangible, interactive experiences. For them, the allure of the store lies in the immersive brand experience it offers, often surpassing the act of shopping itself.

These stores are evolving with consumer preferences and technological advancements, becoming epicentres for storytelling and fostering in-store engagement that translates into online loyalty. The showroom concept has also transformed; today's showrooms are interactive venues for deep brand connection (Servais et al., 2022). They act as conduits between online exploration and in-person buying, enabling a fluid omnichannel journey. The integration of technology is key to enriching the retail atmosphere. Pioneers like Farfetch merge digital with physical retail, creating a 'Store of the Future' through innovations like app recognition, online-connected interactive displays and intelligent mirrors, all aimed at amplifying the shopping experience and fortifying brand loyalty.

However, it's brands like Gentle Monster that continue to push the envelope, consistently reimagining what a physical store can be and setting new standards for retail innovation.

Mini case study

Gentle Monster – destination retail

Gentle Monster transforms its retail spaces into immersive, gallery-like destinations that blend technological innovation with art to engage customers. Each store offers a unique, theatrical experience that narrates the brand's story, turning shopping into a journey of discovery and encouraging visitors to immerse themselves and potentially spend more. These concept stores double as modern art spaces, showcasing fashion-forward eyewear amidst dynamic sculptures and artistic installations, embodying the innovation at Gentle Monster's core, a vision set by founder Kim Han-Kook to redefine eyewear as high fashion rather than just functional accessories.

The brand's name reflects its philosophy: a mix of refined elegance and the pursuit of distinctiveness. The showrooms, curated with art as intriguing as the brand, draw inspiration from diverse domains like comics, science and history. Gentle Monster's success is driven by its diverse team, whose expertise spans from perfumery to robotics, fostering a hotbed of creative and innovative thinking. Their stores are not solely places to shop but cultural touchpoints that prioritise artistic expression over the hard sell.

In an age where the relevance of physical stores is questioned, Gentle Monster's unwavering dedication to reinvention shines through in their 'House Dosan' flagship store. This location epitomises their philosophy of destination retail, inviting the stylish and curious to a place where the act of shopping is elevated to an enriching experience beyond the transaction.

Operating formats – Retailers need to rethink their traditional store strategies in light of digital advancements, weighing the financial impact of large physical stores against the advantages of using digital technologies to improve the shopping process. Rather than simply serving as points of sale, stores are transitioning into versatile spaces that offer immersive experiences and act as fulfilment centres for both physical and online retail channels. According to Alexander and Cano (2020), future fashion stores are likely to diverge from one-size-fits-all models, in favour of a digitally versatile and diversified approach. This is supported by the fact that consumer data is critical for determining the optimal mix of retail format, product selection and services.

Services modes like, 'buy online, pick up in store' (BOPIS), 'curbside pickups' and Nike's Speed Shop exemplify these shifts, combining the convenience of online shopping with the personalised physical experience. Retail advancements extends into services like 'wait and try', a concept that Toshi, a London-based retailer, is pioneering. Established in 2017, Toshi provides luxury customers with the opportunity to try online purchases at their preferred location and time, effectively combining the instant gratification of physical retail with the convenience of e-commerce. This reflects a broader transformation where physical stores are becoming multi-functional hubs, focused on providing experiences, convenience and personalised services (Varley et al., 2019).

This rapid and personalised delivery service underscores the importance of physical stores in the retail ecosystem. They are transforming into crucial nodes within retail networks, facilitating agile inventory management, effective customer relationship management (CRM) and efficient supply chain management (SCM) processes. These locations are becoming more than places of purchase; they are integral to the logistics chain, enabling fast delivery services to meet customer expectations for speed. By addressing the desires of customers who seek the satisfaction of immediate possession, physical retail spaces are broadening their appeal. This adaptability positions retail outlets to cater to a diverse customer base, enhancing their role as vital components of a comprehensive retail strategy. Reflecting on the broader picture, the digital transformation journey in the retail environment is not about displacing traditional systems, but rather augmenting them. The resultant blend offers consumers the best of both worlds, ensuring relevance and resonance in a dynamic retail landscape.

Business model innovation – Fashion retailers of all sizes confront the digital revolution's dual aspects of challenge and opportunity. Proactive retailers harness digital technologies to fuel growth and carve out a market niche, whereas others adjust to counter competitive pressures and meet shifting consumer demands. Defined by Teece (2010), a business model outlines how a company creates, delivers, and captures value. Today's digital environment compels retailers to rethink their delivery approaches to meet continuously changing consumer expectations, beyond just adjusting their product offerings. The impact of mobile, cloud computing, social media, and big data analytics accelerates the pace of change in business models, emphasising the need for businesses to rapidly adapt to remain competitive and relevant.

The way a retailer can apply digital innovation to transform its business model is influenced by its current stage of growth, with strategies varying accordingly:

Stages of growth and digital integration

- **Start-up phase** – Digital tools and platforms offer emerging companies innovative business models, allowing them to present original products and services that align with contemporary consumer expectations. Example: Allbirds, a DNVB footwear brand established in 2014, strategically employs data analytics to gain consumer insights, enabling them to refine their offerings and optimise retail strategies. This integration of digital strategy with innovative offerings has enabled Allbirds' to distinguish itself within a competitive market. Consequently, this approach has fuelled the brand's rapid expansion, allowing it to evolve from an exclusively online presence to establishing physical storefronts globally.

- **Operational phase** – Established businesses harness digital interventions to augment their existing operations, aiming to enhance the overall customer experience. Example: Zara, (part of the Inditex group), originating as a traditional brick-and-mortar store, has seamlessly integrated digital technologies into its operations. By leveraging RFID technology, Zara has streamlined its inventory management and supply chain processes, enabling real-time tracking and quick stock replenishment. This technological integration sustains Zara's commitment to 'fast fashion', facilitating the rapid delivery of new styles to stores. Additionally, Zara has introduced interactive fitting rooms equipped with smart mirrors that recommend complementary products, thereby enhancing the in-store experience.
- **Maturity phase** – For retailers that have reached market saturation, growth starts to plateau, and digital disruptions can be a lifeline, enabling established brands and retailers to diversify, ward off threats and venture into previously untapped ecosystems. Example: In the early 2000s, Burberry, a well-known brand recognised for its iconic check design and heritage aesthetic style, encountered difficulties associated with market oversaturation that put its brand value at risk. In response, the brand took proactive measures, adopting digital technologies to refresh its public image and appeal to a younger, tech-savvy consumer. Burberry was at the forefront of digital trends, embracing live streaming within stores and the, albeit short-lived, 'see now, buy now' model, which facilitated instant purchases straight from the catwalk, catering to customers' desire for immediacy. While some digital initiatives like SNBN failed to meet financial expectations, due in part to the necessity for extensive modifications in traditional buying, merchandising, and supply chain processes, as well as the requirement for increased agility and improved supplier relationships to accommodate the immediate product availability model, Burberry's engagement still soared, with a significant online reach. The brand's mastery in social media, AR, and gamification, including collaborations with popular games like *Honour of Kings*, showcases its ability to innovate and expand into new digital arenas. This proves that even well-established brands can dynamically reinvent themselves using digital tools as an integral part of their growth strategy.

Mini case study

The Mall of the Emirates in Dubai stands out as a premier experiential lifestyle destination. Beyond its 630+ retail outlets, shoppers can indulge in a curated selection of 80 luxury boutiques and 250 flagship stores, while food enthusiasts explore over 100 dining options, from gourmet restaurants to international fast-food chains. For entertainment, the mall offers the Magic Planet amusement arcade, cinemas and an indoor ski resort offering snow activities and penguin encounters juxtaposing with the desert environment. Cultural enthusiasts can immerse themselves in the arts at DUCTAC, a dedicated space for art, theatre and workshops. Adding to its allure, the mall provides direct access to luxury accommodations. The mall's European-inspired sections, the Fashion Dome and Via Rodeo, provide a unique street-shopping ambience, and a bustling events calendar which includes music concerts and luxury fashion shows. Overall, the Mall of the Emirates serves as a comprehensive lifestyle hub, seamlessly blending shopping, entertainment, dining and luxury.

Source: Shaping the Future of Retail for Consumer Industries, World Economic Forum, 2017

TABLE 3.2.1 Retail strategy in the digital age (adapted from Deloitte 2022).

	Traditional Retailers	**Store of the Future**	**Illustrative Examples**
Segmentation	Adoption of mass, demographic-based segmentation	Use data analytics for micro-segmentation • Provide personalised products/services • Targeted communications	Advanced AI-driven analytics to create consumer micro-segments
Positioning	Compete on price and quality	• Expansion of offerings/services • Connected store environment and leisure provisions • Focus on convenience	Digitally enhanced experiential flagship stores
Operating Formats	Predominantly brick & mortar-led with a catchment-focus	Disruptive and innovative formats aided by digital initiatives to expand reach ('phygital' approach)	BOPIS, 'wait & try'
Business Models	Adoption of single dimensional business models	Disruptive business models using digital enablers	Subscription model, on-demand model, mass-customisation.

3.2.4 THE FRONT END: CUSTOMER-CENTRIC DIGITAL TECHNOLOGIES

Front-end technology in retail serves as a bridge, offering customers an enhanced and personalised physical shopping experience. It is contrasted with back-end technologies which silently streamline operations behind the scenes, often without customer awareness. In physical retail spaces, front-end innovations significantly elevate the digital journey of a customer. This transformation is evident through sophisticated digital merchandising, AI-driven promotional strategies and loyalty programmes. These strategies converge at augmented point-of-sale systems which, when integrated with digital wallets, provide a frictionless customer path to purchase. In major cities around the world, it is evident when visiting most fashion retail stores that in-store technologies play a crucial role in influencing customer interactions (Roggeveen & Sethuraman, 2020). Most contemporary fashion shoppers have become accustomed to tools such as 'magic mirrors' and interactive tablets, which, guide fashion decisions and suggest tailored product recommendations.

The design of a store significantly influences its technological integration. Nike Town London exemplifies this by seamlessly incorporating technology into its retail environment. Features like interactive kiosks and customisation stations enhance the shopping experience, creating a highly engaging, technology-infused atmosphere for customers. The retailer's introduction of B.I.L.L. (Bot Initiated Longevity Lab), an in-store robot-augmented system for cleaning, repairing and customising shoes provides a novel experience that combines the practicality of product maintenance with the excitement of technological interaction. Such services transform a standard shopping experience into a captivating event, promoting a cultural shift towards valuing product longevity over disposability. This approach not only enhances customer engagement but also fosters a more sustainable consumer behaviour.

H&M's 'scan and buy' functionality exemplifies the strategic integration of physical and digital retail channels. Through the H&M app, this feature empowers customers to scan a product's barcode in-store and instantly verify its online availability. Such a strategy expertly addresses potential in-store stock limitations and simultaneously ensures a frictionless shopping journey that leverages both the tactile in-store experience and the expansive online inventory. These examples highlight how retailers are transforming the shopping environment using technology, and as a result, positively influencing the consumer's path to purchase.

FIGURES 3.2.3 and 3.2.4 B.I.L.L. (Bot Initiated Longevity Lab) Nike Town London (image credit: Charlene Gallery, 2022).

Customer experience

AR and retail atmospherics – In the context of customer experience, the tactile interaction offered by physical stores is a crucial element. While AR presents a promising direction for retail innovation, its integration within UK stores has been met with mixed results and remains on the cusp of widespread acceptance (Varley et al., 2019). In contrast, AR's adoption in other global markets signals a more optimistic trend. Notably, in Japan, a pioneer in embracing AR, a significant 66% of shoppers express a preference for AR-enhanced experiences in brick-and-mortar stores, underscoring its successful incorporation into the shopping culture since 2009 (Joshi, 2023). Recognising the increasing demand for tactile experiences, fashion retailers are designing spaces that promote product testing and playful exploration, thereby enhancing customer immersion. With AR, customers encounter dynamic visuals combined with supplemental product details, adding layers of interactivity and depth to their in-store visits. For larger retailers, AR even offers navigational assistance. While AR has great potential to enhance the in-store experience, researchers have emphasised that perceived usefulness plays a significant role in consumer adoption. Simply offering entertainment value is not enough to guarantee consumer intention to use AR. Factors such as availability, accessibility and consumer comfort are essential considerations

FIGURES 3.2.3 and 3.2.4 (Continued)

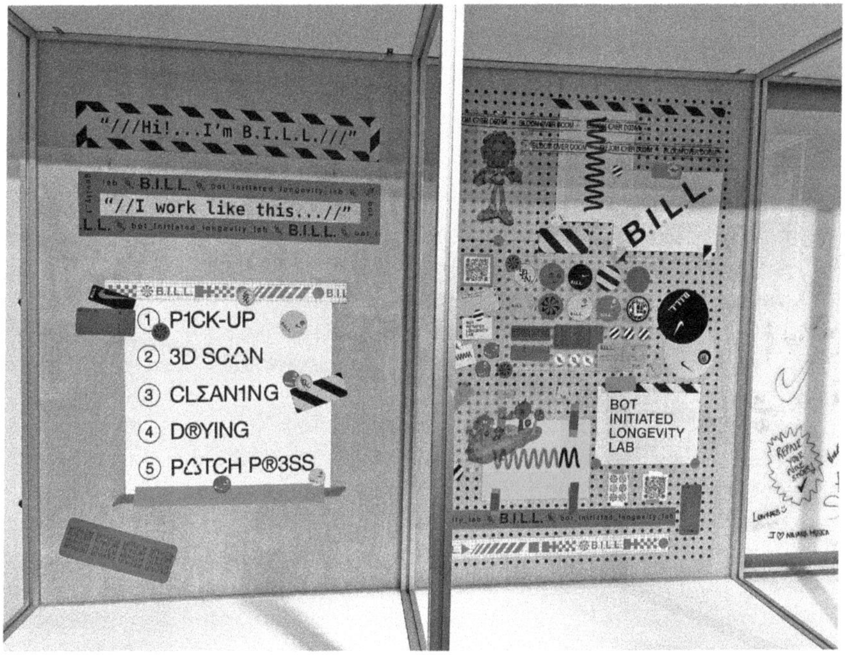

for broader acceptance of AR technology (Li et al., 2022; Boardman et al., 2020). Implementing thoughtful design choices like intuitive user interfaces and aligning with consumer preferences can enhance the overall shopping experience. The combination of technological advancements and tangible experiences suggests a promising future for retail where AR becomes an integral part of the buying journey.

Smart mirrors – A significant innovation in the retail sector is the introduction of smart mirrors. These digital mirrors enhance the fitting room experience by offering personalised interactions while simultaneously collecting valuable data for retailers. By embedded products with RFID tags, these mirrors detect items brought into the fitting room, immediately presenting detailed product information. Smart mirrors can also act as virtual stylists by suggesting complementary products or accessories, enabling customers to visualise complete outfits. If customers wish to try a different size or colourway, a simple touch on the mirror notifies store associates to assist. The smart mirror also lets shoppers build a digital *'wishlist'* for future online shopping or in-store references. When linked to a user's online profile, it can curate personalised recommendations based on previous shopping patterns. However, there are practical concerns to consider, such as the limited availability of smart mirrors, which could lead to a potential in-store bottleneck. A broader perspective suggests that while technologies like magic mirrors might diminish the need for traditional fitting rooms, they cannot replicate the tangible act of trying on an outfit. Thus, the retail landscape finds itself at an intriguing crossroads, where technology and tangibility coexist.

Merchandising

Virtual try-ons (VTOs) – Retailers, including industry leaders like Gucci and Adidas, have incorporated AR and VR into their mobile apps, offering users the ability to virtually 'try on' products. This shift towards a more augmented form of retail is further evidenced by Warby Parker's implementation of face-mapping technology, enabling virtual eyewear try-on. This innovation enhances the user experience and aids informed decision-making. Its popularity is evident in the Middle East, where digital interactions are growing. A 2023 Snap Inc. study indicated that 75% of Middle Eastern users prefer AR for product try-ons, surpassing the global average of 65%. Cultural nuances such as the emphasis on modesty, coupled with regional challenges like high temperatures which deter traditional shopping, contribute to this preference. With advancements in AR, it is anticipated that other regions, such as the UK, will continue to see increased acceptance of these immersive virtual experiences.

Interactive displays and kiosks – i-Kiosks have emerged as essential tools for enhancing in-store shopping. They offer an array of services from accessing product details to streamlining payments and even gathering consumer data. Their adoption is so integrated that many customers now view them as part of their regular shopping journey, rather than a separate digital intervention (Safaryan, 2022). One notable benefit for retailers is the potential for cost reduction. In certain scenarios, these kiosks can replace some of the tasks traditionally done by employees, aiding in overhead cost management. Modern kiosks incorporate advanced blockchain for inventory search. Additionally, the integration of geo-fencing enhances the user experience by providing location-specific offerings and promotions. As retail continues to evolve, the data collection capability of these kiosks will undoubtedly play a crucial role in shaping future in-store experiences.

Loyalty programmes

Personalised experiences – As highlighted in Chapter 3.1, the art of personalisation is essential in cultivating brand loyalty. With the help of technology, retailers are crafting experiences that are not only transactional but emotive and memorable. By leveraging data extracted from a customer's pre-purchase, purchase and post-purchase interactions, they can tailor the in-store interactions to individual preferences, which is a powerful driver for loyalty. For example, when a loyalty program member enters a store, the app might alert the sales staff to this customer's preferred styles or past purchases, enabling them to offer a more tailored service.

Mobile app-based loyalty programmes – Mobile app-based loyalty programs are digital platforms that operate through applications on mobile devices like smartphones and tablets. These programs are designed to reward customers for their repeated business, encourage additional purchases and increase customer engagement. In the context of fashion retail, these programs often offer a variety of benefits to customers, such as points, discounts, exclusive access to sales or new collections and personalised offers.

Beacon technology – Stores can use beacons that connect with the mobile app to send personalised push notifications and offers to customers when they are near or in the store. This could include special discounts on items they have previously shown interest in or reminders about points that are about to expire.

Mobile payments – Loyalty apps can be integrated with mobile payment systems, allowing customers to pay for their purchases via the app. This not only speeds up the checkout process but also ensures that all transactions are recorded for loyalty points.

Blockchain-based loyalty programmes – A blockchain-based loyalty program harnesses the decentralised, secure and transparent nature of blockchain technology to streamline loyalty rewards. Rewards are tokenised as digital assets on the blockchain, with smart contracts automating the distribution and management of these tokens. This approach enhances security, reduces fraud and lowers administrative costs. It also offers customers real-time reward processing and the ability to trade or redeem points across different platforms within the network, improving the overall customer experience. Additionally, the immutable and interoperable characteristics of blockchain ensure that loyalty transactions are tamper-proof and can be integrated with various loyalty schemes, fostering transparency and efficiency in customer rewards programmes.

Pricing and point of sale (POS) systems

Digital in-store technologies significantly influence dynamic pricing strategies by providing real-time data and analytics, which are crucial for making immediate pricing decisions.

Real-time data gathering – Digital technologies such as sensors and smart shelves can track inventory levels, customer foot traffic and buying behaviours in real time. This data allows retailers to adjust prices in real-time, across multiple locations on online touchpoints, to match demand. Digital technologies also enable retailers to monitor competitors' prices in real time and automatically adjust their pricing strategies to stay competitive without engaging in a price war.

Personalised pricing – Retailers can use digital technologies to offer personalised prices and promotions to customers through mobile apps or in-store digital displays based on their shopping habits, loyalty and purchase history.

Demand forecasting – Advanced analytics and AI can predict future demand patterns by analysing vast amounts of data from various sources. Retailers

TABLE 3.2.2 Front end technologies (adapted from Wright et al., 2022).

	Traditional Retailers	**Store of the Future**	**Illustrative Examples**
Customer Experience	Emphasise functionality across touchpoints Focus on the in-store journey	Holistic physical and digital experience across the entire customer journey	Smart mirrors for providing virtual try-on for customers
Merchandising	Focus on customer engagement through: • Visual merchandising • Store layouts	Digital merchandising techniques: • Virtual fitting rooms • Digital kiosks • (AR) • RFID	RFID to provide key product information to enhance the customers purchase decision process
Loyalty Programmes	Focus on: • Traditional loyalty programmes such as physical cards	Shift towards: • Mobile app-based programmes • Virtual Reality tie-ups • Blockchain based loyalty programmes	Blockchain-based loyalty programmes
Pricing and POS Systems	Rely on traditional pricing methods	• Advanced dynamic pricing strategies • Customised engagement and personalised deals for customers	Use of electronic shelf-edge technology

can dynamically adjust prices to anticipate shifts in consumer demand, optimise sales and prevent overstocking.

Instant check-out – Smart mirrors and interactive kiosks are evolving into POS systems by allowing customers to checkout directly via the digital interface, thereby reducing the need for traditional checkout lines. Interactive displays and kiosks also streamline payment processes, offering modern features like contactless payments. In addition, there is a move towards biometric data such as facial and DNA-based recognition which are being trailed in larger retailers. These will be discussed in greater depth in Chapter 3.3.

3.2.5 THE BACK END: DIGITAL-DRIVEN OPERATIONAL EFFICIENCY

There is a collection of back-end technologies critical to retail operations, which, while not apparent to consumers, are indispensable for the integrated online and offline, omnichannel experiences. Given that supply chain management, logistics and demand forecasting are already thoroughly analysed in Chapter 2.4, it would be redundant to discuss them here; rather, this section will divert its attention to in-store inventory tracking systems such as RFID. These technologies streamline operational processes and inventory control, and they open new avenues for ensuring product authenticity and enhancing customer interaction. With blockchain providing a secure and transparent ledger, and RFID offering immediate access to information, both are set to redefine essential operations within the retail industry, leading to improved transparency, security and connectivity.

Shelf monitoring and tracking technology in modern retail – As retailers navigate shifting consumer demands, they are re-evaluating their in-store infrastructure. The aim of contemporary retail is to foster a data-driven, profitable shopping journey that retains the essential touchpoints of face-to-face customer engagements. This balance hinges on merging accurate inventory systems with cutting-edge tracking solutions. To deepen the brand's rapport with customers, investments in digital self-service are vital, while also positioning store associates as expert advisers on products and experiences. Consumers enjoy significant personalisation in online shopping, with website cookies remembering their preferences and purchase history. Brick-and-mortar stores should replicate this level of personalisation, ensuring it does not feel overly invasive to the customer. The synergy between precise inventory systems and unified end-to-end tracking technology is essential. Imagine an in-store shelf, not just any shelf but one that is 'smart'. These shelves integrate an array of proximity sensors, thermal imaging cameras, microphones, RFID tags, NFC, electronically printed labels, LED and IoT sensors. Imagine a shelf that goes beyond traditional standards by incorporating advanced features. Their primary purpose is to constantly monitor inventory levels in real-time. This amalgamation of technologies provides valuable insights into customer buying patterns and essential inventory metrics. For instance, understanding the velocity of product sales – discerning between fast-moving and slow-moving items – becomes easier, and addressing stock-outs becomes more efficient. Companies such as Bossa Nova have utilised image-based analytics to transform inventory management. Using AI and automation, they can provide valuable inventory data, resolving some of the biggest retail challenges for major retailers. Another prominent player in this field is SES-imagotag, a leader in smart digital labels and IoT solutions. With their VUSION Retail IoT technology platform, they have set a new standard by transforming physical stores into real-time connected assets. Through the analysis of images of on-shelf products, these technology providers aim, not only to improve product availability but also to enhance the overall shopping experience.

Part of the inventory tracking ecosystem is RFID, a technology that has gained renewed attention in the retail sector due to the rise of omnichannel

FIGURE 3.2.5 RFID ecosystem and componentry (adapted from Adhi et al., 2021).

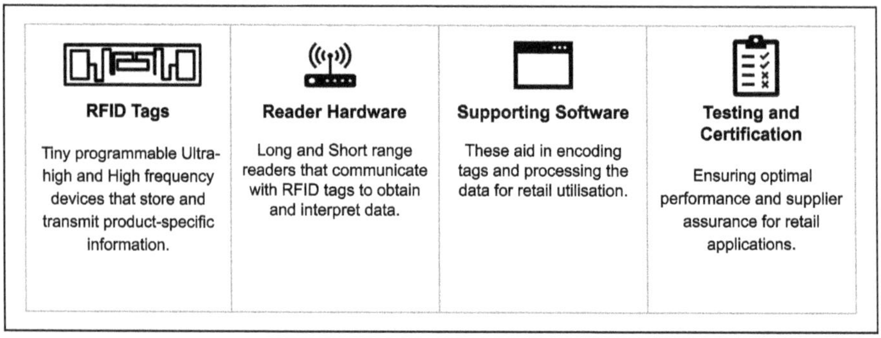

retailing and the need for more accurate and customer-centric shopping experiences. RFID is a technology that uses electromagnetic fields to identify and track tags attached to objects. These tags contain electronically stored information that can be read from up to several meters away, unlike barcode labels which need to be within direct line of sight of the scanner.

The RFID networks consist of several components, including those shown in Figure 3.2.5.

RFID technology has experienced significant advancements over the past decade, including a substantial decrease in costs, making its mass adoption more feasible. This reduction in costs, coupled with improvements in readability and range, has led to tangible benefits for retailers. For instance, improved inventory accuracy, significant reductions in labour hours related to inventory management and a potential increase in revenue. The technology has the potential to advance further. Initiatives like Auburn University's CHain Integration Project (CHIP), demonstrate how RFID is constantly evolving to create a secure framework for sharing data that addresses challenges in the retail industry, such as improving supply chain visibility and damage mitigation.

RFID technology excels in accurately tracking inventory. Retailers vary in their ability to take advantage of RFID technology for inventory management. Vertical integration and selling soft goods, like apparel, make it easier for some retailers to implement RFID tagging upstream. However, multi-brand retailers can also successfully adopt this technology with close collaboration among retail partners and a creative approach. By implementing RFID technology, retailers can improve their inventory management processes and reduce the occurrence of stockouts (Bhattacharya, 2015). Precise product location data not only simplifies inventory management but also enhances customer satisfaction. Consider athletic apparel retailer Lululemon Athletica. Their RFID adoption across their 500 stores resulted in an impressive 98% inventory accuracy (Adhi et al., 2021). Once products are RFID-tagged, the horizon of possibilities expands.

Decathlon, a renowned global sports equipment retailer with 1,600 in over 50 countries, has leveraged RFID tagging on more than 85% of

TABLE 3.2.3 Back end technologies (adapted from Wright et al., 2022).

	Traditional Retailers	Store of the Future	Illustrative Examples
Supply Chain	Linear supply chains	Shift towards a dynamic integrated supply network – digital supply networks	'Always-on' agile supply chain
Logistics & Warehousing	Traditional logistics and warehouse management	Shift to: • Shared logistics capabilities • Digitally enabled logistics services • Continuous automated monitoring	Drone-based deliveries
Finance	Conventional financial reporting and management	Shift towards: • Use of RPA to automate financial functions. • IOT-enabled processes	Crypto currencies such as Bitcoins
Procurement and Vendor Management	Focus on: • Traditional supplier-customer relationships	Shift to: • Collaboration with vendors for success	Blockchain technology for contract management and supplier payments
Assortment-mix & Planning	Decision basis • Experience & Judgement • Ad-hoc assortment prioritisation • Historical baselines	Retailers use: • Data-driven algorithms for store assortment planning • Adopt predictive models and real-time forecasting. • Use dark analytics	RFID chips to make supply chain more responsive

its products, a move that has increased labour productivity and slashed stockouts, boosting revenue by 2.5%. Experimenting with RFID's potential, Decathlon has pioneered RFID-enabled 'scan-and-go' checkout solutions, catering to the modern consumer who values efficiency, frictionless payments and minimal human interaction. While maintaining effective inventory tracking is crucial, RFID's potential in augmenting the customer experience is vast. Fashion brands are increasingly collaborating with third-party e-commerce platforms to enhance the shopping experience and gain valuable insights into consumer behaviour. An example of this is Chanel's partnership with Farfetch, where RFID-enabled fitting rooms create an immersive environment for shoppers. These advanced fitting rooms showcased new styles, provided product information and offered a glimpse into the unique Chanel lifestyle – all within the confines of the room itself. By incorporating RFID technology in their operations, retailers like Chanel can collect data on customer behaviour such as item try-ons and conversion rates for each product. This collaboration not only improves the overall retail experience but also provides actionable insights that can drive business decisions. Additionally, with the rise of e-commerce, the spotlight is on product returns – a vital component of overall customer satisfaction. Considering that nearly one in five online purchases are returned, streamlining the returns process is paramount, particularly as an increasing number of fashion players are collectively shifting towards sustainability. Efficiently reintegrating returned items into available inventory not only conserves margins but also mitigates losses often incurred in the reverse logistics chain.

To fully harness the benefits of RFID systems in retail, collaboration throughout the entire value chain is essential. Retailers need to advocate for widespread adoption, manufacturers must ensure proper source tagging practices are implemented, and integrators play a key role in ensuring seamless system integration. The acronym R-F-I-D sums it up perfectly: **Retailers, Factories, Integrators and Device** providers working in harmony for the greater good of retail.

3.2.6 KEY ENABLERS: THE APPLICATION OF BIG DATA IN FASHION RETAIL: FOSTERING DATA-DRIVEN IN-STORE ENVIRONMENTS

Big data, characterised by high volume, velocity and variety, has become instrumental in the fashion retail industry, underpinning data-centric decision-making processes (McAfee & Brynjolfsson, 2012). It plays a particularly significant role in comprehending customer behaviour, predilections and shopping trends within a physical store environment. Leveraging big data can allow fashion retailers to penetrate the intricacies of customers' desires and expectations, thereby delivering an elevated customer experience and augmenting operational efficacy (Bharadwaj et al., 2013). Big data analytics enable retailers to discern patterns, forecast customer demands and streamline inventory management, ensuring product availability aligns with customer needs (Ransbotham et al., 2015). Furthermore, this quantitative approach permits retailers to customise marketing strategies, promotional activities and product assortments to cater to distinctive customer demographics. Data procurement within the physical retail environment incorporates the use of advanced technologies and tools to gather pertinent information throughout the customer journey. Retailers employ digital touchpoints, encompassing interactive displays, beacons and RFID technology, to monitor customer behaviour, product interactions and time spent within specific store zones (Bharadwaj et al., 2013). Supplementary to this, in-store cameras and heat mapping provide crucial data on customer footfall and preferred shopping zones. Data from these various sources are consolidated and scrutinised using advanced analytics platforms. This integrative process allows retailers to formulate a comprehensive picture of customer behaviour, correlating data from disparate touchpoints to gain profound insights into customer preferences and potential bottlenecks within the shopping experience.

The potency of big data is manifest in its capacity to engender personalisation, creating bespoke experiences tailored to individual customers. With these insights, fashion retailers can offer precise recommendations, targeted promotions and product suggestions that resonate with each customer's unique preferences. Through real-time data utilisation, retailers can engage customers with personalised offerings based on historical purchases, browsing habits and inclinations. This high level of customisation promotes a sense of rapport and involvement, engendering customer fidelity and encouraging repeat patronage (Acharya et al., 2018). Beyond enhancing customer interactions, big data impacts operational efficiency, significantly. Retailers can optimise inventory management, replenishment processes and store layouts predicated on customer demand patterns and product popularity. This data-centric approach ensures product availability aligns with customer needs, reducing stockouts and minimising inventory holding costs (Ransbotham et al., 2015). Harnessing big data within fashion retail's physical environment offers retailers invaluable customer insights and operational efficiencies. By capitalising on big data analytics, fashion retailers can maintain a competitive edge by delivering bespoke customer experiences, optimising in-store operations and staying attuned to ever-shifting customer preferences. As the fashion retail landscape continues to evolve, big data will remain a significant catalyst for innovation and growth within the physical store environment.

3.2.7 THE 'PHYGITAL' EXPERIENCE

In contemporary retail discourse, the term 'phygital', a portmanteau of 'physical' and 'digital', represents the transformative period in the history of fashion retail. Conceptualised as the symbiotic convergence of tactile shopping with the almost limitless scope of the digital domain, it aims to provide a seamless and emotionally resonant consumer experience (Alexander & Cano, 2019). Within this framework, the phygital approach strategically integrates advanced technologies, platforms and **extended realities (XR)** to curate richly immersive experiences. Such an amalgamation has been accelerated by the maturation that most technologies have reached, and, especially within the context of fashion retail, shifts in consumer behaviour (Iannilli & Spagnoli, 2021). Modern consumers are not just passive buyers; shaped by a digital landscape, they are acutely conscious of their influential role in the retail customer journey. In today's consumer landscape, there is a growing shift towards prioritising experiences over material possessions, particularly among price-conscious millennials. According to a survey conducted by PwC, 81% of respondents place equal importance on a brand's experiential offerings as they do on getting value for their money. Furthermore, 42% are willing to pay extra for an enhanced experience (PWC, 2019). Fashion brands acknowledging this shift are recalibrating their retail strategies, ensuring immersive engagement across both the physical and digital domains. The rise of phygital retailing is emblematic of this new consumer mindset (Grewal et al., 2017).

Despite its current prominence, the concept of phygital is not a new phenomenon. Notable scholars, including Dr Wided Batat, have been discussing its intricacies since 2013. However, the significance of phygital has been magnified recently, shaped by increasing environmental concerns and technological integrations. However, phygital is more than a transient response to the changing dynamics of fashion; it signifies a purposeful shift from omnichannel retailing, weaving together the physical and digital to enrich the overall consumer retail experience (Pangarkar et al., 2022).

While both phygital and omnichannel strategies aspire for holistic integrations, their core motivations diverge. The omnichannel approach zeroes in on optimising distribution, which is fundamentally an economic objective. Phygital, on the other hand, casts a broader net, touching multiple areas including communication, branding, advertising, product innovation, pricing and marketing, to provide customers with economic value, along with symbolic and social benefits (Batat, 2022). Phygital aims to deliver enriched consumer experiences that stimulate the senses and reflect cultural and social nuances, while also fostering social interactions. Rather than providing only products, it aims to curate memorable encounters, compelling retailers to infuse value that transcends the convenience of online information and transaction speed to genuinely connect with customers emotionally (Pangarkar et al., 2022).

Phygital retailing curates a journey that fluidly merges digital and physical realms, and connects both tangible (functionality, price, quality) with intangible (symbolic, emotional resonance) aspects of consumer experiences, thereby reshaping established buying patterns. Adapting to the digital era is essential for the retail sector, and embracing a phygital approach has become increasingly important. However, developing an all-encompassing phygital strategy is difficult as it requires a strong emphasis on understanding consumer needs and preferences (Krishnamurthy & Venkitachalam, 2022). Developing effective phygital (physical+digital) experiences demands a nuanced understanding of the allure of physical environments and their digital translation. This process is informed by Holbrook's extensive framework of consumer value, which spans the gamut from extrinsic (economic and social) and intrinsic (hedonistic and altruistic) motivations. Enhancing the physical retail experience involves a variety of experiential values, such as sensory engagement, digital integration, narrative coherence and the creation of captivating experiences. These elements attract customers to physical stores and ensure continuity across various channels. By doing so, retailers can deliver a spectrum of consumer values, from extrinsic factors such as efficiency and status to intrinsic ones like enjoyment and aesthetic pleasure (Rudolph et al., 2023).

However, the retail industry often lacks a structured method for embedding these experiential elements into the store design from the outset. Instead of being an afterthought, creating distinctive in-store experiences should be a priority, integrating considerations like staff interaction, environmental ambience and product curation. The ambition is to surprise and delight customers with elements of novelty and discovery. The store's atmosphere plays a crucial role in this by balancing experiential features with conventional ones, such as store layout and points of sale locations, to meet the desires of consumers who are increasingly seeking holistic, immersive shopping experiences. Understanding and delivering on these immersive elements is key to fulfilling customer expectations in the contemporary retail climate.

In 2022, Wided Batat introduced the phygital customer experience framework (PH-CX), offering a comprehensive tool for strategising the integration of physical and digital customer experiences. This framework is the centrepiece of the paper titled 'What does phygital really mean? A conceptual introduction to the phygital customer experience.' The research illuminates the intricate aspects of the phygital customer experience, encompassing the motivational drivers, the linking elements and the foundational pillars. It is within these details that the PH-CX framework finds its strength, offering a structured approach to blending environments. The model encourages a strategic shift in perspective, acknowledging the dynamic nature of customer value as it transitions between the physical and digital spaces. This shift calls for a more holistic ambition to digital integration than simply achieving positive experiences; it necessitates a deeper dive into the fluid value perception of customers.

Outlined below are the six pillars of the PH-CX framework, which collectively aim to realign business strategies with the evolving landscape of customer interactions:

1. *Practicality* – This pillar emphasises the functional benefits provided to consumers through experiences, aiming to boost usability by combining both digital and physical aspects. For example, in fashion, a shopping app that seamlessly lets users manage orders, process refunds and handle customer service inquiries exemplifies practicality. It merges online and in-store experiences, delivering tangible convenience to the customer.
2. *Sociability* – Sociability is about facilitating social interactions and connections both offline and online, which influence the customer experience. Online socialisation can be enhanced by social media platforms and online brand communities, whereas physical interactions are informed by human customer interactions with brand representatives. In phygital environments, this might manifest as a retailer's fitting room, equipped with virtual mirrors, where users can try outfits, take photographs and share with friends for feedback, prompting social engagement.
3. *Immersivity* – Immersivity is centred on crafting deeply engaging experiences that encompass users within both the digital and physical

dimensions of a brand. As explored earlier, brands are leveraging tools like AR within their apps, allowing consumers to virtually try on outfits. This not only gives them a glimpse of the potential fit and look but also deepens their emotional connection to the brand. Such immersion is not exclusive to digital platforms. In physical stores, captivating designs, interactive displays and engaging in-store events can equally draw consumers into a brand's universe. The overarching aim is to wholly engage customers, fostering a stronger emotional bond to the brand and its products. For instance, a retail app that synchronises online browsing with in-store experiences, offering tailored recommendations and unique deals, can further enhance this immersive journey, merging the digital and physical realms seamlessly.

4. *Technicality* – The technicality pillar underscores the critical role of technology in crafting the customer experience. It's not just about the adoption of technology but the efficiency, reliability and advanced nature of that technology to ensure seamless integration between digital and physical realms. For a genuine 'phygital' experience – a blend of physical and digital – it is essential to weave technology naturally into typically offline interactions. This could manifest as augmented reality in-store displays, NFC-driven product insights, or IoT-fuelled personalised shopping suggestions. Yet, the deployment of such technology should remain intuitive and uncomplicated, prioritising a consistently positive customer experience. It is essential to understand that not all technologies align with every customer demographic. For instance, while facial recognition payments are an integral part of the phygital journey in China, they faced challenges in Europe due to data privacy concerns.
5. *Sensoriality* – The 'sensoriality' pillar highlights the challenge of replicating the multisensory engagement—sight, sound, smell, touch, and taste—found in physical spaces within the digital environment. This is crucial for creating immersive phygital experiences that bridge the gap between the physical and digital domains. Digital platforms primarily rely on visual and auditory stimuli, but the goal for brands is to achieve a consistent sensory resonance across both the physical and digital spaces. For example, the tranquil ambience of a physical store, marked by a soothing aroma, should find its counterpart in a visually calming and harmonious digital interface.
6. *Affectivity* –The final pillar, affectivity, underscores the centrality of emotions in shaping the phygital customer experience. This dimension emphasises the emotional resonance that emerges from interactions in both digital and physical spaces. Brands must ensure the emotions triggered in physical environments, such as joy, surprise, or trust, are also reflected and maintained online. Consistent emotional experiences strengthen brand recall and foster deeper consumer loyalty. As retailers seek to evoke positive emotions across both online and offline touchpoints, they must also recognise the double-edged nature of technology. While technology has the potential to elevate positive emotional responses, it can also inadvertently intensify negative feelings if not implemented thoughtfully.

While the integration of physical and digital elements in the retail space opens new opportunities for immersive consumer experiences, it also poses several challenges. By integrating specific technologies, businesses can gain a more comprehensive view of their customers' needs and craft experiences that resonate on both tangible and intangible levels. The fusion of digital and physical technology provides a powerful avenue to deeply understand and cater to complex consumer needs.

The challenges for integrating the phygital approach within retail have been outlined in Table 3.2.4.

As the concept of phygital experiences grows and continues to develop, businesses must effectively manage these challenges and seize the opportunities they present to deliver real value to consumers in both the digital and physical spaces. As highlighted within this chapter, digital technologies, coupled with a 'phygital' approach opens multiple avenues for retailers to revamp consumer engagement, streamline operations and curate brand experiences that align with the changing landscape of retail. The shift from traditional, purely physical retail to a more integrated mix of digital and physical experiences demonstrates the sector's capacity for innovation. Embracing this shift means that businesses are moving beyond selling products to creating engaging, memorable consumer experiences. For retailers navigating the phygital journey, the focus should be on aligning their strategies with consumer needs, delivering consistent experiences and providing genuine satisfaction at every point of contact.

3.2.8 CASE STUDY: SELFRIDGES: THE PHYGITAL EXPERIENCE

Selfridges & Co., under the strategic vision propelled by Galen Weston's acquisition, has evolved into an illustrious exemplar of how a luxury department store can leverage technology and forward-thinking retail strategies to enhance the customer experience and stay relevant in the rapidly changing world of high-end retail.

In the heart of London, Selfridges' Oxford Street flagship store has undergone a transformative journey, with a £300 million investment that not only redefined its architectural allure but also its technological prowess. One of the crown jewels of this revamp is the 60,000-square-foot accessories hall, which serves as a beacon of interactive retail. With embedded screens and a plethora of digital tools, the space offers customers immersive product discovery journeys. The 4,000-square-foot eyewear department further reinforces this with virtual try-on technology, allowing customers to browse and sample eyewear with the touch of a button.

Selfridges' concession model, a pioneering move in the luxury retail sector, leverages technology to create a harmonious blend of brand autonomy and department store curation. Each luxury brand, from Chanel to Louis Vuitton, benefits from an environment where they can showcase their identity while seamlessly integrating with the Selfridges' digital infrastructure. This grants them the ability to provide real-time stock updates, personalised

TABLE 3.2.4 Challenges and technology solutions within the phygital context (adapted from Batat, 2022).

What	Why	How – tech enabler
Achieving continuity in customer experiences across platforms	To ensure a unified customer journey, it is vital to prioritise seamless transitions between online and offline platforms, address the integration of intuitive experiences that merge digital and physical worlds, and consistently align branding, messaging and experiences across all touchpoints, guaranteeing that consumers consistently encounter a cohesive brand experience irrespective of the channel of engagement.	**Integrated CRM systems**: These systems ensure that all customer interactions, from emails to purchases to support requests, are stored and tracked in one place. This provides a holistic view of the customer, enabling businesses to respond to and anticipate needs more effectively.
Defining the scope of phygital experience	There are problems with defining the beginning and end of the phygital experience, the intensity of the journeys considered and the extent and heterogeneity of the organisational and human resources involved.	**AI and ML**: Advanced algorithms and ML can customise the user experience in real time. AI can analyse a user's behaviour, preferences and past interactions, using this data to offer personalised product recommendations, curated experiences and targeted marketing campaigns, ensuring that customers receive the most relevant information and offerings.
Addressing both tangible and intangible customer needs	Addressing both the tangible and intangible customer needs is a fundamental, yet complex aspect of creating enhanced customer experiences, within physical settings.	**Biometric feedback**: Technologies like facial recognition or even simple camera-based systems can gauge customer reactions in real time as they interact with products or in-store experiences. This can help in understanding both tangible reactions (e.g., picking up a product) and intangible sentiments (e.g., facial expressions indicating delight or dissatisfaction).
Augmenting the sensory and emotional aspects of digital interactions	Phygital retailing should not just be transactional. Establishing an emotional connection, which resonates deeply with consumers, is a crucial challenge.	**Haptic feedback**: Devices equipped with haptic technology can simulate tactile sensations, making digital interactions feel more 'real' and tangible. This can be especially valuable in scenarios where touch plays an essential role, such as experiencing the texture and weight of a product.

customer service through CRM systems and augmented reality experiences that bring their products to life. The Corner Shop at Selfridges epitomises the use of space for innovation. By reclaiming this area, Selfridges created a dynamic platform for limited-time brand activations, which are significantly amplified by digital marketing. From virtual queues for exclusive launches to app-based reservations for special events, technology underpins every element, ensuring a smooth and engaging customer journey.

Catering to a global clientele, Selfridges has incorporated technology that breaks language barriers and provides a comforting shopping experience for international visitors. With multilingual staff supported by translation devices and international payment systems, the store ensures inclusivity and ease of transaction for all its customers. Selfridges' in-store experience is not just about shopping; it's a cultural hub where technology meets art and lifestyle. Interactive installations, like the skate bowl, use technology to engage customers beyond traditional retail boundaries. The store's digital systems facilitate events like gardening workshops or art exhibitions, making cultural relevance a key part of the Selfridges experience.

In alignment with its 'Project Earth' initiative, Selfridges has introduced innovative digital tools to promote sustainability. Features like an online tagging system showcase products made from non-virgin materials, while in-store digital interfaces provide information about the brand's eco-friendly practices and products. Selfridges' use of technology is a strategic endeavour to offer an unparalleled in-store experience. The retailer focuses on creating an engaging, interactive and socially responsible environment where the physical and digital merge. This approach ensures visits to Selfridges are memorable events, integral to the London luxury landscape.

Case questions:

1. How has Selfridges integrated technology within their flagship store to enhance the luxury shopping experience, and what are some specific examples of this integration? Can you map these examples against the PH-CX 6 pillar framework?
2. What strategic advantage does Selfridges gain through its concession model, and how does technology play a role in this approach?
3. In what ways has Selfridges used technology to support its 'Project Earth' initiative, and how does this reflect the store's commitment to sustainability?

Source: Williams, 2023

3.2.9 NAVIGATING THE RETAIL REVOLUTION: AN INTERVIEW WITH ALEX ST. ANGELO

In a period marked by significant retail evolution, Alex St. Angelo, a veteran in the luxury sector, shares her insights into the transformation of retail through technology. With experience at top brands such as Stuart Weitzman, Tapestry

Inc. and Selfridges London, Alex brings valuable expertise to the industry. As a Managing Consultant at MAP Management Academy for Professionals in Reggio Emilia, Italy, Alex has successfully optimised business operations and improved market performance for clients. An expert in phygital retail and customer experience, Alex's remarkable career trajectory showcases her dedication to delivering cutting-edge solutions and driving success in the ever-evolving fashion retail industry.

Interviewer: Alex, your career spans some of the most prestigious brands in luxury retail. How have you seen the industry evolve with technology?

Alex St. Angelo: It's been a remarkable journey. The rise of digital operations has reshaped productivity and brought about a revolution in consumer understanding. For instance, RFID technology has allowed us to track product movement and consumer interactions, leading to smarter merchandising and better inventory management, therefore reducing waste and improving the efficiency of the supply chain. Data has become a cornerstone of strategic decision-making. We're not just collecting it; we're visualising and interpreting it to tailor the retail experience. Data visualisation tools like Tableau have been a revelation in this regard. It allows us to dissect complex consumer data sets and transform them into actionable insights. By understanding purchasing patterns, we've been able to enhance our stock levels, predict trends and ultimately, drive sales with precision previously unattainable. Technology has had a transformative impact on the fashion industry. Retailers have embraced digital innovations to better understand their customers and provide personalised, immersive shopping experiences and the result is a fashion industry that's more connected and faster than ever! As technology continues to advance, I look forward to seeing how it will shape the future of fashion retail.

Interviewer: And since the pandemic, how have consumer lifestyles and retail been affected?

Alex St. Angelo: The pandemic has accelerated a shift towards digital consumerism. Curated apps, like those from Gucci, are now part of the standard toolkit for engaging customers. They offer a blend of shopping, lifestyle and community features that create strong brand relationships. Post-pandemic, consumers expect richer digital experiences. They're looking for engagement that continues beyond the store, which brands are facilitating through enhanced e-commerce platforms and virtual fashion events. Post-pandemic, these digital channels have not receded but have become integral to our operations. Consumers now demand a seamless transition between online and offline experiences – a synergy that we are continually working to perfect.

Interviewer: In this digital age, what role do physical stores play?

Alex St. Angelo: Sure. It's about creating a narrative that customers can step into. Flagship stores are leading this charge. They've become brand cathedrals, places where storytelling and customer engagement are as important as the products themselves. This involves interactive displays and ambient technology that appeal to emotions. The key is personalisation – using technology to understand and cater to individual customer preferences. Real-time feedback and analytics allow for a responsive and dynamic retail environment. And it doesn't end at the store; online platforms need to continue the conversation, offering personalised content and loyalty rewards that keep customers engaged. Retailtainment is the buzzword, where shopping is just one part of a broader, more immersive brand interaction. Today's luxury is no longer defined by lavish displays of wealth. Instead, it focuses on promoting overall well-being and a healthy lifestyle. Brands now prioritise experiences that nurture customers' internal sense of happiness and fulfilment. The new concept of luxury goes beyond material possessions; it emphasises the importance of positive emotional experiences over long-lasting products.

Brands are adapting to changing consumer preferences by utilising micro-influencers and grassroots marketing. Levi's radio show, created as part of their marketing strategy, is an example of this approach, fostering a genuine connection with local communities.

Interviewer: How can retailers craft these immersive experiences effectively?

Alex St. Angelo: The secret is in creating a compelling narrative that customers can partake in. This goes beyond the traditional retail formula; it requires weaving together technology, environment and service to create an unforgettable journey. For example, by utilizing ambient technologies and interactive displays, we can tap into emotions, making the shopping experience both memorable and shareable. Personalisation is also crucial. We employ real-time analytics to tailor the in-store experience to the individual's preferences. And again, it's imperative that this personalisation extends beyond the storefront. Online platforms must continue the dialogue, offering tailored content, recommendations and rewards that align with the customer's in-store interactions.

Interviewer: With the introduction of AI in retail, how are brands leveraging this technology?

Alex St. Angelo: AI has been nothing short of transformative. It's changing the way we engage with customers, predict their preferences, and even the way we design our products. Luxury brands have been at the forefront, creating virtual spaces and personalised shopping experiences that leverage AI's power. Let's take Burberry as an example. They've adopted a 360-degree approach, combining strong digital presence and marketing teams with cutting-edge AI technology. It's incredible what they've achieved, creating virtual worlds, especially in locations such as Korea and China, to offer their customers an extraordinary and captivating luxury experience. Luxury brands such as Gucci are exploring AI's potential beyond gaming, delving into digital experiences like AR and virtual try-on. They've got Avatars and CGI influencers working their magic to engage customers in a cost-effective yet intriguing way. It's such a clever move, allowing them to channel more resources into technology and understand consumer behaviour better.

And keep an eye on Amazon – they've invested heavily in AI and are making big moves in the fashion industry and might just surprise us all as they take on the luxury market!

Interviewer: With increasing use of customer data, how do you maintain trust, particularly with data privacy concerns?

Alex St. Angelo: Trust is the cornerstone of luxury retail. It's imperative for brands to be transparent about their use of customer data and to adhere to stringent privacy standards. Ensuring compliance with global privacy regulations is not just about following the law; it's about respecting the customer. Brands that successfully balance personalisation with privacy will earn lasting customer loyalty.

Interviewer: What is the most important takeaway for retailers today?

Alex St. Angelo: Retailers need to recognise that the future is undeniably phygital. It's about integrating physical locations into the lifestyle of the consumer and ensuring that technology enhances rather than detracts from the human element of retail. Storytelling, personalised experiences and innovative use of technology will delineate the successful brands of the future. It's a period brimming with potential for those willing to embrace change and prioritise their customers.

Alex St. Angelo, 2023
Note: this interview transcript was edited for simplicity.

END-OF-CHAPTER DISCUSSIONS

1. Reflecting on the historical context and recent trends highlighted in this chapter, identify one major challenge and one opportunity for retailers in the current market. Propose a strategy tackles the challenge while capitalising on the opportunity, taking into account both online and in-store environments.
2. Discuss how technology could enhance the in-store experience and consider how retailers can strike a between technological innovation and the traditional tactile experience.
3. Examine the concept of destination stores and discuss their effectiveness in blending experiential retail with state-of-the-art technology. What implications does this have for future retail store designs and consumer expectations?
4. How can digital interventions at different stages of company growth (startup, operational, maturity) serve as a tool for innovation and market adaptation?
5. Reflecting on the integration of RFID technology and big data analytics in modern retail, how do you think these technologies can enhance both the customer experience in a brick-and-mortar fashion retail store?
6. Reflecting on the phygital customer experience framework (PH-CX), which pillar do you think is most challenging for retailers to implement when crafting a phygital experience and why? Discuss how overcoming this challenge could significantly enhance the customer experience.

Bibliography and further reading

Acharya, A., Singh, S. K., Pereira, V. and Singh, P. (2018). 'Big data, knowledge co-creation and decision making in fashion industry', *International Journal of Information Management*, 42, pp. 90–101. doi:10.1016/j.ijinfomgt.2018.06.008.

Adhi, P., Harris, T. and Hough, G. (2021). *RFID renaissance in retail*. McKinsey & Company. Available at: https://www.mckinsey.com/industries/retail/our-insights/rfids-renaissance-in-retail

Alexander, B. and Cano, B. M. (2020). 'Store of the future: Towards a (re)invention and (re)imagination of physical store space in an omnichannel context', *Journal of Retailing and Consumer Services*, 55, p. 101013. doi:10.1016/j.jretconser.2019.101913.

Apparel Resources (2021). 'More store openings than store closures in US in 2021: Report', Apparel Resources. Available at: https://apparelresources.com/business-news/retail/store-openings-store-closures-us-2021-report/.

Axon, S. (2021). *Google is building a new augmented reality device and operating system*. Available at: https://arstechnica.com/gadgets/2021/12/google-is-building-a-new-augmented-reality-device-and-operating-system/.

Batat, W. (2022). 'What does phygital really mean? A conceptual introduction to the phygital customer experience (PH-CX) framework', *Journal of Strategic Marketing*. doi:10.1080/0965254X.2022.2059775

Bertola, P. and Teunissen, J. (2018). 'Fashion 4.0. Innovating fashion industry through digital transformation', *Research Journal of Textile and Apparel*, 22(4), pp. 352–369. doi:10.1108/RJTA-03-2018-0023

Bharadwaj, A., El Sawy, O. A., Pavlou, P. A. and Venkatraman, N. (2013). 'Visions and voices on emerging challenges in digital business strategy', *MIS Quarterly*. 37, pp. 633–661. doi:10.25300/MISQ/2013/37.2.14.

Bhattacharya, M. (2015). 'A conceptual framework of RFID adoption in retail using Rogers stage model', *Business Process Management Journal*, 21, pp. 517–540. doi:10.1108/BPMJ-06-2014-0047.

Boardman, R., Henninger, C. E., Zhu, A. (2020). 'Augmented reality and virtual reality: New drivers for fashion retail?'. In G. Vignali, L. F. Reid, D. Ryding and C. E. Henninger (eds) *Technology-driven sustainability*. Palgrave Macmillan, Cham. doi:10.1007/978-3-030-15483-7_9

BoF (2022). 'Tom & Ruth Chapman – The BoF 500'. Available at: https://www.businessoffashion.com/community/people/tom-ruth-chapman.

Deloitte (2023). *2023 retail industry outlook* . Available at: https://www2.deloitte.com/content/dam/Deloitte/pt/Documents/consumer-business/Retail-Industry-Outlook-2023.pdf (accessed 14 February 2024).

Dubey, R. et al. (2023). 'Dynamic digital capabilities and supply chain resilience: The role of government effectiveness', *International Journal of Production Economics*, 258, p. 108790. doi:10.1016/j.ijpe.2023.108790

Fox, R., Goldrick, M., Green, C. and Rettaliata, A. (2020). *Redefining value and affordability in retail's next normal*. Available at: https://www.mckinsey.com/industries/retail/our-insights/redefining-value-and-affordability-in-retails-next-normal.

Fried, A. (2023). *The next frontier of retail: Contactless kiosks and robots*. Available at: https://www.spiceworks.com/tech/innovation/guest-article/the-next-frontier-of-retail-contactless-kiosks-and-robots/.

Fromm, J. (2022). 'How Gen Z is changing the face of retail sales', *Forbes*. Available at: https://www.forbes.com/sites/jefffromm/2022/07/18/how-gen-z-is-changing-the-face-of-retail-sales/?sh=4544a9bc4317.

Goldman Sachs Intelligence (2016). *Virtual & augmented reality: The next big computing platform*. Available at: https://www.goldmansachs.com/intelligence/pages/virtual-and-augmented-reality-report.html.

Grewal, D., Roggeveen, A. L. and Nordfält, J. (2017). 'The future of retailing', *Journal of Retailing*, 93(1), pp. 1–6. doi:10.1016/j.jretai.2016.12.008.

Henninger, C. E., Niinimäki, K., Blazquez, M. and Jones, C.(2022). *Sustainable fashion management*. Taylor & Francis.

Hollebeek, L. (2011). 'Exploring customer brand engagement: definition and themes', *Journal of Strategic Marketing*, 19(7), pp. 555–573, doi:10.1080/0965254X.2011.599493

Hypebae (2018). *First look at Chanel Game Center in Hong Kong*. Available at: https://hypebae.com/2018/5/chanel-beauty-coco-game-center-hong-kong-pop-up.

Iannilli, M, V. and Spagnoli, A. (2021). *Phygital retailing in fashion. Experiences, opportunities and innovation trajectories*. Available at: https://zmj.unibo.it/article/view/13120

Joshi, S. (2023). '58 augmented reality statistics to unveil AR's growth', G2 Learn Hub. Available at: https://learn.g2.com/augmented-reality-statistics (accessed 14 February 2024).

Kaczorowska-Spychalska, D. (2018). 'Shaping consumer behaviour in fashion industry by the interactive communication forms', *Fibres and Textiles in Eastern Europe*, 26(4), pp. 13–19. doi:10.5604/01.3001.0012.1307

Knitting Industry (2017). *Flat Knitting: Adidas explores localised production with 'Knit for You' pop-up store*. Available: https://www.knittingindustry.com/adidas-explores-localised-production-with-knit-for-you-popup-store/

Kohan, S. E. (2021). 'Customer engagement drives Nike profits up 16%', *Forbes*. Available at: https://www.forbes.com/sites/shelleykohan/2021/12/20/customer-engagement-drives-nike-profits-up-16/?sh=70842b441452

Krishnamurthy, M. S. and Venkitachalam, K. (2022). *The changing face of retailing, 1980–2020*. Available at: https://scite.ai/reports/10.1108/jsma-02-2022-0035

Li, H. C. et al. (2022). *Evaluating the effectiveness of digital content marketing under mixed reality training platform on the online purchase intention*. Available at: https://scite.ai/reports/10.3389/fpsyg.2022.881019

McAfee, A. and Brynjolfsson, E. (2012). 'Big data: The management revolution', *Harvard Business Review*. Available at: https://www.scirp.org/(S(351jmbntvnsjt1aadkozje))/reference/referencespapers.aspx?referenceid=1644568 (accessed 14 February 2024).

McKinsey (2013). *Why retailers must adopt a technology mind-set*. Available at: https://www.mckinsey.com/~/media/McKinsey/dotcom/client_service/BTO/PDF/MOBT32_10-13_NiemeierInterview_R5.ashx

McKinsey (2022). *The tech transformation imperative in retail*. Available at: https://www.mckinsey.com/industries/retail/our-insights/the-tech-transformation-imperative-in-retail

Milanesi, M., Guercini, S. and Runfola, A. (2023). 'Let's play! Gamification as a marketing tool to deliver a digital luxury experience', *Electron Commer Res*, 23, pp. 2135–2152. doi:10.1007/s10660-021-09529-1

PwC (2018). *Customer experience is everything*: Available at: https://www.pwc.com/us/en/services/consulting/library/consumer-intelligence-series/future-of-customer-experience.html

Pangarkar, A., Arora, V. and Shukla, Y. (2022). 'Exploring phygital omnichannel luxury retailing for immersive customer experience: The role of rapport and social engagement', *Journal of Retailing and Consumer Services*, 68, p. 103001. doi:10.1016/j.jretconser.2022.103001

Park, H. and Lim, E. R. (2023). 'Fashion and the metaverse: Clarifying the domain and establishing a research agenda', *Journal of Retailing and Consumer Services*, 74, p. 103413. doi:10.1016/j.jretconser.2023.103413

Polner, A. et al. (2022). 'Automation with intelligence', *Deloitte Insights*. Available at: https://www2.deloitte.com/uk/en/insights/focus/technology-and-the-future-of-work/intelligent-automation-2022-survey-results.html (accessed 16 February 2024).

Pursuitist (n. d.). *Fendi fun pop-up store at Harrods*. Available at: https://pursuitist.com/fendi-fun-pop-up-store-at-harrods/.

Ransbotham, S., Kiron, D. and Prentice, P. (2015). 'Minding the analytics gap', *MIT Sloan Management Review*, 56, pp. 63–68.

Ratchford, B., Soysal, G., Zentner, A. and Gauri, D. K. (2022). 'Online and offline retailing: What we know and directions for future research', *Journal of Retailing*, 98 (1), pp. 152–177. doi:10.1016/j.jretai.2022.02.007

Reinartz, W., Wiegand, N. and Imschloss, M. (2019). 'The impact of digital transformation on the retailing value chain', *International Journal of Research in Marketing*, 36(3), pp. 350–366. doi:10.1016/j.ijresmar.2018.12.002

Roggeveen, A. L. and Sethuraman, R. (2020). 'Customer-interfacing retail technologies in 2020 & beyond: An integrative framework and research directions', *Journal of Retailing*, 96(3), 299–309. doi:10.1016/j.jretai.2020.08.001

Rudolph, L., Suter, B. M. and Barakat, R. S. (2023). *The emergence of a new business approach in the fashion and apparel industry: The ethical retailer*. Available at: https://scite.ai/reports/10.1177/02761467231180456

Safaryan, B. (2022). 'Self-ordering kiosks are grocers' Trojan horse', *Forbes*. Available at: https://www.forbes.com/sites/forbestechcouncil/2022/03/31/self-ordering-kiosks-are-grocers-trojan-horse/

Salpini, C. (2021). 'Adidas aims for DTC to be 50% of sales by 2025', Retail Dive. Available at: https://www.retaildive.com/news/adidas-aims-for-dtc-to-be-50-of-sales-by-2025/596509/.

Sayem, M. S. A. (2023). *Digital fashion innovations: Advances in design, simulation, and industry*. Taylor & Francis. doi:10.1201/9781003264958

Servais, E., Quartier, K. and Vanrie, J. (2022). '"Experiential retail environments" in the fashion sector', The Journal of Design, Creative Process & the Fashion Industry, 14(3), pp. 449–468. doi:10.1080/17569370.2022.2124639

Slack, F. and Rowley, J. (2002). *Online kiosks: the alternative to mobile technologies for mobile users*. Available at: https://scite.ai/reports/10.1108/10662240210430928

Teece, D. J. (2010). 'Business models, business strategy and innovation', *Long Range Planning*, 43(12–13), pp. 172–194.doi:10.1016/j.lrp.2009.07.003.

Van Kerrebroeck, H., Brengman, M. and Willems, K. (2017). 'When brands come to life: Experimental research on the vividness effect of Virtual Reality in transformational marketing communications', *Virtual Reality*, 21. doi:10.1007/s10055-017-0306-3

Varley, R., Roncha, A., Radclyffe-Thomas, N. and Gee, L. (2018). *Fashion management: A strategic approach*. Bloomsbury Publishing.

Vogue Business (n.d.). *Virtual stores: Fashion's new mode of shopping*. Available at: https://www.voguebusiness.com/technology/virtual-stores-fashions-new-mode-of-shopping

Wang, Y., Bell, D. R. and Padmanabhan, V. (2009). 'Manufacturer-owned retail stores', *Marketing Letters*, 20(2), pp. 107–124. doi:10.1007/s11002-008-9054-1

Williams, R. (2023). 'Case study: Can Selfridges future-proof the department store?', *The Business of Fashion.* Available at: https://www.businessoffashion.com/case-studies/luxury/can-selfridges-future-proof-the-department-store-download-the-case-study/ (accessed 16 February 2024).

World Economic Forum (2017). *Shaping the Future of Retail for Consumer Industries.* Available at: https://www3.weforum.org/docs/IP/2016/CO/WEF_AM17_FutureofRetailInsightReport.pdf (accessed 13 February 2024).

Wu, H. (2022). *Enhancements of sustainable plastics manufacturing through the proposed technologies of materials recycling and collection.* Available at: https://scite.ai/reports/10.1016/j.susmat.2021.e00376

CHAPTER 3.3

Retail innovation 2

The future of online selling

Charlene Gallery

The past two decades have witnessed notable advancements, particularly regarding the widespread adoption of the Internet and its associated tools and functionalities. The ubiquity of internet access has levelled the online retail playing field, making it easy for retailers to sell services and products without geographic limitations. Online shopping, webrooming, digital payment systems and mobile commerce have become commonplace, while new innovations continue to disrupt the retail status quo. Anticipated technological progressions in retail suggest that we will witness further developments encompassing artificial intelligence (AI), machine learning (ML), and extended reality (XR), . We can already observe glimpses of this impending technological landscape and how it has the potential to revolutionise online retailing. This chapter will examine the adoption of new-gen technologies and tools within the online retailing landscape. The chapter will the potential of 3D product visualisation, highlighting how AI and AR are opening opportunities for new retail approaches which leverage virtual fashion, from 360-degree digital product development to livestreaming and gamified experiences.

LEARNING OUTCOMES

After reading this chapter, you should be able to:

- Evaluate the role of emerging technologies like ML and XR in transforming the consumer shopping experience.
- Recognise the significance of virtual fashion elements, including 360-degree product views, 3D virtual catwalks and livestreaming, in the digital marketplace.
- Evaluate the integration of gamification in retail strategies and its effectiveness in enhancing consumer interaction and loyalty.
- Understand the role of AI within the context of fashion retail and co-creation.

DOI: 10.4324/9781003364559-12

3.3.1 ONLINE VISUAL MERCHANDISING

E-commerce within the fashion industry has witnessed a remarkable transformation, particularly in 2021 when its global sales surged by 44%, hitting a milestone of $4.9 trillion. This boom, largely accelerated by the COVID-19 pandemic, is expected to maintain momentum, with projections showing a potential increase of an additional 50% in the coming four years. In response, brands are rapidly embracing cutting-edge digital technologies like XR and AI, which are crucial in this paradigm shift, revolutionising consumer online shopping behaviours (PwC, 2020). The early model of e-commerce, characterised by a simple dictum: 'browse, click, purchase', has evolved. Online touchpoints are no longer peripheral but now fundamental to the modern retail ecosystem. A testament to this shift is the surge in social media-based purchases, which have increased by 68% post-pandemic (Dixon, 2023), and a growing consumer inclination towards mobile shopping. Recognising this, brands are advancing their strategies with mobile-centric shopping via apps and presence on third-party online marketplaces.

Chapter 3.1 explored the digital ecosystem's expansion and its influence on consumer behaviour, underscoring the demand for real-time, personalised interactions across brand touchpoints. Alongside this, there is a heightened expectation for comprehensive and detailed product information, aiding consumers in making risk-averse decisions regarding their online fashion purchases. In the preceding chapter discussion, we highlighted the sustained relevance of physical stores and emphasised their new, more experiential role within the customer journey. As explained, these stores now function as interlinking connections in a vast digital ecosystem. Whilst that discussion was primarily centred on how technology is transforming the physical store, the focus of this chapter will be to explore how online touchpoints can be optimised to enhance customer engagement, reflecting on how they can synergise with in-store experience to form a cohesive brand narrative.

By 2027, fashion e-commerce is poised to hit the $1.2 trillion USD mark (Statista, 2023a). As this sector grows, the presentation of products online becomes increasingly significant. Online visual merchandising is the art of organising digital content to captivate shoppers and drive sales, emulating the in-store browsing experience through strategic product placement, search result organisation and intelligent recommendations. This digital rendition of merchandising aims to create a virtual shopping experience that feels tangible.

Visuals are paramount in online shopping. Consumers retain information more effectively through images than text, prompting online visual merchandising to prioritise high-quality visuals and interactive 3D product views. The design and usability of e-commerce platforms play a crucial role in influencing consumer satisfaction and buying patterns. Accessible and intuitive website design is essential, as cumbersome navigation can disrupt the shopping experience and impact sales negatively. Effective product discovery is a cornerstone of online merchandising, as frustration with finding products can result in lost revenue (Ratchford et al., 2022). Retailers must therefore meticulously curate their e-commerce sites, synchronising hundreds of product categories with real-time inventory and sales data to facilitate seamless product discovery. Integrated product discovery tools have become a staple, enabling efficient navigation and personalising the shopping experience to meet consumer expectations.

3.3.2 ONLINE USER EXPERIENCE (UX)

The online visual merchandising interface is crucial in shaping the customer experience, applying user interface (UI) principles to enable impactful interactions between the brand and its consumers. With the absence of physical touchpoints, the digital interface is tasked with delivering a seamless and fulfilling experience across various platforms. User experience (UX) is central to this, influencing the customer's emotional and behavioural response to the digital platform and, by extension, their perception of the brand and its offerings.

A strategic approach to augmenting this experience can draw from Rayport and Jaworski's Seven Cs of customer interface framework, established in 2001, which outlines essential elements for effective website design. Each element is instrumental in creating a user interface that transcends mere transactions to provide an enriching experience. While the framework underscores the importance of coherence and a customer-focused design, modern fashion websites must further leverage advanced digital technologies. This integration results in e-commerce platforms that are not only engaging and intuitive but also deeply immersive.

TABLE 3.3.1 Seven Cs of customer interface framework.

Seven Cs	Traditional Website Design	Website Augmented by Advanced Technologies
Context *Refers to the layout and design of a website*	The layout's architecture and performance, including navigation and page responsiveness, are optimised for ease of use. Aesthetics align with the brand's identity and marketing, enhancing product presentation through thoughtful placement of visuals and promotional material.	Fashion websites can use virtual reality (VR) and augmented reality (AR) to create an immersive context that goes beyond traditional web design. For instance, AR can allow customers to visualise products in a real-world environment, while VR can transport them to virtual showrooms.
Content *Targets the intellect and emotions of consumers*	Homepages feature clear, actionable content, and products are showcased through high-quality imagery and descriptions, capturing details and functionalities that are crucial to informed decision-making. Continual content refreshes keep the platform engaging and relevant.	Leveraging high-quality multimedia content, such as 3D images and videos, can make the exploration of fashion items more engaging. Fashion shows can be livestreamed, and products can be showcased in 360-degree views to provide an in-depth look.

TABLE 3.3.1 (Continued)

Seven Cs	Traditional Website Design	Website Augmented by Advanced Technologies
Community *Encourages user-to-user interaction and collective identity*	By blending interactive forums and chat functions with customer reviews and blogs, a space for both dynamic and static community engagement is crafted. Social media integrations bolster this sense of community, leveraging user-generated content to build brand authenticity and trust.	By integrating social media platforms, fashion websites can foster a community where customers share their styles and experiences. Features like virtual try-ons can be shared to social networks, encouraging user interaction and feedback.
Customisation *Enhances user engagement through personalised site experiences*	Options like account customisation and language preferences cater to individual needs, while maintaining ease of navigation with recognisable elements like the shopping cart feature.	AI-driven personalisation engines can tailor the shopping experience to individual preferences. ML algorithms can analyse browsing patterns and purchase history to suggest personalised fashion recommendations.
Communication *Enables company to consumer dialogues*	The site must offer consistent, branded communication through social media and newsletters while maintaining clear pathways for customer inquiries and feedback, fostering trust through transparency and privacy respect.	Chatbots and virtual assistants powered by AI can provide instant communication channels. These tools can offer styling advice, answer customer service inquiries, and provide personalised shopping assistance.
Connections *Refers to the network of links between sites*	Efficient internal navigation and thoughtful integration of external content provide a seamless and expansive online experience. This fosters reliable consumer connections and supports broader information access.	Fashion websites can connect users with stylists or designers for consultations via live video calls. Also, by linking to related lifestyle content, blogs and partner sites, they can create a network that offers added value to the customer.

(Continued)

TABLE 3.3.1 (Continued)

Seven Cs	Traditional Website Design	Website Augmented by Advanced Technologies
Commerce *Capability of the website to enable transactions*	This involves secure payment gateways, privacy assurances, transparent cost disclosures and streamlined requests for customer information. The rise of platforms like Shopify facilitates these operations, allowing for the creation of engaging and efficient e-commerce experiences.	Integrating advanced secure payment options, such as cryptocurrency or one-click purchasing, can streamline the commerce aspect. Fashion websites can use AI to predict stock levels and manage a dynamic pricing model that reflects real-time demand.

Mini reader task: Analysis of a fashion website

Using the Seven Cs framework, analyse a fashion retailer's website, focusing on design and functionality. Critically evaluate how the elements of Context, Content, Community, Customisation, Communication, Connections and Commerce are applied within the site and consider if they enhance or detract from the consumer experience. Your analysis should be detailed, leading to a report that rates each category and suggests practical improvements. Your final report should reflect the crucial role these elements play in enhancing the effectiveness of an online fashion retail space.

3.3.3 3D PRODUCT VISUALISATION

In the formative days of computing, human-computer interactions were predominantly governed by text commands. The transition to graphical user interfaces signalled an era of two-dimensional (2D) engagement, fundamentally altering our interface with technology (Dix, 2009). However, the limitations of the 2D product visualisation have meant customer expectations of product fabric, colour and texture, along with issues around clothing fit have proved difficult to resolve. Online apparel sales experience extremely high return rates with bracketing, where customers purchase different sizes and colours of an item to try on, a common practice. Presently, the digital landscape is undergoing a transformative shift towards integrated three-dimensional (3D) technologies, poised to redefine our digital interactions. This technological evolution presents significant implications for the entire fashion value chain. As explored in Chapter 1.2, 3D technologies promise enhanced collaboration between designers and manufacturers, paving the way for more agile and accurate prototype assessments. Within online retailing, the potential for creative 3D explorations is magnified, coupled with a promise of augmented digital consumer journeys that elevate satisfaction and increase sales volume. Strategies to help customers develop a comprehensive understanding of the product before purchase are now commonplace. Fast fashion retailer ASOS was one of the first online retailers to use catwalk videos to offer customers a comprehensive look at its products, and many apparel retailers offer this feature along with other features such as additional fit information, the ability to input consumer body measurements to get sizing recommendations, customer sizing reviews, using models with varied body types, and closeup shots of fabric to show texture and pattern. ASOS, along with other innovative retailers also uses 360-degree product views to give consumers an even more detailed understanding of how the product fits and moves on the body.

As Henninger et al. (2022) elucidated, the emergence of 'web atmospherics' through image interactive technology (IIT) offers an emulation of tactile, visual and auditory sensations, paralleling the experience of physical shopping. Traditional static 3D garment representations online are being superseded by dynamic, real-time digital interactions. The introduction of 360-degree 3D technology is emblematic of this change, providing consumers with an all-encompassing, interactive product viewing experience that mirrors the tangibility of brick-and-mortar shopping. Burberry, a fashion industry leader in digital innovation, has integrated advanced 3D visualisation technology into its online platforms. This technology provides consumers with detailed insights into various product attributes and greatly reduces uncertainties associated with online shopping, such as concerns about material quality and size. In addition to the visualisations, Burberry offers high-resolution images and videos that showcase their products in different settings and lighting conditions. The result is an interactive and engaging online shopping experience that sets a high standard for the industry. On the technological front, companies like Cappasity and Threekit are pioneering the development of 3D product visualisation software. Their software solutions allow businesses to create, embed and share 3D visualisations of their products on their websites. Such tools promise to enhance customer engagement, improve conversion metrics and reduce product returns.

However, integrating 360-degree 3D technology into e-commerce platforms presents challenges as this technology requires a high level of graphical rendering which, in turn, demands robust and high-speed internet connectivity. In addition, the process of creating 3D models for each product can be time-consuming and expensive, particularly for businesses with an expansive and ever-changing product range. It is also essential to have expertise in 3D modelling and rendering, which might necessitate additional staff training or the hiring of new personnel. To mitigate these challenges, companies may need to upgrade their website infrastructure to accommodate the increased data load brought about by 3D visualisations, which may entail additional costs, and, of course, all these efforts can be undone at the point of access if the customer's device is not sufficiently powerful to display all the features of the site, or if their internet connection is patchy or low speed.

Taking all this into account, the potential benefits of 360-degree 3D product visualisation in enhancing customer experience and driving online sales are substantial. This technology can play a critical role in the future of e-commerce, making it an important area for further research and technological advancement. As internet connectivity continues to improve globally, and 3D modelling software becomes increasingly user-friendly and cost-effective, more companies will likely adopt this technology, contributing to the digital transformation of the retail industry.

Understanding and improving the customer journey is central to effective online visual merchandising. One way retailers are doing this is through visual eye-tracking technologies. ASOS, a fast-fashion retailer, leverages eye-tracking technology to understand how customers navigate their online store, tracking the movement of the user's eyes as they browse the site. This data is then used to make informed decisions about the design and content placement, with the goal of creating an intuitive and pleasurable shopping experience for the customer. A comprehensive study by Boardman and McCormick (2021) examined the interactions between consumers and online fashion retail websites. Recognising clothing as experiential, the research emphasised the inherent complexities of representing physical attributes, such as fit and quality, online. To counter this, the researchers recommend the deployment of eye-tracking technology as a valuable tool to gain deeper insights into consumer behaviour online.

Diverging from conventional studies reliant on static imagery or manipulated platforms, the researchers advocated the authenticity of real-time consumer interaction analysis. Their proposed methodological approach incorporated the Stimulus-Organism-Response model (Mehrabian & Russel, 1974), with a focus on determining which design elements captivate consumers, how these elements influence cognitive and emotional engagement and the overarching sentiments that affect their online shopping experience.

The study presented in Table 3.3.2 reveals key insights, which have now been extended to encompass actionable strategies for retailers. These strategies are aimed at developing more immersive online experiences that align with current consumer behaviour and preferences.

Boardman and McCormick's research indicates that immersive online product experiences are leading to more intricate customer decision-making processes. This is exemplified by fashion industry leaders like ASOS and Zara, who employ AI and eye-tracking technologies to enhance website navigation. With online shopping evolving as a leisure activity, the imperative for retailers to innovate their digital platforms intensifies. Companies already leveraging digital tools are utilising the rich data from consumer interactions to offer personalised product recommendations, enhancing the customer's unique journey. This evolution in digital commerce signifies a transformation in consumer shopping behaviours and the strategies employed for product promotion and marketing. It also underscores a broader shift towards deepening digital connections, prioritising customer satisfaction and cultivating trust between consumers and retailers.

TABLE 3.3.2 Eye-tracking application to fashion websites.

Eye-Tracking Determinants	Research Insights	Application to Fashion Websites
Viewing Patterns	Users do not always follow the traditional F-shaped or Z-shaped viewing patterns. Website designs need to accommodate diverse consumer attention paths influenced by different design stimuli and individual objectives.	Fashion websites can employ responsive designs that are visually dynamic and engaging. They can use eye-catching elements like videos or interactive content to guide the user's gaze across the page in a way that naturally leads to important information or products.
'Experience' vs 'Search' Products	Decision-making complexities are amplified on websites selling 'experience' products, with consumers devoting more attention to attributes like trend images, sizes and colours.	For fashion items, which are often 'experience' products, websites should showcase high-resolution images, videos and interactive 360-degree views that allow customers to appreciate the textures, styles and colours. Enhanced zoom features and virtual try-on capabilities can give customers a better sense of the products, akin to an in-store experience.
Customisation	Customisation plays a significant role in enhancing consumer satisfaction and simplifying the shopping process, with personalised product recommendations and filtering systems being key tools for achieving this.	To address the desire for customisation, fashion websites can implement smart recommendation engines that adjust to user preferences over time. Features such as AI-driven style quizzes or integration with social media profiles can enable personalised storefronts for users, showing them products that align with their style and previous shopping patterns.
Relevance of Webpages	In contrast to popular beliefs, product listings and information pages hold greater importance than homepages for retailers, highlighting the need for dedicated attention towards them.	Since product listings and detailed information pages are critical, these should be meticulously designed with user-friendly navigation and filters. Websites should prioritise quick load times, clear categorisation and effective search functionality to enhance the ease of finding products.
Concise Consumer Information	Contemporary shoppers prefer concise and practical product information over lengthy textual descriptions, indicating a change in consumer preferences regarding their information needs.	Product information should be clear and succinct, with bullet points highlighting key features. Incorporating user-generated content, such as reviews and ratings with visual elements (photos from customers), can provide practical information and build trust. Additionally, integrating AR to see products in different scenarios can help consumers make informed decisions without the need for lengthy descriptions.

3.3.4 IMMERSIVE ONLINE ENGAGEMENT: LIVESTREAMING AND GAMIFICATION

Whilst the above discussion just outlined effective website design and visual merchandising, the truth is, online fashion retail, for all its convenience and reach, often falls into a pattern of uniformity, with many sites adhering to a standard template of design and presentation. This tendency towards a 'cookie-cutter' approach results in static and uninspiring product displays that lack the engagement of their physical counterparts. Physical stores, in contrast, entice the senses and offer an immediacy and tangibility that online platforms struggle to replicate. As already established, while advancements in 360-degree visuals offer a glimmer of innovation, the overall landscape of online shopping remains largely undifferentiated. This highlights a critical gap between the experiential richness of in-store shopping and the often flat, monolithic user interfaces that characterise digital storefronts. As we seek to bridge this divide, it is essential to examine how online retailers can evoke unique, immersive experiences that are synonymous with physical retail spaces, thereby transforming the online shopping journey into something more captivating and personal.

As consumers continue to adopt new technologies, the imperative to create immersive, sensorial-rich experiences is more pronounced than ever. The notion of 'digital synesthesia' extends beyond aesthetics, suggesting an 'internet of the senses', where fashion becomes a multi-dimensional, tactile experience. As we transition from the metaverse's potential discussed in Chapter 3.1 to the tangible strategies of today's online retail, it is essential to confront the chasm between virtual spaces and proven e-commerce practices (Magnani, 2022). The metaverse, with its immersive environments and interactive experiences, hints at a future of limitless customer engagement. However, despite the excitement it generates, its current contribution to the commercial success of fashion retail remains unproven. The industry awaits concrete evidence of the metaverse's ability to not only captivate but also convert users into customers, suggesting that while the concept is ripe with opportunity, it demands a cautious and measured approach for integration into the established retail ecosystem.

However, two current strategies stand out: livestreaming and gamification. These 'tools' have quickly established themselves as strategic imperatives by transforming the solitary act of scrolling through images into an interactive event, where customers become active participants in a dynamic virtual space. In this next section, we will explore how livestreaming and gamification are essential in designing online retail spaces that are not just seen or clicked through, but rather felt and experienced.

Livestreaming

In China, the 11.11 Global Shopping Festival, hosted by Alibaba, saw participation from over 200 luxury brands, such as Gucci and Maison Margiela. These brands collaborated with Tmall Luxury Pavilion, offering services usually exclusive to physical outlets, including consultations and after-sale services. Mainstream retailers and social media platforms are also establishing collaborations with livestream shopping platforms and influencers. Research by Coresight Research (2023) projected the livestreaming market to touch $6 billion, with an expected growth of nearly fourfold in the subsequent two years. As mobile shopping engagement intensifies, livestreaming evolved into a 'shopatainment' medium, blending entertainment and commerce.

The blend of live events and real-time sales, known as *live commerce* is revolutionising brand-consumer interactions. Social commerce sales, as a result, are forecasted to increase to $600bn by 2027 (McKinsey, 2021a). Popularised in China, live commerce gained significant momentum in Western markets in 2022, generating a $500bn market (Statista, 2023b). Livestream selling signifies a notable shift in e-commerce, marrying real-time purchasing with interactive experiences. Traced back to 2016, Alibaba's Taobao Live event was a landmark, integrating live broadcasts with e-commerce functionalities. This approach witnessed substantial traction during events like China's Singles' Day sales. Luxury division chief and head of Tmall Luxury Pavilion Janet Wang said, 'Consumers no longer think in terms of a break between physical and digital. They want a consistent, unified experience from brands, whether they are shopping online or offline' (Chou, 2023).

Emerging technologies like **livestreaming product recognition (LPR)** leverage ML for real-time product recommendations during livestreams. Despite its potential, challenges in product differentiation persist. For brands exploring live commerce, critical factors include product lifecycle considerations, understanding target demographics, and choosing appropriate formats. Future technologies, such as AR and VR, are poised to further innovate the area of live commerce, introducing immersive virtual interactions and product trials. While Western retailers remain, broadly speaking, in the embryonic stages of live commerce adoption compared to their Chinese counterparts, early entrants such as Tommy Hilfiger have seen substantial gains within this evolving channel. The rise of livestream shopping, particularly within the fashion sector, also underscores an evolutionary shift in the digital commerce arena.

Live commerce merges real-time interactions and online shopping, creating a unique e-commerce experience. Below is an integrated overview of its distinct attributes:

- **Interactive dynamics**: Live commerce transcends the static nature of traditional e-commerce by fostering dynamic interactions. With features like chat and instant feedback, it crafts a more connected and engaging brand-customer relationship.
- **Efficient and instant conversion**: Marked by its ability to catalyse immediate purchasing actions, live commerce uses real-time offers to instigate a sense of urgency, achieving conversion rates that overshadow those of standard online shopping.
- **Expansive demographics and reach**: Initially popular among younger users (Gen Z and millennials), live commerce now appeals to a broader age range. By 2020, it engaged about 265 million users, or nearly 30% of China's internet users.
- **Enhanced brand differentiation and appeal**: Beyond selling, live commerce helps brands stand out. By presenting engaging and enjoyable content, they not only retain existing customers but also attracting digital-native consumers.

- **Enhanced engagement & purchase intention**: The interactivity of live commerce, with its direct dialogue between hosts and audience, heightens customer involvement and intent to purchase.
- **Increased levels of trust**: Navigating the online trust deficit, live commerce uses real-time demonstrations and Q&A sessions to forge credibility with consumers.
- **Social connectivity:** Live platforms support chat features, allowing viewers to communicate with the presenter and amongst themselves. Positive feedback from peers can influence buying decisions.
- **Influence of parasocial interaction (PSI)**: In live commerce, viewers often feel connected to hosts or influencers. This connection can affect how they view products and boost their desire to buy.
- **Sensory experience**: Unlike traditional online shopping, livestreams provide a more sensory experience. With live product demos and audio descriptions, viewers a afforded a more comprehensive understanding of products before purchasing.

Within the concept of livestream shopping, cultural variations play a key role, shaped by entrenched socio-cultural values, consumer patterns and acceptance of technology. The Chinese market offers an instructive example: livestream shopping is built on the foundation of a robust social commerce framework, a society deeply integrated with media entertainment and a high degree of confidence in influencers, or key opinion leaders (KOLs). This success is facilitated by a digital infrastructure, supported by WeChat and Alibaba, that adeptly integrates social networking, entertainment and commercial activities into a cohesive user experience.

On the contrary, Western consumer behaviours, influenced by a different set of historical, cultural and technological determinants, might not be as receptive. The Western audience, traditionally reliant on individualistic shopping experiences and brand-established trust, might approach livestream shopping with a different set of expectations and scepticism. Consequently, understanding these cultural differences is critical for global retailers attempting to implement livestream shopping strategies across diverse markets.

Gamification

The global gaming industry, now worth nearly $200 billion and hosting a burgeoning gamer base, offers a unique duality for fashion brands: a profitable marketing channel and a connection to a tech-savvy youth demographic (Schedey et al,. 2023). The gamer count, as reported by NewZoo (2023), has surged to 3.4 billion, with Asia-Pacific commanding over half of this market. The Boston Retail Partners (2023) indicate that 87% of retailers are poised to leverage gamification within five years, suggesting a pivotal shift in customer experience strategies.

Prominent fashion houses are pioneering this blend of fashion and gaming. Louis Vuitton, Balenciaga and Gucci have ventured into 'Advergames' and Metaverse engagements, marrying traditional luxury with digital innovation. Burberry's 'Burberry B Bounce' and the Tencent-powered 'Burberry

Pocket' are strategic forays into this space, extending their brand experience into the virtual environment (Lau & Chung-Wha, 2021).

Lau & Chung-Wha (2021) observed that gamified VR apps address consumer needs for competence and autonomy, which translates into tangible marketing success. Burberry's mobile game and virtual platforms, Louis Vuitton's 'League of Legends' collaboration yielding both physical and virtual collections, and Taobao Life's 3D shopping universe that converts purchases into points for avatar customisation are all testaments to this effective approach. Physical retail is also ripe for gamification's touch. Nike's 'Reactland' and Fendi's arcade-style pop-ups in Harrods, as well as Chanel's 'Coco Game Centre' in Hong Kong, underscore the potential of in-store gamified experiences to enhance customer engagement (Hypebae, 2018).

Psychologically, gamification resonates due to innate human desires for achievement and reward. Gamification increases consumer engagement by 30% (Gigya). AliExpress exemplifies this with its 'Coins & Coupons' feature, encouraging daily engagement and rewarding users with discounts.

Fashion gamification is propelled by several psychological drivers:

- **Challenge**: Consumers are motivated by tasks and achievements (Deterding et al., 2011 and supported by the success of platforms like the 'Gucci Arcade' app.
- **Progress**: Visible progress enhances user satisfaction, an approach employed by 'Nike+ Run Club' and 'Adidas Running' apps.
- **Competition**: Competitive elements can increase user engagement, seen in Adidas's Metaverse challenges.
- **Socialisation**: Fetais et al (2022) emphasise social connections for loyalty and activity, leveraged by Burberry's and Gucci's virtual platforms.
- **Rewards**: Tangible rewards boost repeated interactions and brand loyalty.

However, the ethical considerations of gamification must be addressed. The risk of inducing impulsive and potentially addictive behaviours, especially in younger consumers, cannot be ignored. Brands need to ensure ethical application, prioritising consumer well-being and transparency (Mandarić et al., 2022)

Mini case study

In 2021, Gucci launched an innovative experience on Roblox, a platform once known for its young audience, now evolving into a major metaverse player. In this virtual Gucci Garden, users explore rooms that celebrate various Gucci campaigns, with the unique twist of having their avatars start as blank mannequins. These avatars then pick up elements from each room they visit, whether it's patterns from the Tokyo Tribe maze or flowers from the central garden room, resulting in a personalised digital transformation by the experience's end.

Roblox, a platform that lets users create and participate in virtual experiences, underlines its adaptability by randomizing the experience, so each user's outcome is distinct. The experience culminates with users observing their avatar's transformation, a concept aiming to match the immersive nature of physical world interactions. This Gucci venture on Roblox not only highlights the platform's capabilities but also signals the game's increasing role in digital fashion retail and user engagement.

Source: McDowell, 2021

3.3.5 EXTENDING THE REALITY OF COMMERCE IN FASHION

The integration of AI, AR and VR is transforming e-commerce by enhancing how customers engage with products. AI utilises vast customer data to tailor personalised shopping experiences, contributing to sales growth – McKinsey cites an increase of 6–10% in this context (Chui et al., 2022). Beyond AI, AR and VR are expanding the possibilities for customer interaction; AR allows users to visualise products in their own space, while VR creates fully immersive environments for deeper engagement.

The AR market, particularly within the fashion industry, is forecasted to grow, with expectations to reach over $1 trillion by 2030 (Grand View Research, 2023). This growth is supported by technologies like WebXR and 5G, revolutionizing retail with more immersive experiences, especially in tech-forward regions like Asia-Pacific. PwC's analysis suggests that AR and VR could contribute £1.5 trillion to the global economy by 2030, signifying their expanding influence in retail. However, while the benefits of these technologies for personalisation and interactivity are clear, adoption rates in the fashion industry vary. Large brands may integrate these technologies with relative ease, but smaller players face hurdles such as financial limitations and a lack of tech expertise.

The industry's heterogeneous nature also means that while some are quick to innovate, others remain reticent, either due to scepticism or a lack of resources. The push factors, however, include heightened customer expectations and the pull of increased sales. The result is a landscape of uneven technological integration, with adoption shaped by individual brand capacities and market demands.

To further understand the spectrum of immersive technologies:

Virtual Reality (VR) – Offers users fully immersive digital environments, facilitated by devices such as head-mounted displays.

Augmented Reality (AR)– Integrates virtual elements into our tangible environment, enhancing real-world scenarios.

Mixed Reality (MR) – A confluence of the real and virtual, enabling interactions with both dimensions simultaneously

Extended Reality (XR)– An overarching term that includes AR, VR and MR, functioning in real-time.

Incorporating AI, AR, VR and related technologies presents the potential for transformative customer experiences and optimised operational workflows. However, this integration necessitates a comprehensive strategy that encompasses every aspect of the business, from product development to retail experiences (McKinsey, 2022). Given the multifaceted and dynamic nature of the fashion industry, it is crucial to approach this evolution with careful deliberation, prioritising investments in versatile technologies that can adapt and scale according to business fluctuations.

The outline below highlights a range of AR and VR applications within e-commerce.

Augmented reality (AR)

According to recent statistics, 71% of shoppers show a preference for AR-enabled shopping experiences. With this number it mind, it is clear that what was once regarded as an ancillary feature, is now very much an essential part of the omnichannel experience. Unlike Virtual Reality, AR integrates digital elements into the real-world view, enhancing consumer interaction through data-rich overlays like product details, reviews and virtual navigation aids (Sayem, 2023).

A 2016 Goldman Sachs forecast predicted that by 2025, 32 million consumers would adopt AR and VR. This estimation, however, was surpassed earlier than anticipated, with 100 million engaging in AR shopping by 2020, and over 170 million users of VR by 2023. The proliferation of AR is significantly attributed to the accessibility spearheaded by tech giants Google and Apple, with their platforms ARCore and ARKit. As a result, over a billion users engage with a multitude of AR apps daily (Alsop, 2022. Echoing Tim Cook's words, AR is swiftly becoming an integral part of daily engagements. As AR evolves into a mainstream tool, fashion retailers must adapt.

One persistent challenge in online shopping is its limited sensory engagement compared to its in-store counterpart. Traditional e-commerce platforms cannot fully replicate the tactile feel of materials or the physical trial aspect of products. AR bridges the sensory gap, providing immersive experiences that mirror the in-store environment. It offers virtual try-ons (VTO), giving customers a realistic preview of how clothes will look and fit, which improves purchase confidence and may reduce return rates. For instance, Charlotte Tilbury's virtual makeup platform not only elevates the consumer sense of immersion, typically attributed to trying on cosmetics in-store, but also resonates with modern hygiene concerns. Similarly, GAP's 'Dressing Room App' demonstrate how AR can blend the appeal of in-store shopping with online convenience.

Even in physical locations, AR adds value. For example, Lily, a Chinese womenswear brand, installed VTO-enabled smart mirrors in a Shanghai metro station, allowing commuters to try on clothes virtually and purchase with a QR code scan, illustrating AR's potential to turn any space into an interactive shopping venue, thus turning the ordinary, into the extraordinary. The practical applications of AR extend to furniture shopping as well, where consumers can visualise products like sofas in their own homes before buying. Similarly, a dress may be captivating on a mannequin, but how does it fit and drape on an actual body? VTO answers these questions, fostering trust and, in the process, cultivating brand loyalty. In an era where returns can significantly impact profitability, facilitating well-informed purchases through VTO becomes invaluable. It enhances buyer assurance, streamlining choices and potentially diminishing product return rates.

Research indicates that AR's incorporation in fashion retail supports consumers' cognitive functions as it enhances attention to detail, boosts memory retention concerning product features, and positively influences purchasing decisions, by reducing the perceived risk typically associated with online retailing (Henninger et al., 2022). Consequently, incorporating AR into online retail can reshape the mobile shopping experience and enhance consumer perceptions by granting them an in-depth appreciation of both product characteristics and brand values.

Several AR applications have been developed to cater to different needs:

TABLE 3.3.3 Types of AR applications, challenges and use cases.

AR application	**What**	**Challenge**	**Use Case**
Marker-Based AR	Involves identifying a specific marker and overlaying a 3D version of the relevant object, allowing users to view it from different perspectives.	Achieving perfect photorealistic images of products is difficult and discrepancies between the physical and digital representations can lead to customer dissatisfaction. AR relies heavily on the device's camera and processing capabilities, however, given that not all consumers possess cutting-edge devices, this could constrain the effectiveness of AR solutions as a mass market strategy.	In fashion, Virtual Try-Ons (VTOs) are a popular application of augmented reality, with leading retailers such as Zara launching apps that allow customers to see how clothes will look on them, thus clarifying some of the uncertainties of shopping online.

TABLE 3.3.3 (Continued)

AR application	What	Challenge	Use Case
Markerless AR	In this method, users have the freedom to place a virtual object anywhere in their environment and adjust its position as they wish.	User-friendliness is crucial in markerless AR. Should an AR application lack intuitiveness, it risks being abandoned by consumers. Inefficient interfaces or convoluted systems can also discourage user engagement.	The 'IKEA Place' app, released in 2017, revolutionised furniture shopping by enabling customers to see how products would look and fit in their own space before buying, thereby reducing the guesswork often involved in online shopping.
Location-Based AR	Leveraging geographic data, this AR displays digital content at specific real-world locations.	Location-based AR needs precise geographic data to correctly overlay digital content onto actual places. When GPS signals are weak or wrong, especially in cities or inside buildings, AR content might not show up in the right spot, which can spoil the experience for the user.	In 2017, Gucci introduced 'Gucci Places' in their mobile app, an AR feature that let users virtually visit real-world spots tied to the brand's heritage. Through this app, users could interact with location-specific digital content on their smartphones (Zargani, 2017).
Projection-Based AR	Projects artificial light onto real-world surfaces, creating interactive holograms or projections.	Projection-based AR can produce impressive visuals, but it may not be as interactive as other types of AR. The experience can be optimal only from certain angles or distances. For example, at a fashion show, someone standing outside the designated viewing area might see a distorted hologram. Also, this AR method lacks the tangible depth of other AR types, since viewers can't physically interact with the projections.	At the 2022 New York Fashion Week, designer Maisie Wilen presented the Autumn/Winter collection using impressive seven-foot holograms. This was achieved with Yahoo's cutting-edge volumetric video technology, which used 106 cameras to capture models in 6K resolution from all angles. The fashion show was available for real-time viewing on mobile devices.

Virtual reality (VR)

VR is a computer-generated simulation that enables users to interact with realistic or imaginative three-dimensional environments in real time. This transformative technology has had a significant impact on the fashion retail industry, revolutionising traditional shopping methods. By offering immersive experiences and replicating lifelike virtual environments, VR allows users to engage with digital surroundings that closely resemble real-life settings. According to Kim & Ha (2021), the immersive environment of VR creates an enhanced sense of presence, which amplifies consumers' engagement levels in fashion retail settings, potentially leading to higher purchase intentions, however, VR experiences can alter consumers' time perception, making them feel like they've spent less time shopping, which can be advantageous for retailers looking to retain consumers' attention. To fully immerse themselves in these virtual worlds, users require specialised equipment such as headsets designed to track their movements and heighten their sense of immersion. Within the fashion retail environment, immersive technologies like VR are employed for various applications including virtual try-on experiences, virtual showrooms, fashion shows and the assistance of virtual shopping advisors. VR's ability to simulate real-world experiences, such as virtually trying on outfits, can significantly reduce purchase uncertainties, leading to decreased product returns and increased consumer satisfaction (Zhang et al,. 2019).

There are two main categories of VR systems: immersive and non-immersive.

- *Immersive systems*, such as the Oculus Rift and HTC Vive, offer a highly realistic experience that requires powerful processors and accurate tracking.
- *Non-immersive systems* are less demanding in terms of resources and are predominantly accessed via high-resolution monitors, providing a somewhat limited virtual experience.

Virtual commerce (v-commerce) uses VR and AR for e-commerce. Unlike e-commerce, v-commerce mimics real-life store experiences using XR tech, needing both a strong internet connection and VR goggles. While e-commerce began as online transactions, v-commerce takes it a step further. Early examples include Amazon's virtual commerce ventures and platforms like 'Second Life' that offer complete 3D virtual environments. Now, many games incorporate virtual transactions, making them v-commerce components. VR in commerce, via VR glasses or smartphones, immerses users in virtual stores and tests new e-commerce features. Companies like Amazon have ventured into v-commerce, with features like 'virtual fitting rooms' using AR mirrors. Marketplaces like Etsy and Alibaba use VR and AR to enhance the shopping experience, while brands like L'Oreal and IKEA allow virtual product tests. Tommy Hilfiger even integrated VR shopping experiences in their stores, offering customers 360-degree catwalk show

FIGURE 3.3.1 Benefits of AR.

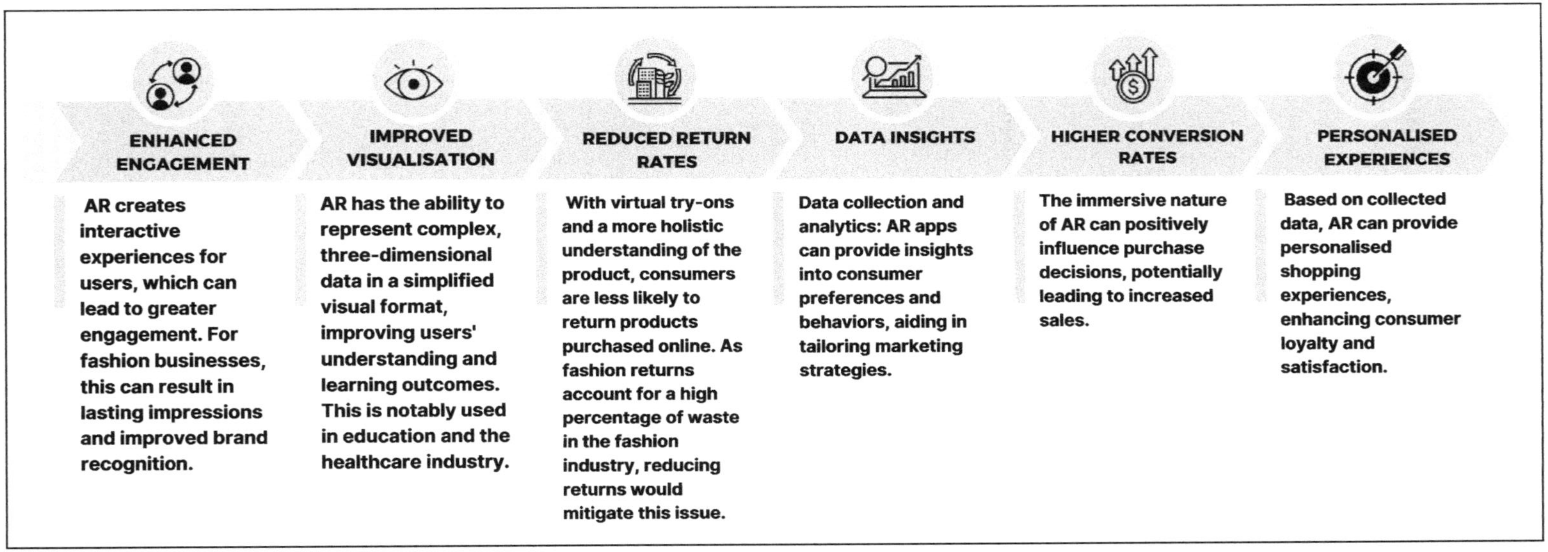

ENHANCED ENGAGEMENT
AR creates interactive experiences for users, which can lead to greater engagement. For fashion businesses, this can result in lasting impressions and improved brand recognition.
IMPROVED VISUALISATION
AR has the ability to represent complex, three-dimensional data in a simplified visual format, improving users' understanding and learning outcomes. This is notably used in education and the healthcare industry.
REDUCED RETURN RATES
With virtual try-ons and a more holistic understanding of the product, consumers are less likely to return products purchased online. As fashion returns account for a high percentage of waste in the fashion industry, reducing returns would mitigate this issue.
DATA INSIGHTS
Data collection and analytics: AR apps can provide insights into consumer preferences and behaviors, aiding in tailoring marketing strategies.
HIGHER CONVERSION RATES
The immersive nature of AR can positively influence purchase decisions, potentially leading to increased sales.
PERSONALISED EXPERIENCES
Based on collected data, AR can provide personalised shopping experiences, enhancing consumer loyalty and satisfaction.

views via VR headsets. Google and Apple, among others, lead in using AR and VR for v-commerce, evident in 360-degree video ads on YouTube.

3.3.6 CASE STUDY: BRANDLAB360 – REVOLUTIONISING RETAIL THROUGH IMMERSIVE VIRTUAL REALITY

Consumer preferences are shifting and expectations are growing. To stay ahead, brands must adapt swiftly to the ever-changing market landscape. As digital products in fashion become commonplace, it necessitates the transformation of their presentation and interaction with a progressively broader audience. Immersive technologies are enabling brands and retailers to reach wider audiences by creating experiences that are not available in the physical world. Blending digital with physical enables businesses to offer the enhanced and engaging shopping experiences consumers want.

The rise of immersive retail signifies a profound shift in the industry. A pioneer in this field is BrandLab360. Their innovative web-based platform can transform any website into a 3D virtual experience, without the need for apps, downloads or VR headsets.

Consumers want more and retailers must react

Shoppers are demanding ever-more sophisticated online interactions from brands. The modern consumer has high expectations. They want to connect with their favourite brands through personalised experiences that not only engage and entertain them, but make them feel part of the brand. These expectations extend far beyond personalisation; consumer experience is everything. Retailers must look past traditional methods of attracting and engaging customers and deliver experiential shopping experiences through immersive technologies. The internet has evolved from offering passive experiences to social interactions and companies like BrandLab360 are now leading the way for the next wave of the internet. Their 3D virtual experiences and stores provide enriched experiences to exceed consumer demands.

BrandLab360 – disruptors of the e-commerce landscape

BrandLab360 has emerged as a world leader in 3D virtual experiences. Their platform enables brands, retailers and wholesalers to create web-based, real-time, interactive virtual spaces. By using 3D photo-realism and 360 virtual environments, brands can create an exact replica of their flagship store, without any restrictions on square footage. This process isn't limited to replication: brands can also engage their creativity to design unique, one-of-a-kind experiences that are not bound by physical constraints. By immersing customers in lifelike 3D environments, BrandLab360 can recreate physical experiences online. Customers can virtually explore products, interact with items and make informed purchase decisions in a unique, gamified and immersive way.

BrandLab360 stands out through its world-leading capabilities. The platform allows users to have complete freedom of movement and seamlessly navigate the virtual space as naturally as they would in their physical

FIGURE 3.3.2 BrandLab360 virtual retail space (image credit: BrandLab360).

surroundings. This elevates the experience for consumers by allowing them to interact more freely with products and experiences, while also offering retailers significant opportunities. The modular functionality allows for instant visual merchandising and assortment building with any virtual element moveable.

This 3D technology, with its ability to create realistic and engaging shopping experiences, allows consumers to visualise products more accurately, leading to confident purchasing decisions. This technology fosters customisation and personalisation of products, with real-time interaction enabling adjustments to size, colour and design. 3D technology also extends its benefits to the supply chain and logistics processes, reducing the need for physical prototypes and aiding in more precise forecasting and demand planning.

BrandLab360 delivers an end-to-end experience for brands and retailers, encompassing all content and transaction capabilities within the environment which creates new sources of consumer insights. Unlike other platforms, customers can make purchases directly within the experience. Live information on product ranges, from stock levels to pricing, and sizing is displayed. This seamless integration ensures an immersive brand experience, leading to increased user engagement and higher conversion rates.

By creating real-world experiences online, brands and retailers can capture enhanced real-time data on user behaviour, not available in physical spaces, stores, or traditional websites. Leveraging these powerful insights enables businesses to make data-driven decisions, inform future trends, optimise product offerings and tailor marketing strategies in real time.

BrandLab360's impact on retail

BrandLab360's pioneering approach to immersive virtual spaces has not only transformed the way brands engage with their audience but also set new industry standards in enhancing customer experiences.

FIGURE 3.3.3 A virtual reality street scene (image credit: BrandLab360).

Mundi Westport, a leading accessory manufacturer and distributor partnered with BrandLab360 to revolutionise their wholesale appointments by creating a world-class immersive wholesale trade and B2B platform. The virtual showroom, along with features like efficient visual assortment creation using full 360 models, not only led to significant cost savings by downsizing the physical showroom but also upheld the brand's essence. This shift resulted in an increase in wholesale orders, improved appointment accuracy, efficient client engagement and fortified brand relationships, ultimately boosting sales and streamlining the wholesale process.

Connectivity is at the heart of BrandLab360's virtual spaces, allowing users to connect with others via integrated voice or video calls. These connections extend beyond mere transactions, fostering a sense of community and shared experiences. Whether it's consumers enjoying virtual shopping with friends, customers seeking guidance from sales assistants, or wholesale sellers engaging in virtual meetings with prospective buyers, these spaces transcend the conventional online shopping experience. They promote not only product discovery but also the development of meaningful connections and a vibrant sense of community.

This element of connectivity can be seen in BrandLab360's creation for Too Faced, 'Maison TooFaced', a transformative virtual retail experience. It seamlessly merges shopping and social interaction, providing solo or group shopping through live appointments, along with virtual consultations and masterclasses for brand engagement. This innovative approach reinvigorated Too Faced's e-commerce strategies, eliminated physical constraints and enhanced the customer experience. Results included increased customer engagement, heightened product launch awareness and a rise in average order value, with #MaisonTooFaced garnering over 100,000 TikTok views, demonstrating the success of this immersive retail experience.

FIGURE 3.3.4 Website browser-based augmented reality for Too Faced Cosmetics (image credit: BrandLab360).

FIGURE 3.3.5 Website browser-based virtual retail space for Mundi Westport (image credit: BrandLab360).

The future of 3D technology and virtual stores

The traditional e-commerce interface has seen minimal evolution with most e-commerce websites adopting a uniform product database format. In contrast, virtual stores provide an online shopping experience that is immersive, visually appealing, personalised and discovery-driven.

FIGURE 3.3.6 Website browser-based virtual retail experience for Too Faced 'Maison Too Faced' with live chat (image credit: BrandLab360).

A common misconception is that digital innovation in retail signals the decline of brick-and-mortar stores. However, 3D technology is poised to bridge the gap between e-commerce and physical retail, integrating physical spaces into the future shopping landscape. BrandLab360's platform's aim is not to replace what we do in real life but to enhance what we do online. While e-commerce brought convenience and efficiency, it also took away the immersive experience of shopping in-store. Utilising BrandLab360's virtual platform enables a unique avenue for brand storytelling, enhancing customer interactions. These visually rich environments are brimming with interactive features and clickable elements to maximise engagement and create memorable encounters. Virtual stores offer the perfect blend of convenience and connectivity. In a rapidly evolving market, BrandLab360 is leading the way in redefining retail with immersive technology. As consumer preferences shift towards interactive, personalised and seamless interactions, the demand for innovative retail experiences is stronger than ever.

Retailers must adapt quickly to meet these evolving consumer desires. BrandLab360's platform, with its unique features and commitment to immersive experiences, offers a transformative solution for brands in the digital landscape. The success of these innovations showcases the path the world is moving towards, aligning with changing consumer preferences and the need for swift adaptation by retailers. In this dynamic landscape, BrandLab360 is at the forefront, offering the key to meeting consumer demands and driving the future of retail.

Q&A with Dan O'Connell, BrandLab360 Co-Founder

Q. What drove the inception of BrandLab360, and what was the vision that shaped it?

Dan O'Connell: BrandLab360 was founded in 2016 with my co-founder Jen Drury and originated from our experiences working in the fashion industry. I had prior experience as a brand owner, while Jen was a buyer. We noticed a gap in the market for a digital tool that could streamline the process of brands selling to retailers. Our initial goal was to establish a B2B platform where small brands could connect with small retailers. Many of these businesses primarily operated through trade shows, and we wanted to provide an alternative for those who couldn't attend in person. This formed the foundation of our 2D concept.

The shift into virtual 3D spaces was driven by fashion buyers using our platform and wanting to replicate 'assortment building'. In real-life, buyers select garments from a showroom with numerous options, even though they may only purchase a portion of them. They physically arrange these garments on racks to visualise how they'd fit in their stores.

We wanted to transition this experience online and developed a gamification platform to make this possible. Our vision was straightforward: facilitate the connection between fashion buyers and sellers online, making it an immersive experience. 3D web was our answer.

Q. How does BrandLab360's technology marry the physical and digital aspects of retail?

Dan O'Connell: Our technology excels by seamlessly merging physical and digital retail environments. We have the capability to generate photorealistic digital replicas of existing stores, offering users access to them online. Unlike traditional approaches, our web-based experiences eliminate barriers such as device limitations and graphics card requirements. In the past, virtual stores often had to compromise on realism and adopt a more gamified, cartoonish appearance. However, BrandLab360 was the first to achieve near-CGI quality photorealism in real-time within a web browser.

Another significant aspect of merging the physical and digital is the ability for people to communicate and collaborate within these experiences. This feature is crucial because while a 3D virtual experience can be impressive, it falls short if it's a solitary endeavour. By combining photorealistic graphics with real-time collaboration within a web browser, we're recreating in-person experiences, online which improves the overall online shopping experience.

Q. Can you share some notable responses of brands to your technology and its impact on their e-commerce capabilities?

Dan O'Connell: Our technology has been embraced by some of the world's leading global brands, including renowned names like Warner Brothers and Harley-Davidson. Many brands have ventured into 3D web environments to future-proof themselves digitally and demonstrate their commitment to innovation, not only from a business perspective but also for PR purposes. Surprisingly, some of them didn't anticipate the tangible commercial benefits they would reap. These benefits include a significant increase in basket sizes. For instance, when a consumer completes a game and earns a discount code, they are a staggering 75 times more likely to redeem that discount, as it feels like a reward they've earned.

Q. What challenges do you encounter in creating photorealistic 3D renders of stores, and how do you overcome them?

Dan O'Connell: While many CGI artists and companies could create photorealistic 3D models or digital twins, the primary obstacles were file sizes and rendering in real-time within a web browser. In films, photorealistic graphics are typically pre-rendered into videos, whereas we needed to render them in real time on the web. We've invested heavily in complex backend engineering and server architecture, along with our proprietary platform. This enables us to optimise and render high-quality, high-poly and large file-sized 3D models in a web browser at impressive speeds.

For perspective, a standard digital twin of a small store in CGI could take up to two and a half hours to load in a web browser, solely for the experience itself, not even considering interactivity. In contrast, we've achieved digital twins of entire streets with loading times as short as five seconds.

Q. How does BrandLab360 see itself shaping the future of retail and e-commerce?

Dan O'Connell: At BrandLab360, we firmly believe that people are inherently wired to interact with each other and form connections. Throughout history, people engaged in commerce by gathering at markets to trade with one another. However, the advent of the internet dramatically transformed our business practices, including shopping. Traditional online shopping, with an individual sitting alone in front of a computer screen, lacks the interpersonal aspect of commerce. Regardless of how immersive online product displays become, they cannot replicate the natural human inclination to conduct business together or shop together. That's where our technology comes into play. Our platform is driving the future of retail as it brings people together online and in 3D. People have the convenience of digital but can interact much like they would in their physical surroundings.

Q. What were some key technological advancements that played a crucial role in BrandLab360's development and success?

Dan O'Connell: Our complex networking and cloud infrastructure have been instrumental in enabling the rapid rendering of high-definition, high-poly and large files within a web browser. This infrastructure ensures that our digital assets are efficiently optimised and delivered to users. Unlike most high-end games that require incredibly powerful graphics cards or specialised devices, we're bringing this level of technology to a wider audience.

Our team is made up of industry-leading experts and their expertise extends throughout our platform's codebase and asset publication. It's the quality of our artistry combined with the sophistication of our cloud streaming platform that has propelled us forward technologically.

Q. How does BrandLab360 plan to further enhance customer retention and community building in the future?

Dan O'Connell: At the heart of our approach is our focus on fostering a strong sense of community. We've seen by offering the necessary technology, users will naturally form dynamic communities within our platform. Our dedication is to establish an atmosphere where users can effortlessly connect, cooperate and interact, fostering a feeling of belonging and shared moments.

Q. How does your technology contribute to more sustainable business practices, and what steps are you taking to further improve this aspect?

Dan O'Connell: Manufacturers and product designers can use our 3D technology to work together in real-time, within a web environment and manipulate 3D products collaboratively. This eliminates the need for cumbersome email exchanges or the sharing of large files.

We are currently involved in substantial projects with some of the world's largest luxury and fast fashion manufacturers. Designers, buyers and other stakeholders can meet in real-time, removing the necessity for travel and enhancing quality assurance. The technology's capacity for traceability and waste reduction is a pivotal aspect of its sustainability contribution.

Q. Could you elaborate on how 3D technology has revolutionised the 'try before you buy' concept in retail?

Dan O'Connell: When shoppers engage with 3D-rendered products, they gain a comprehensive view of the item from all angles. Combining this with our digital store environment, gives consumers a sense of the product's size that closely simulates the experience of physically entering a store.

3D technology has the potential to decrease returns significantly. As 3D technology becomes more integrated into the retail landscape, the impact will continue to increase. Customers can make more informed purchasing decisions, aligning their expectations with the actual product they receive.

Q. How has 3D technology impacted the supply chain and logistics processes in retail?

Dan O'Connell: By seamlessly integrating with digital product passports, smart contract traceability and sustainability initiatives, our technology permeates the entire value chain and operational lifecycle of businesses. Our platform makes processes more efficient which translates to substantial cost savings in the manufacturing phase.

Dan O'Connell, 2023

Discussion questions

1. How has the shift toward immersive virtual retail experiences addressed the changing expectations of modern consumers?
2. In what ways does BrandLab360's technology bridge the gap between physical and digital retail, and what potential benefits does it offer to brands and retailers?
3. What role does connectivity play in the success of immersive virtual spaces, as exemplified by BrandLab360, and how does it impact the overall online shopping experience?
4. How can 3D technology revolutionise the concept of 'try before you buy' in retail, and what implications does this have for reducing returns and enhancing customer satisfaction?
5. In what manner does 3D technology impact supply chain and logistics processes in the retail industry, and how can it contribute to sustainability initiatives and cost savings?

3.3.7 AI IN ONLINE RETAILING

AI has disrupted multiple industries, with fashion being a notable beneficiary. At its core, AI seeks to replicate human intelligence in machines. This involves not just mimicking human behaviours, but also complex cognitive functions like learning, reasoning and problem-solving. Within AI, there a number of intrinsic aspects, two of which are **machine learning (ML)** and **deep learning**. ML empowers machines to learn from vast datasets without being explicitly programmed for a specific task. It utilises algorithms that assess data, discern patterns and consequently make informed decisions. Deep learning, a more advanced facet of ML, employs multi-layered (hence 'deep') neural networks, modelling its approach on the human brain's functionalities, and allowing it to 'learn' from large amounts of data. While a neural network with a single layer can make approximate predictions, additional hidden layers can help to refine and perfect those predictions. The intersection of AI with fashion primarily capitalises on the rising consumer demand for personalisation. AI-driven predictive technologies, through algorithms, use past behaviours and trend analysis to predict potential future actions. As Kumar et al., (2019) highlighted, this can lead to more intuitive user online interfaces, personalised advertisements and even virtual dressing rooms that suggest outfits in real time.

The impact of AI-driven tools on the fashion industry is becoming increasingly evident. Notably, McKinsey (2023) reported a compelling conversion rate of 70% from AI-generated product suggestions. Highlighting an upward trajectory, The Insight Partners (2019) valued the global AI in fashion market at approximately 357 million USD in 2019, with a projection to reach 4.4 billion by 2027. This indicated a substantial CAGR of 37%. While recent data specific to the fashion sector remains limited, the broader AI market's valuation in 2023 approaches a significant 100 billion USD (Thormundsson, 2023). Given this context, the valuation of the AI-driven fashion segment appears modest in comparison. This underlines the potential of Al when integrated into omnichannel touchpoints.

Yet, a significant challenge in integrating AI with human interactions is understanding the nuance of human language and emotion compared to the systematic, code-driven machine language. Humans communicate through words, emotions and expressions filled with depth and subtleties. In contrast, machines operate on codes, starting from basic binary sequences and evolving into complex programming languages. For AI to effectively serve sectors like fashion, it's imperative to bridge this divide. It must adeptly interpret human emotions and requirements and convert them into actionable data (Luce, 2019). While humans learn through experiences, sensations and emotional responses, machines primarily rely on data, pattern identification and algorithmic adjustments. The promise of AI within fashion lies in its potential to transform human-centric experiences into data-driven strategies, enhancing the user's interaction with technology. The fashion industry's adoption of AI signifies a move towards superior operational approaches, particularly evident in areas such as personalisation, smart search and trend forecasting. This influence is particularly substantial in e-commerce, where AI reshapes core processes, enhancing customer experiences, search functionalities and pricing strategies.

Despite AI's evolving presence in the fashion sector, it's useful to highlight its applications in omnichannel retail. Here, we explore several AI-driven strategies and how they've been actualised within the fashion industry.

Applications and real-world integrations

Personalisation and prediction – AI has significantly redefined the fashion industry's approach to personalisation and predictive analytics. No longer relying on broad-strokes targeting, companies now offer finely-tuned recommendations by analysing detailed customer data. For example, ASOS crafts personalised shopping experiences based on users' interactions, while Stitch Fix uses AI to curate style selections tailored to individual tastes.

Predictive technologies further enhance this personalisation; algorithms adjust websites to users' sizes, align ads with personal styles and power virtual fitting rooms that anticipate preferences. McKinsey (2021b) reports a connection between precise AI recommendations and increased consumer spending. A projected 60% of retailers are set to increase their AI investments in the upcoming years, as per 'The State of AI in Retail and CPG' (2024). However, the Business of Fashion's 2022 study warns of the risks of imprecise recommendations, which can, of course, erode trust. Ethical data handling is critical in this age of personalisation. McKinsey (2022) found that personalised recommendations prompt 40% of consumers to overspend, while Accenture notes a 70% conversion rate increase with tailored suggestions. Yet, imprecise recommendations can deter users, (Morris, 2023), therefore striking a balance is crucial. While AI-driven insights enhance the user experience, mishandling can be seen as intrusive, risking customer churn. Beyond e-commerce, AI's role in trend prediction is growing, with firms like Edited using digital insights to identify emerging fashion trends. In the fight against overproduction and waste in the fashion sector, AI driven personalisation and prediction also offers a solution. Zara, for instance, uses AI to predict demand, optimizing production and subsequently reducing waste. This move towards an AI-enhanced

Forecast-Design-Sell-Make model, and away from the traditional Design-Make-Sell, may provide a pathway towards sustainability in the industry.

Smart search – Navigating the vast expanse of online shopping can be daunting for consumers. In today's fast-paced world, we are time-poor, increasingly impatient and demand instant gratification. AI-driven search functionalities offer a solution to these demands, making e-commerce platforms more responsive and aligned with user intent. Enhanced search algorithms have shown a direct correlation with increased customer satisfaction and higher conversion rates. Given that a significant share of online traffic to fashion websites, nearly one-third, is attributed to site search (Econsultancy, 2022), the strategic advantage of efficient search mechanisms is evident. Brands who leverage site search experience up to a 50% rise in conversion rates compared to those who do not.

However, optimising these search systems is challenging. Constant updating of algorithmic responses, consistent product catalogue synchronisation and adapting to changing user queries add layers of complexity. Manual oversight for each search scenario is not only resource-intensive but also cost-inefficient. Hence, many businesses are transitioning to AI-optimised search solutions. These AI tools, equipped with features like predictive autocomplete and **intelligent faceting**, aim to provide a more fluid and intuitive user experience. Amazon, for example, uses intelligent faceting to generate and personalise facets for its product catalogues based on the user's search behaviour; this is why we receive push notifications of new product ideas, based on our search histories. ASOS is also an early adopter of AI. The retailer's visual search capability, which uses a combination of **natural language processing (NLP)** and **computer vision (CV),** allows users to upload images and receive product recommendations, exemplify the innovation in this space. Yet, despite these advancements, the importance of human judgment remains paramount. This duality, where AI systems work in tandem with human strategic oversight, ensures that business goals and evolving customer expectations are seamlessly met. The goal is not just improved search; it is consumer direction, guiding them towards optimal purchase decisions.

> **Computer vision (CV)** enables machines to interpret and act based on visual data. It allows computers to identify objects, patterns and, facial gestures and even emotions from images and videos.

> **Intelligent faceting,** powered by AI, enhances the precision and relevance of search results. It auto-generates facets, personalises them for individual users and updates dynamically in response to user search patterns.

Virtual style assistants (VSA) – For many, the 1995 film *Clueless* offered an introduction to the concept of a virtual stylist. In the film, the protagonist,

Cher uses a computer to help her select her outfits, marking a prelude to today's technological evolution in fashion. VSAs are still in their early stages of development, but they have the potential to alter the way people shop for fashion. There are a handful of brands venturing into this space. Levi's VSAs, for example, uses an AI chatbot that helps customers find the perfect pair of jeans based on their fit, rise, amount of stretch and wash. Nike enhances the customer experience by enabling a virtual shoe try-on feature. Leveraging computer vision, data analytics, ML and sophisticated algorithms, the app meticulously measures the entire shape of both feet to determine an accurate fit. This sizing information is integrated into the consumer's Nike Plus profile, ensuring consistent size recommendations across shopping platforms and minimizing return probabilities (Barseghian, 2019).

Tech start-ups are also disrupting the fashion industry, exemplified by platforms such as YesPlz, which tailors clothing recommendations for users and Save Your Wardrobe, another notable initiative which integrates AI to digitally catalogue a user's existing wardrobe items. This application is worth greater focus as its core objective is to mitigate overconsumption (LVMH, 2023). To achieve this, it offers users access to local aftercare services, from alterations, repairs, eco-cleaning to upcycling, thereby promoting garment longevity. This digital platform, while facilitating a circular approach, also optimises the post-purchase experience for brands and retailers. Key features include automated logistics, efficient operational management, streamlined customer communication using NLP and real-time data reporting, all curated to enhance garment lifespan and customer engagement.

Conversational commerce – The consumer adoption of voice interfaces, exemplified by Apple's Siri and Amazon's Alexa across smartphones and smart speakers, is expanding. According to a report by Statista (2020), there were over 4 billion digital voice assistants in use worldwide as of 2020, with this number predicted to double by 2024. Such data positions voice assistance, or conversational commerce, as a potential disruptor within the omnichannel landscape.

> **Conversational commerce** utilises natural language interactions through chatbots, messaging apps, and voice assistants to streamline the shopping process, offering a more intuitive and user-friendly experience across different platforms.

In the fashion industry, conversational commerce, though a relatively nascent technology, is gaining momentum. Leveraging NLP, it deciphers and mimics human language, fostering more authentic interactions between users and systems. In online platforms, chatbots and AI stylists have become essential tools, serving as intermediaries in messaging interactions with consumers. This allows users to receive tailored recommendations, product care information and customer service, streamlining purchase processes. Since 2017, the use of these tools has increased significantly. Inventor of the hashtag, Chris Messina, who first coined the term 'conversational commerce', described it as the use of chat, messaging and natural language interfaces for two-way interactions. This goes beyond just text; it includes graphical elements like buttons and images to simplify user interactions, which streamlines product discovery.

One of the recurring consumer complaints for online shopping is the difficulty in finding specific products because they do not know the correct search terms (McDowell, 2023). For example, searching for a 'winter coat', might return a set of tweed coats, even though the customer did not specify 'tweed'. NLP would therefore mitigate this issue, eliminating the hassle of navigating through multiple filters by allowing users to input their specific requirements directly. Notable implementations of conversational commerce are Net-A-Porter and Kering, who have released online shopping tools powered by generative AI, which empowers customers to use natural language for product searches. For example, customers can input requests such as 'Find a black evening dress for my wedding in August' or specify price ranges and colours in their search like 'Men's trainers in yellow and white under £200', resulting in more tailored product recommendations. Whilst the backbone of these efficient systems is a synergy of ML and AI, adept at understanding and delivering on customer intent, they still have limitations related to generic suggestions based on the retailer's inventory.

In omnichannel operations, chatbots stand out as a significant tool within conversational commerce. We have all most likely interacted with a chatbot, and while the experience occasionally lacks finesse, the value of chatbots is undeniable. Recognising this early, the fashion industry leveraged AI and ML to create cost-effective, personalised experiences (Grewal et al., 2017). AI-driven fashion chatbots, available on many websites, often outperform what a human counterpart might offer, with more accurate, efficient and comprehensive support (Landim et al., 2022. Chatbots can typically be categorised into two types: scripted and AI-driven. Scripted chatbots, operating within a predefined set of instructions, are commonly what most of us interact with. Due to their rule-based programming, they occasionally fall short in addressing our queries. In contrast, AI-driven chatbots, designed to understand human language, are more responsive and adaptive. The fashion industry, in particular, has adopted these AI-driven chatbots for online retail; however, we are also seeing its application within other online interfaces such as within virtual reality retail environments. Through a mix of visual AI and ML, these chatbots refine their responses and suggestions over time. Based on user feedback, they quickly offer related items from extensive product listings, thanks to fashion tagging. This capability optimises recommendation engines that monitor and react to purchasing patterns. By considering variables like style, size and even cross-brand size correlations, these chatbots assist customers in making prompt decisions, which can lead to reduced churn rates. Prominent brands, such as ASOS and Farfetch, deploy AI chatbots to provide continuous customer support, addressing questions about products, shipping and sizing 24/7.

As conversational commerce technology matures and finds a firmer footing within the fashion industry, its potential will open doors to increasingly diverse applications. Consumer resistance to chatbots is a potential challenge that businesses still need to overcome (Kallel et al., 2023). With the rapid advancements of AI, ML and NLP, such innovations mark just the beginning of how conversational commerce will evolve.

3.3.8 CO-CREATION AND DESIGN

The intersection of AI and fashion, as we have previously already established, presents a myriad of opportunities for fashion retailers. While AI has proven valuable in retail, a new and exciting aspect, generative AI (GenAI), is gaining momentum. This section looks at how GenAI, still in its early stages, is creating opportunities for innovative collaboration between customers and brands in the constantly changing world of omnichannel retail. In 2018, artist Robbie Barrat made waves in the fashion industry by designing a collection with AI, inspired by Balenciaga. The designs were rough and blurred, but they caught the industry's attention. Since then, and in just a few short years, GenAI tools have become more accessible, accurate and flexible, allowing almost anyone to design their own fashion line. GenAI works by using ML to create new content. After learning from large amounts of data, these tools can identify patterns and create without being directly told what to do. For instance, DALL-E 2 and Stable Diffusion can create images; ChatGPT can generate text; and Runway can produce videos. They all share the ability to create content from text descriptions, showcasing their adaptability.

McKinsey & Company forecasts a significant rise in GenAI's influence on fashion within the next three to five years, potentially boosting profits in the apparel and luxury sectors by $150 to $275 billion (Harreis et al., 2023). This transformation is already beginning to shake up various aspects such as design, marketing and customer service. However, it appears the application of design is where GenAI may have the most potential in the fashion industry, as these tools will give designers the speed and agility to explore countless design possibilities, mixing different ideas and styles based on consumer purchasing behaviour and online interactions across social media. Interesting projects are already underway in this area, such as Tommy Hilfiger's collaboration with MIT to create adaptive clothing using GenAI, and the Metaverse Fashion Week (2023) where Hilfiger's AI design contest led to a digital wearable sold on DRESSX (Van Gastel, 2023). H&M has introduced a GenAI tool allowing customers to co-create products (refer to the case study for details). However, the long-term success and impact of this initiative remains to be seen. Yet, the adoption of GenAI brings challenges and risks, including ethical considerations and the necessity for industries to adapt to new technological landscapes.

While promising, integrating GenAI in fashion comes with challenges. The complexities of choosing fabrics, constructing garments and refining AI-generated designs mean GenAI is best as a support to human creativity, rather than a replacement. In summary, GenAI is ushering in a new wave of innovation and personalised experiences in fashion. It paves the way for a future where co-creation is standard, with brands and consumers collaborating in new creative ventures. As the fashion industry approaches this tech revolution, it's the blend of human skill and GenAI's potential that will create limitless opportunities.

(Source: DRESSX, n.d.)

3.3.9 AI ETHICAL CONSIDERATIONS

In 2023, Casablanca, a French Moroccan label, unveiled its spring/summer campaign, 'Futuro Optimisto', created entirely by AI, featuring photorealistic avatars set against lush, exotic backdrops. Yet, this leap forward into AI-generated fashion marketing campaigns raised significant ethical concerns concerning its appropriation of Mexican heritage, and its replacement of human creativity.

AI's capacity to inadvertently perpetuate biases poses a real concern. For instance, there is the danger of AI systems promoting certain body ideals or perpetuating harmful stereotypes, potentially sidelining diverse body shapes, ethnicities or other protected characteristics. Beyond design, the extensive data harvesting that AI enables could impinge on privacy, affecting not only consumer behaviour but potentially influencing vital aspects of individuals' lives, like credit or job prospects.

Fashion companies embracing AI must tackle these issues with vigilance and transparency:

- *Open communication* – Transparency about AI usage and data sourcing can foster consumer trust, enabling customers to make informed decisions about their engagement with AI-enhanced services.
- *Ethical AI practices* – Developers must prioritise equity in AI design and conduct ongoing audits to identify and correct biases, ensuring AI tools serve a diverse customer base fairly.
- *Consumer data control* – Customers should retain control over their personal data with clear options to opt out of data collection and straightforward channels to express their data privacy preferences.

AI's potential to transform fashion is tremendous, but it must be balanced with ethical considerations. Brands are tasked with deploying AI judiciously, ensuring that tech's integration into fashion remains not only trendsetting but also fair and inclusive.

Case study activity – H&M Group's Creator Studio and the age of GenAI in fashion

H&M Group, renowned for its global fashion footprint, took a leap in the area of co-creation through its platform, 'Creator Studio'. Introduced in 2021, the platform initially catered to businesses and select creators. However, its evolution saw the integration of Stable Diffusion, an open-source GenAI model, opening doors for the masses to actively participate in design. The AI tool aids users in manifesting professional-looking designs, sidestepping the need for advanced software knowledge or inherent artistic prowess. With the combination of H&M's expansive manufacturing and logistics prowess, users can see their digital designs transform into wearable fashion, shipped globally.

Capabilities and concerns – GenAI's integration is not without its challenges in the fashion landscape. The ability to conjure images based on textual prompts makes it easier for individuals to create designs reminiscent of established brands. For instance, the AI tool was noted to create a design bearing likeness to Louis Vuitton's iconic logo. While not an exact replica, such designs wade into murky waters concerning intellectual property rights. H&M Group acknowledges these potential pitfalls. The company relies on a mix of human moderators and technological interventions to identify problematic designs. This ensures that even if a design is generated, it may not necessarily culminate in a tangible product.

Strategic vision – The underlying objective of integrating generative AI into Creator Studio stems from H&M Group's aspiration to democratise fashion design. By removing digital skill barriers, the company encourages a wider audience to engage with fashion in a participatory manner. As Dinesh Nayar, managing director of Creator Studio, highlighted, merchandising has seamlessly woven itself into the fabric of contemporary culture. From musicians to influencers, merchandise serves as both a revenue source and an expressive medium. H&M's initiative aims to strengthen this trend, allowing individuals worldwide to order custom merchandise effortlessly.

Reflective discussion question

Q. While technology democratises fashion creation, it also presents intellectual property challenges. How can brands ensure a balance between promoting creativity and safeguarding proprietary designs in the age of generative AI?

Case study has been adapted from the Business of Fashion (Bain, 2023).

END-OF-CHAPTER DISCUSSIONS

1. Reflect on the advancements in online retailing technologies such as 360-degree 3D product visualisations and eye-tracking. How do these innovations contribute to solving the challenge of representing physical product attributes like fit and quality online?
2. Discuss the potential trade-offs involved in implementing advanced technologies for both retailers and consumers.
3. How do cultural differences influence the adoption of livestream shopping between China and Western markets?
4. Identify the key technological advancements mentioned in the chapter and discuss how each of them contributes to addressing the specific challenges faced by the fashion retail industry. Reflect on how these technologies can be strategically implemented to enhance customer engagement and satisfaction.
5. Discuss the ethical considerations and potential societal impacts of AI in the fashion industry,
6. Consider the ways in which AI might contribute to sustainability efforts.

Bibliography and further reading

Accenture (2022). *Widening gap between consumer expectations and reality in personalization signals warning for brands, Accenture Interactive Research finds*. Available at: https://newsroom.accenture.com/news/2018/widening-gap-between-consumer-expectations-and-reality-in-personalization-signals-warning-for-brands-accenture-interactive-research-finds (accessed 19 February 2024).

Alsop, T. (2022). 'Global mobile augmented reality (AR) user devices 2024', Statista. Available at: https://www.statista.com/statistics/1098630/global-mobile-augmented-reality-ar-users/ (accessed 13 February 2024).

Bain, M. (2023). 'H&M Group's new AI Tool Lets anyone play designer', *The Business of Fashion*. Available at: https://www.businessoffashion.com/articles/technology/hm-group-is-using-ai/ (accessed 13 February 2024).

Barseghian, A. (2019). 'How Nike is using analytics to personalize their customer experience', *Forbes*. Available at: https://www.forbes.com/sites/forbestechcouncil/2019/10/07/how-nike-is-using-analytics-to-personalize-their-customer-experience/?sh=686191a1611c.

Boardman, R. and Mccormick, H. (2021). 'Attention and behaviour on fashion retail websites: An eye-tracking study', *Information Technology & People*. ahead-of-print. doi:10.1108/ITP-08-2020-0580.

Cheung, M. Y., Luo, C., Sia, C. L. and Chen, H. (2009). 'Credibility of electronic word-of-mouth: Informational and normative determinants of on-line consumer recommendations', *International Journal of Electronic Commerce*, 13(4), pp. 9–38.

Chou, C. (2023). Alibaba's Janet Wang outlines key innovations in China's luxury market set to feature in 11.11 shopping festival, Alizila. Available at: https://www.alizila.com/alibaba-janet-wang-china-luxury-innovation-1111-shopping-festival/#:~:text=%E2%80%9CConsumers%20no%20longer%20think%20in,Luxury%20Pavilion%2C%20for%20designer%20brands (accessed 4 June 2023).

Chui, M. et al. (2022). 'The state of AI in 2022—and a half decade in review', McKinsey & Company. Available at: https://www.mckinsey.com/capabilities/quantumblack/our-insights/the-state-of-ai-in-2022-and-a-half-decade-in-review (accessed 13 February 2024).

Coresight Research (2023). *Livestreaming E-Commerce*, Coresight Research. Available at: https://coresight.com/livestreaming/.

Deterding, S., Dixon, D., Khaled, R., & Nacke, L. (2011). 'From game design elements to gamefulness: Defining gamification', *MindTrek'11: Proceedings of the 15th International Academic MindTrek Conference: Envisioning Future Media Environments*, pp. 9–15. doi:10.1145/2181037.2181040.

Dix, A. (2009). 'Human-computer interaction'. In L. Liu, and M. T. Özsu, (eds) *Encyclopedia of database systems*. Springer, Boston. doi:10.1007/978-0-387-39940-9_192

Dixon, S. J. (2023). 'Topic: Social media use during coronavirus (COVID-19) worldwide', Statista. Available at: https://www.statista.com/topics/7863/social-media-use-during-coronavirus-covid-19-worldwide/#topicOverview (accessed 13 February 2024).

DRESSX (n.d.) *DRESSX*. Available at: https://dressx.com/ (accessed 16 February 2024).

Econsultancy (2022). *Stats roundup: The impact of covid-19 on ecommerce*. Available at: https://econsultancy.com/stats-roundup-the-impact-of-covid-19-on-ecommerce/ (accessed 13 February 2024).

Epsilon (2022). *Create real customer connections*. Available at: https://www.epsilon.com/us/products-and-services/epsilon-peoplecloud/messaging.

Fetais, A. H., Algharabat, R. S., Aljafari, A. and N. P. Rana (2023). 'Do social media marketing activities improve brand loyalty? An empirical study on luxury fashion brands', *Inf Syst Front*, 25(2), 795–817. doi:10.1007/s10796-022-10264-7

Grewal, D., Roggeveen, A. L. and Nordfält, J. (2017). 'The future of retailing', *Journal of Retailing*, 93(1), 1–6.

Goldfarb, A. and Tucker, C. (2011). 'Online advertising, behavioral targeting, and privacy', *Communications of the ACM*, 54(11), pp. 25–27.

Grand View Research (2023). *Augmented Reality Market Size, Share & Trends Analysis Report By Component (Hardware, Software), By Technology (Marker-Based, Markerless), By Application (Retail, Gaming, Healthcare, Aerospace & Defense, Industrial), By Region, and Segment Forecasts, 2023–2030*. Available at: https://www.grandviewresearch.com/industry-analysis/augmented-reality-market (accessed 20 February 2024).

Harreis, H., Koullias, T., Roberts, R. and Te, K. (2023). 'Generative AI: Unlocking the future of fashion', McKinsey & Company. Available at: https://www.mckinsey.com/industries/retail/our-insights/generative-ai-unlocking-the-future-of-fashion (accessed 13 February 2024).

Hypebae (2018). *First look at Chanel Game Center in Hong Kong*. Available at: https://hypebae.com/2018/5/chanel-beauty-coco-game-center-hong-kong-pop-up.

Henninger, C. E., Niinimäki, K., Blazquez, M. and Jones, C. (2022). *Sustainable fashion management*. Taylor & Francis.

The Insight Partners (2019) *Artificial Intelligence in fashion market trends & growth by 2027*. Available at: https://www.theinsightpartners.com/reports/artificial-intelligence-in-fashion-market [theinsightpartners.com] (accessed 20 February 2024).

Kallel, A., Mouheli, N. B. D., Chaouali, W. and Danks, N. P. (2023). 'Hey chatbot, why do you treat me like other people? The role of uniqueness neglect in human-chatbot interactions', *Journal of Strategic Marketing*, pp. 1–17. doi:10.1080/0965254x.2023.2175020.

Kim, J. and Ha, J. (2021). 'User experience in VR fashion product shopping: Focusing on tangible interactions', *Applied Sciences*, 11(13), p. 6170. doi:10.3390/app11136170

KPMG (2017). *The truth about online consumers*. Available at: https://assets.kpmg.com/content/dam/kpmg/xx/pdf/2017/01/the-truth-about-online-consumers.pdf (accessed 19 February 2024).

Kotler, P. (1974). 'Atmospherics as a marketing tool', *Journal of Retailing*, 49(4). https://www.researchgate.net/publication/239435728_Atmospherics_as_a_Marketing_Tool

Kraus, S., Jones, P., Kailer, N., Weinmann, A., Chaparro-Banegas, N. and Roig-Tierno, N. (2021). 'Digital transformation: An overview of the current state of the art of research', *SAGE Open*, 11(3). https://doi.org/10.1177/21582440211047576

Kumar, V., Rajan, B., Venkatesan, R. and Lecinski, J. (2019) 'Understanding the role of artificial intelligence in personalized engagement marketing', *California Management Review*, 61(4), pp. 135–155. Available at: doi:10.1177/0008125619859317.

Landim, A. R. D. B et al. (2022) 'Chatbot design approaches for fashion e-commerce: An interdisciplinary review', *International Journal of Fashion Design, Technology and Education*, 15(2), pp. 200–210. doi:10.1080/17543266.2021.1990417

Lau, O. and Ki, CW. (2021). 'Can consumers' gamified, personalized, and engaging experiences with VR fashion apps increase in-app purchase intention by fulfilling needs?', *Fash Text* 8, 36 doi:10.1186/s40691-021-00270-9

Lee, Y. E. and Benbasat, I. (2004) 'A framework for the study of customer interface design for mobile commerce', *International Journal of Electronic Commerce*, 8(3), pp. 79–102. doi:10.1080/10864415.2004.11044299.

Luce, L. (2019). 'Basics of artificial intelligence'. In *Artificial Intelligence for Fashion*. Apress. doi:10.1007/978-1-4842-3931-5_1

Luckel, M. (2017). 'Gucci's new app is perfect for fashion history-slash-travel buffs', *Vogue India*. Available at: https://www.vogue.in/content/guccis-new-app-is-perfect-for-fashion-history-slash-travel-buffs.

LVMH (2023). 'Save your wardrobe wins 2023 LVMH innovation award grand prize at Viva Technology', LVMH. Available at: https://www.lvmh.com/news-documents/news/save-your-wardrobe-wins-2023-lvmh-innovation-award-grand-prize-at-viva-technology/ (accessed 13 February 2024).

Magnani, C. (2022). 'Revisiting fashion online: The past, present, and future of immersive fashion digital experiences', *The Fashion Studies Journal*. Available at: https://www.fashionstudiesjournal.org/digital-engagement-a/2022/8/15/revisiting-fashion-online-the-past-present-and-future-of-immersive-fashion-digital-experiences.

Mandarić D., Hunjet A. and Vuković D. (2022). 'The impact of fashion brand sustainability on consumer purchasing decisions', *Journal of Risk and Financial Management*, 15(4), p. 176. doi:10.3390/jrfm15040176

Mangold, W. G. and Faulds, D. J. (2009). 'Social media: The new hybrid element of the promotion mix', *Business Horizons*, 52(4), pp. 357–365.

McDowell, M. (2021). 'Inside Gucci and Roblox's new virtual world', *Vogue Business*. Available at: https://www.voguebusiness.com/technology/inside-gucci-and-robloxs-new-virtual-world (accessed 13 February 2024).

McDowell, M. (2023). 'With generative AI, luxury hopes to finally crack digital clienteling', *Vogue Business*. Available at: https://www.voguebusiness.com/technology/with-generative-ai-luxury-hopes-to-finally-crack-digital-clienteling (accessed 13 February 2024).

McKinsey & Company (2021a). *It's showtime! How live commerce is transforming the shopping experience*. Available at: https://www.mckinsey.com/capabilities/mckinsey-digital/our-insights/its-showtime-how-live-commerce-is-transforming-the-shopping-experience.

McKinsey & Company (2021b). *The value of getting personalization right—or wrong—is multiplying*. Available at: https://www.mckinsey.com/capabilities/growth-marketing-and-sales/our-insights/the-value-of-getting-personalization-right-or-wrong-is-multiplying.

Mehrabian, J. and Russell, J. A. (1974). *An approach to environmental psychology*. https://psycnet.apa.org/record/1974-22049-000

Mitchell, C. (2022). 'Gartner Magic Quadrant for personalization engines 2022', *CX Today*. Available at: https://www.cxtoday.com/data-analytics/gartner-magic-quadrant-for-personalization-engines-2022/.

Morris, M. (2023). 'Will brands ever get product recommendations right?', *The Business of Fashion*. Available at: https://www.businessoffashion.com/articles/direct-to-consumer/will-brands-get-product-recommendations-right/ (accessed 13 February 2024).

NVIDIA (n.d.). *State of AI in retail and CPG: 2024 trends*. Available at: https://resources.nvidia.com/en-us-retail-cpg-ai (accessed 12 February 2024).

Parasuraman, A., Zeithaml, V. A., & Malhotra, A. (2005). 'E-S-QUAL: A multiple-item scale for assessing electronic service quality', *Journal of Service Research*, 7(3), pp. 213–233.

Park, C. H. and Lee, T. M. (2009). 'Information direction, website reputation and eWOM effect: A moderating role of product type', *Journal of Business Research*, 62(1), pp. 61–67.

Pew Research Center (2019). *Internet/ broadband fact sheet*. Available at: https://www.pewresearch.org/internet/fact-sheet/internet-broadband/ (accessed 19 February 2024).

Pine, B.J. and Gilmore, J. H. (2020). *The experience economy*. HBR Press.

Ratchford, T. B., Soysal, G., Zentner, A. and Gauri, D. K. (2022). 'Online and offline retailing: What we know and directions for future research', *Journal of Retailing*, 98(1), pp. 152–177. doi:10.1016/j.jretai.2022.02.007.

Rayport, J. and Jaworski, B. (2001). *Introduction to e-commerce*. McGraw-Hill.

Schudey, A., Kasperovich, P., Ikram, A. and Panhans, D. (2023). 'Game Changer: Accelerating the media industry's most dynamic sector', BCG Global. Available at: https://www.bcg.com/publications/2023/drivers-of-global-gaming-industry-growth (accessed 13 February 2024).

Statista (2020). *Number of digital voice assistants in use worldwide from 2019 to 2024 (in billions)* [Graph]. Available at: https://www.statista.com/statistics/973815/worldwide-digital-voice-assistant-in-use/ (accessed September 28, 2023).

Statista (2023a). *Fashion e-commerce market value worldwide from 2023 to 2027*. Available at: https://www.statista.com/statistics/1298198/market-value-fashion-ecommerce-global/#:~:text=Global%20fashion%20e%2Dcommerce%20market%20size%202023%2D2027&text=In%202023%2C%20the%20global%20e,trillion%20U.S.%20dollars%20by%202027.

Statista (2023b). *Market size of live streaming in China 2016–2026*. Available at: https://www.statista.com/statistics/874591/china-online-live-streaming-market-size/.

Thormundsson, B. (2023). 'Artificial intelligence market size 2030', Statista. Available at: https://www.statista.com/statistics/1365145/artificial-intelligence-market-size/ (accessed 13 February 2024).

Van Gastel, T. (2023). 'AI's role as fashion design assistant: Tommy Hilfiger, AI Fashion Week, and Text-to-Design', *Jing Daily*. Available at: https://jingdaily.com/artificial-intelligence-fashion-design-assistant-tommy-hilfiger-midjourney/.

Zargani, L. (2017). 'Gucci launches Gucci Places Project', *WWD*. Available at: https://wwd.com/feature/gucci-launches-gucci-places-alessandro-michele-10947617/ (accessed 13 February 2024).

Zhang, T., Wang, W. Y. C., Cao, L. and Wang, Y. (2019). 'The role of virtual try-on technology in online purchase decision from consumers' aspect', *Internet Research*, 29. doi:10.1108/IntR-12-2017-0540.

PART IV

Future skills development in the digital age

The book concludes with Chapter 4.1, titled 'Digital Skills in Fashion', which is a comprehensive exploration of the significant juncture at which the fashion industry finds itself due to digital transformation. This chapter recognises the pervasive impact of digital transformation across the fashion value chain, as previously highlighted throughout the book. It addresses the acute digital skills deficit that has emerged as a direct consequence of the rapid advancements brought forth by Industry 4.0. The chapter emphasizes that, while basic digital literacy is now a fundamental requirement, the industry's more pressing need is for advanced digital competencies. This growing demand for higher-level digital skills is projected to increase, bringing to the forefront the urgency of upskilling within the fashion sector. The narrative delves into the implications of this skills gap and the necessity for individuals in the industry to acquire and enhance their digital skill sets to remain relevant and competitive. The chapter serves not only as an analysis but also as a practical guide, offering an array of digital resources. These resources are designed to enable readers to effectively engage in the digitally driven marketplace and to carve out successful careers in this new fashion landscape.

By the end of this chapter, readers are expected to gain a multifaceted understanding of the digital transformation in the fashion industry. The learning outcomes include a comprehensive grasp of the scope of opportunities within the fashion industry, an understanding of the emerging skill requirements in a future-facing fashion environment, the identification of relevant technical skills applicable to the changing industry and strategies to enhance digital skillsets in preparation for a career in the future fashion landscape. This chapter is essential for graduates and aspirants in the fashion industry aiming to navigate and succeed in the rapidly evolving digital era.

DOI: 10.4324/9781003364559-13

CHAPTER 4.1

Digital skills in fashion[1]

Charlene Gallery, Panashe Katema, Momoyioluwa Olatokun, Alina Zhakenova and Jo Conlon

Fashion is at an inflection point. Throughout this book, we have highlighted how digital transformation has impacted fashion across the spectrum of the value chain. The fashion industry confronts an acute digital skills deficit as Industry 4.0 reshapes the business landscape. Basic digital literacy has become a baseline requirement; however, the sector's pressing need lies in advanced digital competencies. This trend is projected to accelerate, underscoring the urgent call for upskilling within the industry. This final chapter will highlight the importance of digital skills within the fashion industry, outlining the essential skills requirements within the global fashion environment and providing a range of digital resources which will enable the reader to engage effectively in the digitally driven marketplace and carve out a successful career in the new fashion landscape.

LEARNING OUTCOMES

After reading this chapter, you should be able to:

- Understand the scope of opportunity within the fashion industry and the drivers impacting change.
- Understand the emerging skills requirements required within a future facing fashion environment.
- Identify a range of technical skills which are applicable to the changing fashion industry.
- Enhance digital skillsets in readiness for a future fashion career.

1 This chapter has been developed in collaboration with University of Manchester undergraduate researchers, Panashe Katema, Momoyioluwa Olatokun and Alina Zhakenova.

DOI: 10.4324/9781003364559-14

4.1.1 THE SCOPE OF OPPORTUNITY

The fashion sector stands as a critical engine of the global economy and a barometer of societal shifts (Conlon & Gallery, 2023). It is a dynamic, fast-paced industry that influences how we live and interact with the world around us. Integral to both economic growth and cultural evolution, fashion encompasses everything from textile production to global retailing. It impacts labour, trade and consumption patterns, shaping industries from luxury to mainstream retail. The reach of fashion is extensive, affecting employment, innovating trade practices and setting cultural norms. As it perpetually transforms, fashion holds its place as a powerful force in creating economic wealth and defining cultural identity.

The textile, clothing and footwear industries are critical to the global labour market, engaging a significant 300 million workers in a myriad of roles that cut across design, production, distribution and retail. According to the Ellen MacArthur Foundation (2019), these sectors are not just employment powerhouses but also span a vast array of professional domains, from creative to logistical. They encompass the talent of artisans and the innovation of designers in crafting products and involve supply chain experts and retail personnel in bringing these goods to market. The importance of these sectors extends beyond the sheer volume of employment they provide, deeply influencing the socio-economic fabric of nations worldwide.

Economically, the fashion industry was a tour de force before the pandemic, amassing global revenues close to $1.7 trillion, as reported by Statista (2023). This figure highlights the industry's colossal impact on the world economy, asserting its role as a primary driver of international financial dynamics. In the UK, the fashion industry, traditionally a beacon of creative ingenuity, is navigating a transformative phase where digital skills are becoming as indispensable as traditional design abilities. Recent findings point to a significant skills gap, particularly in digital proficiencies, among industry professionals (Conlon & Gallery, 2023). This deficit is mirrored by the concerns of many graduates who feel underprepared for the technological demands of the modern workforce. The implementation of advanced digital tools in fashion opens doors to sustainable practices and improved customer relations, but it also demands that leaders and educators in the field equip their teams to meet these new challenges. The necessity goes beyond adopting the latest technologies; it involves cultivating a workforce that is proficient in using these tools to their full potential. As Industry 4.0 principles become entrenched in fashion, the sector must ensure that its employees are ready to operate in this new digital-led environment.

There are several determinants impacting fashion careers:

Impact: Digital first

The ongoing transformation in the fashion sector, expedited by the pandemic, has required a shift away from established norms in design, marketing and retail. As a result, there's been a considerable impact on career trajectories within the field. Job profiles traditionally central to fashion are evolving, and new roles are surfacing in response to the industry's digital direction. Proficiency in 3D design and digital marketing is increasingly sought after, reflecting a broader demand for digitally skilled professionals.

In response to these industry shifts, the nature of fashion work is being redefined. Companies are increasingly reliant on digital resources to optimise their workflows, ushering in an era of more dynamic and cooperative methods. The sector now favours those with a strong grip on digital tools like CAD and 3D software, and an ability to integrate such tools with their inherent creative skills to lead the charge towards innovation and operational efficiency.

This digital wave has created niches such as digital product design and fashion-specific digital marketing – fields poised for growth and indicative of a digital-centric business model. The workplace itself is transforming; digital solutions promote teamwork and flexibility, prioritising a workforce that is both adaptable and continually upskilling in digital technologies. For those in the fashion industry who can navigate and harness these digital shifts, the prospects are promising.

3D graphics skills with the highest projected growth in demand job roles that utilise these skill sets are also growing faster than the job market overall and new job roles are emerging. Mastering interactive 3D skills can benefit students and workers interested in career mobility and provide them a competitive advantage in the job market (Unreal Engine, 2021).

Impact: Social responsibility

The landscape of business has expanded to embrace corporate social responsibility (CSR) as an integral aspect of operations. Companies are increasingly integrating ethical, sustainable and eco-friendly considerations into their products and practices. The establishment of dedicated CSR teams has become a standard for forward-thinking organisations, driven not only by altruistic motives but also by the strategic advantage that robust CSR initiatives offer. They enhance a company's reputation, which can translate into increased profitability. However, professionals in the fashion industry face the challenge of recognising and addressing ethical issues within their supply chains. Neglecting to do so can lead to significant repercussions, affecting not only economic outcomes but also brand credibility and consumer trust.

As CSR and ethical practices become more prominent in the job market, companies are leveraging these initiatives as unique selling points (USPs) to attract top talent. A company's commitment to responsibility is often a decisive factor for job seekers with a strong sense of corporate ethics.

In procurement, for example, a deep comprehension of industry standards and ethical policies is increasingly demanded. Interviews for such roles now frequently include assessments of candidates' understanding of

CSR-related elements, such as supplier evaluation on CSR policies, adherence to standards like the ETI Base Code, and compliance with regulations on modern slavery, bribery and health and safety standards, exemplified by various ISO accreditations.

A firm grasp of these areas is essential – not just for the sake of compliance but to safeguard against potential financial pitfalls. Ensuring that both employers and employees are knowledgeable about these policies is becoming ever more vital in today's market, highlighting the role of CSR as a foundational element in the ethical and sustainable evolution of the fashion industry.

Impact: Sustainable innovation

The growing importance of sustainable innovation in the fashion industry underscores the pressing need for environmentally friendly approaches and creations. Professionals entering this field should possess a strong understanding of sustainable methods and technological progress to effectively contribute to positive change. An important focal point is the advancement of bio-fabricated materials, which have the capability to transform the industry significantly.

Central to reducing the environmental footprint of textiles is the selection of eco-friendly materials. The substances chosen for fabric production carry consequences that extend from the manufacturing process to the end-of-life of the garment, including how it interacts with human skin and its disposable nature (Wu & Li, 2020). Industry professionals are therefore tasked with prioritising sustainable textile fibres that are free from pesticides, manufactured with renewable energy, water-efficient, chemically safe and dyed in an environmentally responsible manner.

The commitment to sustainability extends beyond the selection of materials to encompass the entire production lifecycle. Professionals need to scrutinise each phase of production for potential waste and inefficiency (Pedrose-Roussado, 2023). From the design of patterns to the process of cutting and putting pieces together, there are many opportunities for improvement. Implementing even small changes at each step can result in notable decreases in waste, especially within mass production environments.

Staying abreast of the latest innovations is not just advantageous but essential for those dedicated to a sustainable fashion industry. Through continuous learning, professionals can adopt cutting-edge methods that improve material efficiency and diminish waste. Environmental certifications such as ISO 14001, FSC/PEFC, life cycle assessments and water footprint measures are integral to industry standards, guiding companies along sustainable trajectories (Waheed & Khalid, 2019).

Technological innovation significantly impacts the fashion industry, particularly in production and logistics. Investing in technology improves communication, data management, and process optimisation, contributing to reduced rework and waste, enhancing overall efficiency and sustainability. Digitisation now allows for virtual modelling and sampling, thereby reducing the reliance on physical materials and lessening environmental impact.

Graduates aspiring to work in sustainable fashion must have a comprehensive understanding of how companies utilise technology. This knowledge is crucial for gaining better control over the supply chain and its impact on the environment. With the fashion industry experiencing growing demands for transformation, the combination of technology and sustainable strategies equips professionals with the means to bring about significant and enduring change.

Mini case studies: Sustainable innovation

Modern Meadow

Modern Meadow is at the forefront of sustainable innovation, developing bio-fabricated materials that offer eco-friendly alternatives to traditional products. Utilising biotechnology, they create materials with reduced environmental impacts, avoiding animal products and toxic chemicals. Their multidisciplinary approach, blending design with biology and material science, is pioneering new, sustainable pathways for product development. This company exemplifies how collaboration across various fields can lead to significant advancements in creating high-quality, sustainable products for the market.

Mango Materials

Mango Materials produces bio-polyester from renewable resources, aiming to revolutionise the textile industry with its eco-friendly approach. Their proprietary technology converts methane, a potent greenhouse gas, into poly-hydroxyalkanoate (PHA) powder, a biodegradable biopolymer. This material, which can degrade in various environments, offers an alternative to traditional plastics and is used in products ranging from textiles to cosmetic packaging. As the demand for sustainable products increases, Mango Materials is at the vanguard, providing a solution that not only reduces environmental impact but also turns harmful emissions into valuable, earth-friendly materials.

Frumat

Frumat is pioneering a sustainable transformation in material science by converting apple industry waste from Northern Italy into an eco-conscious alternative to leather named Apple Skin. This ingenious material is borne out of a need to tackle the environmental concerns associated with both agricultural waste and the synthetic material industries. By repurposing the remnants of local apple production, Frumat is hitting two birds with one apple, so to speak. Apple Skin, deriving its base from cellulose, offers a gamut of textures and can undergo various finishes such as embossing or laser printing, showcasing its adaptability and suitability for bespoke manufacturing. Frumat's catalogue includes two variants of Apple Skin: one, a suppler composition crafted for the fashion sector, apt for garments that demand flexibility and softness; and the other, a robust concoction made of 32% recycled apple fiber, 34% organic cotton and 34% recycled polyurethane (PU), which is ideal for creating enduring products like footwear, luggage and furniture upholstery. This bifurcated strategy by Frumat does more than just meet diverse sectoral demands – it represents a shift towards a circular economy where waste is a starting point for new, more sustainable production streams.

Source: Modern Meadow, 2023Source: Mango Materials, 2023 Source: Appleskin, n.d. (https://moea.io/pages/appleskin)

4.1.2 THE SKILL EVOLUTION: NAVIGATING INDUSTRY 4.0'S IMPACT ON FASHION CAREERS

The current technological landscape, as extensively covered in this text, is a fertile ground for innovation, providing companies with the potential to reap significant benefits. These include enhanced operational efficiencies and a deeper transparency across their supply chains. However, these advantages are contingent upon having a workforce adept in contemporary, often rapidly evolving technological domains. A persistent hurdle for businesses and educational institutions alike is ensuring their workforce is equipped with the necessary skills to handle new technological tools and processes (Wong & Ngai, 2021). As technology advances, the demand for certain skill sets surges, often outpacing the availability of professionals who possess them. According to a survey by Gartner (2021), 58% of organisations struggle to find candidates with the required modern skill sets, and nearly a third of these organisations have seen the skills gap widen over the past year.

Amidst this talent shortage, the concept of upskilling becomes a strategic imperative. Monster's 2022 analysis highlights that upskilling can be a potent solution, one that is not just about filling immediate skill voids but also about investing in the workforce for longer-term benefits. Notable among these are the retention of institutional knowledge and top-tier talent, which was emphasised by 52% of those surveyed. The practice of upskilling signals to employees the potential for varied career trajectories within the organisation, also cited by 52%. Financially, 46% regard upskilling as the more economical choice when compared to the costs of recruiting and training new staff (Monster 2022 global report, 2022).

Monster's research highlights the economic benefits of upskilling current employees compared to hiring new ones, with costs potentially 70% to 92% higher for acquiring new talent. This significant cost difference makes upskilling a strategic and economic necessity, particularly in a technology-driven business landscape, prompting companies to consider their options carefully.

Addressing the skills gap in organisations, especially in dynamic fields like fashion where technological proficiency is increasingly important, often boils down to two primary strategies: hiring new talent or training existing employees. Each approach comes with its opportunity costs and challenges:

- **Hiring new talent** – While bringing in new employees can bring fresh skills and perspectives into the organisation, it is not without its drawbacks. The recruitment process can be lengthy and expensive, and there is no guarantee of finding the perfect candidate. The integration of new hires typically involves substantial onboarding and training before they can fully contribute, adding to the time before the investment pays off.
- **Training existing employees** – On the other hand, upskilling current staff ensures that experienced employees who are already familiar with the company's culture and processes enhance their capabilities. However, this approach also has opportunity costs. It requires investment in training programs and possibly a temporary reduction in productivity as employees take time away from their regular duties to learn new skills. There's also the risk that the training may not meet all the company's skill requirements or that employees might leave the company after acquiring new skills at the company's expense.

Both strategies necessitate a careful evaluation of costs, benefits and the long-term impact on the organisation's human resource capabilities. Firms must balance these factors against their immediate needs and future goals to decide the most effective way to close the skills gap in their workforce. Graduates entering the fashion industry face numerous career paths which, while offering vast opportunities, also present the challenge of choice. Navigating this diversity requires being well-informed and strategic, aligning one's skills and interests with industry needs while staying adaptable to swiftly changing trends and technologies. Proactive engagement in continuous learning and professional development will be key to their long-term success and ability to make a meaningful impact in the fashion industry.

Skills audit framework: 21st-century digital skills

The following framework is adapted from van Laar et al., 2017. Digital skills will continue to evolve with advancements in digital technologies and the requirements of society, and therefore this is intended to provide individuals with a self-audit tool rather than a definitive list. The elements are listed in two categories: core skills and contextual skills. The core skills are seen as fundamental for performing tasks in a broad range of occupations, whereas contextual skills are dependent on the environment the skill is being applied in and tend to show sector or industry variation.

TABLE 4.1.1 Framework with core and contextual 21st-century digital skills (adapted from van Laar et al., 2017).

Core Skills	**Description**
Technical	The skills to use digital devices and applications to accomplish practical tasks and recognise specific online environments to navigate and maintain orientation.
Digital literacy	Mastery of both foundational and advanced digital tools goes beyond the basics to encompass a thorough understanding of the digital landscape.
Information management	The skills to use ICT to efficiently search, select, organise information to make informed decisions about the most suitable sources of information for a given task.
Communication	The skills to use ICT to efficiently search, select, organise information to make informed decisions about the most suitable sources of information for a given task.
Collaboration	The skills to use ICT to develop a social network and work in a team to exchange information, negotiate agreements and make decisions with mutual respect towards achieving a common goal.
Creativity	The skills to use ICT to generate new or previously unknown ideas or treat familiar ideas in a new way and transform such ideas into a product, service or process that is recognised as novel within a particular domain.
Critical thinking	The skills to use ICT to make informed judgements and choices about obtained information and communication using reflective reasoning and sufficient evidence to support the claims.
Problem solving	The skills to use ICT to cognitively process and understand a problem situation in combination with the active use of knowledge to find a solution to a problem.
Contextual Skills	
Ethical awareness	The skills to behave in a socially responsible way, demonstrating awareness and knowledge of legal and ethical aspects when using ICT.
Cultural awareness	The skills to show cultural understanding and respect other cultures when using ICT.
Flexibility	A flexible mindset and the skills to adapt one's behaviour to changing ICT environments are imperative in an industry characterised by rapid technological change.
Self-direction	The skills to set goals for yourself and manage progression toward reaching those goals to assess your own progress when using ICT.
Lifelong learning	The skills to constantly explore new opportunities when using ICT that can be integrated into an environment to continually improve one's capabilities.

*ICT is an abbreviation for information and communication technology

Mini task

Find five different examples of fashion graduate entry-level vacancies and review the requirements of the job specifications against this framework. Are all these skills listed? Are alternative names used? Are examples provided? Are examples of the level the skill is required at given (beginner, intermediate, advanced)? What alternative additional skills are also listed?

Assess your capabilities against the framework and job specifications. If you were to apply for these positions to what extent are you a good fit to the specification? What training might enhance your application further?

4.1.3 DIGITAL SKILLS IN FASHION: RESOURCES

As highlighted earlier, there is a rising demand for fashion graduates to possess a wide range of digital skills; however, this places a significant burden on students to learn a wide range of complex software. Despite this complexity, embracing this technology and making it an exploratory process can benefit students. Fashion professionals equipped with current skills enjoy higher demand, better career prospects, and higher salaries. The shift in fashion education towards these new needs is crucial, with institutions encouraged to adopt modern digital tools and software in their curricula to prepare students for the evolving industry landscape.

As indicated by our database analytics, the following technological areas show significant growth within the industry:

1. Computer-aided design (CAD), 2D and 3D design software
2. Data analytics
3. Web development & e-commerce

Computer-aided design (CAD), 2D and 3D design software

CAD and 3D design software have become indispensable tools in the fashion industry, enabling designers to create, visualise and modify their designs with precision and efficiency. These technologies facilitate a more sustainable approach by minimising material waste during the design phase. The adoption of these tools is reflected in job market demands, with around 17% of fashion industry positions requiring CAD or 2D design software proficiency, and nearly half of these roles necessitate skills in both areas (Worldskills, 2021). As such, proficiency in these software tools is highly valued in the fashion industry, and individuals equipped with these skills are well-positioned for a wide array of career opportunities.

Here is an overview of key 2D CAD/Vector Graphics software and their roles in the industry:

TABLE 4.1.2 Popular 2D CAD/Vector Graphics software used in fashion.

Software	Application to Industry
Adobe Photoshop	Used for editing and creating images, Photoshop allows designers to colour sketches, develop textile patterns and retouch photos. Its extensive range of tools supports the detailed creation of design elements for fashion.
Adobe Illustrator	This vector-based software is essential for crafting technical drawings and scalable fashion illustrations. Illustrator is preferred for its precision in creating flat sketches and complex design elements like logos and embroidery.
Lectra	A suite of solutions for fashion and apparel design, including pattern making and textile design.
CorelDRAW	Part of the CorelDRAW Graphics Suite offers a range of tools for vector illustration, layout and typography.
Affinity Designer	A popular vector graphic design software with capabilities similar to Illustrator.
Canva	An online design and publishing tool with a drag-and-drop interface. Offers vector graphics features but is generally more template-driven and suitable for non-designers. (This is increasingly being adopted within marketing roles in the fashion industry)

3D virtual prototyping in fashion

As the fashion industry navigates its path in the 21st century, there is a clear inclination towards leveraging technology for innovative, sustainable and efficient methodologies. One of the most transformative advancements within this domain is 3D virtual prototyping. Stemming from the rudimentary foundations of 2D CAD, this technology offers immense promise to reshape the fashion sector' modus operandi.

3D virtual prototyping can be defined as the digital creation and manipulation of garment designs in a three-dimensional space. Unlike traditional 2D designs where only flat sketches and patterns are generated, 3D virtual prototyping brings these designs to life, enabling a comprehensive view and understanding of the garment's fit, drape and overall aesthetics.

Benefits of 3D virtual prototyping in fashion

1. **Sustainability** – The iterative nature of fashion design often results in material wastage. By prototyping designs virtually, designers can make swift modifications without the need for physical resources, leading to a substantial reduction in material wastage.
2. **Efficiency** – This technology cuts down the time between ideation and realisation. Designers can rapidly iterate, test and finalise designs, thereby compressing the time-to-market and increasing agility.

TABLE 4.1.3 Popular 3D prototyping software used in fashion.

Software	Application to Industry
Style3D	Specialising in fashion design and garment simulation, Style3D offers tools for designers to create, adjust and visualise clothing items in 3D, streamlining the fashion design process and allowing for rapid prototyping and adjustments.
CLO Virtual Fashion	CLO is a powerful software used for fashion design that simulates fabrics and patterns in 3D, enabling designers to create and alter clothing in a virtual environment, which enhances the design process and reduces the need for physical samples.
Blender	Blender is a free, open-source 3D creation suite supporting the entirety of the 3D pipeline. It is highly versatile, being used for modelling, animation, simulation, rendering, compositing, motion tracking, video editing and game creation.
Rhinoceros 3D	Rhinoceros (Rhino) is a 3D computer graphics and CAD application, known for its mathematical precision in creating and editing curves and surfaces. It is widely used in architecture, industrial design, jewellery design, automotive design and more due to its versatile modelling capabilities.
SketchUp	SketchUp is known for its user-friendly interface and is widely used for architectural design and planning. With a vast library of plugins and an extensive 3D warehouse of models, it's a go-to tool for quick 3D modelling of buildings and in-store layouts, spatial planning and interiors.
Substance 3D (Adobe)	While Adobe's Substance 3D is more known for texturing, it is part of a suite that also includes modelling tools. It's commonly used for 3D painting, material creation and texture mapping, integrating well with other Adobe products for a streamlined workflow.
V-Stitcher (Browzwear)	A stalwart in the industry, known for its in-depth detailing and realistic fabric simulations. Browzwear University launched as a response to COVID-19 and the changing educational landscape, Browzwear University offers an online platform for methodological learning in fashion. It also provides a guide page for students to showcase their portfolios.
Accumark3D (Gerber)	Known for its robust pattern design and grading tools, Gerber's Accumark3D offers an intuitive interface for 3D garment visualisation.
Modaris 3D (Lectra)	This solution from Lectra focuses on ensuring a garment's fit is accurate by providing detailed virtual representations.
Optitex3D	Provides a comprehensive suite for 2D pattern design which seamlessly translates into 3D mock-ups.

3. **Cost-effectiveness** – Reducing the number of physical samples leads to tangible savings in terms of materials, labour and shipping.

3D virtual prototyping tools in fashion

3D modelling has become a cornerstone in many industries, such as gaming, film, architecture and fashion, for creating detailed and lifelike digital representations. Below are several notable 3D modelling software providers, along with descriptors highlighting their features and industry applications.

Each of these providers caters to different aspects of the 3D modelling industry, offering a range of functionalities from general-purpose modelling and animation to industry-specific solutions like fashion design and architectural visualisation.

Mini case study

Hugo Boss and Adobe Substance 3D: Pioneering digital transformation in fashion

Hugo Boss has significantly invested in digital transformation, particularly through the integration of 3D design technology, which has been part of its strategy since 2012. This long-term commitment has established the brand as a forerunner in the digital space within the fashion industry. On their German campus, a dedicated team of over 500 specialists works with cutting-edge 3D technology, particularly utilizing tools from Adobe Substance 3D, to advance their design and production processes.

The partnership with Adobe Substance 3D has been pivotal, providing a suite of tools for 3D painting, animation and rendering. These tools have enabled Hugo Boss to produce highly accurate, photorealistic visualisations of their products, capturing the finest details such as fabric textures and logo embroideries with precision. One standout application is the development of 'virtual try-ons', leveraging body scanning technology to reduce the guesswork for customers shopping online and subsequently decreasing return rates – a significant concern in the realm of fashion e-commerce.

Adobe Substance 3D's Painter has revolutionised how Hugo Boss approaches fabric design. By allowing designers to experiment and finalise patterns digitally, Hugo Boss has reduced its dependency on external textile suppliers and physical samples, which historically slow down the fashion supply chain. The move towards digital samples has brought about unprecedented accuracy and flexibility, transforming how the brand approaches its design-to-production cycle.

As a result of these advancements, Hugo Boss has significantly increased the efficiency of its design process. Over 60% of its design operations are now executed with digital tools, and the brand aims to push this to 90% within the next year.

Hugo Boss's strategic alliance with Adobe Substance 3D stands as a testament to the power of digital technology in redefining fashion processes. This collaboration showcases the brand's innovative spirit and serves as an inspiring case study for the rest of the industry, pointing towards a future where digital solutions are integral to fashion design and retail.

Sources: Douglass, 2023; Adobe, 2023

Real-time 3D technology

Interactive 3D technology is transforming industries by enabling immersive experiences far beyond traditional media's capacity. As real-time engines become crucial for adding interactivity and life to 3D models, industries are seeing an unprecedented surge in demand for professionals with real-time 3D skills. This demand spans various fields, from industrial design to entertainment and education, indicating that proficiency in real-time 3D is quickly becoming a valuable asset in the job market.

To ensure that the workforce can meet this demand, education and industry practices must evolve. Educational institutions need to incorporate real-time 3D and interactive media into their courses, creating a curriculum that mirrors the interdisciplinary nature of the field. Training in specific tools, such as Unreal Engine, is essential since the need for these skills is expected to grow significantly.

Real-time 3D technology has become integral to various industries, revolutionising the way we create, interact with and experience digital content.

The table below lists popular real-time 3D technology providers along with brief descriptors:

TABLE 4.1.4 Real-time 3D technology (interdisciplinary usage).

Software	Application to Industry
Unreal Engine (Epic Games)	Unreal Engine is a highly advanced real-time 3D creation tool, Unreal Engine offers a comprehensive suite of development tools for anyone working with real-time technology. From game developers to architects and filmmakers, it's renowned for its high-fidelity graphics and extensive support for VR and AR content creation.
Unity Technologies	Unity is a flexible and powerful development platform used to create multi-platform 3D and 2D games and interactive experiences. It's well-known for its accessibility to indie developers, extensive asset store and its ability to deploy across more than 25 platforms.

(*Continued*)

TABLE 4.1.4 (Continued)

Software	Application to Industry
CryEngine (Crytek)	CryEngine is known for pushing the boundaries of graphical fidelity with its full suite of development tools. The engine has been behind some of the most visually stunning video games and is available for developers who want to achieve high-end visuals.
PlayCanvas	PlayCanvas is an online game development platform known for its cloud-based workflow, which allows for collaborative real-time editing. It is specifically tailored for creating 3D games and immersive experiences on the web.
O3DE (Open 3D Engine)	O3DE launched by the Linux Foundation, this open-source engine focuses on high-fidelity graphics and is designed for building games and simulations. It offers flexibility for developers looking for a community-supported engine alternative.

These providers offer a range of tools tailored to various needs within the real-time 3D content creation spectrum, from game development to simulations and virtual productions. Each has its unique strengths and focuses, making the choice of engine as much about the specific needs of the project as about the overall capabilities of the software.

4.1.4 ADVANCED TOOLS: UNREAL ENGINE AND STYLE3D

Unreal Engine, originally a creation for gaming, has quickly been integrated into fashion due to its ability to generate high-fidelity, interactive 3D environments and garments. The software excels in bringing digital creations to life with advanced realism, which is crucial for designers looking to showcase their work in the digital space.

Its importance in fashion lies in its utility for designers to visualise and iterate on designs in real-time, enhancing creativity and productivity. It allows for a seamless blend of art and technology, enabling designers to create immersive virtual showrooms and fashion shows. This kind of technology has become a necessity for brands aiming to stay relevant in a digital-centric market where customers expect rich, engaging online experiences.

Unreal Engine has expanded its influence into the fashion industry, offering a suite of uses that have proven invaluable for design, marketing and customer engagement:

- **Design and prototyping** – Designers use Unreal Engine for creating and refining 3D models of clothing and accessories. The software's advanced rendering capabilities allow for detailed textures and realistic lighting, which are essential for evaluating how a garment will look and move in reality.
- **Virtual fashion shows** – With in-person events often being costly and limited by location, Unreal Engine enables fashion brands to stage virtual fashion shows. These can be streamed to a global audience,

offering an interactive and immersive viewing experience that can go beyond the constraints of the physical world.

- **Interactive retail experiences** – Brands are crafting interactive digital showrooms and retail spaces within Unreal Engine, allowing customers to explore collections in a virtual environment. This approach merges e-commerce with an immersive in-store experience, potentially increasing engagement and sales.
- **Gamification** – Video games like Fortnite have introduced fashion into their virtual environments through partnerships with brands like Moncler and Balenciaga, showcasing Unreal Engine's flexibility. Additionally, companies like Timberland have developed their own virtual worlds, demonstrating the engine's broad applicability.
- **Marketing and digital assets** – The software is used to produce high-quality visual content for marketing campaigns. It enables the creation of striking, photorealistic images and videos that can be used across various digital platforms, from social media to online advertisements.
- **Customisation and personalisation** – Unreal Engine can power apps that allow customers to customise and personalise products in real-time, seeing their choices rendered immediately. This enhances the shopping experience and allows for a more personal connection with the product.
- **Sustainability through visualisation** – By visualising designs in a virtual space, brands can reduce the need for physical samples, which contributes to waste reduction. It's a step towards more sustainable practices in the industry by minimising material usage and waste.

The incorporation of Unreal Engine into the fashion industry is not just about the appeal of technology but also about addressing practical needs such as cost efficiency, sustainability and the demand for innovative customer experiences. It's a tool that's reshaping the industry, opening new possibilities for designers and retailers alike.

The Unreal Engine website features a diverse and extensive range of free tutorials, courses and other learning resources. www.unrealengine.com

Style3D

Style3D specialises in creating cutting-edge 3D modelling software tailored for fashion designers and brands. Their platform enables the digital creation of clothing, accessories and footwear, allowing designers to visualise and modify their creations in a virtual space before proceeding to the production stage. With Style3D, fashion and apparel designers can create 3D clothing simulations with high visual and functional fidelity. The software allows users to create patterns and arrange them on a virtual model; adjustments to the patterns and fabrics are immediately reflected in a 3D sample that can be rotated and examined from any angle. This real-time rendering capability accelerates the design process, enables rapid prototyping and reduces the need for physical samples, leading to cost savings and a reduced environmental impact.

Style3D's platform is known for its realistic fabric simulation, extensive material library and powerful tools that mimic traditional patternmaking and design techniques in a virtual environment. The software is utilised by individual designers, educational institutions and global fashion brands to innovate, collaborate and streamline the product development cycle. With features that support design, draping, pattern making, fitting and animation, Style3D is at the forefront of the digital transformation in the fashion industry, promoting efficiency, creativity and sustainability.

Style3D offer a range of free training workshops, courses and video tutorials. www.linctex.com

4.1.5 CASE STUDY: DEVELOPING DIGITAL SKILLS: A FASHION BUSINESS MASTERCLASS IN VIRTUAL 3D PROTOTYPING WITH STYLE3D AT THE UNIVERSITY OF MANCHESTER

The use of 3D DPC software changes the design process and enables greater collaboration across disciplinary roles, reshaping the required soft skills and subject-specific skills that are needed by digital product development professionals (Casciani et al., 2022). Today, businesses are increasingly searching for new hybrid professionals with combined digital, fashion and business backgrounds (Kalbaska and Cantoni, 2019). Increasingly, all stakeholders need to have a more well-rounded understanding of digital technologies, costing and manufacturing to ensure production feasibility (Sun and Zhao, 2018). The creation of a manufacturable garment using 3D design tools requires a set of advanced interrelated skills and knowledge, including technical product expertise, material understanding and an appreciation of garment fit. Individuals with this skillset and knowledge are key to establishing and advancing DPC workflows and integrating digital twins (Harrop, 2023). This highlights that for DPC to scale and achieve its potential, organisations need to go beyond investing in technology and to review the collaborative processes in the extended enterprise and address the upskilling of staff to leverage digital tools to do their best work. Accordingly, universities offering fashion programmes are increasingly including the educational experience of DPC to better prepare future professionals with the right foundational capabilities and thereby improve employment outcomes of graduates with specific work-relevant skills and competencies.

In this research, we collaborated with Style3D to explore the potential of a short industry-facilitated 4-day masterclass to inform curriculum development. The collaboration with Style3D enabled the rapid evaluation of potential learning benefits and barriers of this type of digital technology. The masterclass consisted of fashion business students (n=22) and aimed to enhance their understanding of 3D technologies and consider the digital transformation of the industry. The masterclass consisted of an introduction to the topic and orientation to the software and three classes totalling approximately nine hours of experimentation. During the masterclass, students worked collaboratively to 1. select and digitalise a fabric, 2. modify a T-shirt block pattern, 3. select and modify a 3D avatar for product rendering and virtual catwalk of the masterclass garments and 4. (optional) investigate the potential of non-fungible tokens (NFT). During the interactive masterclass, the participants, with minimal technical expertise, used Style3D virtual modelling software for the process of 2D-to-3D design, product visualisation, simulation and marketing of virtual fashion products.

FIGURE 4.1.1 3D Kimono design using the Style3D software. Design is shown on avatar providing front, back and side views.

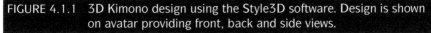

According to the study, the fashion business students saw many advantages in participating in the non-credit-bearing masterclass and made rapid progress in developing new 3D virtual prototyping skills. The fashion business students reported the experience as helpful in understanding the potential of 3D software technologies within more sustainable product development processes, and to understand their roles as fashion marketing and/or management professionals within DPC workflows. They were able to evidence their new skills with digital assets and a certificate of participation. The masterclass helped to make connections between existing knowledge and ideas, but further support in garment and pattern construction was needed. The study suggests that the integration of virtual prototyping in the fashion business curriculum can provide innovative learning experiences and enhance students' understanding of 3D technologies and their potential for impact as workflows evolve and mature.

This case study is intended to demonstrate the rapid progress made during the 4-day course and to encourage others to invest time to upgrade their 3D design knowledge. Many software companies offer the opportunity to personalise learning through online learning courses to develop 3D design skills through individual, independent and flexible study.

4.1.6 DATA AND ANALYTICAL TOOLS

Data analytics is a critical skill for fashion industry graduates. It sharpens trend forecasting and deepens understanding of consumer behaviour, key to making informed decisions. This analytical capability is vital for managing supply chains, optimising stock levels and streamlining production. In e-commerce, it helps craft targeted marketing strategies and improve user experiences. Analytics also supports sustainable practices by ensuring efficient use of resources and sustainable supply chains. It aids in managing risks by providing insights into market changes. With the rise of smart textiles and new technologies, analytical skills are necessary to harness their potential. Therefore, proficiency in data analytics is essential for fashion graduates to effectively contribute to the industry's progress.

Table 4.1.5 provides a list of data analytics tools used widely within the fashion industry.

These tools offer a blend of capabilities that can be harnessed to make data-driven decisions, enhance customer experiences, optimise operations and maintain a competitive edge in the fast-paced world of fashion.

TABLE 4.1.5 Data analytics tools used within fashion.

Software	**Application to Industry**
Tableau	Tableau is a powerful and fast-growing data visualisation tool used in the Business Intelligence Industry. In fashion, it helps brands visualise their data to understand patterns and insights, facilitating better decisions on aspects like inventory management, sales trends and customer preferences.
Google Analytics	Widely used for tracking and reporting website traffic, Google Analytics is also a vital tool for e-commerce platforms in the fashion industry to analyse customer online behaviour and optimise marketing strategies.
Adobe Analytics	This tool provides detailed insights into customer behaviours on digital platforms. For fashion retailers, it allows for an in-depth understanding of how users interact with their online presence, aiding in personalisation and targeted marketing efforts.
SAS Analytics	Providing advanced analytics, SAS helps fashion brands to manage, analyse and interpret large volumes of data to inform trend forecasting, supply chain operations and customer relationship management.
Microsoft Power BI	A suite of business analytics tools that deliver insights throughout an organisation. Fashion brands use it to connect to hundreds of data sources, simplify data prep and drive ad hoc analysis.
Looker	Now part of Google Cloud, Looker supports data exploration and insights. Fashion brands use it for its robust data modelling and powerful analytics capabilities that inform decisions across the supply chain.
QlikView/ Qlik Sense	Qlik's associative engine allows for in-depth, custom reporting and analytics, enabling fashion retailers to build their own data analysis applications with guided storytelling functionalities for more informed business decisions.
SPSS (IBM)	This modular, integrated, full-spectrum analytics software platform enables fashion businesses to address the entire analytical process, from planning to data collection to analysis, reporting and deployment.
Minitab	Minitab is statistical software that helps businesses predict trends and find solutions to their most challenging business problems. In fashion, it's used for quality control and to optimise design and production processes.
Alteryx	Alteryx provides end-to-end data analytics for data blending and advanced data modelling. It is useful for fashion brands looking to delve deep into customer data and operational performance without the need for complex code.

4.1.7 WEB DEVELOPMENT AND E-COMMERCE

Awareness of web development and e-commerce tools is increasingly indispensable for fashion graduates due to the digital transformation of the industry. A strong command over these skills enables graduates to create and maintain a brand's digital identity, optimise online retail operations and engage customers through enhanced online experiences. In an omnichannel retail landscape, proficiency in digital tools equips graduates to drive traffic, analyse consumer data and manage sales strategies effectively. This knowledge is also economically advantageous, reducing reliance on external agencies and fostering cost efficiency. Additionally, an understanding of digital platforms is crucial for ensuring a brand's competitive edge, facilitating global market access, and endorsing sustainable business practices. In essence, for those entering the fashion sector, expertise in web development and e-commerce is a powerful asset, enriching both the brand's value and the professional's adaptability in a dynamic market.

Table 4.1.6 lists some of the most popular tools and platforms used in the fashion industry:

TABLE 4.1.6 Web development and e-commerce development tools.

Software	Application to Industry
Magento (Adobe Commerce)	A leading open-source e-commerce platform, Magento offers powerful and flexible features that are highly customisable for complex online fashion stores, enabling advanced marketing, search engine optimisation and catalogue-management needs.
WooCommerce	An open-source e-commerce plugin for WordPress, WooCommerce is favoured by fashion start-ups for its simplicity and customisable platform that integrates seamlessly with WordPress websites.
BigCommerce	Serves as a scalable e-commerce solution for online stores. It offers various built-in features and is adaptable for both small businesses and large enterprise-level fashion brands.
Squarespace	With its design-oriented website builder, Squarespace is a hit among fashion brands that prioritise aesthetics. It provides sleek templates that are ideal for creating visually appealing online stores.
Wix/EditorX	Wix is known for its drag-and-drop builder that allows for easy creation of simple e-commerce sites. It is suitable for small fashion retailers that require an intuitive platform with moderate customisation.
Salesforce Commerce Cloud	Formerly Demandware, Salesforce Commerce Cloud is a cloud-based e-commerce solution offering a range of features for CRM, AI, and data-driven customisation for larger fashion retailers.
Adobe Dreamweaver	A long-standing web development tool, Dreamweaver is for those who have more technical knowledge and want to hand-code their e-commerce platform for ultimate control over their design and functionality.

Each of these tools caters to different needs, from ease of use and design flexibility to robust data handling and extensive customisation. Fashion brands typically select the platform that best aligns with their size, technical expertise, customer engagement strategies, and long-term digital goals.

4.1.8 THE FUTURE DIGITAL SKILLS IN FASHION: AN INTERVIEW WITH DR. MONIKA JANUSZKIEWICZ

Dr. Monika Januszkiewicz, a prominent figure in fashion technology and 3D body Scanning, shares her insights on the future of digital skills in fashion and how to bridge the perceived gap between industry and academia.

Interviewer: Could you provide a brief overview of your background and experience in the fashion technology field?

Dr. Januszkiewicz: My journey began at the University of Huddersfield, where I was studying 'Textile Buying Management' with my dissertation focused on designing a 3D-printed dress using the Selective Laser Sintering method. This piqued my interest in fashion technology, leading me to a PhD at the University of Manchester, where I delved into the ergonomics of 3D body scanning technologies. I then ventured into the start-up world in Germany as a Product Manager, applying computer vision and machine learning to virtual fit and mobile scanning solutions and exploring the interoperability of 3D assets on the POS blockchain. Currently, I'm part of the immersive technologies team at PWC UK, overseeing its operations and providing technical and regulatory expertise for various projects.

Interviewer: In the areas of fashion product development, material innovation, and technology, what are the essential competencies or skills that students should aim to master?

Dr. Januszkiewicz: The field can be segmented into three pillars:

1. **Anthropometry and biomechanics** – Grasping human measurements is vital for creating apparel that's not just stylish but also functional and comfortable. Technologies like 3D body scanners and volumetric capture equipment play a significant role here.
2. **Textile science** – Beyond understanding the body, there's the cloth. Grasping the intricacies of various fabrics and materials, their interactions with each other and the body, and translating this knowledge digitally is paramount. The digital representations need to reflect the real-world behaviour of these fabrics to be effective.

3. **Business acumen and manufacturing** – Once designs are finalised, they need to be produced. This involves a deep knowledge of the supply chain, manufacturing processes, PLM, and technologies that optimise materials. The inclusion of robotics, CAD & CAM, and even blockchain can further streamline this process.

Interviewer: There's a perceived skills gap between the fashion industry and academia. What steps should be taken to better prepare students for the industry's evolving demands?

Dr. Januszkiewicz: The gap might be more perception than reality. Big fashion brands sometimes mistakenly view technology as a simple plug-and-play solution. They think that by hiring a contractor, the work will be completed seamlessly. However, the reality is different. From my experience, many fashion technology start-ups employ individuals from computer science backgrounds rather than those with a deep understanding of fashion. While these individuals might excel in programming or developing models, they often lack a nuanced understanding of fashion dynamics. For instance, when designing a virtual sweater for try-on, engineers may devise an excellent mathematical model for generating wrinkles. Still, they may overlook how fabric weight and pattern structure influence the type of wrinkles.

To bridge this gap, it's essential to foster collaboration between fashion students and those from different fields. Interdisciplinary efforts, like hackathons, where participants come from varied backgrounds, can be invaluable. These events will allow participants to understand each other's vocabulary and learn how to work together effectively. Most importantly, the fashion industry needs specialised training datasets for large language models (LLM) to capture its unique requirements fully. Relying on borrowed datasets, especially from the medical field, is insufficient.

Interviewer: Are there any emerging technologies or trends that you believe should be incorporated into the university fashion degree programmes?

Dr. Januszkiewicz: In fashion, direction is crucial. If you're working with pattern drafting, body scanning and processing technologies are essential. Knowing software like ZBrush or Maya to edit body scan models gives you a competitive edge. Textile-focused individuals should be familiar with software like Clo3d and gain experience in digitising fabric. If you're going into manufacturing, understanding smart contracts and blockchain can be helpful, especially when auditing factories. And for marketing, extended reality or augmented reality could be useful to enhance storytelling. The choice of technology depends on your goals.

Interviewer: How can universities collaborate better with industry professionals to keep fashion education relevant?

Dr. Januszkiewicz: At straiqr, we partnered with a few universities. Collaborating not just with traditional fashion houses but also with tech startups is key as they offer universities deeper insights into the rapidly evolving industry. Participating in events with industry professionals can provide students with an unparalleled hands-on experience, enabling them to brainstorm real-world problems. Another essential aspect is bridging the gap between theory and practice. Universities could encourage students to approach their degrees as portfolios. Rather than focusing solely on theoretical knowledge, students would benefit from understanding the practical applications of technologies and their current use in the industry. They should be driven by purpose and think about what skills and technologies they want to master and the problems they find interesting to solve.

Interviewer: What are the industry-specific software tools you recommend students familiarise themselves with?

Dr. Januszkiewicz: It depends on the direction. For 3D body scanning, one should be familiar with software from scan providers and 3D editing tools. For fabric design, simulation software like Clo3D is useful. If working with manufacturing data, understanding PLM systems and blockchain basics will place you ahead of the competition.

Interviewer: What's your take on the integration of metaverse in the fashion industry?

Dr. Januszkiewicz: Metaverse can be described as a three-dimensional virtual world with a social and economic system in which people interact as avatars with each other and with software agents. It is underpinned by extended reality (XR), 5G, cloud computing, artificial intelligence (AI), and the Internet of Things (IoT). XR encompasses augmented reality (AR), virtual reality (VR) and mixed reality (MR). However, creating a virtual workspace that can effectively animate human interactions and emotions in real time presents immense technical and ethical challenges. Yet, that is not to say the underlying technology isn't transformative. The existing applications permeate various sectors such as education, healthcare, gaming, entertainment, arts, and civic engagement. At PwC, we look at the prospective advantages of the Metaverse, which include amplifying educational and professional training experiences, assisting in medical research, nurturing community and art platforms, and offering expanded venues for events and commerce.

Fashion, in my view, lags slightly behind. It seems the industry is more drawn to the 'hype' rather than earnestly striving for innovation. A vivid illustration of potential cross-industry collaboration came from the automotive world when Aston Martin collaborated with Varjo XR and the Unreal Engine. Together, they used VR to foster collaboration between designers and engineers to iterate car designs in a shared virtual space. This kind of integrated design approach could be revolutionary for the fashion sector. However, understanding the technology is paramount. Consider the popular topic of blockchain in fashion. Many articles project an overly simplified or incorrect perspective on how technologies like NFTs work in conjunction with the blockchain. For instance, many believe that an entire 3D graphic can be stored on the blockchain securely in a decentralised manner, which isn't the case. Most often, what's placed on the blockchain is essentially a 'pointer' to where the actual asset is stored, usually on centralised systems like AWS. My advice for fashion professionals would be to dive deep into these technologies. Avoid getting swept up solely by the hype. It's essential to spend time genuinely experimenting with and understanding the technology, not just in theory but hands-on. For the metaverse and 3D fashion tech to truly integrate and thrive in the fashion world, we need iterative experimentation. It's about taking gradual steps, understanding the barriers, whether they be in data collection or processing, and figuring out how to overcome them for seamless integration.

Interviewer: Do you believe the metaverse is going to have a long-lasting impact on the fashion industry? What are the specific benefits and challenges of implementing it?

Dr. Januszkiewicz: The concept of the metaverse is still in its early stages and not yet clearly defined. However, I genuinely believe in the potential of blending the digital and physical realms to achieve more sustainable outcomes in fashion. If we want to label that amalgamation as the 'metaverse', that's fine. But naming isn't the crux here. The essential aspect is how these digital technologies can be utilised to reduce waste, a significant issue in the fashion industry right now. The goal should be about genuine sustainability and not just employing technologies as marketing gimmicks, as we see with some uses of NFTs or 3D avatars in digital fashion. For instance, generative AI is a recent buzzword. Brands are leveraging it to generate their fit models, touting increased diversity and inclusivity. But why was this not accomplished with real individuals, and what happened with photographers whose work was used to train these models but often received no compensation for their work? The underlying motive, unfortunately, often revolves around cost-cutting rather than true innovation. Brands might sidestep hiring real models for photoshoots under the guise of 'embracing technology'.

The industry can't solely focus on optimisation. Consider brands like Shein; their business model is hardly sustainable. Merely ramping up efficiency isn't the solution. We must explore alternatives and educate consumers about the value of sustainable fashion. For instance, body scanning and digital sampling are (currently) quite labour-intensive because we still need standards but can yield more sustainable and fitting products. The challenge lies in convincing consumers of the value of these products, especially when juxtaposed with fast-fashion giants. Perhaps positioning these innovations under the 'metaverse' umbrella could act as a catalyst for change. The term might draw attention and interest. It's early days, but the potential and challenges are significant.

Dr Monika Januszkiewicz, 2023
Note: This interview has been reformatted for clarity and conciseness.

4.1.9 TASK: DIGITAL READINESS FOR FASHION 4.0 – PREPARING FOR A CAREER

Considering the significant digital transformation in the fashion industry, readers are encouraged to reflect on how these changes impact their own future career ambitions. Below is a list of key tasks that you can do to prepare you for your careers. Remember, although your degree or course may be creative, it may not have the agility required to equip you with the most up-to-date digital skills. Therefore, as the conclusion to this book, we highly encourage you to undertake the tasks below in preparation for your future careers within the digitally evolved fashion industry. This project will encompass research, practical skills development and career planning, all aimed at equipping students with the knowledge and skills for emerging digital roles in fashion.

Independent skills building tasks

1. **Self-assessment** – Evaluate your current digital skillset against industry requirements. Research relevant careers in line with your future ambitions, read the job specifications and identify any gaps in your knowledge and skills that need to be filled.
2. **Research and exploration** – To stay up-to-date, research the latest trends in fashion technology, sustainable innovation, and digital marketing strategies. Follow fashion tech platforms like The Interline, join webinars and subscribe to journals that focus on the intersection of fashion and technology.

3. **Learning new tools and technologies** – Enrol in online courses to learn about 3D design software (e.g., Style3D, Clo3D, Adobe Substance), AR/VR applications in fashion and digital pattern making. Experiment with these tools to create your own designs and understand their application in the design-to-retail process.
4. **Build your network** – Connect with professionals in the digital fashion space on platforms like LinkedIn or through virtual meetups and conferences. Engage in discussions and forums related to fashion technology to build your professional network.
5. **Practical application** – Identify relevant competitions or find industry projects where you can respond to a real-world scenario relevant to your future career pathway. If possible, secure an internship, an industry placement or volunteer in roles that allow you to practice digital skills in real-world settings.
6. **Portfolio development** – Compile a digital portfolio of your work that highlights your digital skill proficiency and include any relevant projects or collaborations that showcase your ability to adapt to and innovate in the digital fashion environment. Build your own online portfolio using free, easy to use software such as Wix.com, TheDots, Behance.
7. **Brand yourself** – Create a personal brand that emphasises your unique combination of creative and digital skills. Develop an online presence that showcases your work and knowledge in digital fashion spaces.
8. **Career strategy** – Develop a career strategy that includes short-term and long-term goals. Consider where you want to be in the next five to ten years within the digital fashion landscape. Map out the steps you'll need to take to achieve these goals, including further education, certifications, and networking opportunities.
9. **Stay current** – Commit to lifelong learning to keep your digital skills up to date as technology evolves. Regularly review and refresh your knowledge to stay ahead in the competitive fashion industry.
10. **Final reflection** – Write a reflective summary that articulates how you envision your role in the future of fashion, considering the digital competencies you've developed, and how you can contribute to the industry's growth and transformation.

Through engaging in these tasks, you will build a strong foundation that aligns with the technological advancements in the fashion industry, ensuring that you are well-prepared for the digital demands of future career opportunities.

Bibliography and further reading

Adobe (2023). *Hugo Boss improves design times by 85% with 3D – Adobe*. Available at: https://www.adobe.com/products/substance3d/magazine/hugo-boss-leverages-substance-for-3d-fashion-design.html.

Appleskin (n. d.). *MoEa*. Available at: https://moea.io/pages/appleskin (accessed 21 February 2024).

Casciani, D., Chkanikova, O. and Pal, R. (2022). 'Exploring the nature of digital transformation in the fashion industry: opportunities for supply chains, business models, and sustainability-oriented innovations', *Sustainability: Science, Practice and Policy*. 18(1), pp. 773–795.

Conlon, J. and Gallery, C. (2023). 'Developing digital skills: A fashion business masterclass in virtual 3D prototyping with Style3D', *International Journal of Fashion Design, Technology and Education*, 17(1), pp. 76–85. doi:10.1080/17543266.2023.2247425

Cresswell, K. (2023). *From runway to gameplay: The rise of fashion in gaming*. Available at: https://www.anzu.io/blog/fashion-brands-in-game-advertising

Douglass, R. (2023). 'Hugo Boss partners with Adobe to power 3D design methods', FashionUnited. Available at: https://fashionunited.com/news/business/hugo-boss-partners-with-adobe-to-power-3d-design-methods/2022102050257 (accessed 14 February 2024).

Ellen MacArthur Foundation (2019). *Fashion and the circular economy*. https://www.ellenmacarthurfoundation.org/fashion-and-the-circular-economy-deep-dive

Epic Group (2023). Home page. Available at:https://www.epicgroup.global/corpinfo21v1/index.php/corpinfo21v1

Fibre2Fashion (2021). Interview with Ranjan Mahtani. Available at:https://www.fibre2fashion.com/interviews/face2face/epic-group/ranjan-mahtani/13089-1

Gartner (2021). 'HR research finds 58% of the workforce will need new skill sets', Gartner.com. Available at: https://www.gartner.com/en/newsroom/press-releases/2021-02-03-gartner-hr-research-finds-fifty-eight-percent-of-the-workforce-will-need-new-skill-sets-to-do-their-jobs-successfully (accessed 13 February 2024).

Harris, S. (2008). 'Catwalk goes techno (wearable technologies)', *Engineering &Technology*, 3(18), 28–30. doi:10.1049/et:20081801

Harrop, M. (2023). 'Why digital twins will be essential to building end-to-end workflows', *The Interline*. Available at: https://www.theinterline.com/2023/08/15/why-digital-twins-will-be-essential-to-building-end-to-end-workflows/ (accessed 13 February 2024).

Husband, L. (2023). *Relentless pursuit of better: What's really disrupting the fashionindustry*. Available at:https://www.just-style.com/interviews/relentless-pursuit-of-better-whats-really-disrupting the-fashion-industry/

Inside Fashion (n.d.). *Where, why and how: A 2020 perspective on global sourcing*, Ranjan Mahtani, Chairman, EPIC Group. Available at:http://inside-fashion.net.tempdomain.com/FASHCON/FASHCON2020Program/Speakers/tabid/232/ArticleID/1029/Where-Why-and-How-A-Global-Perspective-on-Sourcing-for-the-Next-Decade.aspx

InteliStyle (n.d). *The ultimate guide to fashion digital transformation*. Available at: https://www.intelistyle.com/the-ultimate-guide-to-fashion-digital-transformation/

Joy, A., Zhu, Y., Peña, C. and Brouard, M. (2022). 'Digital future of luxury brands: Metaverse, digital fashion, and non-fungible tokens', *Strategic Change*, 31(3), 337– 343. doi:10.1002/jsc.2502

Just Style (2023). Q&A – Ranjan Mahtani, Executive Chairman, Epic Group. Available at: https://www.just-style.com/awards-rankings/thought-leadership/qa-ranjan-mahtani-executive-chairman-epic-group/#catfish

Kalbaska, N. and Cantoni, L. (2019). 'Digital fashion competences: Market practices and needs'. In R. Rinaldi and R. Bandinelli (eds) *Business Models and ICT Technologies for the Fashion Supply Chain: Proceedings of IT4Fashion 2017 and IT4Fashion 2018* (pp. 125–135). Springer International Publishing.

Mango Materials (n.d.). Home page. Available at: https://www.mangomaterials.com/ (accessed 13 February 2024).

McDowell, M. (2021). '2021: The year in fashion-tech', *Vogue Business*. Available at: https://www.voguebusiness.com/technology/2021-the-year-in-fashion-tech.

McKinsey & Company (2020). *Fashion's digital transformation: Now or never*. Available at: https://www.mckinsey.com/industries/retail/our-insights/fashions-digital-transformation-now-or-never

McKinsey & Company (2022). *State of Fashion Technology Report 2022*. Available at: https://www.mckinsey.com/industries/retail/our-insights/state-of-fashion-technology-report-2022.

McKinsey (2023). *Generative AI: Unlocking the future of fashion*. Available at: https://www.mckinsey.com/industries/retail/our-insights/generative-ai-unlocking-the-future-of-fashion

Modern Meadow (n.d.). Home page. Available at: https://modernmeadow.com/ (accessed 12 February 2024).

Monster Government Solutions (2022). Monster 2022 Global Report (2022) . Available at: https://www.monstergovernmentsolutions.com/docs/The-Future-of-Work-2022-Global-Report.pdf (accessed 14 February 2024).

Movement Strategy (2022). *Web3 Demographics: The Users Behind Web3*. Available at: https://movementstrategy.com/editorial/users-web3-demographics/.

New Forum (2022a). *Regina Turbina shares her perspective on digital fashion, NFTs & wearables in the metaverse*. Available at: https://medium.com/@newforum/regina-turbina-shares-her-perspective-on-digital-fashion-nfts-wearables-in-the-metaverse-61433fa26bb2

New Forum (2022b). Regina Turbina Shares Her Perspective On Digital Fashion, NFTs & Wearables In The Metaverse. [YouTube]. Available at: https://www.youtube.com/watch?v=foOKyFPQCUI&ab_channel=NEWFORUM

Noris, A, Nobile, T., Sabatini, N. and Cantoni, L. (2020). 'Digital fashion: A systematic literature review. A perspective on marketing and communication', *Journal of Global Fashion Marketing*. 10.1080/20932685.2020.1835522.

Pedroso-Roussado, C. (2023). 'The fashion industry needs microbiology:Opportunitiesandchallenges', *mSphere*, 8(2). doi:10.1128/msphere.00681-22.

Petkova, I. (2018). 'New institutional entrepreneurs in the fashion industry'. In I. Petkova (ed.), *Engineering legitimacy* (pp.17–48). Springer International Publishing. doi:10.1007/978-3-319-90707-9_2

Replicant (2023). *Digital fashion*. Available at: https://en.replicant.fashion/digitalfashion

Rubin, R. (2023). *The evolution of digital fashion and the impact on sustainability*, Available at: https://keiseimagazine.com/the-evolution-of-digital-fashion-and-the-impact-on-sustainability/

Siakam, C. (2022). 'Web3 market-statistics for 2022–2023', METAV.RS. Available at: https://metav.rs/blog/web3-market-statistics-2022-2023/

Statista (2022). Dangers of the metaverse 2021. [online] Available at https://www.statista.com/statistics/1288822/metaverse-dangers/#:~:text=The%20metaverse%20could%20lead%20to%20some%20unintended%20consequences [Accessed 21 Jul. 2023].

Statista (2023). *Clothes & apparel: Top brands in the world 2022*. Available at: https://www.statista.com/statistics/1207840/top-apparel-clothes-brands-worldwide/#:~:te xt=According%20to%20the%20ranking%20of%20most (accessed 21 June 2023).

Sun, L. and Zhao, L. (2018). 'Technology disruptions: exploring the changing roles of designers, makers, and users in the fashion industry', *International Journal of Fashion Design, Technology and Education*, 11(3), pp. 362–374. 10.1080/17543266.2018.1448462.

Turbina, R. (2022). 'Replicant Fashion', TechRound. Available at: https://techround.co.uk/marketplaces-24/12-replicant-fashion-regina-turbina/

Unreal Engine (2021). 'New report shows high demand for real-time 3D skills in global job market'. Available at: https://www.unrealengine.com/en-US/blog/new-report-shows-high-demand-for-real-time-3d skills-in-global-job-market (accessed 13 February 2024).

Van Laar, E., Van Deursen, A. J., Van Dijk, J. A. and De Haan, J. (2017). 'The relation between 21st-century skills and digital skills: A systematic literature review', *Computers in Human Behavior*, 72, pp. 577–588.

Waheed, F. M. and Khalid, M. A. (2019). 'Impact of emerging technologies for sustainable fashion, textile and design'. In W. Karwowski and T. Ahram (eds) *Impact of emerging technologies for sustainable fashion* (pp. 684–689). Springer Nature Switzerland. doi:10.1007/978-3-030-11051-2_104.

Webster, A. (2022). *Gucci built a persistent town inside of Roblox*. Available at: https://www.theverge.com/2022/5/27/23143404/gucci-town-roblox

Wong, T. D. and Ngai, W. E. (2021). 'Economic, organizational, and environmental capabilities for business sustainability competence: Findings from case studies in the fashion business', *Journal of Business Research*, 126, pp. 440–471. doi:10.1016/j.jbusres.2020.12.060.

Worldskills (2021). *Worldskills Annual Report 2021*. Available at: https://api.worldskills.org/resources/download/18181/19965/20929?l=en

Wu, X, J. and Li, L. (2020). 'Sustainability initiatives in the fashion industry', IntechOpen eBooks. doi:10.5772/intechopen.87062.

Yu, Y., Choi, T.-M., Hui, C.-L. and Ho, T.-K. (2011). 'A new and efficient intelligent collaboration scheme for fashion design', *IEEE Transactions on Systems, Man, and Cybernetics - Part A: Systems and Humans*, 41(3), 463–475. doi:10.1109/TSMCA.2010.2089514

Zvekic, D. (2023). *The drivers and challenges of fashion's digitization*. Available at: https://material-exchange.com/drivers-challenges-fashions-digitization/

Zwieglinska, Z. (2023). *Brands are pairing customer service associates and AI to improve the shopping experience*. Available at://www.glossy.co/fashion/brands-are-pairing-customer-service-associates-and-ai-to-improve-the-shopping-experience/

INDEX

Note: Locators in *italic* indicate figures, in **bold** tables and in ***bold italic*** boxes.

For Product Safety Concerns and Information please contact our EU representative GPSR@taylorandfrancis.com
Taylor & Francis Verlag GmbH, Kaufingerstraße 24, 80331 München, Germany

www.ingramcontent.com/pod-product-compliance
Ingram Content Group UK Ltd.
Pitfield, Milton Keynes, MK11 3LW, UK
UKHW050930180425
457613UK00015B/357
9781032428475